Linka's Diary

A Norwegian Immigrant Story in Word and Sketches

Mavin G. Slind,
Diary Editor

Gracia Grindal,
Sketch Editor

Lutheran University Press
Minneapolis, Minnesota

Linka's Diary
A Norwegian Immigrant Story in Word and Sketches

Marvin G. Slind, Diary Editor
Gracia Grindal, Sketch Editor

Library of Congress Cataloging-in-Publication Data

Preus, Linka, 1829-1880
  Linka's diary : a Norwegian immigrant story in word and sketches /
Marvin G. Slind, diary editor ; Gracia Grindahl, sketch editor.
      p. cm.
  ISBN-13: 978-1-932688-28-3 (alk. paper)
  ISBN-10: 1-932688-28-5 (alk. paper)
  1. Preus, Linka, 1829-1880 2. Lutheran Church--Biography. 3. Norwe-
gian Americans--Biography. 4. Norway--Emigration and immigration.
5. United States--Emigration and immigration. I. Slind, Marvin. II.
Title.
  BX8080.P68A3 2008
  284.1092--dc22
  [B]
                                    2007045417

Lutheran University Press, PO Box 390759, Minneapolis, MN 55439
Manufactured in the United States of America

Contents

Caroline Dorothea Margrethe Keyser Preus (Linka)

Foreword

Marvin G. Slind: This translation of Linka Preus's diary is a collaborative project. Although I am its general editor and translator, I would not have been able to undertake the project without the assistance of Eva-Kristin Urestad Pedersen and Ragnhild Hjeltness, two students from Norway who attended Luther College, and who agreed to work with me on this undertaking. They made initial, "rough" translations of the diary and letters, respectively. (In addition to working with all of the letters, Ms. Hjeltness also provided translations of some sections of the diary that were not available while Ms. Urestad Pedersen worked on the diary.) Without their native understanding of Norwegian idioms and culture, this translation would not have been possible.

After reviewing their translations, I then compared their transcripts to the original manuscript, and put them into their current form. The holdings of Luther College's Preus Library include a number of Norwegian-English dictionaries published in the late nineteenth and early twentieth centuries. They often helped to clarify terminology that was difficult for speakers of more modern Norwegian to translate precisely (Preus Library is named after Hermann, their son, Christian Keyser Preus, and three grandsons).

My initial intent was to avoid comparing any of our text to J.C.K. Preus's edition of the diary, published in 1952, until I had completed our translation. However, I soon found it useful to consult that edition to see how he had translated references to currency or distances, as well as some passages that we found difficult to read or translate. I immediately discovered that he had severely altered the sense of many sections of the original diary, and thus came to suspect many aspects of his translation. Yet, in his translation of the diary, as well as in a family history that he compiled, he was nonetheless able to offer insights about familial relationships that were not available elsewhere. In most cases, he provided enough information that his annotations could easily be corroborated by secondary sources published in Norway or the United States. J.C.K. Preus also transcribed some sections of the original diary into a version that was much more legible, which sometimes helped me to decipher passages that were extremely difficult to read in Linka's handwriting.

I also sought advice and insights from numerous colleagues in Norway and the United States regarding particular wordings or phrases. I am particularly grateful to the advice and information provided by Øyvind T. Gulliksen and Kari Gronningsæter, from the *Høgskolen i Telemark* in Bø, Norway; Dina Tolfsby, Director of the Norwegian-American Collection at the *Nasjonalbiblioteket* in Oslo, Norway; Solveig Zempel, Associate Dean and Professor at St. Olaf College, Northfield, Minnesota; Kathleen Stokker, my colleague at Luther College, Decorah, Iowa; and John R. Christianson, Luther College Professor Emeritus of History. Suzanne Bunkers, from Minnesota State University, Mankato, also provided invaluable insights into the problems of editing diaries.

Because of my access to additional resources, or because of advice from other colleagues, the final wording of my translation occasionally differed from that of Ms. Urestad Pederson and Ms. Hjeltness in ways other than simply American idiom and syntax. And just as their native knowledge of Norwegian facilitated their initial translations, my own native American English use of idiom and language skills are represented in this translation. While they provided the initial translations, I bear ultimate responsibility for the text as it appears here.

Throughout the life of this project, I have received the enthusiastic assistance of the Luther College Archivist, Rachel Vagts. Furthermore, this translation would not have been possible without the award of a Berg Grant and other supplemental funding provided by Luther College. I am indebted to my colleagues at the Vesterheim Norwegian-American Museum for locating photographs of Linka and he family, and to Jim

Skree, who provided the photographs of Kari and Tarje Kraagnes. The project would not have been completed without the efforts of our publisher, Leonard Flachman, who was able to organize two very different genres, edited by two individual from different disciplines, to form a coherent publication. For such assistance, and for the support and encouragement of my colleagues at Luther and many other institutions, I am extremely grateful. But even with all of that support, I owe an even greater debt to my wife, Mickey, whose support, encouragement, and advice have been unwavering throughout this project.

Gracia Grindal: During a summer in which I was doing some work in the Preus Library Archive, I was looking for more materials documenting the lives of the early Norwegian-American pastors' wives. One day, Martha Henzler, the archivist at Preus Library, came to me with a box of Preus memorabilia. I watched as she picked the Norby sketchbook out of the box. As we paged through the sketchbook, we knew we were viewing a familiar past through fresh lenses. As I have continued to study them, their historical detail continues to reveal new and interesting perspectives on an age long since disappeared into the musty pages of time.

After the first book was discovered, I gave a paper on the drawings to a group of Scandinavian-American scholars. At that conference, the daughter of Ole Rølvaag, Ella Valborg Twedt, noted that she had a little book of drawings left to her by her father. A year later, she brought them to me and they were indeed drawings by Linka. They were in a smaller book that contained some forty-seven sketches of the years from 1858 to 1864. Since that time, others in the family have found drawings in their own collections. Agnes Preus, granddaughter of J. W. Preus, Linka's youngest child, found twelve drawings in her

memorabilia. All told, there are more than 100 drawings extant and very likely others stashed away in attics in Norway and in the Midwest.

So that others can enjoy this unique woman's view of a world now lost to us, Linka's sketches are being printed along with her diary. I have arranged them in the order in which they appear in the books, starting with the forty-seven drawings in the Rolvaag collection, to which I refer by numbers preceded by an R. These drawings were found in a little 3" by 5" book. There are some loose-leaf sketches on letters, etc., which I mark as LL. There are sixty-eight sketches from the Norby collection, on rich stock paper of various hues. The sketches are landscape, about 15" by 8.5", and identified by an N. The twelve loose-leaf pieces from Agnes Preus, referred to as AP, are on individual pieces of paper the size of the Norby collection.

In order to make these pictures accessible, I have translated the titles and conversations recorded on the sketches, plus sought to determine the identities of the people in each picture and their significance to the larger history. Because many of the sketches are like cartoons, with conversation bubbles above the characters, those who cannot understand Norwegian or read the sometimes-illegible script need to have translations that make sense. The text next ot the sketch number is a translation of what appears to be the title of the drawing, That is followed by the text in the drawing, done from left to right so the reader can understand what is being said or noted in the drawing. It is possible to discover who is speaking by connecting the name of the speaker in the picture with the text attributed to them in the translation. Underneath the translated text, I have included a brief description of the picture, listing the main characters and the dramatic situation of the sketch. Then, if the situation warrants it, I include commentary on the picture so that those who are not steeped in Norwegian-American culture of the nineteenth century have some idea of what Linka is portraying and its important in the life of the family, the culture, or ecclesiastical situation of the time.

I am most grateful to the librarians at Luther College: Leigh Jordahl and Martha Henzler. My colleagues at Luther College endured my telling stories when I would emerge from the archives with news from an elegant past. I am thankful to them for their help and support. Now, with the new translation of the diary, these sketches take their rightful place beside her writings. I am most grateful to Marvin G. Slind, Associate Professor of History at Luther College, and the library and archivist Rachel Vagts for giving me the chance to communicate some of what I learned during my many summers with nineteenth-century Norwegian Americana where I lived with "my ladies." Thanks. *Soli Deo Gloria!*

Introduction

Caroline Dorothea Margrethe Keyser, known throughout most of her life as Linka, was born in Kristiansand, Norway, July 2, 1829.[1] She was the second of seven children. Their mother died in 1840, when Linka was ten; their father died in 1846.[2] Linka and her five younger sisters moved to live with their grandmother in Uranienborg, which was then on the outskirts of Oslo.[3]

Linka's circle of friends and family acquaintances included some of the most prominent individuals in Norwegian society, including high-ranking leaders within the Church. Her grandfather was a bishop, and her father was a pastor and professor. Most of the people in Norway whom Linka mentions in her diary are included in the *Norges Biografisk Leksikon*, which is essentially a "Who's Who" of Norway in her time. For example, her great-uncle was Wilhelm Christie, one of the most prominent figures in early nineteenth-century Norwegian politics. With his support, Anders Monsen Askevold studied art under a leading painter in Bergen and ultimately became a prominent landscape and animal painter. He was apparently such a good friend of Linka's that in 1851, four years after he had begun his art studies in Bergen, she arranged for him to paint Hermann's room. (His painting skills were apparently not limited to the canvas.)

She was clearly part of the *kondisjonerte*, or "people of status," in Norwegian society. After her marriage to Hermann Preus in 1851, she immigrated to America, where she had the general prestige of a pastor's wife, which her husband's rising position in the newly emerging Norwegian Synod quickly enhanced. Almost all of their friends and colleagues in America are the same individuals who figure most prominently in every historical study of the early Norwegian Lutheran church organizations in America. Elizabeth Koren, for example, was another pioneering Lutheran pastor's wife. She became Linka's close friend, and often referred to her as "Aunt Linka."

This is not the first translation of Linka's diary to be published. Her grandson, J.C.K. Preus, published a translation in 1952. His perspective in editing his grandmother's diary was clearly influenced by the church environment in which he lived and worked. In J.C.K. Preus's translation of Linka's diary, almost all of his descriptions of her relatives or acquaintances include numerous superlatives to describe their positions or status. The modern reader might easily conclude that his descriptions represent family pride more than an accurate representation of their actual positions in Norwegian or Norwegian-American society. A comparison of the original diary with the 1952 edition shows the role that J.C.K. Preus played in shaping the character of that publication. In his introduction to *Linka's Diary*, he discussed the question of publishing his grandmother's personal papers. His father had quoted from the diary in his reminiscences, and J.C.K. asked him why he had not published the complete diary, "since pioneer material was of interest to a great many people." His father replied, "I hardly think I would do that . . . at least not yet. You see, so much of it is rather personal and intimate."[4] J. C. K. then described how he later inherited the diary and also discovered a collection of letters that helped to fill in missing sections of the diary: "As I read the diary, I soon discovered why Father had decided against its publication at the time I asked about it, some forty years ago. It was the self-revelation of a young pioneer woman—who happened to be his mother. For want of an intimate friend to whom she could unburden herself, she had confided to the pages of her book the deep and sacred thoughts of her lonely heart."[5]

Linka's diary can be divided into three broad sections. The first reflects the observations of an adolescent, commenting on the events taking place around her. Some entries focus on significant developments affecting her family and friends, while others are little more than references to mundane daily occurrences. In the second section, she is a mature young woman, describing events related to her engagement, marriage, and immigration to America. The entries in the final section are sporadic. She wrote much less frequently after she arrived in America. In particular, she made few diary entries after the birth of her first child, Christian Keyser Preus, in 1852. The character of the diary also changed during that period. Instead of describing the events of her life, she focused most of her attention on her own religious faith. In some cases, she devoted almost entire entries to her fears of her own weaknesses and possible sinfulness, and her faith in God's saving grace. While she did not write in her diary often after she arrived in America, she increasingly documented her experiences through her sketches. During this period, her observations of the events around her are preserved in her sketches, rather than in text.

Linka's sketches, most of which have never been published previously, are included here with annotations by Gracia Grindal. The combination of a new translation of Linka's diary and letters with her sketches, provides an significant glimpse into the life of a prominent Norwegian immigrant in the mid-nineteenth century — an important set of historical documents.

The diary begins in 1845. Part of the winter and early spring of that year was spent with relatives at Askevold, near Bergen, where her uncle, J. Carl Christie, was pastor. Her last entry ends abruptly in mid-sentence in 1864; if she wrote more, it did not survive or has not been located. The bulk of the diary precedes her emigration in 1851. Unfortunately, there is a gap between December 31, 1845, and November 27, 1849, when there are no extant diaries. However, many of her letters from that period survive. Although the letters have a different purpose than the diary entries, the character of the letters is often very similar to her diary. She describes daily events, teases her relatives, comments on contemporary developments, and shares some of her personal and religious thoughts.

Because the letters offer the only insight into her life for the period for which there is no extant diary, J.C.K. Preus included parts of them in his edition of the diary. However, his editing of those letters was quite drastic. For example, she sometimes wrote teasing comments to her aunt, but with the unsophisticated humor that is often typical of teenagers. Such comments were not included in the 1952 edition. The letters are included in their entirety in this edition.

Linka and Hermann Preus became engaged during the period from which no diaries exist. They were cousins, and had apparently known each other most of their lives. When the diary resumes, she frequently refers to Hermann and their impending marriage. She also describes her feelings about aspects of their developing relationship. At times she is even critical of his attitudes or behavior. Most of those comments were also excluded in the 1952 edition of her diary.

Because of her parents' deaths, she spent time with different relatives. When she began her diary, she was living with her uncle and aunt, Pastor J. Carl and Rosa Christie, in Askevold, on an island north of Bergen. She then lived with her grandmother, Dorothea Carlsen, at Uranienborg, which was then on the outskirts of Christiania (now Oslo). She returned to Askevold to help her aunt, Rosa, care for her young, growing family, and then returned to Uranienborg again before she married Hermann in 1851. They emigrated soon thereafter.

Her journey to America was far more typical of the *kondisjonerte* than of the average Norwegian emigrant. Prior to their departure, the ship owner, Ole Irgens Duus (who was also the Danish Consul), hosted them in his home. Once on board, they were in a cabin, while almost all of the other passengers were below deck. From her descriptions, it is clear that the Norwegian farmers respected the young pastor and his wife, and the couple continued to receive deferential treatment from other emigrants throughout their journey.

Ironically, the period in which she wrote the least was also the period that historians of Norwegian-American Lutheranism might find of most interest. Because of her husband's preeminent position in the newly emerging Norwegian Synod, she was an observer of many of the critical developments in that body's history. But she makes only a few general references to those events. Similarly, although she relates some anecdotes associated with the life of a pioneer woman, she includes much less of that type of information than is found in Elizabeth Koren's diary.

In her study of "Private Writings of Midwestern Women," Elizabeth Hampsten points out a number of problems with published versions of private diaries, especially when family members edit them. Editing can often alter the sense of time or perspective found in a diary. For example, brief, repetitious comments about unchanging weather or days with nothing to do may be combined or excised in order to give a more coherent or interesting flow to the published work.[6] There is also the issue of publishing something that was written as a collection of one's private thoughts. Few authors of private diaries write them with the intent of having them published. Yet Thomas Mallon argues "that no one ever kept a diary for just himself." While a diarist may not have a specific audience in mind, there is always the expectation or hope that it will be read by someone, which in a way gives life to the diarist's ideas. [7]

Similarly, Suzanne L. Bunkers notes, "Any diary that has been edited for publication, whether by a family member, an academic editor, a scholarly press, or a mass-market publishing house, bears the unmistakable marks of the editor(s) as well as the diarist." While the diarist may write the diary, the editors actually select the specific elements of the diary that ultimately appear in print. Some entries may be modified or excluded entirely.[8] Bunkers also believes that "most diarists have a clear sense of audience, whether defined or indeterminate." Based on her examination of nineteenth-century Midwestern women diarists, she concludes that they kept diaries "for reasons that are not unlike the reasons why women continue to keep diaries today: to define the self, to understand how one's self is shaped by interactions with others, to express emotions otherwise repressed, to view one's life and work as important, and to create a forum for commentary on relationships, institutions, and events."[9]

Linka Preus's diary does not fit easily into any single category of diaries.[10] However, it illustrates a tendency noted by Margo Culley: "Most diarists do not write consciously or explicitly in defiance of death or what Bashkirtseff calls 'oblivion,' but we can see how the smaller 'deaths' or dislocations have often prompted journal keeping. Marriage, travel, and widowhood are all occasions creating a sense of a discontinuity of self—I was that, now I am this; I was there, now I am here. Keeping a life record can be an attempt to preserve continuity seemingly broken or lost." In particular, this is often found in diaries of women who traveled to the American West. Their diaries and journals may be seen as a means of maintaining connections or networks that were otherwise broken. Such women, Culley believes, "were strongly informed by a sense of audience that shapes their accounts of wondrous and unfamiliar sights and their efforts to come to grips with a new life."[11] Linka Preus's diary is an example of such an effort to relate new experiences to her own broken connections. In particular, her life in Norway was deeply affected by the loss of her parents, and her subsequent separation from her siblings. Furthermore, the diary seems to undergo a significant transformation after her arrival in America.

Although she often referred to religious themes in her earlier entries, religious concerns come to dominate her writings in America. Similarly, once in America, she seems to espouse temperance sentiments that were clearly not present in her earlier materials.

Diaries express the diarists' views and feelings at the time of writing. But, as Linka Preus's diary illustrates, if what is considered socially acceptable behavior changes in the period between a diary's creation and its publication, the publication may reflect the views and mores of the editor, rather than of the author. J.C.K. Preus's edition of the diary, for example, carefully edited out behavior that did not seem to conform to the puritanical standards of Norwegian-American Lutheranism in the mid-twentieth century, such as dancing, card playing, or drinking alcohol.[12]

Bunkers believes that the editor must address the problems created when one attempts "to 'rescue' a particular diary (and, by extension, its writer) from apparent oblivion by bringing the text to the attention of present-day readers. While this desire is not inherently bad, it could lead to problems if I develop what might be termed a co-dependent urge to control the text and its writer by my selective editing and presentation of the diarist's words and ideas."[13]

These problems can be compounded when a diary deals with particularly religious themes. Thomas Mallon identifies several categories of diarists, including a group he classifies as "pilgrims." He notes, "A breed apart from the diarists who write simply to collect the days or preserve impressions of foreign places are those who set out in their books to discover who they really are. These are generally serious people, more in the way of pilgrims, with inward destinations, than mere travelers."[14] In many ways, Mallon's description fits Linka Preus. While she does write about events surrounding her life, a constant theme throughout the diary is her faith and belief in God.

Fortunately, while he severely edited portions of the diary, J. C. K. Preus recognized its value, not only to himself and his family, but also to others interested in the insight it provides into a young woman's life, particularly on the American frontier. (The folder containing the diaries carries a touching notation, apparently in his handwriting, labeling the collection "Very Precious.") Nonetheless, the picture he created of his grandmother was an artificial construct, portraying her in the light of his own mid-twentieth century environment.

Bunkers describes the editor's role in publishing a personal diary as "the construction of the writer's life." She notes that "in my interaction with the writer's text, in my interpretation of the significance of what she said and didn't say, in my analysis of what the diary as a whole reveals about her personality—in all of these ways I am creating my construct of the diarist, a construct influenced as much by who I am as by who I perceive the diarist to be."[15] Margo Culley also cautions, "We must remember that diaries and journals are texts, that is, verbal constructs. The process of selection and arrangement of detail in the text raises an array of concerns appropriately 'literary,' including questions of audience (real or implied), narrative, shape and structure, persona, voice, imagistic and thematic repetition, and what James Olney calls 'metaphors of self.'"[16] If an editor plays too much of a role in shaping the content of a diary, that construct can be totally altered. This edition of Linka Preus's diary attempts to let its author's voice be heard, with as little influence from the editor and translator as possible.

As Linka notes in her diary, she often supplemented her diary writings with sketches. (Unfortunately, many of her early drawings, which she mentions in her diary, have not survived.) After she arrived in America, her sketches more and more became her primary method of recording her observations of the world around her. Her writings in America were increasingly devoted to religious thoughts. To understand what she was experiencing in America, one must turn to her sketches.

Linka had learned sketching as part of her education as a young girl of her class in Norway. In addition to the typical domestic arts of managing the parsonage farm and household, Lutheran pastors' wives and daughters were expected to excel in arts and letters to add a gracious sheen to parsonage life. Their education, transmitted to them by their mothers and aunts, aimed to make them gracious ladies of the kind we read about in the novels of Jane Austen. Most Scandinavian Lutheran pastors' daughters of Linka's class, after learning the Scriptures, Luther's Small Catechism, hymns, and other edifying literature, felt it was necessary to gain facility in several living languages, fine needlework, singing, playing the piano, and pencil drawing. These sketches were considered more of a craft than an art since, at the time, women were not usually considered artists in their own right.[17] Sketching taught them to observe and record scenes they wanted to remember, especially scenes from touring or family life.

The young Linka Keyser enjoyed the art of sketching. We read in her diary comments about her practice at sketching and her own sense of her skill at the art. The conventions of her art, known as "genre" painting, involved more than creating recognizable semblances between people and scenery; they also had to tell a story. Although Linka's pen may fail to move us with its artistic skill, her sense of the drama of the scene is unerring. In each drawing involving people, we see her wit revealed. She portrays her own failings, her extra weight, and her preference for beer over brackish water. She also portrays herself having to engage in tasks in the home she would never have thought of doing in Norway, such as cleaning the intestines of an animal after slaughter for sausage. Linka shows us the overbearing nature of Diderikke Brandt, a pastor's wife of her class, who is always pushing them on, the overweening self-possession of Pastor Ulrik Vilhelm Koren, Gustav Dietrichson's weight, Hermann's bumbling detachment from family scenes, Uncle Nicolai's difficulties assimilating, her son C. K. goofing off, and Laur. Larsen's formality. The only one who escapes her gentle ribbing is Elisabeth Koren, whose quiet mien she captures in all of the sketches she does of her. Her dramatic insight and wit capture our attention as we see her pictures of scenes in Norwegian Americana for which there are few visual records. Instead of the formal picture of the dedication of the new Main Building at Luther College, we have her homey scene of the church supper afterward, with three intimate portraits of human interchanges: Diderikke with a farm woman who helped with the meal, Laur. Larsen chasing off an Irish interloper looking for food, and Elisabeth Koren's serene conversation with a big supporter of the college. It humanizes the history because it gives us more than the formal history of the men; instead, we see the distaff view of the same event. Linka's sketches document the early life of the Norwegian immigrants, especially moments in the history of the Norwegian Synod. She gives us her views of life on the Mississippi; scenes from the early log cabin parsonages on the frontier; intimate insights into the life of the family; church; work on the farm; the impact of the Civil War on the immigrants; encounters with Native Americans; and visits to Niagara Falls, Cleveland, and New York, as well as their trip to Norway in 1866-1867.

Because Linka saved most of the letters she received from her friends among the pastors' wives, especially those from Elisabeth Koren, it was possible to read the pictures for a fuller sense of what was going on in each sketch, since these letters give an almost monthly record of what was happening in the lives of the women from 1854-1874. They help to set the sketches in their context. Linka's letters to Mrs. Koren were very likely lost in the fire that consumed the Koren parsonage in the early 1870s, so there is much less from Linka's side. We do, however, have the diary and these sketches.

So that others can enjoy this unique woman's view of a world now lost to us, Linka's sketches are being printed along with her diary. It is hoped that this combination of a newly translated text and the sketches, most of which have never previously appeared in print, will provide a more complete understanding of Linka Preus's life, as well as the times in which she lived.

The Historical Context

Linka's diary has historical significance at several points. It not only provides insight into the life of a young nineteenth-century Norwegian woman, but also gives a perspective on the lives of several prominent relatives who played a significant role in the history of the church.

Her grandfather, Johan Michael Keyser, had served as bishop in Kristiansand from 1805 to 1810. Her father, Christian Nicolai Keyser, was also a pastor, and eventually served as professor of sacred theology at the University in Christiania (Oslo). In 1851, she married her cousin, Hermann Preus, who was a young Lutheran minister. (Marrying one's cousin was not uncommon in the mid-nineteenth century; several of the family members mentioned in the diary also married cousins.) That same year, the couple emigrated, settling at Spring Prairie, Wisconsin (now DeForest), where she died on September 19, 1880.[18]

Hermann Preus's position in the emerging Norwegian-American society was a significant one. As the number of Norwegian immigrants grew in America, a few Lutheran pastors emigrated from Norway to meet the needs of their fellow countrymen in the new land. Hermann Preus was one of the dozen pastors to immigrate, accepting a call to the new Norwegian-American community in Spring Prairie, Wisconsin. Most of the Norwegian pastors worked together to form the Norwegian Evangelical Lutheran Church of America (generally known as the "Norwegian Synod") in 1853. It became one of the main church organizations among Norwegian-Americans in the nineteenth century. Unlike their counterparts from Sweden and Denmark, Norwegian Lutherans formed a number of synods; by 1876, there were at least five, and others would form, merge with others, or gradually decline as a few came to the fore. Some of the disputes were over major theological issues such as lay preaching and "election" (predestination), while others involved organizational or even personal disputes. Union of the various synods came slowly; even in the early twentieth century, it was only partially achieved when three of the largest synods joined in 1917 to form the Norwegian Lutheran Church in America. [19]

Even before its formation in 1853, Hermann quickly assumed a prominent role in the development of the Norwegian Synod. In their history of Norwegian-American Lutheranism, E. Clifford Nelson and Eugene L. Fevold note that soon after his arrival in 1851, Hermann "was to be the acknowledged leader of the Synod for the next generation" and that "his leadership was presently to be felt in the emerging church on the American frontier." He was elected president of the Synod in 1862, a position he held until his death in 1894. In his history of the Preus family, J. C. K. Preus describes his grandfather as "the man who occupied a most important position of leadership in the organization and development of the Norwegian Synod through the first half of its existence."[20]

J.C.K. Preus was Linka's grandson. His father, Christian Keyser (C.K.) Preus, was Hermann and Linka's oldest child. He had also played a leading role in the Lutheran Church. C.K. was his father's assistant pastor at Spring Prairie from 1876 until Hermann died in 1894, and continued as pastor there for another three years. He then taught religion at Luther College from 1898 until his death in 1921. C. K. Preus also served as the college's president for most of that period, from 1902 to 1921. He was also vice president of the Norwegian Synod from 1911 to 1917 and vice president of the Iowa District of the Norwegian Lutheran Church in America from 1917 to 1921.[21]

Like his father and grandfather, J.C.K. Preus was also prominent in Lutheran circles. He graduated from Luther College in 1902 and attended Luther Seminary, Johns Hopkins University, and the University of Chicago Divinity School. After being ordained in 1905, he served as a parish pastor in Wisconsin and Minnesota until 1931. Then he began a long administrative career, which included serving as executive secretary of the Evangelical Lutheran Church's Board of Education from 1931 to 1956.[22]

Linka Preus and her siblings:

Johan Carl Keyser ("Kalla"), born August 10, 1828, died in 1904

Caroline Dorothea Margrethe Keyser ("Linka"), born July 2, 1829, died
    September 19, 1880

Anna Waleska Keyser ("Hexa," also "Hex"), born February 25, 1831, died in
    childbirth in June, 1853. (J.C.K. Preus indicates that she was also known as
    "Eska." He states that she died on June 28, but in her diary notation of June
    30, 1854, Linka notes, "Today it is exactly a year since sister Hex died.")

Ovidia Wilhelmine Keyser ("Lillemamma"), born October 10, 1832, died
    December 6, 1916

Hanne Marie Keyser ("Hanchen," "Hanken," or "Henny Penny" *Hønepøne*"), born
    September 25, 1834, died November 9, 1893

Rosa ("Rosemette") Keyser, born 1837, died in 1881

Agnes Keyser, born 1840, died at age 94.

Source: Johan Carl Keyser Preus, *Hermann Amberg Preus: A Family History* (n.p.:
Preus Family Book Club, 1966), 10-11.

Children of Hermann and Linka Preus:

Christian Keyser Preus, born October 13, 1852, died May 28, 1921

Rosine Pauline Keyser Preus, born October 21, 1854, died 1918

Agnes Wilhelmine Rudolpha Keyser Preus, born September 2, 1859, died May
    12, 1927

Johan Wilhelm Keyser Preus, born October 21, 1861, died October 19, 1925

Carl Christie Preus, born October
    21, 1861, died October 22,
    1863

Paul Preus ("Palle") born April
    24, 1867, died Thanksgiving
    Day 1883.

All of the children were born at
    Spring Prairie except Paul,
    who was born in Norway,
    where the family was visiting.

Source: Johan Carl Keyser Preus,
*Hermann Amberg Preus: A Family
History* (n.p.: Preus Family Book
Club, 1966), 15.

Part One

A Young Norwegian Woman

(1845-1849)

Autumn 1844 — *January* 1845

I left my home, my father, and my brothers and sisters at 10 a.m. Monday, August 19 [1844], headed for Uranienborg.[1] The entire party going to Askevold[2], plus the people seeing us off, was leaving from there. The party included Aunt Lodviska[3] and Wilhelm Bøg; Aunt Lillebessa sat in Aunt Rosa's big calash[4], Bøg and I sat in a gig. There were no mishaps before the first relay station, Stabek, which we passed without even changing horses. However, something fortunate did happen to us between Uranienborg and that station. At Skomagervold, Aunt Maren and Uncle Carl Carlsen were waiting with their little boys to say good-bye to us. They'd brought something from Ullern[5] which was ten times better than the kisses we got—at least I thought so. Aunt Maren had a big basket of black cherries for us to enjoy on the journey. She complained that she hadn't been able to finish a cake for us to take along, but she said that it should be done shortly. So if we could wait about a quarter of an hour, a messenger would bring it. Aunt Rosa, on the other hand, said that we couldn't wait, but since she thought that the cake would be done soon, she could send the messenger to Berum. We'd be waiting there for a little while, since Lomse[6] was coming with us. (She thought it would be good to bring a cake.) So this was how it was, and we continued on our way after having said a <u>beautiful</u> and <u>loving</u> good-bye to the people at Ullern. Ha, ha, ha!

I don't know how it went for the people sitting in the calash. But I do know that even though I was a little sad that I had to be away for such a long time, without being able to see Father or my siblings, I enjoyed sitting in the gig. I had the basket with black cherries in my lap, and they weren't saved, that's for sure. I don't know whether or not Bøg had a good time, but he helped me eat the cherries as much as he could. He also talked nonstop, which amused me a lot.

Up to this point, we had no accidents. But what happened when we got to the long Steensbakken not far from Berum? The big wagon split on both sides. However, there was a piece of metal or something—I'm not sure what—that kept the wagon together until we got to Berum. And how lucky was that? When the wagon did break, it broke when we were near Berum.

Song for Stiftsamtsmand Christie's Student Jubilee November 7, 1844

Melody.: Once upon a Time There Was a Brave Man

I

The entire world untold
The student though sincere
Yielded not in times of need
For rights and truth he fought
Therefore thank you friend that you today
The student paid respect
Came faithfully to be with friends
As faithfully you studied

II

We gathered then in Axelstad
Our senses are delighted
To this you added willingly
To joy and happiness
A real student, that you were
Honest were you too
Lived as happy students do
But did not forget the book[7].

III

For fifty years you've been a student
Now it's time to party
You've earned your civic* garland
Now the golden cup is needed
To you each student jubilating,
You are our prize, so join
More years we have still to come
And good, old memories to share!
                    —Sagen

*As known, double meaning.[8]

Askevold, January 1, 1845. I spent the first of January at Tysse, where I had been since December 27. I spent my time that day hiking, playing various games and walking around the floor arm in arm with Andrea Landmark. Uf, I've written incorrectly — New Year's Day I was in Fagervigen, at Attorney Landmark's[9]. The party was for dinner and the evening, and what I just described happened there.

January 2 — I was at Tysse, at Judge Landmark's. As I already noted, I'd been staying there since December 27. In the morning, while I was sitting knitting my mitten, Barbra Landmark came up to me, tugged on a tuft of my hair, and said, "Linka, how would you like a sleigh ride right away?"

"Oh, yes, thanks," and with that I went out in the hallway to put on my warm clothes, and then hurried out into the yard. Barbra and Andrea Landmark were already sitting there in their sleighs,[10] and mine stood empty — but I was soon sitting in it. Since all three of us had good horses, we practically flew down the road. My horse was the best one; I had the judge's "Foxen."

After an hour or so we were back home, and we had barely had time to sit down before *candidatus theologie* Johan Daniel Landmark[11] walked through the door and said, "Barbra, I've been through all of our books, and they include a few short comedies. Remember yesterday, we discussed how we should put on a comedy like that here at home before Linka leaves? I don't think there are any that would be better than *The Boarder* (*Kostgjengeren*), and if you haven't read it, I'll be glad to read it to you."

Her answer was "no," whereupon Landmark sat down to read with all his might. But when he was almost halfway through, Barbra couldn't sit still any longer. Landmark stopped reading and went down to the office where, without having asked Barbra, he started to write out the cast. When he had written for a while, Barbra came down and when she saw the *candidatus* sitting there writing, she said, "Johan Daniel, you aren't sitting here writing out that boring play you were reading? I have one here that is more worth doing — it's *Power and Cunning (Hagl og List)* by Johan Ludvig Heiberg."

He now looked over the characters in this play; they fit the actors who would play them *very* well. In the play, all the characters were big, strong people. We actors were little nobodies, but the play was still taken favorably. The characters were divided among us, and I was supposed to be a twenty-four-year-old "animal."

That day nothing more worth writing down happened, except for my playing billiards that afternoon with *Cand. Bar.* Anders Lem and Nils Land Fagervigen.

[12] *January* 3rd, as well as the following days until the 11th of January, I spent one day like the one before: I got up at eight in the morning, drank my cup of coffee a little after I had my cup of tea, and ate breakfast. Afterward I sat down to dictate my part to Landmark. After a day had lapsed, I sat down to read a little of it, since we were having rehearsals the next day and all the other days until the 12th of January. That's when the play would be performed for a very large audience, namely the judge and his wife, six little boys, and the attorney's wife and six children. In addition to these, there were some uninvited members of the audience standing outside the windows, but as they thought they did not see well enough from there, they tiptoed into the living room to see this beautiful and <u>very well</u>-performed play, ha, ha!

January 4 — The Landmarks went to Doctor Landmark's at Tros[13], and I came along. When we arrived, we went into a room where we could get changed and made up for a ball, since the doctor was having a ball that evening. I really enjoyed myself that evening.

January 5 — I was still at Tros, and that day I did nothing but knit, eat, drink, and play games with Eva Rasch. Since it had had rained all morning, we could not go out at all, but in the afternoon the weather got better and we went over to the palisades by Pastor Lund's for a long, yes, four-hour-long, visit. Afterward we went back to Tros where we spent the evening eating apples and cakes. After that, we started dancing. We danced until we got bored with that, and then went to bed.

January 6th started just like the 5th, but as the weather got better in the morning, we went over to Dale for a visit with Vonen, the blacksmith. Since he had said earlier that he was going to have a ball, we gave him obvious hints that we wanted the ball to take place that very evening, which it did. That is why I found myself at a ball at Vonen's that evening. It was great fun, as we danced not only the regular dances from the cities, but also *Springerdanser.* I got everybody to join in on *Reven lakker til Bondens Gaard,* and we danced it several times as they delighted in this dance. The last time was the most enjoyable one. When we were all down on our knees, I suddenly rose and pushed a few of the others down, so that they ended up lying on the floor. I was the only one of the ladies who drank all of my beer; the others said it was only because Vonen wanted me to, not because I was thirsty. At 4 a.m. we all left after having danced so much the walls were shaking.

January 7 — I got up very late, like everybody else, and after breakfast, Eva Rasch and I took a long walk on the big wide country road. In the afternoon we sent for Lieutenant Daal, asking him to spend the evening at Tros. When he came, we sat down and played "*Halvtoll*" until supper. After we ate, we started dancing, even though there were only three and a half couples. One person had to play the pianoforte, namely Mrs. Landmark from Tros. After a while, it was finally time for bed, and I slept well after Andrea Landmark promised me a birching[14] the next morning — which she never gave me. That day I sent Vonen an imprint from a signet my uncle wanted to give me for Christmas.

January 8 — The people from Tysse and I returned to Tysse. The weather was really nice. I waited all morning and afternoon for visitors from Askevold, but none came that day.

January 9th started with my having my cup of coffee in bed, then getting up and getting dressed and having breakfast. Afterward I started dictating roles for the others, as my own was already done. That day all the roles for the play were finally done, and everybody started reading over their parts, since we were having a rehearsal in the afternoon. The rehearsal was a lot of fun, even more fun than the real show. I didn't have to be so serious at the rehearsal; I could play tricks and laugh. There was a lot of laughter in all the rehearsals, but especially in the one that I am about to describe. It took place down in the office in the evening, and we had about eight or ten candles there. The first act came along really well, and at the end of it we realized that the Judge was standing in the doorway. Following him were a group of boys and when they entered the door they said "Ahhh!" This was supposed to be a secret for the Judge, so his presence down there was rather unwelcome. So he said, "I really did not want you to be down here, my children, because there are so many papers here. But you can stay here tonight, but only if you are careful with those candles. By the way, it was not my intention to come down here and surprise you. After all of that writing you have been doing, I could not help but guess what was going on. But if anybody else asks me, I'll pretend I don't know a thing. All right boys, off we go!" With that, they left. The rest of us had been eating apples Barbra had given us, but when the Judge left, we could not help but laugh, since we had told everybody else except for the Judge about what he thought was now his "secret."

The actors themselves caused the rest of the breaks in the rehearsals. Whenever we were supposed to kiss someone's hand, we either spit on it or punched it instead. Whenever we were supposed to hug someone, the embrace consisted of punches and avoidance. I was, by the way, the unhappy actor who had to hug someone I simply could not embrace..... so instead of hugging her I ran to the opposite side of the room. She followed me and we ended up running around the room like that for a little while, me laughing heartily, she deadly serious, since for some reason she really wanted this embrace to take place. The others found this good entertainment, except for J.D. Landmark, who did not. This funny scene ended with me taking her by the neck in order to push her down on the floor. She would have ended up on the floor if I had not arranged it so that she ended up in her dear J.D. Landmark's arms. However, the only thing I got for having entertained the others like that was that the person I would not embrace, Miss Rein, was angry with me. But I really didn't care if she was. It all passed the next day, though. When the rehearsal was over at last, all the actors went to bed and slept well.

January 10 — I received a letter from Aunt Rosa in which she told me that I should come home. If the weather was too bad to go over on the troller, I could walk from Heller. There were also a few lines from Uncle, though, and he told me to come home when I felt like it. Some time ago, I really wanted to go home, but neither the people at Tysse nor the weather would allow it. We had a rehearsal that day, too, but we kept it early enough to have time for a game of whist afterward. That same day I also sent a pair of mittens home to Wilhelm.

January 11 — We worked on the stage, since we would be performing the play the next day. J.D. Landmark and Lem worked with the sets, while the rest of us read our parts. I probably would have gone home that day, if it had not been that the others begged me to stay. If I had left, they wouldn't have been able to put on the play the following day.

January 12 — We had the dress rehearsal in the morning, and in the evening we played to a full house...ha, ha, ha, hi, hi, hi, ho, ho, ho!

January 13 — In the morning I rode home to Askevold, together with J.D. Landmark and his girlfriend. Landmark had brought his gun in order to shoot some game on the way. After a lot of trouble he did get two *Teister.*[15] We arrived at Askevold with this great bounty at about two in the afternoon, enjoying the most beautiful weather on earth. Doris was the first one to see me as we came up Søveien, but right after her came Auntie and Uncle. What a warm welcome I got from Auntie! Instead of just greeting me formally, she said to me, "So it finally pleased Little Miss here to come home?" Then she kissed me and soon I was sitting in the living room, and it was even nicer there than usual. To my great pleasure, in the evening they lit the Christmas tree. I thought it would have been taken down a long time ago.

Happy to be back home, I went to bed in the evening. On our way from Tysse to Askevold, we met the boat Auntie had sent to get me. But it had to return without Linka, because I was already sitting quite comfortably in my boat.

January 14 — This was the first day of the New Year I spent at Askevold. The first thing I did when I came down in the morning was obviously to eat, after which I sat down to knit. But since the weather was so fine, I went for a walk along *Søveien.* The memorable thing about this walk occurred when I came back into the yard: I saw a bridal party coming from church. I stood there for a while, looking at how the bride and groom were dressed. I couldn't keep myself from laughing when I saw the bride's outfit, even though I thought it was a pretty style. She had a black bombazine skirt and a flat black jacket. Outside of this she had a piece embroidered with gold and silver, covering her entire chest. Below this she had a big white apron, which was just as long as the skirt. On her head, she wore a silver gilded crown, about one and a half quarters high. Every point of the crown had bells hanging from it, so that when I saw her, I couldn't help but think of a jester's cap. For the finishing touch of her finery, she had broad ribbons, nearly four feet long,[16] in all possible colors. They were fastened to the crown and hung

down her back. The groom was dressed in blue homespun wool and wore a shiny hat with a golden ribbon tied around it.

Eventually the entire party went down to the bishop's big lounge to dance and drink beer. It was amusing to me, watching the bride dance. Following the usual custom, she had to put on a serious and almost sad expression, when she really had a lot of trouble keeping herself from laughing.

When the party had been dancing for about an hour, they wanted to go out in a boat, but they had to wait for the bride, who wanted to go upstairs and give my uncle a drink. When she came back down, they all left, with two violins leading the way. The bride was eighteen years old and the groom was twenty, but Uncle said the oldest of them had just been confirmed and that she was rather dumb, so he told her that even though she was now a bride, she would probably have to learn her catechism next year in church with the rest of the confirmands from her class.

After a little while, J.D. Landmark, his girlfriend, and I went fishing, but even with my new fishing line that I used for the very first time, I did not catch any fish. The same evening a terribly drunk Ole Storevigen came to the parsonage and made a fuss about two shillings he claimed I had promised him, but he was too drunk for me to give them to him.

January 15 — I went out fishing with J.D. Landmark again, but I soon got bored when I did not get a single fish that day, either. Instead of fishing, I started rowing, which I was really good at. Once I fell backward over the thwart. In the evening we lit the Christmas tree again, to the great joy of the visitors as well as to the rest of us young people.

January 16 — Landmark and his girlfriend left. I started working in the house. I got some veal, and I did a really good job making veal *Karbonarer.*[17] Nothing funny really happened that day. I got a letter from home.

January 17 — Nothing of importance took place, besides my burning all the food I was supposed to prepare. Oh, yes, in the evening Ole Storevigen, who was still here, scared a man, "His Royal Highness King Ole." He had put up a white shirt outside his door, next to the road that leads down to his house. The shirt was frozen stiff, and when the man came home, he thought the shirt was a ghost. He had enough courage (ha, ha!) to go up to the door, and he practically fell in through the door, pale with terror. When he came in the door like a madman, his wife asked him "What's wrong with you?" He told her about he ghost, but she laughed at him. "Go see for yourself then!" he told her. "I'll go look, that's for sure," she replied. She went outside and laughed even more when she came inside and told him it was a frozen shirt.

January 18th was the first day this year that I started studying with Uncle. I got up at 6 a.m. and looked over some homework I was to be examined on from 6:30 to 7:30 p.m. When this work was somewhat done, I went down to have breakfast. I did some sewing after breakfast, but I did not get time for much, as it was soon time for dinner, and I had to help with the food. After dinner I went to do my homework more thoroughly, and when that was done, I had my coffee and then sewed until it got dark. I started knitting a pair of mittens for Doris, who had developed such a terrible cough that my aunt thought it was the whooping cough, and she was afraid that the other two children also had it.

January 19 — I spent this day like the 18th. Auntie bought a live wild duck from Bertel Ask, Dorthea Prestøen's boyfriend. They put the duck in the hen house. It couldn't be outside, or it probably would have flown away!

January 20 — I spent the day as peacefully and quietly as a flower in a meadow. It was not quite as peaceful outside, however, as we had a rather furious wind from the south.

January 21st passed just as quietly as the 20th had. Nothing amusing happened.

January 22 — I felt like a grown-up, responsible young and responsible girl. In the evening I went for a walk with Auntie, who wanted to buy some firewood.

January 23rd was also a quiet and peaceful day. I spent it just as I had the 22nd.

January 24 — I spent just the 23rd, except that I couldn't go for a walk because it was raining. But even though it was raining, Uncle went to Aafjorden!

January 25th was exactly like the 24th of January.

January 26th was like the previous days had been, very quiet. But since it was Sunday, I did not sew at all. Instead, I read the second part of my book. In the evening I played the piano for nearly two hours.

January 27 — We had a terrible wind storm, but it was only about a fourth as bad as it had been during the night, when the entire house was practically shaking. Uncle was supposed to return that day, but he couldn't because of the bad weather. In the evening, after having spent my day like I had the 26th, I also played the piano.

January 28 — The weather was better, and Uncle got back home. Otherwise, for me the day was like the previous ones.

January 29 — This was the most unpleasant day I have spent here at Askevold. What made it so bad didn't really happen until the afternoon, though. That's when Carl Andreas Carlsen Christie broke Auntie and Uncle's lamp, while I was supposed to be looking after the boy. This happened in Auntie and Uncle's own room. They were sitting in the living room, but they came running when they heard the noise. They were really upset when they saw that their lamp was broken. It was not only functional but also very pretty. Auntie was especially upset, since that lamp had been a gift from Grandfather Carlsen. However, they had to pretend to be in a good mood since Doctor Landmark and Sergeant Haugland were visiting. I did some sewing during the day and knitting in the afternoon.

January 30 — I wrote my grandmother and a few words for Kalla and Hexa. While I was writing, Doctor Landmark glued the lamp, so that when I came back down the lamp was standing there, good as new. But of course if you looked closely, you could see that it had been glued. The doctor said that the children did have the whooping cough. Both the doctor and the sergeant left the same afternoon.

January 31 — I got a letter from Grandmother, in which she told me that *Bya* was *well!* I could hardly believe my own eyes when I read it. I also received a letter from Hanken[18] in which she said that both she and her siblings were healthy.

February 1 — I spent my morning very sensibly, finishing up the neckband of a shirt that I had embroidered for Dorthe. In the afternoon I did my homework and when I was done, I went down to try out the ice on some of the smaller ponds. After the last rain, we got colder frost, and I was happy to discover that the ice was just solid enough for me to try on my skates. I ran up to the house, fetched my skates, and — down onto the ice goes Linka. Despite the bad ice, and even though it was the first time I had been skating in two years, it went really well and I had a lot of fun. I had so much fun that I stayed on the ice until dark. It was a good thing I took advantage of it and stayed that long, because it snowed that night, and the next morning skating was impossible.

February 2 — We had bad weather, but I didn't really mind, it being Sunday and all. Uncle was preaching that day, but only for twenty or thirty people — all men, except for two women from his own parsonage. I spent that day partly reading *Redgauntlet*,[19] partly eating stolen apples, partly playing the piano, and partly playing whist. It's a pleasure (playing whist) that I enjoy almost every evening. The last thing I said this evening was "watch out (Auntie and Uncle), because tomorrow you'll get a taste of some Shrovetide wood!" [20]

February 3 — Shrove Monday. I carried out my threats from the night before. I got up at 3:30 a.m. Krafting, the maid, was the first to taste the sting of the branches I'd put together the night before. After I'd been hitting her for a while, she finally woke up and screamed so much that I had to stop or she would have awakened everybody else. She already had awakened Auntie and Uncle. I was practically dressed, and after threatening the maid that she would taste my branches again if she went back to sleep, I went down to give the man and woman of the house a taste of it.

The first person I met as I approached the girls' room was Dorthe. She was kneading some bread dough. I asked her if she'd heard anything from the children. She hardly had time to say "no" before Doris started coughing so badly that both Auntie and Uncle got up to make sure she was okay. I waited a bit, and when I was sure everybody had gone back to sleep, I slowly approached the door. I unlatched it very, very gently, and I thought nobody had heard me. But just as I opened the door, Wilhelm started coughing, and I was left with a long nose.[21] This happened three or four times: every time I'd made it to the door, Wilhelm started coughing, and every time I was more disappointed than the time before. I finally got tired of being down there without accomplishing anything, so I went back upstairs to my own room to read. The first thing I did when I got back in was to hit the maid a few more times for having gone back to sleep.

After half an hour or so, I went back downstairs to see if I might have more luck this time, but as soon as I got into the kitchen, I could hear that someone was awake in the other bedroom. I sat down on one of the benches in the kitchen, watching the flames in the fireplace. I was deep in thought, but Auntie interrupted me when she came into the kitchen and saw me sitting there. The first thing she said was, "Oh, Linka, let's have our coffee together, I see Dorthe has made some."

"Oh, it's you, Auntie, good morning! But what are you doing up this early, it's not even 4:30!"

"I'm going to make you all some Shrovetide buns, but first I want my coffee! Hurry up, will you dear, when I ask you!"

I got the coffee on the table right away, and we both sat down. It really tasted good! After the coffee, Auntie started kneading the dough for the buns. While she was working, I made a quick trip into their bedroom and gave Uncle a good taste of my bundle. Afterward I went back through the girls' bedroom to watch Auntie.

I had only been standing there for a little while when she said, "Now, Linka, you have to watch the dough. Be sure to turn it every now and then when it's standing there by the oven. I'm going back to bed."

"Yes, I'll do that, Auntie, but first you have to show me exactly how I'm supposed to turn the dough."

"Uf, you split hairs more than anyone I've ever met, Linka. Of course you don't turn the dough, but the *bowl* the dough is in! When the bowl is completely warm, you can move it away from the oven! I'm going now. Do exactly as I've told you, otherwise you won't get any Shrovetide buns!"

"Good Night, sleep well, sweet dreams, etc. What a sleepyhead of an aunt you are!"

With this, Auntie left. But she soon came back and earnestly asked me not to surprise her with my bundle of branches. She hadn't been able to sleep all night, and now she finally felt calm enough to fall asleep, but only if I wouldn't come in and wake her up. I promised not to surprise her, and she went back to her room.

I went to my room, too, and sat down to write a description of my journey from Christiania to Askevold, but I obviously didn't get it done. I had Auntie's travel notes to look at. I interrupted my writing to go down and turn the bowl full of dough. When daylight finally came, I heard Uncle in the living room, and Auntie and the kids in the bedroom. So I went downstairs with the bundle under my arm, and all the noisy people in the bedroom got a taste of "Peer Erik." Among the Shrovetide buns Auntie had made, I found the biggest one, and asked Auntie if I could have it. I stuffed it as full of candied fruit as I could. The buns were soon done, but I couldn't eat mine that day.

I thought Shrove Monday was a good day for being lazy, and I took advantage of it. I was so lazy that I didn't even do any of the lessons Uncle had given me, but gave myself a little vacation that day instead. We played whist in the evening.

February 4 — I was a very hardworking and good girl, except when I started weaving Dorthe's cloth. It was snowing rather heavily all day. We still went to Hinn, though, where they said the herring fishing had begun. It is, by the way, superfluous to add that we played whist in the evening, as Auntie always makes sure that we get a game of cards every single evening.

February 5 — I took advantage of the good skiing conditions and was able to borrow a pair of Finmark skis that were really good, and out on the hills I went. The hills weren't really that steep, but I still fell a lot — not because I was clumsy, but because there was so much frozen horse..... that I was supposed to go around. As you might expect, I didn't always get around it. A pole should have helped, but since this was the first time I ever used a pole, it didn't help me at all. I don't want to use a pole anymore.

February 6 — I got a letter from Papa, Kalla, and Lillemamma, which said that they are all well. Bya is getting tall, fat, and healthy. She's started to read with Hexa.[22] Otherwise, I spent the day eating, drinking, cooking, and sewing, and in the evening, playing whist.

February 7th passed exactly like the previous day had, except that I didn't get any letter from home.

February 8 — For me the day went exactly like February 7th.

February 9 — The most exciting thing that happened this day was that Auntie and I walked up to Askevold, despite the terrible weather. It was raining so much that there was a lot of water under the deep snow. On the way up it went fine, but on the way down, Auntie fell in a ditch and got drenched. Apart from this, the day passed like the previous ones had, but since it was Sunday, I read, instead of sewed.

February 10 — The day was like the 8th of February. I was weaving a little on a linsey-woolsey that Auntie has set up now.

February 11 — News from the herring fisheries came here from Kinn. They said there hadn't been so many herring in many years, but they were so badly paid that they didn't get more than sixteen shillings for 100 herring; last year you could get two spesiedaler and twelve shilling for 100 herring.[23] That's because there were so few buyers. Today Uncle sent someone out to Kinn to bring him the fish tithe that's due.

February 12 — It was snowing heavily and Uncle said that there hadn't been this much snow here at Askevold since the year 1840. I was outside trying out the skiing conditions this day, but they were so bad I went back inside and continued with my usual occupation.

February 13 — I wrote home to Father, and he learned a lot about the fishery at Kinn.

February 14 — Uncle was supposed to have been in Aafjorden, but his ride wasn't home from Kinn yet, and there weren't any other men here to give him a ride, as they were all at the fishery except for a few old, old men. A few boats from Kinn arrived, but most of them wouldn't have dared go out this day because of the fog.

February 15 — All the men who had been at Kinn fishing came home since it was Saturday, and according to custom, everybody has to be home on Sunday. It was very amusing to watch how one boat after another came into the bay here. Once I saw fourteen really big boats sailing by under full sail, one boat weighed down more with herring than the next. Uncle's tithe boat came too, but Uncle was a bit surprised that he didn't get more than twelve shillings for some herring and eight shillings for others, but he had to sell almost all of his tithe over there since he had such a small boat that it couldn't take more than 2,500 herring. That evening they were all prepared (*prekeverede*, as they say here). I thought it was very amusing to watch once I got out in the brew house (*ildhuset,* as they say here). Eight or ten people Auntie had gotten together were sitting in a circle around a pile of herring, cleaning them. Their mouths were going just as fast as their hands, even though those were moving pretty quickly, since the herring had to be prepared (cleaned, salted, or hung up for smoking) the same evening. Auntie was not all that pleased with the herring fishery this spring, since she hadn't been able to borrow a big enough boat to take the herring home, instead of selling it for six shillings. But all the bigger boats were used by the owners themselves.

February 16 — I read *Morskab* all day (it was Sunday) when I wasn't out skiing. But since skiing conditions were excellent, a great part of the day was spent with this amusement.

February 17 — Most of the men who came home from Kinn on the 13th went back to the same place to fetch the load of herring they had left ashore there since they couldn't load it onboard the first time. Auntie and I took a ride into Tristad, but there was a lot of snow to drive in.

February 18 — The day was spent very quietly. But I had a big surprise when a freight carrier brought letters from home. They were definitely a bit old: some were from the 11th of November, others from the 14th of November 1844. The letters were from Eika, Lillemamma, the maid Brandt, and also from Kalla. In this last one were silhouettes of all my siblings except for Hanken's and Rosa's. I got Hermann Preus's, too. I also got a white dress, which had been a present from Miss Holfeldt to Eika, but which the folks at home thought was for me. The carrier had been to Bergen, and he brought back a watch that I had sent to Bergen to get fixed a couple of months ago.

February 19 — The day passed without my doing anything but the usual.

February 20 — The day flew by just as the 19th of February had. The evening was fun, because then my uncle told me several anecdotes. The one I liked the best is the one about Count Wedel. He traveled around to look at the more distant parts of his forests. One evening, on one of these journeys he met a whole row of coal-drivers in a hill close to Berum (his land). The count yelled to them, "Get off the road!" But what did the men do? (They were angry with the count for reasons not worth mentioning here). Instead of moving out of the way for the yelling man, whom they knew very well, they drove in the middle of the road so that it was impossible for the count to get through.

But for each of these coal drivers who drove past Wedel, the impudent ones gave him a stroke on his back with their whip. The insulted could, however, live with the strokes, but when he got to Berum he asked one of the lieutenants living there, "Would you loan me your Damascus sword? Also bring me the two strongest blacksmiths." The man went out and returned with the blacksmiths and the blade. The count then instructed the blacksmiths to fetch the coal drivers, who had just arrived, and place them in a side room. Everything was done as he had ordered, and each of the coal drivers had to go before the count in turn. As each came in, the count asked him, "Do you know the man you attacked on the road?" The answer was "Yes" — a sad "Yes." With that, the coal driver got a few swats with the blade, and afterward everything was all right again. After I heard this anecdote, I went to bed.

February 21 — Aunt Rosa got a letter from the people at Uranienborg. They were all well. Also a lot of boats came in from Kinn, the same ones that left some days ago. Auntie was told by some people that when they came to Kinn, the herring hadn't gone yet, but they didn't want to fish more than they already had. They also said that the herring hadn't stayed at Kinn for so long in a long time. They had been at Kinn for _____[24].

By the way, it was calm and quiet here. Daarthe[25] started weaving a new linsey-woolsey, and Auntie and I were busy winding thread into balls, though I needed all of my patience to finish one ball, since the thread was so poor. I was happy when I'd finally finished one ball, and then I said I had to go upstairs to read.

February 22 — The morning passed peacefully, but in the afternoon I had fun skating. When I'd had enough, I stopped to go with Auntie to Ask to see if we could hire a man from there to go into the city with two lepers. They would be going together with one of the hired men from the parsonage, who goes by the name of "The Admiral." We really didn't need to take the trouble to go all the way to Ask, because we couldn't get anyone there who was willing to go, because they were afraid they would miss the fisheries at Buelandet. We ended up getting a man from one of our closest neighbors, a *Tys* called "Little Lars." Finally Auntie and I went home. When we came into the living room, we were surprised to find Uncle sitting on the sofa, since he had been lying down the rest of the day.

February 23 — We had such a strong wind that the city people I mentioned were unable to leave. I amused myself for quite a while watching a large number of skiers and skaters who were practicing near the parsonage. After I'd watched long enough, I went up to the barn with Auntie, and looking out on the water from the road here, we could see the steamer *Constitution*, which was out on its first trip to get reports from the herring fisheries. It docked at Saugesund, not far from here. Uncle was not well this day either, though he was better than yesterday, and he told me I should write my letters if I wanted some of them to get to Bergen, since the Admiral was leaving tomorrow, if the weather would allow it. I went upstairs and wrote a long, long letter to Anne Elin Christie. After having done that, I went to bed.

February 24 — The much-mentioned city people left, even though they were very displeased as they had heard that the fishery at Buelandet had started, and every man in the area went to the fishery. The linsey-woolsey was started today, and it was a lot of fun to help get it set up.

The children got a bunch of cough drops from Governor Christie,[26] but I didn't get any.

February 25 — I was working very hard in the morning, but not so much in the afternoon. In the evening we drank a toast to sister Hexa, since it was her birthday. My toast for Hexa was as follows: "May she not practice too much witchcraft in her 16th year!"[27] This evening I had so much liquor that if I couldn't take a lot, I'd have been drunk.

February 26 — Nothing worth writing down took place except that we got very good reports about the fishery at Buelandet. Yes, they were so good that my uncle wants to go out there to have a look, and I'll get to go with him. The trip is supposed to take place in two days.

February 27 — This day Uncle wanted to send people out to the fisheries to collect the tithe. But first he wanted to have accurate reports about how the fisheries were going. So he sent his servant, Jens, over to Saugesund. The message he came back with was as follows: the report about the excellent fisheries at Buelandet is not quite true. The herring had come into the sound, but Rosendahl had closed it with some seines, so that most of the herring school, which was outside the net, left the sound. Herfurt had made what looked like good casts, but regardless of how good they looked, every last herring had gotten out of the net before he raised it. This was really not all that strange, since something unfortunate always happens to him. Uncle didn't send anybody to him for the tithe.

February 28 — Uncle's people left for Buelandet to get the tithe, despite the very uncertain reports he had received. Doctor Landmark came today, and he said that the whooping cough hadn't really been too hard on the children. Carl was the one who looked the worst, whereas Wilhelm looked best. Afterward the doctor left.

March 1845

March 1 — I made the acquaintance of two young merchants who came here from Buelandet to discuss the herring tithe with Uncle. One was Dancher Roggen, brother of *stud. the.* [theological student] Johan Roggen; the other one was Rosendahl. He used to be a seaman, but he had more interest in being a merchant than a seaman, so he left the seamen's ranks. In the evening, Auntie and I went out for a walk with the two of them, but when Auntie saw my skis, she asked Roggen if he wanted to go skiing. He had never been skiing before, so I had to teach him. I thought he was a very good student, because he was soon skiing as well as I was. After we'd been skiing for a while, we went back inside, where a Boston table was ready for the four of us who had been outside; Uncle was not well enough to play. We played cards until *fløielsgrøten*[28] was set out for supper. Shortly after we had eaten, I went to bed, so I don't know what happened between when I left and when the young men went upstairs to bed.

March 2 — Auntie was going to examine my hands for frost and she advised me to put them down in the snow, but then my fingernails hurt so much that that I barely made it into the kitchen before I fainted. Despite all the other sufferings I endured before I fainted, they didn't help with the frost at all, which was very annoying. In the afternoon, the two visitors were supposed to go back where they had come from, but Uncle would not let them. He said he would very much like to have them here until tomorrow, and they agreed. We went skiing, too, and Roggen got very good today. As the previous day they also played Boston, but I was excused, because Uncle was able to play his own cards.

March 3 — The snow was so deep that the visitors couldn't possibly leave. So they had to try to pass the time today as well as they could here at the parsonage, reading, skiing, and playing cards.

March 4 — They finally left and they had beautiful weather too. After Auntie and I had walked them to the boat, we happened to stop by Uncle's boathouse. To our great surprise, we found a cod nearly four feet long and a foot wide.[29] The boy in the warehouse said it was a present from Rosendahl. Both Auntie and I had to admit it was the biggest cod we had ever seen. When they had left, I returned to my usual pursuits.

March 5 — Hendrik (the man who had been in the city) came home, and among a lot of other things, he had a big pile of letters. Among those there was also a letter for me from Governor Christie, which I really appreciated. In the letter, he invited me to come to Bergen in the spring. At the same time, I also got a bag, which was a present for me from Anne Holfeldt. It had been in Bergen for quite some time, but because of the neat knit-work in it, Aunt Thrine[30] had kept it to use as a knitting pattern. I also got two very good pencils that I had written home for. All of this took place in the morning. In the afternoon, the men who had been at Buelandet to collect the tithe for Uncle came home. This time they only brought money for about one-sixth of the tithe (if Uncle sold all of it, fresh), Uncle thought. The remaining five-sixths he was to get from Rosendahl, I think. Hendrik brought home some linsey Auntie had sent to Bergen.

March 6 — They spread fertilizer in Auntie's garden. While they were doing that, she was busy cutting a dress for me out of the linsey Hendrik had brought. I started the skirt right away, and the housemaid started the bodice, since the dress was supposed to be done on Monday.

March 7 — Uncle went to Aafjorden in spite of the fact that he was clearly not well enough to go. Auntie could not get him to stay at home, even though she used all of her eloquence on him. Auntie and I walked him to the boat, and he set out after having heard several times that under no circumstances should he leave Aafjorden unless the weather was beautiful. Aunt Lodviska's birthday was celebrated very solemnly at Askevold; the entire staff at the parsonage was treated to coffee.

March 8 — We saw starlings for the first time in the new year. A big starling was sitting in a large ash tree right outside the living room window, singing beautifully. By the way, nothing really exciting happened that day, at least as far as I know. I was indoors all day, hard at work.

March 9 — It was Sunday. I read all day, and thus had an excellent time.

March 10 — Uncle was supposed to come home from Aafjorden, but because the weather was so bad, we didn't think he would come. A little after noon we were very surprised to see Uncle's boat (the one he takes to church at Vigen). Auntie and I went down to the pier. The boat had already arrived, but there was no Uncle. Instead, one of his carriers brought a letter for Auntie, in which he said that he couldn't leave the harbor or the inn at "Korssund," but he let his carrier go. If the weather would allow it, though, he would get a ride from "Korssund" in the morning. He also said that Auntie and I could go to Tysse the next day for Judge Landmark's birthday. With this we went back up to the house, and had to accept the fact that no minister was coming.

March 11 — In the morning, my linsey dress was done, and a little bit later Auntie and I went to Tysse. When we arrived, all the guests were already there. At 2 p.m. there was dinner and as we drank the Judge's toast, we heard six cannon shots, source unknown. Afterward the women and the men were separated and the first group went to the office to play cards and the last group went into the hall to spend time doing one thing or another until the evening, when the dance began. The music was very good, as we had three musicians, Attorney Landmark on the violin, Doctor Landmark on the flute, and minister — or more accurately, Curate — Friis on guitar. The three were among those who had been playing cards, but they had gotten tired of that, especially Friis. So now they came up to treat us to some music, to which we partly danced, and partly listened. It was really very beautiful. The beautiful music soon stopped though, because Pastor Lund, who had started the game of cards and was the most eager of them all, came up and asked them to stop playing music, and instead continue the type of playing he preferred (cards). Even though they would have rather kept on playing for us (since all three really enjoyed music), the doctor and the attorney went along with him. But Friis did not want to, so he got someone else to take his place. Meanwhile, he began singing, accompanying himself on the guitar. Finally the Boston players came back up and we started dancing again, but since it was getting late, we soon danced ourselves to bed.

March 12 — Everyone who had been at Tysse on the 11th spent the day there again. In the morning, the men started playing cards again right away, while the women went over to the office to play billiards. Later in the day, the magistrate came in and asked us if we wanted to go for a ride, the conditions being so good. We all went; there were several sleighs, and we had a great trip. We drove past a big mountain called *Storebautaen*, and later we passed another mountain called *Lillebautaen*. At the top of it some boys were playing the lur[31] — it was really fun to listen to. We crossed a little inlet, entirely surrounded by high mountains except at one end. We turned when we had crossed the inlet, and came back to Tysse just in time for lunch. In the afternoon all of us laid down to have a nap, but Barbra and I laid together, and we made so much noise it was impossible for everybody in the side room to sleep. Finally we all went down to have coffee, but Aunt Rosa, who was not well, stayed back to see if she would be able to sleep. When it got dark enough to light the candles, the women started playing *Halv Tolv*. But after we'd been playing a little while, a maid came in and told me that Mrs. Christie was very ill; I could almost guess what it was. I ran down to Doctor Landmark and asked him to come right away, because Auntie was ill. He threw his cards down immediately and ran upstairs with me. There was Auntie, lying on the floor with cramps. Several people helped lift her up into her bed. Although the cramps were severe, they didn't last all that long, and after three hours or so had passed, Auntie was able to eat some oatmeal and crackers.

March 13 — Although Auntie was not completely over her headache, she wanted to go home. But the doctor and the other people here wouldn't let her go — partly because she wasn't well enough, and partly because she must not be the first one to break up the group. I had a good time that day, but I would have enjoyed myself even more if Auntie had been well.

March 14 — Auntie and I went home to Askevold, where the children were very happy to see us. Now my regular activities started again: cooking, reading, sewing, knitting, and in the twilight, either playing the piano myself or dancing to what Uncle Minister played. I danced with Doris, since I had taught her how to waltz.

March 15 — Aunt Rosa's birthday came and went very quietly, just like any other day, except that we had *Prinsessepudding*[32] for dinner.

March 16 — Sunday we had terrible weather. There were hardly any people at church, in all not more than twenty or thirty, and Uncle had to have the service for them. Auntie and I sat and read all day.

March 17 passed without anything in particular happening.

March 18 — Likewise.

March 19 — Uncle went to Aafjorden to hold services there Maundy Thursday and Good Friday. In the afternoon we got visitors; Rosendahl came to spend Easter here.

March 20 — Maundy Thursday came and went quietly inside the house, but less quietly outside, where it was blowing hard.

March 21— Good Friday was likewise quiet inside while there was a storm blowing outside. <u>Nevertheless</u>, Uncle came home from Aafjorden today, but he and his men were not far from perishing in Vilnæsfjorden. The boat was full of water several times.

March 22nd passed quietly.

March 23 — Easter Sunday the weather was so bad that only seven men came to church. As a result, Uncle didn't hold a service.

March 24 — Uncle went to Vilnæs to hold a service there. We had quite beautiful weather today.

March 25 — We had very nice weather here, and the children could be outside on the hill a bit, for the first time since they got whooping cough.

March 26 — It rained, but it was still quiet here. Today I started reading the small letters with Doris, though she showed very little interest in this. I guess she would rather have me tell stories about wolves, or let her play with Wilhelm, her younger brother. But that didn't happen at all.

March 28 — Uncle Christie's birthday passed just like one of the previous days, both for me and the others.

March 29th also went by without the slightest amusement taking place.

March 30 — Likewise.

March 31 — Sunday I went to church. I spent the afternoon reading.

April 1845

April 1st passed quietly. I will now stop writing for a long time (for a couple of weeks) until they start working with the soil, sowing, etc., since at that time there is always something going on that is worth writing down.

April 11th, 12th, 13th, 14th, and 15th passed without anything special taking place.

April 16 — They started plowing as well as sowing at the farms around here. Today I wrote home to Uranienborg, to Aunt Constance.

April 17 — They continued the farm work, but they haven't started here at the parsonage yet.

April 18 — A day of prayer. I went to church, and in the afternoon I read.

April 19 — I was outside with Auntie, sowing timothy in a large field. But I didn't get permission to sow in the field, so instead, I found an open area among some trees and planted my seeds there.

April 20 — Sunday Uncle was at Vilnæs. I spent the day walking around outside, as well as reading and drawing.

April 21 — They started sowing here at the parsonage. They began digging on the hill, too, and they also put up a hotbed there.

April 22 — Uncle taught me how to graft, which I found very enjoyable. I also helped Auntie clean strawberries, but since there were so many, we weren't able to finish them today.

April 23 — I got a letter from my siblings (Kalla, Eska, Lillemamma), after a month of waiting in vain for a letter from home.

April 24 — A whole load of trees — spruce, beech, and also ash — came from town, and they were all replanted the same day. The spruce were barely six inches tall.[33]

April 25 — Auntie was going to sow flower seeds in her hotbed, but they were nowhere to be found, even though we looked for them almost all day. Uncle went to Aafjorden today.

April 26 — I started looking for the seeds again, but it was all in vain; they were gone. I gave up looking and started diligently working on a dress shirt for Doris.

April 27 — It was decided that our trip to the city would take place when the steamer *Nordkap* makes its second trip. Aunt Rosa, Uncle Carl, Doris, Wilhelm, Carl, and Linka are the ones who are supposed to go to Bergen.

April 28 — I have to stop my diary writings for a while. I have so much work to do before our trip to Bergen that I won't have time to write a thing.

My Stay in Bergen at Governor Christie's

For the first three or four days I did not do anything but go with Aunt Rosa and Uncle to visit people. We went to Hagerup's, Grieg's, Konow's, Smith's, Minister Bruun's, Herler's, Riis's, Mohnen's, Marten's, and finally Bishop Neuman's,[34] where he took us to his garden. When we said good-bye, he told me that when I wrote home to my father I had to tell him that "you have been with me in my garden."

The first Sunday I was in the city was May 25th, when I went for a ride with Anne Eline Christie. Our trip took the Stradgaden and Porten (City Gate) out on Kalfareveien, past Nygaardsveien, Arstad Lunggarden (that's the source of the name Lunggardsvand, which is close by), Kalfare, Kautaa, until we came to our destination, situated a quarter mile[35] outside of Bergen, namely Friedalen, home of Customs Collector Christie[36] (brother of the Governor). Here I met a very nice and decent family, and each time I was up there, I had a great time. There were so many children, both young and old, that we had no trouble to playing. The names of the thirteen children are Wilhelm, Hans, Johan, Andreas, Anne, Christian, Magdalene, Edward, Werner, Benjamin, Butz, Hans, and finally Catharine.[37]

May 26th, 27th, and 28th, I was out visiting — very unpleasant work.

May 29th, I was at Nygaardsveien for the first time. This begins right when you leave the city and there are big, thick trees on both sides of the road, creating a very broad avenue. The road is mostly used by walkers and it ends down by a lake called Nygaardsvannet. It passes upper as well as lower Nygaard.

May 30th, I was at home, and the day went by without any variation from my usual activities at home.

May 31st went by just like the previous day, but the weather was beautiful, so I took a walk to Sverresborg where I listened to the music, although I thought it could not be compared with the military music in Christiania.

June 1 — I went to a party at Secretary Smith's where I had a really good time.

June 2 — I was at home. It was raining, but every now and then it stopped, and I went down to the customs wharf to look at the ships from foreign countries that were there. Also I enjoyed looking at the big *Nordfarere*[38] sailing in.

June 3 — Went by quietly, although I went to some of the shops along the Strandgade, which is terribly narrow.

June 4 — I went for a ride to Friedalen.

June 5 — A Danish corvette came to Bergen. I heard them say that the ship in itself was not pretty, and I didn't think the cargo the ship brought was much worth, either; it was inch-high cadets with blue-striped pants, blue shirts with some red decorations on them, plus a small sword at their side. There were also some knock-kneed non-commissioned and commissioned officers, plus a snuffling, lisping captain. They were all ugly, that's for sure.

June 6th was quiet.

June 7 — The cadets were going to the museum, and Governor Christie guided them around. But all the Danish cadets were claw-fingered; they handled everything that was not locked in. Christie took the captain and showed him around, and after he had been looking at the turtles, his eyes landed on a *klumpfisk*.[39] "Oh look, there's another turtle!" the captain said. "That is a *klumpfisk*," said Christie. "Then I must say it is very similar to a turtle!"

June 8 — We had bad weather, so I was taken good care of at the customs house.

June 9 — I got a lovely parasol from Governor Christie.

June 10 — I walked to Nævegaarden with Anne Eline Christie. We went through Strandgaden, across the marketplace and Tyskerbryggen, where several *Nordfarere* were unloading, through Oregaarden down to Sandvigen, down Ladegaardsbakken, and after a half mile[40] of walking, to Nævegaarde. There we had a beautiful view over the city.

June 12 — I went to Friedalen and climbed a mountain close by called Ravnebjerget, from which you can see to Korsfjorden.

June 13 — I was at home doing all sorts of things.

June 15 — I was at Sverresborg again. I was supposed to have been at Korskirken that day, but I was too late.

June 16 — I was at home, but in the afternoon I went to the museum for a while. I had a lot of fun looking at and hearing about all kinds of things. Among other things, it was fun to blow on a lur[41] they had there.

June 17 — I was at Tyskerkirken[42] listening to a sermon as part of Mission Day. I went to a party at Minister Bruun's later, where I became acquainted with Elen Bruun and Lena Halven. The corvette left today.

June 18 — I was at home.

June 19 — The same.

June 20 — I was at a party at Minister Daal's. I also went to the museum.

June 20 — I was at the museum. In the afternoon I went up to Fride and spent the night there.

June 22 — I took Wilhelm Christie (son of the customs officer) on a trip to *Sortediget* early in the morning. We were supposed to have been at *Uldrikken* today, but the weather had been too bad the day before, so instead we decided to take a trip to the parsonage Tanøe, which is situated two miles[43] south of Bergen. At 10 a.m. next morning, the Christies from the customs house, plus Auntie and Uncle, came to Friedalen, and all of us went to Minister Daal's at Tanøe. In the morning when we were leaving, it looked foggy, but later on in the day we got the most beautiful weather you could wish for. The largest farms we passed were Landaas, Paddemyren, Natland. When we were a bit more than halfway there, we came to Kallandspakken from which you have a very pretty view over Kallandsvandet and the farms surrounding this lake. After another half hour we stopped at a farm to eat. We stayed there an hour, and afterward we continued on our way to *Tanøe*, where we arrived at about three in the afternoon. Here I met a very old minister, Daal, and his wife, both in very good health in spite of their age — the minister seventy-four and his wife sixty-something. We had a little meal here and afterward we went home. We took a different way than the one we came, though. The biggest farm we passed was *Steen*. At eight in the evening we came back to Friedalen and left from there to the city at ten.

One thing I have forgotten: When we left *Tanøen*, old minister Daal walked us out and yelled "Hurray!" as we let our trusty horses run off. "Heida!"

June 23 — I was at Steerling's at *Nalland* and looked around there.

June 24 — I went to a dinner party at Hagerup's at *Landaas* and had a very good time. Early in the morning, Aunt and I were packing, since we were leaving with Nordcap the next day.

June 25 — We left Bergen, and when we came onboard the steamer, the two noisemakers we were supposed to take with us to Askevold were already there. They were Mrs. Martens with her son and her sister — the noisemaker maid Amalie Eriksdatter Pettersen. (She saw me write this.) I only made acquaintances among a few young girls in Bergen — which always smells of herring. But those I liked the best were Maria Hertzberg and Laura Grieg. With the former I went to a concert, and I was up to Lassen's with both of them. I also became acquainted with Ida Kühle's family.

July 1845

July 2 — My birthday. I got a very pretty ladies' signet ring from Aunt Rosa.

July 12 — Mrs. Martens left us, but they didn't take the steamer. We had convinced them to stay eight to ten days longer, and then leave the next Saturday overland to Leervig (*Bøefjorden*). On Sunday, they took the steamer *Constitutionen* from there to Bergen.

The woman with the family was coming to Tysse, Judge Landmark's farm, accompanied by Rosa Christie. When they arrived there, they found a letter for them saying that everything was well at home. They continued the journey, and Aunt Rosa went with them to the first relay station, "Flekke."

July 13 — In the morning Auntie came home, and we met her at the wharf. But we were soon even happier. No sooner had Auntie greeted us than we saw maid Amalie Pettersen come up from the boat where she had been hiding beneath some coats. We agreed on what we wanted to do to honor Governor Christie's family when they came to see us on the 16th of this month. Amalie and I convinced the others that we should make an *Æreport*[44] for them. It would stand by the garden gate at the base of the hill.

July 14 and 15 — We had so much rain we were afraid our arrangements would come to naught. In the meantime, we spent our time quite comfortably indoors.

July 16 — We had beautiful weather, so we got busy with the *Æreport*. It would consist of two small birches placed by the garden gate, their trunks surrounded by a thick garland which would also create an arch between the two trees, right below their tops. Thanks to Auntie's help, the *Æreport* was done early, but since we had the time, we agreed to make a flag. We took a square piece of white cloth, sewed a thin wreath around its four edges and a little bit thicker one in the middle, where we had sewed Governor Christie's initials (W.C.). The flag was done just as the steamer came in Saugesund, and when the boat with our visitors was in the middle of Vigen, we ran the flag up a big flagstaff at the top of the bishop's house. We now greeted our visitors at the wharf, but neither the governor nor his sister (Aunt Thrine), nor his niece (Anne Eline) came. But his son, W. Christie, and his brother, Customs Officer W. Christie with three of his grown sons, Wilhelm, Hans, and Johan, were there.[45] So it was for these people that we had run up a flag and made an *Æreport*. However, we were lucky with the initials in the flag, as they were the initials of three of the visitors.

We spent that evening just talking.

July 17th, 18th, 19th, 20th, 21st — yes, each day until the 26th, Amalie and I were simply living in whirl of activity, because during the day we were out fishing with the customs officer's sons, and in the evenings after dinner we were outside, doing whatever we came up with. We made a lot of noise, that's for sure!

July 26 — The sad moment of good-bye was here. The entire staff at Askevold walked the guests down to the wharf, and when they set out from the quay, the people on shore (the ones from Askevold) yelled "hurra" three times, and we got the same reply back from the boat. Shortly before Wilhelm Christie (the governor's son) left, he gave me a beautiful brooch for my confirmation, and Wilhelm C. (the officer's son) gave me a tatting needle that he owed me.

July 27th, 28th, 29th, 30th, and 31st — For the most part, Amalie and I were sewing and reading. But every now and then in the afternoons, we went out fishing. We were very good at catching this ugly type of fish (skate), which belongs to the flatfish family. The male has three long tails, but the female's are not as long.[46]

August 1845

August 1, 2, and 3 — We stayed within the four walls.

August 4 and 5 — The same, except that instead of sitting, we were walking inside the four walls. We were very busy because Governor Christie and family were coming.

August 6 — Governor Christie's family arrived, though his son, Wilhelm, did not come, to my great sorrow. It helped, however, when Aunt Thrine said, "Linka, I know you're sad that Wilhelm is not here, but he had too much work to be able to leave the customs office. However, it will comfort you to know that he's coming on the next steamer, in about three weeks, and will stay here until we all go back to Bergen on *Nordkap*. We've brought a little girl who probably can compensate for Wil's not being here, at least for a while."

"Oh, Aunt Thrine. You talk as if I'd never met Anne Christie (the Customs Collector's daughter).[47] But I have, and I'm very surprised to see her, because when her father was here, he answered with a definite 'No, thank you' when Aunt Rosa asked him if Anne could come along with you."

August 7 — Anne Christie and I amused ourselves as well as we could. One day was like the other, but we did have a lot of fun from the day she arrived until she left on September 14th.

August 16 — Amalie Petersen went back to Bergen, after having been here for two to three months. I think she had a lot of fun. At the same time, my uncle, Pastor Christie, went to Bergen, too. He went for reasons of his health, as well as to help manage the housekeeping. But he went mostly to be company for Wilhelm, who was still there.

September 1845

3rd of September W. Christie came, but Anne and I got neither more lazy nor more hardworking for that reason. When W. did not want us to come fishing with him, we went out with Acting Minister Friis, who was here to fill in for Pastor Christie while he was in Bergen. Otherwise, he lives in Førde, where he is curate for his father, Minister Friis.

September 14 — All of the Christies left. Before their departure, all of them except the governor visited Magistrate Landmark and his big family at Tysse.

September 15 — From now until the last day of September, I studied religion with Friis in the afternoons. Before Uncle went to the city, he had asked him to do that. I can't deny that I was a bit anxious before we started studying together, but after the first afternoon, all this anxiety had flown away, since I liked him very much — not very much, but at least a lot.[48] I also liked it when we were not studying, because I was not alone.

September 30 — Friis went home, and Auntie went with him to Tysse.

October 1845

October 1 — Uncle came back home, feeling quite good after having been in rather poor health during his stay in the city. He studied with me once, and when we were done he said a couple of words to me regarding my forthcoming confirmation.

October 12 — I was confirmed. I wore a very long skirt for the first time. I think I stepped on it four or five times until I made it to my place. Because I had told Uncle that I had problems standing still for a long time, I had a chair brought into the church, on which I could sit when the hymns were sung and when Uncle was with the confirmands further down. I thought, and I am sure everybody else thought so too, that the sermon that day was excellent. A few days later I asked the schoolmaster and parish clerk Mons Andersen what he thought about the sermon. He answered "Oh yes, that's a man who knows how to do it."

We had beautiful weather that day, so we could expect visitors from Tysse. They had not yet arrived when Auntie, Uncle and I went to church, but they arrived a little bit later, so when Uncle and I came back from church, we saw Auntie and the entire company in the living room: Mrs. Landmark, her daughters Barbra and Andrea, plus another Mrs. L. They told me they had arrived just as the minister was questioning the first of the boys. Later in the afternoon, I had to smile when Barbra said, "How annoying that the minister had already questioned you when we arrived." The reason I smiled was that when Barbra had been here fourteen days earlier, she said she wanted to come out for my Confirmation Sunday, and I answered her, "Oh yes, please come, but I know you won't be in time to hear me answer anything, I know you that well!" "Oh, I'll see to that, Miss Smarty"

Oh, I can write what was sent to me this day, except for letters from Grandmother, Father, siblings, and aunts, plus girlfriends, cousins and friends — ha, ha, ha, ha!

From Grandmother I got a brooch, from Father I got a necklace with a diamond lock and a little ring. Both were very precious to me because my mother had worn the ring on her confirmation day, and also the necklace. Siblings: from Kalla I got nothing, from Hexa a chemise plus a couple of ruffles. From Lillemamma I got a handkerchief, from Hanken a needle case, from Rosa a beautiful box in which I should put all of these things, and from Liden a lock of hair and a long letter. From the aunts: from Lodviska I got a ring she had gotten from Momma, from Maren a silver bracelet, from Constance a little golden needle, from dear Aunt Rosa (wife of the minister at Askevold) I got two earrings with pendants, from maid Brandt I got a ring, from Marie Keyser an embroidered handkerchief, from Doralise Smith a ring. From Governor Christie I got a brooch, and from Hermann Preus smooth[49] earrings. However, what should have been mentioned first comes at last: from Uncle I got a hymn book, and from his daughter Doris a couple of tortoiseshell combs for my hair. I could have written a lot more about this extremely important day, but it is not necessary, as it never will be erased from my memory. Even if I could not be at home with my father and my siblings, I did not miss them, because Auntie and Uncle are so kind and good, and I am extremely fond of them.

October 13 — Doctor Landmark's wife and Andrea left, but the Magistrate's wife and Barbra stayed. They were planning to leave two days later.

October 14 — I sat inside most of the time, talking to Mrs. L. and Barbra. We were also out in the garden, eating lots of red currants and gooseberries. Gooseberries are a rarity this time of the year; you can't find them anywhere but here at Askevold, and we get them every year.

October 15 — The same.

October 16, 17, and 18 — We did the slaughtering, and I had a lot of fun stuffing sausages and mashing the meat — that was what was most fun, I thought. When I came inside in the evenings, I was amused listening to our two previously mentioned guests, who were complaining about the terrible weather which had kept them back for two days. It even seemed like we would get the same weather the next day. On the 18th they were able to leave, but not really without concern for the weather; when the squalls came, the waves were dangerous. Before Barbra left, she gave me a very nice ring.

October 19 — It was Sunday, and I almost always spend Sundays in the same way: reading, drawing for the kids and telling them stories about wolves. They don't want to hear any other stories.

October 20, 21, yes right to the 31st — My occupation one day was the same as the next, but I think what I did the most of was telling the children stories about weasels and wolves, plus teasing them some in between. I thought I only teased them a little, but my Aunt Rosa had a different opinion.

October 24 — I went to God's table for the first time in my life.

October 29, and also 30 — Auntie was in bed with an earache. She placed three leeches behind each ear. I was sorry that the earache had to come at this particular time, since it had been agreed that on the 30th, Auntie and I would accompany uncle four miles[50] into Dalsfjorden to Ousen, a farm where Pastor Rennord[51] lives. We would then go a half mile[52] from there to Bogstad, the church that was to be dedicated on Sunday, November 1st.

October 31 — Auntie was well enough to leave for the dedication with Uncle and me. We had such a terrible wind, though, that the boatman and Uncle weren't sure we could travel, but as we had fair wind getting out on the fjord, we went quite fast. However, as we came out to Granesundet (close to Askevold and an island called Prestøen) there was so much wind that they took the sail all the way down for a little while. When we found shelter by Prestøen, we lay quite still for about fifteen minutes until the rain and the wind had calmed down. While we were lying there, they were talking about going back, but we never did, because the boatman said that as soon as we had passed Dorghellen's Point, there would be no more danger. The sail was hoisted again, and in a little while we reached the point the people were talking about. It was not as harsh there as in *Granesundet*, not at all. Instead, I thought it was very enjoyable to sail here, since there was a pretty high groundswell. (?)[53] When we reached Tysse, we left Auntie on shore there and Uncle and I continued toward Ousen. We arrived there at five in the afternoon. I got a friendly welcome but I didn't enjoy the evening very much, since I was sitting at a table all by myself, sewing. The ministers had so much to do before the dedication the next day.

November 1845

November 1 — Bogstad church was dedicated. I went there in Dean[54] Rennord's boat.[55] When the seven ministers entered the church, they put on their surplices, while the bishop (Dean Lund) also put his _____[56] on. Afterward the ministers each read a selection from the Bible. Then there were several speeches from the chancel by Dean Friis and the parish clerks Friis and Halager.

Lund gave the dedication speech from the pulpit. There was not the slightest bit of devotion in God's house that day. First, the church was stuffed with people. Second, these people made so much noise you could hardly hear what the speaker said. However, that was mostly because the gallery was so full of people it threatened to fall down. To prevent this, military guards were sent up to get people down from there.

A very amusing little scene took place in the church during the dedication. Mrs. Rennord could not come to church as early as the rest of us, and thus arrived later. She happened to come into the church right when Dean Friis was giving his sermon from the chancel. As she carefully walked up the aisle, she wanted to pass him quietly. But she walked past the old minister at the moment that he said "Amen." He stepped aside, took a deep bow, and said to the passing minister's wife, "Would you please be so kind as to step up, Mrs. Minister." She was quite embarrassed by this charming little church scene, and took a seat near the altar, where the rest of the women were sitting.

After the dedication I went back to Ousen, where I had a lot of fun that day. In the afternoon I saw old Pastor Rennord, but when I saw him, a shiver ran through me; he looked, if I dare say, like a ghost. He said that his health would not allow him to take part in the great joy of the Bogstad church dedication. But he thanked God for being lucky enough to see his parents' church, then old and run-down, now as his property, new and rededicated. Later I heard that he suffered from tuberculosis and that he himself was waiting to die. He had even had work started on his coffin.[57]

November 2 — we left Ousen and when we said good-bye, Pastor Rennord asked the six or seven ministers present if they would to come back (soon) to carry his body to its last resting place. Uncle and I went with Pastor Lund to Bjergene parsonage, where we were meeting Aunt Rosa, since Auntie and Uncle were going to Communion together the next day. I can't deny that I was a bit worried at five in the afternoon, when I got to the parsonage Bjergene, a quarter mile from Tysse (no, I guess it is half a mile[58]), and there was no Aunt Rosa to be found anywhere. Uncle and I thoroughly discussed the possible reasons for this, for if she had been sick, there should have been a messenger at Bjergene to tell us. Finally, at 7 p.m. two rather big women came into the living room, and who were they other than Mrs. Landmark and Aunt Rosa? She had been so ill earlier in the day she did not want to leave, but as she got better later on in the afternoon, she went, and Mrs. C. Landmark came with her. Just as I had been ready to cry earlier in the day, now in the evening, I was just as happy.

At 11 p.m. I went to bed.

November 3 — Auntie and Uncle went to Communion and while they were at church, Barbra L. and I went looking for nuts under the nut trees. But most of the nuts we found were inedible. When we finally got tired of this, we went home, where we found the church people. We had dinner and spent the day at the parsonage.

November 4 — In the morning we set off in Pastor Lund's boat for Askevold, although we stopped at Tysse to let off Mrs. Landmark and Bieland. In beautiful weather, and in an even better mood, we reached our beloved Askevold at two in the afternoon. I was happy to be home, because there's no place with our neighbors that's as nice as it is here at Askevold parsonage.

November 5 — Everything followed its usual routine.

November 16 — For a long time now I haven't been writing, but I'm basically a fool[59] who sits herself down to write, because I really have nothing to write about, since I don't want to just write down the things that happen here every single day.

November 17 — Auntie gave birth to a beautiful little girl.[60]

December 1845

December 7 — The little girl was baptized at home. Auntie held her, and the little children and I were close by when we heard her receive the name Agnes Louise.

December 17 — Christmas preparations started here. This night (I mean the night of Wednesday, December 17th) the slaughtering started. It included two fat pigs, one ox and one cow. The last one was lean and ugly, but the first one was big and fat, since for six weeks before Christmas it was fattened up. And this summer it was grazing out on Alden, an island with beautiful meadows. They say that Bernt Alden (the farmer, who is reportedly a rather strange, changeable fellow) has sheep on the island that have not been sheared or brought indoors for several years; they are out there summer and winter. When Uncle got his ox back home and saw what great condition it was in, he asked Bernt Alden if he could graze a couple of animals there next summer, too. To this Bernt answered "No, Father, I don't want any more of your animals out here; they teach mine tricks!" Uncle laughed and with that the case was settled. Wednesday was spent slaughtering the creatures and salting them, and I was there to see how all this was done.

December 18, 19, and, 20 — We were also working with the slaughtering, but finally, Saturday afternoon, we were done.

December 21 — Sunday passed quietly.

December 22 — Baking began. We made *Flatbrød, rygbrød, fattigmandsbakkels, gode raad, julekage* and *sandbakkels*. We were done baking on *Lille Juleaften*.[61] While the entire baking fuss was going on, maid Muller and I were sewing on a carpet, which was to be placed in the bedroom Christmas Eve morning. We did not get done until 3:30 a.m. the night before Christmas Eve, but at midnight that night, life was good, since Aunt Rosa and the girls were making *fattigmandsbakkels*. We could have finished the carpet earlier, but we wanted to — and we were also supposed to — take part in the baking in order to learn. I watched how both the slaughtering and the baking were done. The carpet project was kind of funny, since on *Lille Julaften* of December 1844, maid Krafting and I were sewing on another carpet until early morning. That carpet was supposed to go in the living room.

December 24 — Christmas Eve, I was busy. First of all I had to put up curtains in the living room and the bedroom, then I put up curtains and made it look nicer in my own room. I was busy doing this and other little tasks all day until it was time to get the Christmas tree ready. The worst part of this was fastening the lights to the pine bush. (It's hard to imagine, but there is not a single spruce to be found in this area, and in order for us to have a pine tree, our servant boy had to travel almost nine miles.[62]) However, I was soon done with this, as well as putting up the gilded eggs, the roses, and the apples, plus the presents.

As soon as I was done, I lit the lights and opened the door to the living room (the Christmas tree was in the room toward the garden, next to the living room) where Auntie and Uncle were, with Doris, Wilhelm, and Carl, as well as little baby Agnes. The first five were having tea, while six-week-old little Agnes was sitting at the nursemaid's lap in the rocking chair, which is in the living room. When they first saw the Christmas tree, the children's faces flushed with joy, and they sat quiet and happy for a little while. But they soon came down from their seats and started screaming and running around the Christmas tree.

The presents I got were a collar and a couple of shirt cuffs from Governor Christie, a collar from Grandmother, a collar and an apron from Aunt Rosa, and a cup from maid Muller. But I got nothing from Papa and my siblings, the reason being that Papa had just been ill. But it was a great, yes a very great, gift that he was already well. From Wilhelm Christie I got a little bar of soap. I gave Aunt Rosa, my lovely and nice Aunt Rosa, a couple of shirt cuffs, Uncle Carl, kind as he is, got only a bottle of eau de cologne, the children got an eight-shilling watch each, and maid Muller a silver crochet hook. Here, as home, Christmas Eve was nice and enjoyable. I do not think we got to bed until 11:30 at night.

December 25 — Christmas Day, I went to church. That day, as the other days this winter and fall, we had bad weather. Because of this, Aunt Rosa was unable to go to church. Apart from this, the day passed quietly.

December 26 — The weather was too bad for Uncle to go to Vilnæs. In the evening, we lit the Christmas tree again.

December 27 — Uncle went to Aafjorden in beautiful weather. Maid Muller and I also left Askevold this day. Maid M. went to Aasnæs to her parents, and I went to Tysse for a Christmas visit. We were both supposed to come home the 2nd of January. This was not really according to my wishes: I would have preferred being at home New Year's Eve. Farewell, dear Aunt Rosa—it's your own fault that you are going to be home alone until Uncle comes back from Aafjorden, since I would much rather have been home with you than leaving!

I got to Tysse in the afternoon, got a cup of coffee then, and for the rest of the evening I did nothing but eat, drink and talk. I was with Mrs. Landmark, who was ill, for a long time. I amused myself until seven in the evening, but after that I really had a lot of fun. That's when the old Judge started reading one of Holberg's comedies; to everybody's great delight, he read it in a very funny way.

December 28 and 29 — I went for a ride both mornings. In the afternoons, I was reading, knitting, walking, talking, and playing games. I had a lot of fun. I enjoyed myself most in the evening when the Judge was reading Holberg's comedies.

December 30 — I was at a party at Attorney Landmark's in Fagervigen, where I enjoyed myself.

December 31st was like the 28th and the 29th, except that we were invited to a party at Doctor Landmark's at Leite.

Linka's Letters — 1846

[Ed. Note: After the December 31, 1845, entry, there are no extant diaries covering the period until November 27, 1849. There are, however, a number of her letters that survive from that period. Their format and character are obviously not the same as her diary entries; in particular, they have a specific audience identified. However, the tone of the letters is often similar to that of her diary. Because they provide the only insight we have regarding that period, they are included here.

Most of these letters were also included in J.C.K. Preus's edition of the diary, but in most cases, not in their entirety. In some cases, teasing or joking references to her aunt or other family members reflect the unpolished sense of humor characteristic of a teenager. Most such passages — and in a few cases, entire letters — were omitted in the 1952 edition. All of the letters are included here in their entirety.]

Askevold, May 5, 1846

My dear Auntie!

I have nothing funny or new to tell you, since Uncle wrote about all that. However, I would like to remind you of something that I forgot to talk to you about before you left. I think you remember it, but I will tell you just in case. It's about Grandma's slippers. Remember, we talked about finding something like that or something similar for Papa? You can decide whatever you think. You know I'll be happy with whatever you come up with. Then there is something else that I think you have forgotten, and that is the silk (I believe you said "Flock silk"[63]) for the ribbons like Aunt Constance was working with here. I would like to have the latter, but it's not necessary. You know enough about the narrow black silk cord for the watch. *Und nun nichts weiter...*[64]

I hope you haven't gotten worse after your trip, oh no, I really hope not! Both of your children are well and alive, I bet you take such good care of them that they are not, nor will they get, sick. Tell Doris from Carl and W that she was naughty to leave them without saying good-bye! That was because she was so heartsick about another person — how foolish!

C and W are sleeping so soundly that they snore, but if they were awake, they would definitely say "Say hi to Momma from us and give her a kiss." Did it taste good? Every time Carl cries, he yells for "My Titi," so you have to say hi to her from him.

Grandmother sowed carrots today; the weather has been too cold for that the past few days. She says "hi" to you with great enthusiasm.

I haven't seen Linka, but I see the minister's wife (several people think I am the wife of the minister) every day. She is like she was the day before you left, but not as the day you left — no, no!

Adieu, Aunt Rosa

With many greetings from your own

Linka

Greet Governor Wilhelm and everybody else from me.

Aker's Parsonage,   *June* 22, 1846

My dear Aunt Rosa!

•'m finally home — thank God! Papa is feeling better — he doesn't look as bad as I'd imagined. Today he instructed the confirmands, eighty-two girls, and tomorrow he'll instruct the same number of boys. Papa said today that he did not feel any pain when he was reading with them; it was a pleasant diversion and I think it will do him good. Every evening he goes out for a drive, but because of dust, the country road has been filled with stones, so he can hardly stand it. (That is how I understood it, but maybe that's wrong.) I wish he could get a better night's sleep so that he would not feel as weak as he does.

Grandma thought I looked just the same as two years ago, but she didn't believe me when I told her that she didn't look old. "You are clever enough not to tell the truth," she said, but I really meant what I said. Aunts L and C[65] are just as before — No! C is prettier. My siblings are all well; Eska and Lillemamma are almost as tall as I am now, but I guess everybody has grown. Bya looks so healthy, and I can feel that I have a cold coming up, and I do not want to infect her. Kalla works hard. I think he has an upcoming exam; Hermann told me today that Kalla will take his final high school exam in August, but when I asked him himself, he said "next year." He's studying privately with three different people, and Papa says he's working very hard.

Imagine how surprised I was when I arrived in Drøbak, and Kalla and Hermann came aboard the steamer. We had a lot of fun on the tour; it was, in fact, the last day Amalie and I spent a lot of time together, though she was sleeping almost the entire day. She was seasick as usual, even though the weather was beautiful.

June 23. In a moment, this letter will be sent. Yesterday as I was sitting and writing, Papa called me, and then Uncle W. Keyser[66] and Constance came, so I totally forgot your letter. Please excuse me; you can imagine how busy I am so soon after coming home. At least you will get to know how we all are doing after reading these lines. There is only one more thing I have to add, and that is my greatest thanks to you and Uncle for my stay with you. You know I normally don't give speeches, so you would have to make one up yourself.

No, no more time! Affectionate greetings to you and Uncle from Papa, Grandma (she and F met me with "The Ark" at the pier on

Sunday), and everybody else. Don't forget to say hi to Uncle and the kids from your

Linka

Greet Maid Müller.

Adieu, my Aunt Rosa!

Christiania (now) Aker, July 4, 1846

My own dear Aunt Rosa!

This letter might be a little out of date when you receive it; I don't know if I'll send it in the mail next week, or if I'll send it with "Jensen."

Even though I'm coming right from the tub, and should be well enough to write, I am wondering what I should tell you. Oh, what a shame, I do have a lot to tell you, and now you'll hear it.

On June 30, we were with Grandmother until dinner, but at five in the afternoon we went to Ullern where there was a party, Aars and Rings as well as Kavug-Mathissens, Grandmother, Lillebessa, and Linka — the noblest last, of course...! Doralise and Mathissen went to Heddemarken with Kalevig and his wife. Doralise and Mathissen will probably come back in a couple of days, but the two others will keep traveling.

Kind Aunt Rosa. Linka went downstairs. Your Eska. Now I'll catch it![67]

No, that Hexa is a big monster! You weren't so harsh that you said anything like that to me when I scribbled in the letters you were writing!

Doralise has been at Ullern for a long time now for her health. She hasn't gotten any worse. You can be sure that we both thought the other looked good when we first saw each other again in Kløds store. Doralise hardly recognized me at first, because she thought I'd become so ugly. So when she turned her back to me I said to Nasa, "How Doralise has changed, she looks so terribly bad today." "You're right," Nasa replied, "It's rare to see her as ugly as today, she looks very different." That was true, because she looked beautiful at Ullern.

Everybody had expected me to come home both fat and tall, so they were so surprised when they saw me that they said, "But Linka, you aren't any bigger than Agnes Smith, and we expected you to be taller; people have described you as a regular milkmaid."

I regret that I chose this sheet of paper to write on, because I can't find a pen that works on it. Now I will try a steel pen...

Agnes and Waleska are going to go to Nittedalen, while Uncle goes on his little trip to Fredriksvern, I think that's where he's going. Oh, these pens are driving me crazy!

Papa is the same as when I got here. A couple of days ago he started on a milk cure, he is to drink three quarts a day. We will get a cow here from Grevsen, which we can milk three times a day, because it's hard to keep the milk fresh in this heat, and it's supposed to be as fresh as possible.

(Hexa is chatting so much that is it impossible to write without errors.)

I have not been to Grevsen yet, so I can't tell you how I'll find it, but here it is beautiful. If only our Lord would give us some rain, because everything in the garden is burning up and we will hardly get any sweet cherries [morellos] or cherries, and no apples at all. But we'll have a lot of plums, currants, and gooseberries, so we should be satisfied. We also have a lot of roses, and we would, no doubt, also have had wallflowers if the man who cut the grass the day before I came home hadn't been so long-armed that he cut the tops off of all the plants. Yes, that time my children were watching out for their things well.

Soon I will go out on a drive with Papa. Our usual tour is around Ladegaardsøen[68], for it's less dusty than the country road, where the horses are walking in dust up to their knees. It doesn't matter if I exaggerate a little...

Oh, Hexa is so full of nonsense today that it is almost impossible to write, but I want to finish the letter before I go. Please excuse my handwriting as well as my corrections. Papa, the kids, and many others send their greetings to you and Uncle. Tell Uncle that I have talked to Constance about the widow's fund. If I meet A. S. I will tell her that she should write to you with Jensen, although I may not see her soon because I don't go to the city often. I've been there three times since I came home, and then I've hurried all I could. How boring the city is. Uncle Carl will not meet St[?][69] in Plysbyen, because his leg hurts so much. I don't know what it is.

Now Hexa and I will go with Papa. She and Lillemamma are now banging on the walls. Little Waleska at Ullern has become so beautiful, you would not recognize her if you met her. She is prettier than Doris, but they look alike, both the aunts and I agree. Adieu Aunt Rosa! Give my greetings to W.C. and the Governor's family from me, and my loving greetings to you, Uncle, and the kids, from your

Linka

Aker's Parsonage, July 5, 1846

My own dear Aunt Rosa!

I'll send the letter I wrote to you yesterday by mail, but today I really felt like scribbling, so I figured I could scribble down some words for you to send with "Jensen," together with some little trifles. I've told my sisters to write to you, too, but I don't know if they will do it, even though they replied, "Yes, we want to write to Aunt Rosa, to scold her for being such a naughty person!" There, you can put that on your bread and butter.

So how is Uncle doing? We hope he's well again.

Conrandie just went over to see Papa, who's resting; if Papa isn't asleep yet, he's most welcome, because he's so clever. Hjort was here this afternoon; he's our family doctor now, since both the Preuses are away, but he was very upset for a while because his son was doing so poorly. He was really distressed about that, and Papa talked to him, so now both he and Conrandie come to see him. Not that he is worse; on the contrary, Hexa and I think the swelling has gone down a little, but we don't talk about it to Auntie. We don't understand these matters and we keep it to ourselves. God grant that he'll soon get better. He's cheerful and sometimes makes jokes; that is such fun. I'm glad to be home, because now I can help Hexa take care of Papa. When it's too much work for him, we're both familiar with the office work; that is, Hexa writes in the Ministerial book, and I write sexton's slips for people who want to get their child baptized, before Papa or Boyesen have arrived at the office. It's really something to have <u>forty</u> baptisms on one Sunday (Pentecost).

Oh, we are all as poor as church mice here. Imagine, on my birthday, Papa didn't give me anything because he didn't have any money, but he'll give me something soon. Grandmother gave me a ribbon and embroidered sleeves, Mother Tulin gave me a bracelet; from Agnes Smith I received a teacup, and Kalla gave me a mother-of-pearl quill pen. The others gave me little things they themselves had been given.

I will really try to get some money and buy something that I can send you to surprise you, like two or three bunches of large hairpins, some lemon cookies for Uncle, and some peppermints for Aunt Thrine. But it won't be a lot, because, because… I also want to send some knickknacks to the little ones. Do the little rascals ever talk about me? Yes, I'm sure they do, because I was so kind to them, I think they would remember me.

Kalla is studying hard; it's a pleasure to notice how thin he is becoming. Hexa got to see the beautiful letter I wrote to Maid Müller, and it was so well written that she had to run and show it to Papa. She just came in to me to tell me that I have to send his greetings to Aunt Rosa and Uncle, and tell them that he would really like to write to you, but his side gets so tired when he sits for a long time. You can be sure he would like to write to you, to thank you for making me so gentle. Here everybody says, "Linka sure is not as quick-tempered as when she left." Of course, now in the beginning I try to be as loving as I can! Grandmother says, "I can understand that Mrs. Christie has learned how to take you the right way, but I don't think she could ever be angry. I've never seen such a happy and satisfied wife. She looked so gentle." "Oh no, Aunt Rosa was never mean to me and she never had a reason to, either." So now you know how kind everyone thinks you are, but in reality you were really mean to me!

Well Aunt Rosa, I can imagine you are sick of me now, so I'll stop. I'm surprised to see that I am actually writing the fourth page of this letter. Auntie, you are bad; how can it be that I am sitting here talking to you for so long. It isn't because I love you, oh no, not indeed. If you only were here, then I would…

A kiss from your own

Linka

"I bet Carl has become a pretty boy now," Bya says. "Linka, I remember so well when I saw him and Doris in Uranienborg that Sunday." Poor Carl! I can imagine you spoil him now, since I'm not there to tell you when J. is mean to your little boy. He probably will be a little crybaby like ____ is. I don't dare mention her name; Aunt Thrine would no doubt be offended.

I wish Doris could come here and keep Bya company; they're both two wildcats. The Sunday I came home, Bya had tricked Anna Falsen up into a manure pile. She looked beautiful when we finally found her and Bya!

Kalla sends you his greetings; he'll write to you soon, but right now, he doesn't have time.

[*Linka's father died July 21, 1846. Linka then went to live with her grandmother, Dorothea Carlsen, at Uranienborg*]

Uranienborg, August 17, 1846

My dear Auntie!

There has been a great change in our family since last time you heard from me. Oh, how sorrowful the thought of being orphans is for us; that never again will we be with our parents as we travel on this earth. But we can be thankful that when our days down here are over, we will again meet our loved ones, who now have gone before us! How deep are our thanks to our Father in Heaven, that we could be together, and that we have found a home with our dear grandmother.

Please thank Uncle for the letter I received from him on August 8th. Both of you are so kind to ask if one of us would like to live with you, but Grandmother has to decide. She knows what is the best for all of us.

Like us, I am sure you are glad to hear that Kalla has passed his exams. He got 3-3-4 on the written part and the oral part went well, too. Before the grades were decided, he was so sure he would fail.

Since Grandmother and Aunt Lillebessa are also writing to you right now, I don't have to write much more. I don't really feel like writing more today either, but you will hear from me another time.

Uncle Hoffmann, who planned to leave tomorrow, says he will stay for a few more days, because all of us walk in such an ugly way. He will teach us to walk better, and says that I walk just like you.

I am so glad the kids are well; I just wish that Uncle would be completely well, too. Here we all are in a good health.

You don't have to ask why my handwriting suddenly became so bad; it's just because Grandmother said that we had to start sewing now. I will write you more, and more neatly, later.

I'm sending you the little knife, with nice blades, I believe. You shouldn't carry it in your pocket without keeping it in its case; otherwise, it might get scratched. You have to be concerned about it, you know, so it will look nice when I see you again.

Adieu Aunt Rosa

Your Linka

Please give my greetings to the little ones and Uncle from me, and all the others. Greet the Governor, Aunt Thrine, and W. Christie many times. When Kalla comes today on his way to Uncle Wilhelm's, he'll get the letter that, after looking at the signature, we think is from W.C.

Your Linka

Uranienborg, September 18, 1846

My dear Aunt Rosa!

While I'm writing this letter, all my sisters are lying around me snoring. And why don't they have to get up for quite a while? We were at a party last night at Smith's[70], because of Doralise's birthday. There I received the dear letter from my Aunt Rosa from September 4. Thank you so much. I was planning on writing before, but now I'll tell you why it didn't happen: Even though I haven't been away from home since I was in Christiania, I've been gone four times this week: at Smith's on Doralise's and A's birthdays, then at Petersen's, and today I am going to Mrs. Holst (not Mrs. Thea). I had a great time yesterday at Smith's; all the people there were nice people I know well. We didn't forget to toast the Christies. Doralise sends her love, she will write you soon, she said.

You asked me many questions in your letter, which I now will answer. However, first I will ask you to tell Uncle that he must excuse us for not having told him more about the Widow's Fund. The reason is that I misunderstood my dear grandmother's "soon." She told me that she is going to Aars soon, where she will talk to him about it. Uncle will learn about it in the next letter from me, I promise.

You talked about the auction at Aker. It happened so soon after it was decided that there wouldn't have been enough time to tell you about it. For Kalla, the timing was really inconvenient — it was in the middle of his examinations. He sends his love; you know he is with Uncle Wilhelm Keyser, and walks to town every day for his lectures. Sometimes he comes here before he is off for town in the morning, and each time he tells me I have to sew him a cap, since the cockade and badge don't look good on the one he has. "Yes, I guess I can sew you one, but I can't buy you silk lining, as my monthly allowance tells me you should have wool lining. And you still haven't gotten the necessary badge."

Now to the auction: the Probate Court was very reasonable with Grandmother, Uncle W. Keyser, and us. Norbeck said that since Hexa and I had always used the two dressers (the two nicest ones), we should each keep one. Likewise, with our new piano, Lillemamma could keep it because Papa once told her that she could have it and that Kalla was to have the old cabinet. By the way, we kept all the things that were ours. When the belongings were all being totaled up, we hid the big pretty porcelain bowl that we gave Uncle W. Keyser. Grandmother, Uncle Hoffmann, and other family members bought back a lot of things that all of us wished would remain in the family, old furniture for instance. For Constance, Grandmother bought the dainty tea or chocolate set, and I got our damask really cheap. People paid good money for our things, except when we bought them ourselves. When the auctioneer heard any of us bid, he would strike his hammer quickly. Grandmother and Hoffmann were the most eager buyers; they bought every little thing. I asked Grandmother if she would give you a waffle iron that used to be ours; I'm sure you can have it, but she didn't answer me. Give my greetings to Aunt Thrine, Uncle, and everybody — and yourself, from your

Linka

Uranienborg, October 1, 1846

Dear Uncle!

I'm ashamed that I haven't yet written to you about what is remaining in the Widow's Fund. Finally, I've found out and I will tell you that you are to pay seventy Spd.[71] I assume you know that it has to be paid before December 11th. If you had paid in the month of June, you would have had sixty-eight Spd. seventy Skilling, but adding the interest, the total amount due in December will be seventy Spd. You might know all this, but since I received the message, I thought that I should deliver it to you. Enough about that!

I have to tell you everything that is new in town. You know that eight days ago the king[72] came to town on the steamer. When he arrived, the pier was nicely decorated, but in the flurry of looking at the king, people forgot to shout "hurrah." That was miserable, but it got better by the Palace. When he was in the theater on Sunday, however, the cheering was just as it should be. Here at Borgen,[73] nobody was planning to go to town to see the king, but we went after all, since Mother Tulin invited everybody down in the afternoon. However, everyone else felt fooled, because the king was driving in a closed carriage. But Constance and I went to Uncle Smith's to watch as he drove to see the Viceroy.[74] So we saw a little of him and Prince August. Today the guilds are having a torchlight procession with singing outside the Palace, I think, and some other night the entire student singing society will sing for the king and the prince, but they don't want to have a torchlight procession before he is crowned; thus they're waiting for the moonlight. Oh, I forgot, when the king went back home in the afternoon, the streets he drove through were illuminated.

Have I really written a whole page about the king? You must have gotten tired of it a long time ago.

Marie Meyer and Tomas Johannes Hefty will get married soon, but they're doing it very quietly, as the family is in deep sorrow after the death of Anette Hefty. She died on a trip abroad with her mother and brother. She got typhoid fever and died when they were in Dresden. Poor Madame Hefty, who now has to leave from there. She arrived with the steamer yesterday, and probably went right to Løkke where Cathrine Løvenskjold and Madame Hefty's sister awaited her. Constance says Cathrine did not know what to do, she dreaded her mother's sad return so much.

Thank God, here we all are well, with the exception of Grandmother's rheumatism. Lillebessa's headaches and eyes are doing better, even though she had some pain today and could not write to her Aunt Rosa as planned. How are you doing? Is your breast better? I guess it's almost time for communion and the confirmations; that will be hard for you. Auntie and the kids are well I hope, say hi to them all from me. Mentioning my Aunt Rosa, I remembered the potatoes — are yours diseased?[75] Askevold parish has not been mentioned in the newspapers. Here the potatoes aren't diseased, but they are few and small; Grandmother's garden won't even provide many. With Uncle at Ullern, they just started to harvest, but they will also have a poor crop. He hardly sowed any grain, mostly planted potatoes.

Send my greetings to everybody. Adieu, your

Linka

Uranienborg, November 2, 1846

My dear Aunt Rosa!

Eight days ago, Grandmother wrote a letter and she told me it was for you. But last night, I asked Lillebessa if she thought that Grandmother had written to you, and she said, "I think everything with that letter was so secretive, so I think Grandmother has fooled you." Today I asked Grandmother if I could write to you, as it has been a long time since you have heard from us. Then she said that she had written to you, but put the letter in another letter. But I didn't find out which one.

We live here quietly; if we go somewhere, it's to Ullern. Yesterday Grandmother and four of the kids went to Ullern (oh yes, all of them are bigger than me). Aunt Lillebessa and I kept house for Kalla and Lomse until coffee time, when they left, and for Bang in the evening. Bang is called the cloister parson for the cloister girls. Imagine! They've given him that name because he'll be here this winter to defend the girls. People can be so impertinent at times!

I bet you want me to tell you some news, but I know little. Well, I guess I can tell you something terribly funny, I hope Bidani didn't tell you already. Hanne Muller had twins; two girls, and when Grandmother was visiting her, she thought one of them resembled Hanne Muller, and the other one resembled Falsen because of her big curved nose (how bad that must look). The oldest girl had a little stub nose. Well, wasn't that a funny story! If only they were a boy and a girl.

Hagerup might come soon, if not before then maybe after New Year's, to take the Practicum examination. I really wish he would come, as Constance often is in a bad mood, because when she reads a letter she's gotten from him, we aren't even allowed to ask her how he's doing. Four-page, closely-written letters—what can they find to write about!

Bya just came in and asked me to say hi to you. She's doing so well, walking around in the sunshine with big water boots every day. Hanchen, on the other hand, is not doing that well. She'll probably start taking cod-liver oil again, and today she has toothaches.

We have such a busy time right now. One hour a day, the four oldest of us are the most hardworking, as it is Aunt Maren's birthday the 28th. Hexa is sewing a handkerchief, Lillemamma a pair of cuffs, Hanchen is knitting a sofa pillow, and I'm embroidering a cushion for her bathroom table. We aren't allowed to embroider more than one hour a day, and this is the hour we work so hard. However, today we have embroidered the whole day, because we're working on a tablecloth like yours. We are not to talk any language but German, but when Grandmother and all of us are in a good mood, we can speak easily. Rosa is participating, of course, but Hexa is the master of us all, as she is taking private lessons. I suppose I ought to be the most proficient, since I am now schoolmistress and am teaching both German and French, but I'm not. Grandmother wanted me to learn more languages, but that is unacceptable; she could never afford such an expense.

Lillemamma is doing well with her music. Hexa and I, or Constance and I, often play duets, and Hexa is teaching me English.

Oh, I almost forgot to tell you something Lomse told me yesterday to ask you. Would you please weave something nice and thick homespun that he can get in the spring? He told me to ask you just like that. Kalla sends his love. He was here for a short time this morning, as he spends the entire day attending lectures. His second exam is getting close.

Everyone sends their greetings. Your

Linka

Uranienborg, November 19, 1846

My kind Aunt Rosa!

It seems like it's been a long time since I heard from you, but every time I say that, the others answer, "We got a letter from her in the middle of October, so we can't expect another letter from Askevold already!" But I think that was a long time ago.

Oh, before I write something else, I have to ask you to congratulate Agnes for me. I suppose you had a great banquet that day, with wine and everything. Here we celebrated her day in an unusual manner. Aunts Lillebessa and Constance attended a party, and since it was supposed to get over later than 12:30, Hexa and I asked Grandmother if we could sit up and wait for them, so that we could hear all the ball stories "fresh," as we said. (To our surprise) she allowed us to, and we sat up eating apple cake, which Bang treated us with after all the others had gone to bed. We told each other jokes and laughed until the partygoers returned; then we made even more noise.

Talking about balls, on the eighth of this month Kalla attended a ball at the Viceroy's. Before he went there, he stopped by here in the afternoon to learn the "Francese," but he told us the next day when he came back that it wasn't at all necessary. All four of the "Francese" dances were a complete mess. Agnes Smith was there, too. She is the one who attends the balls most frequently, and people say she is almost the best dancer.

Grandmother sends her greetings, and many, many thanks for the herring you sent her, and you must also greet and thank Uncle for her, too. She has been of the opinion that you also sent her the cakes, so we had to bring out your letter and show her that they were from W.C. and not from you. If you are to write him soon — oh, never mind, I 'll probably write him myself. The skipper is still not here, but we're expecting him soon, as W.C. said in a letter to Kalla that he left Bergen in October (at least I think so).

Grandmother has been in bed with rheumatism and chest pain, but now she seems relatively healthy and is up walking again, thank God. It was in the middle of the slaughtering (a great slaughtering, not like the little affair you were going to have), as here we killed one tough old cow. For Christmas, we're going to slaughter a couple of pigs, too, I believe, so then there will be a lot more to do.

I don't think I've told you that Claus Heiberg had a daughter. His wife is relatively well, but I suppose she is still in hospital. "Heiberg looks so contented," a friend told me after he met Heiberg on the street. I wonder if in my next letter I'll have a similar story to tell you about someone else, since three things bring good luck. I think you know that

Mrs. Ingstad had a little one, as it happened a month ago. And do not tell me any similar news from your house; I admit that little Agnes is one year old, but remember, I've <u>forbidden you</u> to get sick.

Now I want to tell you some gossip! Every time I talk about housework at Askevold, that dull Lillebessa says, "Yes, they live well at Askevold." And yesterday afternoon when we talked about your fish balls with butter sauce, she said, "Yes, Rosa uses a lot of sauce, but you can see how big she's gotten." And Rosa isn't big at all. There, now you know how mean she is toward you! However, she's not as mean to you as I sometimes am to your Doris. Constance says I talk too much. We don't call Constance Aunt except when we call her Aunt Tressa, as she is angry several times a day. But we always make her happy again, as she doesn't mean to be difficult.

Yesterday I went downtown wearing my new winter clothes, a black velvet hat and a black French merino coat (half length, with fringes below and on the two small collars). Oh, it's so stylish, and not very expensive. I use the brown cloak for driving, so that's why we made the three-quarter length cloak. Bya and Rosa have new furs, too. The latter trips off to school every morning in a bad mood, since she is afraid of getting there late. In these foggy days, one should follow her to the town, as she can easily get lost in the Palace Park. She never tells us anything about school, but one day she got home and said that Mamzel Lotz had said she was "*eine kleine Puppe.*"[76]

How is Doris doing with her reading? I look at Bya and think of little Doris, who has come so far considering her age. Poor little Bya, she still can't read. If she doesn't get sick this winter, I will teach her. We all hope she will remain well; we all take care of her and with God's help she should get over the little cold. Soon she will know how to read, and later also write, and then she says she will write to Doris. Maybe Doris will beat her to it.

I have a feeling there is something more I should tell you, but I can't remember what. Give our love to Uncle and the little ones and everybody else!

Kalla will take his second exam in the beginning of December. He has studied well for this one.

Greetings to you all from your

Linka

No, not you, my Aunt Rosa! You didn't send any of us greetings in your last letter. Imagine — we've all sewn ourselves wool skirts. Well, I didn't like it and said so, too. (But Linka had to do it anyway…)

Uranienborg, December 19, 1846

Dear Uncle!

You'll probably receive this letter around Christmas, so first I want to wish you, Auntie, and all the others a Merry Christmas. I also want to thank you for all the good things from this year, and wish you a happy New Year! Oh Uncle, please excuse my handwriting, you see, I'm using a steel pen that's not worth a cent.

You've probably read in the newspapers that there was to be a student ball at the Masonic Hall yesterday, the 17th. I really have to tell you a little about it. None of us planned to go to the ball, but suddenly both Kalla and Lomse wanted to go. Kalla is now done with two parts of his second exam. He's upset because he got a 4 in Greek, as that kept him from getting an overall grade of "Laud." So he might take the whole exam over again in May. He and Lomse invited us to the ball, and Aunt L. and C. went with them, and I did, too. I didn't think that I could have a lot of fun at the first grown-up ball I attended, but, using Grandmother's expression, "I made my first entrance into the world." There was also comedy at the ball, and Lang-Bøgh was very amusing. Apart from that, everything was so-so. I danced well: I entered the ball at 6:30-7 in the evening, and came home at five in the morning. Wasn't that a lot of dancing…?

Don't you think that Kalla is a fool not to celebrate Christmas with us, and instead, he's going to our cousin Pauline Breder in Fredrikshald[77] with the Preuses? Oh well, he probably would have stayed home if we had acted sad when he told us. He leaves on December 23 and will probably come back January 6/7. He isn't quite well either, that is what he tells us, and thus he has to leave.

Another time I will write more and not so messy, but now goodbye dear Uncle. Greetings to you, Auntie, and the small ones from all of us here. Your

Linka

Linka's Letters — 1847

Uranienborg, January 7, 1847

Dear Aunt Rosa!

It hasn't been more than fourteen days since you got the last letter from me, but I would like to write you some words for the New Year. However, I won't give you a lot of good wishes for the year now, because later you'll get a printed New Year's wish that will be so beautiful that you won't believe it. You'll admire my good taste.

Grandmother is lying on the sofa taking her siesta, saying, "Wasn't the drawing I sent you beautiful?" She just asked me to send her best greetings to you and Uncle, and tell you that you'll soon be getting a letter from her, if her eyes are good enough.

Constance would like to have written to Uncle today and thanked him for his letter, at least I'm sure she would have enjoyed that a thousand times more than writing to the one she is writing to right now. She has to thank a Mrs. Hagerup for a diamond ring she received as a New Year's present at KM.

Yesterday I was in the theater and watched *The Devil's Part*, and while I was enjoying myself, I thought about you a lot. It's been a long time since you've had that kind of enjoyment, as long as it had been for me. Yes, I had a lot of fun watching; actually, it was the most enjoyable evening this Christmas. Oh, we had a good time Christmas Eve, too; Hexa and I fixed the Christmas tree for the little ones. Imagine, Auntie, Grandmother got the collar I started on when I was with you. I was contented, but later when I saw how happy the little sisters were, I couldn't help getting quiet, and I had to go out to cheer up a little. I think you can imagine what I was thinking of and why I got quiet. Well, enough about that. Aunt Rosa, Christmas Eve I scribbled a little note for you, but then Constance didn't write, and since my words were to be included with hers, I didn't send it. The family was here Christmas Day, and the next day, it gathered at Ullern. I stayed there for four days, and then Grandmother said I couldn't stay any longer. Hexa stayed for eight days to be with Auntie when Uncle left. New Year's Eve, the family was at Smith's.

Now I've brought a candle in here and wonder if I should throw away the entire letter, since it's so badly written, but I think you can see that it has gotten worse since the daylight disappeared.

Kalla will be back today or tomorrow. I got a letter from him New Year's Eve, and he has celebrated Christmas quite merrily. He was just going to attend a ball, to look at the pretty ladies, as he said. You can see what he's become!

I don't have anything new to tell you. Saturday, Hexa is going to a ball at Wegner's, Kalla will go, too, if he's back by then. At least that is what people who have seen the guest list tell me. I don't know why they haven't invited me, perhaps because I haven't visited them, but I don't care. I care less about balls, and I would stay away with great, great delight if I were ever invited to such a party. People are so critical toward simple young ladies such as myself, that I'm quite scared. I did enjoy the student ball, because it was so crowded there that everyone had enough to do just taking care of themselves.

Well Aunt Rosa, send my greetings to Uncle and everybody, from your

Linka

Uranienborg, February 4, 1847

Dear Rosa!

[Today I'll try to write to you, although my eyes are not at all good. God knows how it will end; I probably will not be able to use them _____[78] any more. Lodviska]

February 11

Well, it's true that Lillebessa's eyes are bad, but her headache is better. — Dear Aunt Rosa: It seems like I'm not very welcome in this letter. Aunt Lodviska's eyes are not good, so she won't be able to finish this today. I told her to dictate it to me, so I can write the letter for her, and only what she wants me to write, but no. The things she wants to tell you are so important that she cannot tell me, but I am quite sure I know everything she would have written about, that is how conceited I am. I think I will suggest to her that she write a couple of lines every day, in that way she would get the letter done, and you would get to know all the things she wanted to tell you.

Now Hagerup has gone, and a few days ago, Constance received a letter from him. It was sent from Lærdal, and the trip was better than he'd expected. The extract[79] and the pancakes were delicious, and when

Grandmother heard that, she immediately said "Oh, if only we had given him more! He could have gotten more, if we had only used a bigger pail."

There was a great deal of emotion when he left (February 1), for both him and Constance in the few preceding days. We came on the day of his departure, and there were many touching scenes, although none of us was as emotional as the two of them. People claimed that I had to go in the stable to give the hens grain just because I was so touched. Oh well, when everything was ready for him to leave, and the transportation had arrived, it was quite difficult. (You have experienced that yourself.) Grandmother started, Lillebessa sat down in a corner and started thinking about what was happening, and then everybody got all touched and emotional. I ran out the door immediately, got some grain and went to the stable where I had a banquet with the hens prior to Hagerup's departure. While I was standing there, I heard the bells coming up from the road, and I ran out and gave him my good-bye kiss. And then — then he was out of the gate. I realized too late that I should not have been the one to give him the last kiss, but I gave Constance the kiss back absolutely fresh! It is obvious that love is affecting her; C. has become so skinny while her W. has been here that it is a shame, but now I can see roses in her cheeks again. I bet you also have lovely roses in your cheeks, Aunt Rosa, as your children are still young enough to give you some really good kisses. See, there you have one from me ——!

Oh, I'm just talking nonsense today, but I feel so well again after being in bed for a couple of days, so please excuse me. I expect the doctor will allow me to go out tomorrow, and if only he could come up here right now so that I could get back into the corner room. Imagine, Auntie, in the spring we'll move from aforementioned room and spend both summer and winter down at the "Rose" room and the bedroom (I should have said former bedroom). Professor Thaulow[80] has rented the entire ground floor of the main building, including the kitchen. In our part of the house, the kitchen will be in the maid's bedroom and the maid's bedroom will be in the attic. We will furnish the attic and build stairs down to the kitchen. So there will be construction and masonry work here again.

I don't have any news from town—well, except that Cathrine Løvenskjold (Hefty) is in blessed circumstances. Uncle must not...

"So?! When you write nonsense like that, you'll soon have four to six pages finished!" Lillebessa is saying. Now I don't know if I should send this letter or not, and I tell her to tell me something funny. We were very surprised to hear that you hosted a ball, but you don't mention if you were in condition yourself to dance. You know, we have all these funny dreams here, and you know the conditions of the 9th.

The ruffles you got were from Lillemamma. We've had a market here; Hexa was there the two opening days. Lillemamma, Hanchen, Rosa, and Bya were with Aunt Gitta, while the rest of us were at home, and we waited and waited for treats.

Everybody is here these days. We have a sickroom, and all the kids are sent in there, with the Aunties following, and finally the doctors. I'm not allowed to leave the room, and have to stay in with little Rosemette, who also has a cold. She is or has been close to getting croup. Bya is well, thank God, and Grandmother has been quite well, too. Last Monday she attended "*Dramatikken*,"[81] and unfortunately, I was sick; otherwise, she told me, I could have gone with her. But I would not have gone no matter how well I'd been. Agnes, Doralise, and many other acquaintances were there.

You can get a couple of barrels of early seed potatoes from Uncle Carl; they're still good but he can't tell how well they'll last. You don't need to set them until May or June, as they'll mature anyway, but you should get them as soon as possible.

Send many greetings to Uncle; you have to tell him that oats are very expensive here, from eleven to thirteen marks per barrel. Uncle Carl's (Ullern) oats are so old and deteriorated; he's stored them for more than ten years so they're not good. Send my greetings to the little ones from your

Linka

Grandmother and everybody tell me to send their greetings to Uncle and you. Mattissen and his fiancé Doralise just came; they both asked me to send their greetings. Doralise would like to write to you, but her eyes hurt. Papa, sisters, and Mattissen are well, and send their greetings to your Agnes . . . Hurry up visit us!

Uranienborg, March 4, 1847

Stupid cruel Aunt Rosa! (Red Cow)

I assume you understand that I title you so nicely because this is supposed to be a birthday letter. I would be pleased if it reaches you in time, because I want to tell you that you, early on the morning of the 15th, have to imagine that I come into your room when you lie in your comfortable bed (well, I guess it is a little too narrow), tease you a little (but just out of love), and say "I wish you a happy birthday." Well, enough about your day. But I assure you that we will all drink a toast for you, if not with red wine or Sauterne, then I guess we can always use goose wine,[82] if we have any, of course! And you can just forget about getting a present from me! (Don't you think I am being nice to you...?)

Now I have started attending balls. Last Tuesday I was in the Society[83] for the first time, and I assume I will soon go to the Dramatic Society, too. Yesterday I attended a large formal soiree at the home of General Consul Wegner; the place teemed with Wedlers and Løvenskjolds and a great many others, but Agnes Smith was the only one of my friends there. I don't count Kalla among them, although he may make a nice lady. He would probably claw my eyes out if he read this! I did not arrive at the party with Agnes, so I had to enter a large hall alone. Dignified older ladies (wearing turbans, etc.) were lined up along the walls. I didn't see a single person I knew, so I started talking to a lady I was introduced to and didn't know at all. She was a very amusing person, and we soon got to know each other. Later Agnes came and she didn't know many people, either, so the two of us stayed together. We talked to some gentlemen (curates whom we had met at children's balls in the past) and other people, too. I enjoyed myself a lot, but I'm not sure if Agnes did. There was singing and music; we both were dressed in white. Wearing gloves is hard on my monthly allowance; it really is a luxury. But we wash and clean them as well as we can — I must keep myself from falling in debt.

I will soon write to W.C. — I'm not sure if Kalla has heard from him. He is so good at remembering to tell us things.

Hanchen is in bed today and Grandmother thinks she'll get the measles. It's probably better that she gets them now rather than later. Rosa and Bya will most likely get them, too. There are a lot of children who have gotten the disease these days, and Doralise is so afraid of catching it. "I couldn't stand it, uff, I would go crazy with impatience," she says. She is well and as before.

Everything is also going well with the small boys at Ullern and their home teacher; they're not as naughty as before. (There is a big difference between these boys and yours.) My students are not improving very quickly. They are so incredibly naughty, and I've lost the hope that Bya will learn how to read this year. She is just like your Doris: she will play and be naughty rather than learn how to sew and knit. You know, we're all working hard spinning now. Constance is the best, then Lillebessa and I, so we help ourselves, but Hexa, Lillemamma and H. are all beginners. I tell them that you, Auntie, should not take the credit for my talent of spinning, because when Uncle says that you should (ha ha) buy a spinning wheel for me, what do you say, mean Auntie, sitting there with five — no, four — naughty boys who deserve a little cuff on the ear or a kiss from me. Well, both taste equally good or bad (like to take the pincers out, or the same as Uncle says about your milk soup).

Lillebessa, Eska, Hanchen, Lillemamma, Rosa, Bya and Kalla (if only he knew it was your birthday) all send their greetings on your day. Your

Linka

Uranienborg, April 7, 1847

Mrs. Rosalide Isabella Christie,

Well Auntie, this letter will not reach you in eight days, but I needed a break from darning stockings. Besides, when the cat's away, the mice will play, which is what happens when Grandmother goes to town. Oh well, it is not like we turn the house upside down, but we're not working as efficiently as we should. Instead of tidying up, for instance, Constance has curled herself up in the green chair with a porridge poultice on her swollen thumb, and is sitting there reading *The Antiquarian* that she took from me. So now I don't know anything fun to do other than what I am doing right now! Haha! This is a strangely thick piece of letter...

Hopefully, you'll get a small case of the measles with this letter, as Rosa's skin is peeling after hosting these uninvited guests. Little Bya is lying in bed blossoming so beautifully. She kicks around her all the time so that one of us always has to be there with her, almost up in the bed with her. She is a naughty child. I don't think she will ever grow up to be a decent person. Rosa is still halfway decent, since she is allowed to be up late at night, but she used to be a real monster. As Grandmother's favorite pet, she always defended her, although all the aunties and siblings said "Rosa is a little grumbler". Grandmother would reply "Oh, you are so mean to her."

Now it is the Smiths' turn. Waleska has gotten the measles, and Uncle walks around her all day taking care of her. I think Doralise had gotten them when I wrote the last letter for you, and she is still in bed. She has gotten a hoarse throat, which Uncle says is due to carelessness. He keeps on telling Wallik, "Please be more careful than Dora, so you can get back on your feet soon." The conditions down there are not very pleasant now, although they cheer up when one of us comes to visit, which happens every day. At Ullern they still haven't been infected by the measles.

On April 1 I sent a letter to W. Christie. Oh, Grandmother's coming right now, now, now...

— *April* 13

Today, dear Auntie, is the first day we've spent in the small rooms. We moved in yesterday. It will be difficult for Thaulows to move in, as both his wife and children are in bed with the measles. Oh, I have a bad head cold, I would like to give some of it to Uncle.

Last Sunday we hosted a farewell party in the corner room. There were a lot of ladies present, but only two gentlemen; the others of that kind had been here the Monday after Shrovetide. I don't have more time now. (April 14) I bet Uncle was in the door for Doris at Shrovetide. Did you stay up till three to bake? Oh, people are coming and going all the time here, as we still are not completely settled after moving. But I can assure you that it looks splendid with our two living rooms (the red room and the old bedroom), both with new wall coverings. Well, the red room is the finest living room. The walls are covered with deep crimson red velvet, and on one wall all the family portraits are hanging. The only thing that could have made it better would be more portraits of the same kind, with golden frames. You and Uncle are not at all flattered by those pictures. You look like you could be in the same circumstances as you are now! Haha. How can you think, you fool (in all respect), that you can make me believe that you are even thinner now than before. You are getting cruel. Yesterday, when I was sorting clothes, I came across some pants of yours, and I got this strange wish that Lillebessa and Constance would tell me "Linka, you are an incomparable beast."

Grandmother is today, thank God, quite well. She walks around indoors and outdoors, but yesterday she didn't leave the living room. It is so difficult to write something about her, as she is doing well one day and is sick the next. During the whole process of moving her mood has not been good, but now that everything is settled and the money does not disappear so fast, I am sure it will improve. Oh dear!

I'm excited for the summer. Constance and I have so many plans. About the garden, however, …

Oh, you should have seen the face of Aunt L. when she read in the last letter that Grandmother had said that Viska might visit Askevold this summer. Neither Viska nor any of the rest of us had heard anything about this trip, so we started laughing, and Auntie started scolding Grandmother. But the end of the story is that every day, we talk about the trip to Askevold, and Nasa (I have never before written this name), and me, too; we talk about what we are going to do this summer. You will probably soon get a reasonable letter from the two only reasonable people among all the individuals here at Borgen (Grandmother and Aunt L.). It's true, too, as C. is dreaming about marriage, and the rest of us are like mad hens. Madame Ring has actually gotten a little one, and the same goes for Cathrine (Hefty) Løvenskjold. Severin Løvenskjold is about to kiss this ugly child to death. Mother Ullern is getting rather excessive, that is what C. told me just now. She is sitting writing a letter to W.H., and at the same time I hear her shout, "Oh, the mean chief administration officer!"

Hexa is getting confirmed this fall. Lillemamma is still acting like a mad goat, so she has to wait for a few more years. She is getting so tall and slender and pretty that you will fall all in love with her when you come to visit and see her.

Well, all greetings to you from the whole company, with Grandmother and the aunties first of all. Give my greetings to Uncle, the kids, and everybody, including Your Highness, from your

Linka

Ca. April 20, 1847, *Uranienborg*[84]

Yes, Aunt Rosa, I have to say I'm deeply insulted because you don't believe my important news, but think I'm joking. I assure you that Aunt Maren is so plump and round that I'm sure she can't get any bigger. I didn't expect you to be so mean.

Grandmother is so busy these days with the spring work and the garden; in addition she suffers from bad arthritis, so she can't write to you, but only sends you her greetings. And in three or four weeks, Aunt Spess, I'll have a very nice mission, because I have a secret that I shouldn't even know about, and much less write about. But since I know that you and Uncle can keep quiet, I guess I dare to tell you that Matthiesen is applying for a position for 300 Daler; I think it is for the Assurance Company. This evening it will be decided if he gets it. We all have a certain hope, but I don't want to get you too excited in case you will later receive contradicting news. If he gets this position he will have 500 Daler, and then he'll probably get married as soon as possible. Uncle Smith is ready to jump out of his skin in pure happiness, and about Doralise, I don't know anything except that she feels the same way. Kind Auntie, please do not pass this on, as I would not like to be the one who divulged the secret.

Agnes is still bothered by headaches and when she was allowed to go out again after her measles, the continuous and harmful running in the street immediately started. To prevent this, she is now up at Ullern where she will have some blessed stability. If only it helps, but I think she longs for the city when she is up there; now she has been in the city for two days to hear about the position.

Aunt L. will also get a few words from me this evening; therefore, good-bye and greetings from

not *Your Linka*.

Why do you have to be such a stubborn person? Thank God that you didn't take responsibility for all the farm duties; I did not like you when I found out that last fall you persuaded Uncle, etc.

Uranienborg, April 29, 1847

Hurray for the 17th of May, my Aunt Rosa!

Aunt Lillebessa has promised that she will visit Uncle Hoffmann and Askevold. If she really goes, as we all hope, it will be on May 17th. Oh, it would be fun to watch you and Lillebessa as you meet each other — Aunt L. would have to get up on her toes to kiss you. You are presumably too stiff to bend down to her. Uncle should not go to Aafjorden that day, because otherwise I wouldn't find out how amusing the meeting between you two was. You shouldn't start to talk about the return journey right away.

Yesterday I received a letter from W. Christie, he will go hunting this summer, too. He and Aunt Lillebessa will not spend much time together, as Auntie does not plan to be in Bergen for more than the night. She says she will rather stay there a few days on her way home. I think for sure that Uncle Carl will be coming to the Bergen area in August, so then he and Auntie will spend time together in Bergen for a few days. Uncle said so cunningly yesterday, when he heard that Auntie was serious with her plans of making the journey, "Yes, I will go to Bergen in the fall for sure, but not now, as I have to do the spring work, and not during summer, for Maren's sake." I would be glad if both of them went on their journeys, but first Auntie will stay two weeks at Uncle Herman's… haha!

There will be busy times here at Borgen when C. and I will be in charge, as they promised us. I have already told Nasa that she can take care of the kitchen and I will be outside and oversee the workers. It would be no problem if only Grandmother were well. It would be even better if her mood could also improve, and the same goes for Constance. Every time she receives and sends all these confounded love letters she is really a little tearful, and what is the point of that nonsense anyway.

Uf, the ink is too thick! I had planned to write better, but first of all I am competing with C. who is writing to "WH" — I'm trying to finish before she does, and second it is nothing but scribbling, but I hope you can read it…?

Oh, spring is coming so late this year! Imagine, there is still ice on the water and in the soil. Hopefully all these dreadful things will go away soon, as it has been snowing the first couple of days this week and later raining, but tomorrow is the last day of April! You, mean Auntie, laughed at me when I brought my wading boots, but they will be of great use this wet spring. I'm sure you can come some other time and see for yourself. A lot of people have great pleasure in watching me walk up the alley in the sunshine; when Matthissen sees me he says, "Well, look, there is Rosa in the cabbage!" Of course I don't understand it. All of our family's ugly patients are now back on their feet. A.S. is allowed to go out, but Doralise is told to stay inside. Since Dr. Paulsen's housekeeper (Smith) has moved out, however, she goes to the kitchen daily. She does as much inconvenience to herself as possible to keep uncle from getting food from the eating area. She hasn't yet gotten any worse after all the walking in the kitchen.

Louise Martens will come on Sunday, that is what Amalie told me the other day when she was here to look at Grandmothers pianoforte, which now will be rented out for one and a half Spd per month. She liked it and now Pettersen will have it, and we can put up with the loss. Lillemamma uses her own piano, and as we only have room for one, Grandmother could not have come up with anything better.

Cathrine Løvenskjold is still not well; she has the thing same that you had last summer when you had to go to Bergen to get treatment. Make sure that you are careful this year, no, that is not what I wanted to say. Make sure you are a good wife this summer!

Lomse was here last Sunday. He was quite concerned as he thought that Grandmother must have felt scared in these small rooms and missed the corner room. Yes, it is odd to see strangers in our old living room, but we all find the new place really nice and this summer we'll spend most of the time outside and in the cotter's cottage, which Grandmother has kept to herself this year. Thaulows will, of course, have the garden behind the house.

If everyone in the house, young and old, were not sound asleep right now, they surely would shout together, "Send our greetings to Carl and Rosa, Uncle and Auntie, from us!" That is what Nasa and I are shouting, the only ones awake, as real farm people. Adieu, Aunt Rosa, and here is a cuff on the ear. You expected to get a kiss now!

Greet everybody from your *Linka*

One o'clock in the morning

The last day of *April*:

Good morning, Aunt Rosa! How did you sleep last night? I didn't sleep very well, as I dreamt about Lillebessa's journey. And the first thing Auntie asked me this morning at the tea table was, "Well, Linka, did you tell Rosa that I will go on a journey?" Those were her own words. We're so busy here, as Auntie is going to stay with utter strangers and needs help with sewing and getting ready. She wanted so badly to bring Hanchen, but that will not be possible, partly because of the costs, and partly for all of Hanchen's many lessons. She is good to have at home, too. Rosemette also had the measles, but Monday she will attend school.

Hexa will be confirmed next fall; she will have Pastor Tangen. We were in "Slottskirken" Sunday to hear his final sermon, but we and many others did not think much of it.

Well, I just had to say good morning to you, but now I will leave the rest of the page to Lillebessa and Constance.

Adieu, your

Linka

Uranienborg, May 20, 1847

Thank you so much, dear Uncle, for the greeting to the "madcaps" in your last letter. Just so you know, I took it to heart. Well, I don't write to you just to thank you for that, but to tell you about a great, great event. Aunt Lodviska Josephine Carlsen boarded the steamer on May 17th and started her journey to Bjelland, where she will stay until she has to leave for Bergen. She is to be in Bergen on June 12th; thus she will stay with Uncle H. for approximately three weeks. I think it depends on Aunt Rosa if she will stay in Bergen for one day or more. She can't stay there for Pentecost unless Aunt Rosa really wants her to, as she can't shorten the stay at Bjelland. So now you are reading and hearing about Lillebessa's departure. People think that she will turn her eyes toward home after three weeks at Bjelland, but neither she nor any of us hopes that will happen. With you, she'll follow rules of good health, and she'll probably start a strange cure as soon as she comes to peaceful Askevold. She and you should get together, as neither of you is supposed to eat salty food. Do you think you will believe your eyes when you see Aunt Lillebessa come out of the steamer, whether you are in Bergen or in your boat in Langesund? Yes, I believe that will be an exceptional sight. Just try to kiss her and you will soon recognize her toss of the head. Oh, how I wish I could see Auntie when she arrives; I sure would laugh, just as I laughed at myself when I said good-bye to her at the steamer and my eyes got watery. Actually I was so happy that I would not have minded dancing with her right then.

Although L, has left, everything is as usual here at Borgen. The last couple of days Constance, or I guess I should have said "Aunt Constance" as we have decided to call her ("Aunt Nasa" was better), has spent the entire day in the potato field. Grandmother and I have been handling things inside the house, and I had the pleasure of weeding the strawberry field for two days until I was done. I suspect that the increasing amount of work for Aunt Constance is the reason for her surprisingly good mood; there have been no clouds visible on the horizon, and that is good. There was a small scene the evening before Aunt L. left, because she was in bad spirits, but now she is fine. The two of us have still not been arguing, which usually happens every now and then; you know my bad (but funny) habit of being a big tease!

I have some news to tell you. Mr. Henrik Jenson, Grandmother's former favorite, recently got engaged to Ms. Mona Morgenstjerne, a good choice (as you know, she's very beautiful). She is the daughter of the clerk Willhelm Morgenstjerne and the former Wilhelmine Libern. Those are two very prominent families.

In good weather we spend time in the cotter's parlor, but here it is now so freezing cold that it's snowing at Frognersæter and in the Grefsen hills. Today Hexa was at Aker and registered for confirmation next fall.

Now, farewell, dear Uncle. Greetings to you and your loved ones, from everybody here. Your

Linka

July 6[85]

My dear Aunt Rosa,

I have to start this letter so that I can write down everything I've forgotten to tell you and ask you in the other two.

First, I have to tell you that I have not, as you wrote to me while I was in Bergen, received my pearl necklace. You wrote that it came in the same package as the linsey-woolsey shirt, but it did not. Please make sure you sent it to me, as well as my knitting needles. Well, now I don't remember more for the moment.

— *July* 7: Some people tell me, "Miss, you seem to have lived well on milk at your aunt's; what was the name of the farm again?" "Well, we didn't go as hard on the milk as on the cream," I reply.

Please send me the little petite leaf border that is sewn around the (purple, isn't that what the gray steel color is called) gray-violet steel-colored fabric. You know I was supposed to have finished it. Let me have it as soon as possible (for example, in a letter you write for me); I would like to have it immediately, so I can use it as a sample pattern.

Have you ever seen such a foolish human being as myself, who can forget to give W.C. the clock key, which now is sent to you?

— *July* 9: I've left my green coat in Bergen. The lemon cakes should go to Uncle and the burnets to Aunt Christie, but if you would like some of each it is understandable if you take some. I would love to send more (much), but money??? Greetings to all of you from your *Linka*.

I don't have time to write to Doris.

Uranienborg, July 18, 1847

My dear Aunt Rosa!

Grandmother, Constance, and all the kids are at Ullern today. I don't have any good book handy, so what else is there to do but sit down and talk reasonably to you, especially since it's raining and my man just left me. I had the pleasure of having him for dinner, and I made him fricassee. What tasted the best were the stolen goods, the strawberries that I had taken from the garden and that we weren't supposed to eat yet. None of us has eaten more of them this summer than we can count; imagine, Grandmother is so thrifty with them that I was not even allowed to send him a few for his birthday. It's different with you, Auntie, you have so many. But we had enough to make Lomse pleased with the "thieves' dish" at dinner today; when the cat is away, the mice will play!

You should have heard more about Behrens's[86] wedding in my previous letter.[87] Don't think you'll get away with only that — oh no, I remember exactly where I last stopped. I talked about Constance's feelings as a bridesmaid, and I wanted to tell you how much better it must be to be a bridesmaid when one is not engaged. One may easily get jealous—just ask Lillebessa, she knows as well as I do. There were, of course, some touching scenes after the ceremony, but they gave way to the joyful celebrations at the party. We ate until the food was up to our throat, and then we danced. Oh, I forgot to tell you that during dinner there were many toasts given. First we toasted in champagne to the bride and groom, and then one champagne cork after the other hit the ceiling. Toasts were given to the ladies, to Uranienborg, and to the quartet. The latter was requested by the bride. And before we were done eating, we heard singing outside. Behrens opened all the windows, and song after song was heard. The bride and the groom went to the window, bowed and curtsied for a loud "hurrah!" Then silence outside, though not inside, as we all started dancing. You can imagine that the bride, Constance, and I were popular on the dance floor as the only young girls there; well, actually the bride was a wife then. I was especially popular when I danced with an old, huge, big-bellied man, the merchant Gjertzen from Bergen. He was a really funny man.

I guess you were sick of this wedding a long time ago, but you have to be patient and listen until I am done. Constance and I were the last ones to leave; we stayed long after the other guests said good night. We talked about Behrens's house and that he could not move in on Saturday the 17th. Until then, the couple had to live separately. We offered to take him home when we left, and that was definitely very polite of us, but for some strange reason he declined. Can you understand why he would do that, Auntie? You have to tell me or explain that to me in your next letter, which I hope I will receive on this side of Christmas. And tell me how you can stand to weed the flowering manna ash, and what is it really good for? And how can you do that when you can't even handle sitting bent over for sometime writing letters to us?

I thank you on behalf of Grandmother for your wish of happiness for your uncle and aunt. She didn't ask me to do that for her before she left, as she obviously didn't have any idea that I would sit down to scribble down a letter to you so soon. I hope she doesn't mind my action. I also have to thank you for congratulating me, and thank Aunt Lopes for the same and for her words (not letter). The farmers must have had an idea that it was my highness's birthday, since Johannes' wedding was so joyful. Oh no, Auntie, how I bother you…

I forgot to tell you that this morning, we sent a vase with lovely roses down to Behrens and wife, before they got out of their bedroom. In this vase we put a lady of porcelain supposing to be the virgin surrounded by greens. We had her arm holding onto "Rules for Young Spouses." In it was an overture, which I will send you, so you can get a little laugh. I wrote it down this morning, as the one I wrote on the ground had become so wrinkled. This one turned out so well that the first one got thrown away.

Since the last time I wrote to you, I've also been on a fishing trip with Reinhart (he arranged the trip) and some other acquaintances. Several times I thought about Askevold and how many times I used to be in a boat with you. Now I sailed for the first time since I came here. It was so delightful and a lot of fun, although I didn't get more than one fish. We sailed more than we fished, and we drank wine and ate cake. When we were to eat in the evening we went to Blegøen and ate a veal steak, a ham, cucumber salad, etc. We had drinks in abundance, but the men even became a little cheerful. We got to sail more, as they turned the boat just as we reached the pier, and we sailed back out.

Dear Auntie, you ask me so seriously if I can write something about Bya. The reason for not doing so is not because I don't think about her — actually, she's the one of my little sisters that I worry most about, about how she will be when she gets older. She now has a great deal of Nøkken and Maren's instruction in her, but if she remains faithful to the truth, I think she will be fine. We can't expect her to be different; the teaching will come to her if we give her some time. In Rosa's breaks they play school with Thaulow's children. I think that is good for them, as they have to learn their lessons.

Everybody is as usual. Kalla has been at Ullern this week. In the next letter I may be able to tell you that he's been lucky enough to get a position as a tutor. You can laugh at this, but as soon as he gets a final answer, the first thing I'll do is to write to you or Uncle, as it would really be great for Kalla.

You are greeted by your

Linka

My dear little Carl! Calleboss![88]
Your mama and your future Auntie tell me you are being so naughty, but I can never imagine you, who were so obedient when I left, are behaving so badly now. I suppose I believe so because I am not with you, but you have to promise me to be a good boy until you get the next letter from me. During that time you have to read these words each day, otherwise I fear that you might forget my admonition.

Now I will draw some nice horses for you, and if you also want some other small animals I will draw those for you, too. But first I have to go to feed the hens. Come, come, come! Ka, ka, ka! See now, I'm done with that. You know, when I was with the hens, two of them were dancing the waltz together! You should have seen that, ha ha. I think the best is if I first give you a dog who looks like your Rinaldo. I guess the last thing you want is myself, and you will get that, too! Don't you recognize me, you little fool?

You are greeted from your

Linka

Uranienborg, August 12, 1847

Dear "whoever cares to read this scribbling!"

For a terribly long time now, I haven't been in the mood in the morning to talk to people who live far away. Thus I will try to get started now while the living room people are sleeping and the kitchen staff are making noise with the plates. Can you guess what time of the day it is? It would be excellent if I could make the pen go as fast on the paper as our mouths go in the afternoon, when we all go outside in the garden and let the staff run around inside. Grandmother and Bang talk together seriously, Hexa and Jensen lightheartedly, and Constance and Knudsen quite slowly, and without doubt, about love matters. During the entire conversation Knudsen kicks with his legs, and the more eager he gets, the higher he kicks. Constance should almost fear for her eyes. Finally Magnus starts talking to me, and we eagerly converse about our physical and moral concerns. In conclusion, I think I'm the one who has the most reasonable conversation, at least on this particular afternoon.

The royals are in town, I know, but I think you know as well as I what they look like. I have never seen any of them and I do not really care. I have heard that they are at the Palace today, even though it is far from ready; some of the scaffoldings are gone, though.[89] One of the best things Grandmother has done, was some time ago when she went to look around in the Palace, she came back and told us that she hadn't seen it well enough. "And there were also a lot I never got to see," she said. Constance, on the other hand, was more than pleased and found many things beautiful, except the three hundred birch chairs in the dining room which were both ugly and heavy. Grandmother was also there when the Queen Dowager was here. It was convenient, since the Queen drove right pass Smith's Lodge. She stays at Sexton Svensen's new farm. Because of her highness, Svensen and his wife struggle to learn French two hours a day.[90] "Oh, if only I could listen to the conversation between the married couple and the Queen," Mother Christensen is thinking... ha ha!

The Queen Dowager was given many times greater acclamation than the King. Everything was splendidly decorated for her reception, with banners, etc. She looked many years younger and prettier than last time she was here (thirteen years ago), dressed in white from head to foot. She bowed in all directions, and when she saw old white-capped ladies behind the windows she doubled her greeting. She was welcomed in her lodgings by the royal family, and the kisses were overflowing by the gate. She gave the princes a kiss on their hands and the king one on the forehead. Enough about that...

I will inform you about a new and pretty engagement. Anders Bull (son of Arilissen) has gone to Dresden to visit or get his dear Ms. Dahl (daughter of professor Dahl). Lomse has been on a health trip to the well of love for one or two days, but I do not think that his wife should have any reason to be jealous, as what he attended was a long-lasting ball.

From one thing to the other: this morning Kalla was going to Ullern, but on his way a woman with a cariole appeared on the road. When he recognized the traveler, the previously mentioned Mother Christensen, he turned his back on his favorite place and marched back to town. Now I will not write more until I hear any news from Ullern.

Ha ha! Well, now the pastor's wife at Askevold will soon get started! Now at 9:30 Grandmother received a letter from Ullern, and can you guess what it said??? At 6:30, a pretty little, well-shaped, crying girl was delivered to Auntie and Uncle. I guess she came with the mail in a little package from England, tell me, isn't that how they come to this country? Or do the children at Askevold come from Spain? (Shame on you, Linka.) Uncle Karl writes in his letter that he will come here this afternoon to tell Grandmother all about it. I really hope that everything turns out for Aunt Maren as well as it did for Maren the maid. The second day she felt very bad, but the third she was up in the morning to make coffee and the fourth day she was up and felt much better. I was thinking she seemed just like Aunt Rosa.

Friday morning: Kalla is leaving Monday for Jarlsberg. Consequently, he should be quite busy now, but he seems so calm and relaxed about it, and I assume that is the best. What Aunt L. said was true, that if I sew ten stitches a day you may call me a cat. I have worked on the corset forever. I'm glad we'll soon be done with the rye field. And the oats that Aunt L. looked at before she left, trying to see how far it had come, are partly in the barn and partly eaten, along with the vetches.

Last time I was at Ullern, Uncle told Auntie, "Maren, you have to hurry now, so I can go on my journey to Bergen August 23rd." Now Auntie is ready, and with God's help everything will be fine and Uncle can leave.

Bya is busy these days fixing an apron she managed to tear; she's not allowed to go outside until she is done. She has been grounded for three days now, and she will probably be grounded until Christmas is over, poor little girl. She asks me to give her greetings to Doris, Karl, and Dorthe; the latter is still referred to as the beautiful girl in her national costume. By the way, Grandmother and the entire company at Uranienborg send their greetings to everybody at Askevold.

Dear Uncle! I am sorry the fishing jig still hasn't arrived; Saturday I was at Ullern, as they sent the boots on Sunday, and I asked Lomse to tell them where the jig is and that they need to send it. To my great irritation, Lomse forgot all about it, so do not say "what an unreliable person she is!" about your

Linka

Uranienborg, September 30, 1847

My Aunt Rosa, we're really surprised not to have heard from you and Uncle. We assume that you have provided the parsonage with another "queer duck[91]" of a little person; however, I can't congratulate you until I get my suspicions proven. I have to hurry with this letter as I will write another letter to Kalla before Constance is done with hers to …, and as you can imagine or figure out by experience, that takes a long time…

What I was going to say was that when you read these words, Auntie has probably left you already. I have a feeling you did not previously consider lying sick in bed for a month, but now you can enjoy it as you got the nice rarities from Major. He joked so much about Askevold the last time I spoke to him; he said he liked your home, but I found that hard to believe. (Maybe because I think the opposite??)

Poor Constance, she struggles with her writing. She is tired after the busy days preparing for a confirmation that we will have here on Sunday. Doralise has been here to make her famous fish balls. I have been chopping suet, which was so raw that anyone with a little less patience than me would have put it right into the meat, which Hanchen, Constance, and Helene were scraping. Hexa is sewing on a little white skirt and studies religion, French, German, and English in between. Lillemamma is with Madame Luur struggling with her confirmation dress; Rosa goes to school and studies; and poor Bya, in these busy times, goes with Grandmother to the potato fields; she is delighted that we will have a good harvest this year. I have actually been out in the fields today, but Grandmother was there all day yesterday, forbidding us to relieve her. She wanted us to take care of the work indoors, such as hanging up curtains, etc. Grandmother was tired when she came back, but I think being outdoors is the best for her. She is definitely healthiest and in the best mood when she is outside. However, don't think that we are so stupid that we let Grandmother be out when it rains or is windy.

We still haven't harvested all the potatoes, only those that are easily available for thieves. The rest will be harvested next week. All the potato greens have been cut off and hung up in a drying rack that Grandmother had built in the back yard. Uncle Carl is also busy harvesting his potatoes, but unfortunately his field has been hit by disease, so he said, "Yes, unfortunately that's the case. There will probably be over one hundred barrels of bad potatoes from the fields." Auntie is now well; we hope to see her here Sunday, as the first time since...

I often think that it must be strange having a confirmed sister, as I assume Hexa will change and become a little more serious after taking the big step in a couple of days. I do not exactly mean that she will become more serious, but I think that she will be thinking much, much more about the future than she does now. But enough about this, we should not think too much about the future...

A friendly greeting to you and Uncle from us all, by your

Linka

Please make no remarks about this letter, Auntie, as it is written in the greatest haste, and my thinking machinery has gone mad this evening.

Uranienborg, October 13, 1847

Dear Christie,

I'm finally home after fourteen days on my journey from Askevold, and have found all my loved ones. (Loviska)

Pinch pennies, scrimp, and save, Auntie Rosa, that's why you get a letter from me that's started by Aunt Lodviska. We can't overcome our consciences enough to steal more than two pieces of paper from Hexa, and since L. said that what she had written was so bad, we exchanged pieces. And I also had to make the tea service (water) ready before I could start writing.

Now I let the pen run again. I have two bits of great news to tell you, and I assure you that you don't have the faintest idea of what they are. Hexa is confirmed according to the accepted practice, and I now have a grown-up sister. However, she might be confirmed, but she's still a child, although she might think more seriously about the future. That's something none of us really can predict, and something she may not see even in the brightest light. We have lost our dear beloved ones, but praise the Lord, we still are together and happy as before!

Aunt "Little Healthy"[92] is home, which is the second great and unpredictable thing I have to tell you! Sunday we were all so happy that we jumped around, and could hardly sit still, although we had to be polite to people visiting. Every second we ran up to the officer on duty in the billiard room to look for the steamer, but no matter how much we looked, the steamer did not come until four in the afternoon. It had to stay in Moss for four hours due to fog. So Auntie arrived exactly at tea time, which I had arranged here, and Constance, Lillemamma, Hanchen, Rosa, and the little cart with Dølen and Ole were down there to welcome her. And imagine our annoyance when she did not come driving up the main road, as any rational person would have done, but rather walked up through the garden. All the work Hexa and the maids had done putting up two flags by the gate was a waste. But as the people by the barn said: on the other hand, we all were happy when we saw her face in the door. And Grandmother, who had been in bed Friday and Saturday, suddenly became well and ran to the door. The welcome kiss rang so loud that the walls echoed, just like Constance's kiss. I'm not exaggerating.

She had hardly been home for half an hour when a gentleman in a full uniform (on a sweaty horse) came riding through the gate. It looked very suspicious. I wish I could express on paper the same words and with the same pathos and passion that he presented. "Good day, my dear Lodviska. Welcome home! How have you been during the long time since I last saw you?" And then almost an embrace, anticipated with his legs. "Good day, farewell my love." (Uff.) Wait! Out the door, on the horse and away as fast as the wind. (Please read this with emotion. Your voice should be a little shaky...)

Oh, these kids are nagging to go to town! Lillemamma is getting better at sewing school; she sewed Hexa a beautiful confirmation dress, edged with blue silk, and the pattern sewn with light blue silk. I presume you are also better than me in all possible household tasks, but when Auntie is back, they put away "*mir nichts dir nichts!*"[93]

Yesterday we showed her all the unpleasant things of Uranienborg. I assume the "Little Healthy" is going to Ullern today; they live well up there. Sunday, Auntie went to church and on the Sunday of confirmation she had dinner here with us, and she had to leave again in the afternoon. We were busy here that day. Grandmother and Lillemamma took Hexa to church and the rest of us worked at home. There were many people for supper; I think you know who. Uncle S. and Ag. were at Nittedalen with Magga, who also got confirmed. I really prefer taking it easy on days like that instead of having a party. It seems like a bad tradition.

Here none of us really thought about Auntie being gone for the winter, and consequently we were surprised when she said that it was very close: We congratulate with the newborn! Grandmother says you would give birth yesterday or today as the moon is full.

Don't get mad, Auntie, because you see the beginning of this letter. I apologize, I can see you are disappointed after expecting some words from Lodv., but as she was going out, she couldn't write anymore. You'll hear from her by next mail delivery, and I write you to tell you that she is home safely and in one piece. Kalla is well! Greetings to you and Uncle from everybody here, from your

Linka

Uranienborg, November 2, 1847

My dear aunt Rosa!

God bless you and all your children, and may He give you all health and happiness! If the anecdote had said that the man with the wings of wax could fly, I would fly to you and talk to you, since you have been sick for a long time. Uncle would be at Aafjord and you would lie in *Your* bed being bored, because if I know you well, you are too careful to lie down to read. When you receive these words, however, you will probably be back on your feet, but maybe not yet outside? Please be a nice careful wife...

Aunt Lodviska wanted to write to you, but I won't allow her to write more with the light today, as she has already written to Uncle Hoffmann. I have not seen anything of Doralise for several days now. She probably has a little cold, so Agnes will go to "Dramatikken" by herself. I should try to go to a lot of balls this winter, so that after a while I will get as excited as Hexa. She gets so excited about attending a ball, but at first I don't think she would go to public balls.

Auntie, I have a bone to pick with you, if it has to happen on the kitchen bench or on the coach in the living room. Have you ever, dear Auntie, felt that it is fun to receive things, even if they are unimportant, from a place that you love? So how could you laugh at Aunt L. when she brought me a box of Askevold treats. I still have a few left and every time I want to have something special I eat a couple. I have another bone to pick with you, too: why don't you use the cushion for the bathroom table I sent you? I hope you don't think it's too ugly to look at for everyday use. And when it is worn out I assume you won't consider me useless, and will expect to get a new one.

From your

Linka

Linka's Letters — 1848

[*The fall of the French "July Monarchy" in February 1848 led to a chain reaction of events collectively known as "the Revolutions of 1848." In Denmark, liberals pushed for a political change, and German nationalists pushed for a new constitutional relationship for the Duchies of Schleswig (Slesvig) and Holstein. When the Danish government failed to grant the reforms they sought, the German nationalists in the Duchies declared their independence, which led to the "Three Years' War," essentially between Denmark and Prussia (supporting the German nationalists in the Duchies). Following a Prussian victory, Oscar I agreed to send 15,000 Swedish and 3,000 Norwegian troops, and by early July, he helped negotiate a temporary armistice. Some of the following letters written in 1848 reflect the fear of impending war in Scandinavia.*[98]]

Uranienborg, May 1, 1848

Highly esteemed Mrs. Christie,

Good day, my dear Aunt Rosa. I am pleased to again have a conversation with you; I think it has been more than fourteen days since the last time I wrote. Unfortunately I cannot check my little notebook to see when I last wrote, because in these terrible times when we have so much to worry about, it should not be surprising that I have forgotten to note down the letters I have sent.

I can almost imagine sitting in my old room in your house, Auntie, as the ocean is right in front of me. Lately I have not had such a view. When working, I mostly look outside at the chestnut trees which are still standing immodestly bare; a boring sight. I'm gazing at the bay, a little broader than that at Askevold, and one big ship crosses the other. You have only fishing boats to watch. Now, for instance, "Nordstjernen" is here, enjoying herself for a little while. She will stay here in the bay until next week, cheering up my depressed and melancholic spirit. Puff! Puff! — A corvette repeats this eight times after a similar salutation from a passing steamer. Oh, what a wonderful room the billiard room is! I hope we can keep it if Knutson and Magnus do not come. (The former leaves for liquor control and the latter has gone abroad with consul Faye regarding the state loan.) There is to be a new lodger, Mr. Thoresen, a handsome medic. Gossip says it's strange how Mrs. Carlsen rents out rooms for young gentlemen; it is bad for all the young ladies currently staying at Uranienborg. Oh, I would never bother to be busy gossiping, like professors, wives, young and old ladies, coffee ladies, men, etc., do. They are being ungrateful and wishing for things that are not thought through well, and how bad it is for the people being talked about.

Borgen's summer guests, Hals, together with Thoresen and Bang, will be the gentlemen marching up and down the avenue with nine ladies this summer. Won't they enjoy that!

No one can say that people at Ullern are well nowadays. All the children here are coughing the best they can; we only hope that they won't get as bad as the little charity girl is. She has a terrible cough; the entire household wakes up and worries for her at night. God knows what will happen to Aunt Maren if the children get that ill, as all of them sleep with her in her bedroom. Yet a maid sleeps with them on the coach (Uncle has moved to the guest room), but she is busy with little Doris, who has just gotten accustomed to … Auntie has Waleska on one side and Bassen on the other side of her in the king bed, and as she is not very strong, she will undoubtedly become even weaker from all the nightly disturbance. Of course Doralise is there, but she only helps during the day.

Aunt Maren and Doralise were here for Constance's birthday; imagine, they arrived in heavy rain and surprised us all in middle of a most pleasant afternoon nap. We laughed so much, and so did they, and Auntie was both well and fit. She is not often in town; when I last saw her, on Maundy Thursday, it had been more than a month and a half since the last time. Grandmother does not want us to go to Ullern often, which is one of the many things I cannot understand. I do not like it, as I do not like the constant questioning whenever I take ten steps. I'm afraid I'm the same old stubborn goat I was a few years ago, as I am not at all as meek… well… as I was when I left you. "Yes, Linka, you will get far by being soft," I guess you are saying now, dear Auntie, but it is not that easy. Whether I admit it or not I cannot be what is always the best. And now that I, without really being aware of it, have brought up a topic I never thought I would ever come near, I guess I can take the opportunity to say that you, as well as myself, since you know me better than anyone else, do not really understand me. Yes, I am a very strange person.

Please excuse the last paragraph, dear Auntie, I didn't ever expect that sentence would come on paper.

Saturday Aunt L. got a letter from Miss Hohlfeldt; she is well and will be coming this summer.

In your last letter you talked about Uncle Carl's trip this summer. (Thanks for the greeting I never got.) Before he got the whooping cough, he was quite determined to leave at the end of June, but now he does not know how things will turn out. If possible, he will go, but don't get too-high expectations.

I have to write a comment regarding Doralise's marriage; as I have told you before, it will take place this coming fall. It's quite tentative yet. Matthiessen told Dora, who could predict such a slackening in the old man's business; thus the wedding might get cancelled.

As soon as the crew on the corvette docked on the 28th, Nicolai Moe went right up to Uncle Smith, who was very surprised to see him. But after the first cheerful greetings, Uncle had to inform him of his mother's death. He sent a letter to the captain earlier this winter, but the news was not to be told him unless he showed concern for the conditions at home.

Bya has again caught her spring cold; hopefully it will not get any worse and I think she will recover soon, as she felt much better today. The rest of us are doing pretty well, except for Grandmother's rheumatism, which I guess I will have to tell you about in every letter.

Lomse is already starting to get some bachelor notions, and I assume these will increase instead of decrease like they should. Kalla writes nonsense and is enjoying life. Talking about enjoyment, Constance got a lady's desk from Mrs. Hagerup (still at the customs house) on April 27th, and in a letter from Wilhelm there was an odd ring, formed like a serpent entwined with roses and forget-me-nots. This was put on crepe wrapped in a note saying, "To my dear Wilhelm's beloved Constance from your gracious mother, Benedicte Hagerup."

Reply soon, *your Linka*
Greet Moe and the children

[comment on margin: Haven't I done well, Auntie? Constance can't write three lines without mentioning politics, but I have put together three pages without using that word, which should never be used by ladies, because they play tricks and talk nonsense about it.

NB: Behrens received a daughter on the 29th of April.

NB: On the 27th, Constance got a teakettle with a chafing dish and a brass coffeepot from Mrs. Hoeflye.]

Tuesday morning, May 2, 1848

Are you saying, dear Uncle, when you read these words, "Oh no, another letter of Linka's political nonsense." Yes, Uncle, I 'm telling you, this is exactly how it is going to be. You can choose whether you want to read it or save your brain from my rubbish.

This morning I was very astonished when hearing, "Do you want to go to town to see the King's arrival on the steamer today?" Ever since the Parliament got extended, it has kicked over the traces, due to the Cabinet change as well as the war. The Cabinet therefore felt it had to write a letter to His Majesty and ask him to come here, and he is to arrive today. I will go, although I might not see His Highness himself, but at least I will get to watch all the hysteria. People say, as though it is a big thing, that Mr. Stabel has retired, and many of the farmers have abandoned their position, because of a speech by Cabinet Member Riddervold to members of the Parliament. The masses are threatening to level his residence to the ground on May 17th. Indeed, that dishonorable man should be ashamed of himself. He has been embarrassed before, but if he doesn't get enough votes from Parliament to send his formal address to His Majesty, he will feel even more ashamed. This would please our city, where even the least interested and deadest people in the world now are all enthusiastic, partly for their own sake, partly for the poor Danes. Yesterday, upon request, there was a meeting at the Exchange (there were several thousand people there, so the Exchange grounds were as full as the hall). It concerned a letter to the Parliament and the King, saying that Norway should help Denmark. There were several speeches given by the different administrators, one more enthusiastic than the other. Never has a gathering of so many people (educated men as well as non-educated, like all kinds of craftsmen, not to forget the hired men who are profound politicians. We have a boy here, the foremost nincompoop, who yesterday said to me, "Miss, if the Holsteiners should win over the Danes, I suppose we Norwegians would also have to go to war, otherwise the Germans will come here, too.")

Well, back to the party at the Exchange Market, to which I would like to add that such a large crowd has never agreed more. They were burning with enthusiasm the entire time, but after Attorney Dunker's speech, they all went mad. They were standing in groups of twos and fours, and swore to genuinely help the Danes. Finally the meeting was over, but discussions continued at every street corner. Many students went straight to the students' association and signed up to participate in the fight against the Germans, leaving as soon as possible to fight side by side with their brothers. Chief Magistrate[95] Blom's three sons are also going, along with a whole lot of others. So even if the Parliament decides not to declare war on Germany and the King does not send support troops down, there are already volunteers, workers, and students, ready to leave.[96] The latter are going to at least preserve their own honor, as there are not enough of them to preserve their country's, and the former maybe for the same reason, or because they prefer this way of dying to starvation. The Army has received its new breech-loading muskets, so there is no lack of weapons. Anyone who wants to can enlist in the general militia, which is going to begin drilling in a couple of days. The students do not want to form a separate corps for themselves anymore, the prelates and artisans will join them. The ladies will probably have to take the plough and harrow and let the men go, and we will follow the example of the wives from Stril.

Imagine, Uncle, last night Grandmother got so tired of all our politics and spiteful talk about the Germans that she went to bed, after unsuccessfully attempting to shut our mouths. Things are not going well for the Slesvig-Holsteiners up here, Thaulow and wife (naturally); when the Germans lost, they were so meek and did not know which side to favor, but now things have changed and Grandmother cannot hear Danish or Norwegian talk without getting sad or leaving the room. Thaulow becomes vehement and says, "The Danes are stupid and will get nowhere." If he insults us we are no better, but in the end the Danes will get help, or Frenchmen will overrun Germany.

There were several other things I wanted to tell you about, but the pen and all my words have gone away from me, so it is impossible for me to gather my thoughts and put them in a bag.

Today Rosa bought me grafting wax, and I have already made eight experiments, but I do not think they will succeed. Enough for now, dear Uncle.

Your Linka

Ullern, September 14, 1848

As far as I recall, kind Aunt Rosa, it was a lovely spring day, or even one of the first days of summer, when I last wrote to you. That is a long time ago now, but I have talked to you and I will be pleased if this letter delights you as much as it pleases me to write it. You might still be angry with me for not writing in a while, but I was thinking that "why should I write? Aunt Rosa has gone to Bergen where she can read from Uncle Carl's letters how we live; she knows that he will come there in a few days and then she will receive a real letter, better than ten others." That was the reason, and enough about that. I hope you banish any frown on your forehead or your pursed lips.

This Sunday, it has been fourteen days since Uncle Carl got home. There was an understandable longing for him when he was gone, thus when he got back there was an understandable happiness in the family. Someone from Uranienborg met him at the dock and waited there, while Uncle and Mathissen drove up here. Auntie, all the small ones, Doralise, and I met him at the door; this was at dinnertime, and later in the afternoon Grandmother, State Auditor Smith and his family, and others came, too.

We were all pleased to hear that you live well and are fit as a fiddle, which we hope still is the case. Uncle complained of the bad weather on the trip, but apparently, it had not been any better at Askevold. His impression of this place, a foreign place to you, was very similar to that of Aunt Lodviska: "A beautiful oasis in a desert;" although you got offended by that comparison... Both Uncle and Auntie asked me to give their greetings to Uncle and you; I have not heard Uncle say anything about writing to Askevold, but today he writes to the chief administration officer. Lomse wanted to come here to meet Uncle after his arrival, but the hunting has prevented him from leaving. Well, I guess the adage, "When you speak of . . . " is right; as we were talking about him this morning, Lomse stepped into the room., "Good morning, Carl!" Uncle Carl told him about the homespun cloth he brought from you, but he would not believe it at first. However, when he got to see the cloth, he had to smile and finally exclaimed, "Although it was late, it was strongly needed! I was going to go to town today and buy me some clothing for my legs." If he were here now, he would have asked me to say thank you, but he ran downtown after half an hour here and will be back late tonight. However, I think I am doing the right thing by telling you that he was very thankful for the cloth and he would have given you a kiss for it if you were here.

Everybody is well at Uranienborg now, but earlier this summer, the little sisters were not good. Hanchen had a bad cough; it was taken very seriously, and it is now over. Rosa had a sore throat and chicken pox, which Agnes also got. Agnes has, by the way, been wild and frenetic as usual. When I visited Uranienborg Wednesday, Grandmother sat in the potato field and was in a bad mood because of the many diseased potatoes. For each two carts of good potatoes, she got two carts of diseased ones, and this was the best field; she does not expect it to be better on the other fields. Constance received a letter from Hagerup and Lodviska was busy as usual.

Aunt Maren is good, well, except for today; she has a very bad headache. She has been busy this summer, worked hard and been outside all day, but that did her good. Now she has again shut herself in the house in her usual way, as Uncle is here and everything is back to normal. The family tutor has still not arrived, so I think I will have to stay here for another fourteen days to read with the boys. I've been here for a long time and don't doubt that the staff at Borgen would die of longing for me if I didn't visit them twice a week when in town for drawing lessons. Please don't let it be too long until we hear from you. Give the boys and Uncle greetings from

Your Linka

You must greet Moe for me, and thank her for her letter

Uranienborg, November 22, 1848

These are hard times; I hope you in the countryside also feel that, though it is doubtful that you complain about the same things as I do. I think I can imagine how you worry about the times, but my worries are nothing like that. One of my big concerns these days is that I cannot send messages to town whenever I would like to, thus I have problems with all the letters I want to send. This was the case the other day when I got up from my nice warm bed to write you a letter. I struggled hard to get it done and Aunt Lodviska was going to take it to the post office on her way to the butcher shop. Whatever happened, she spent so much time going in and out giving and receiving orders that she left the house too late to have time to take Linka's unusually <u>beautifully written letter</u> to a person called Mrs. Rosa Christie to the post office. It was very disappointing having to give the letter away to the fire instead of to the mailbox, but it didn't hurt me; I survive although I have to write a letter twice. However, in the meantime, I know that you've been disappointed the last two times you've opened the red mailbox, looking hopefully inside it to see if there is any letter from Christiania. I hope there are fewer and fewer wrinkles on your nose and forehead when you find a letter for you this time. Your grimace disappears completely for a moment as you see it is from Uranienborg, but then the sail breaks and what a disappointment; the letter is from Linka. Why couldn't Viska or Constance write so I wouldn't have to trouble my head and eyes with the nonsense this fool makes up. I don't really need to read this as I remember her last letter, since they are all the same… I'll throw it in the stove. No, dear Auntie, please hold on for a moment! You've tested your patience with me so many times, please do it this time, too; I think you would like to know how the people here are doing. Well, unfortunately I don't have anything positive to tell you, as people here are ill as usual (I can't differ from my other letters on this matter). No, we expect that when a person here starts to recover from an illness, another one gets ill. It has not been more than eight or fourteen days since Hanchen and Bya left their bedrooms after having colds, and now Grandmother lies in bed with a cold. The doctor found her much better today, so I hope that we'll soon see her on the couch in the living room. It seems as if little Rosemette feels sorry for Grandmother who is sick and all alone in her bed; the little clown has a sore throat. Today she's out of bed and will soon get back to school again, where she is doing pretty well. By the way, the family is well, and at Ullern they're going to have a slaughter next week; I'll be there to work in the house while Auntie takes care of the slaughter in the kitchen.

Oh, how excited I am for next Saturday (the 23rd)! My two sisters and I just received tickets for the Ole Bull concert; it will be delightful to hear him stroke his fiddle, something I've never heard. What a shame that you can't be here; indeed, since it's impossible for you to be here, I might just as well say that I would have given you my ticket...

While I was staying at Ullern this summer, Pastor Jensen[97] and his family moved to town — a family well acquainted with the people in this house. They have visited Uranienborg several times, and the team at Borgen has visited them back, but due to my absence I've never had the opportunity to spend time with them and get to know them. However, since I came back here, I've had the pleasure of seeing, hearing and talking to them, and I actually like them a lot. The other day Aunt Lodviska, Constance, Hagerup, and I visited the Jensens in the Old Town; it was very nice and enjoyable, really enlivening. The pastor's wife is nice when she does not talk too loud, and the pastor is the same as he has always been, and thus not very ecclesiastical. We danced a little in the afternoon as Petter Andreas yearned for a dance; he was in trouble last week when we were in "Dramatikken." Grandmother was there with us and he went over to her several times, saying, "Uf, Mrs. Carlsen, why can't I dance with you, I have an incredible desire to!" She was sitting at the gallery; then he ran down to us and said, "Oh, it really is [hard?][98]." "Can't you step into a steady Quadrille?" "No, there will be no dance, neither waltz nor gallop." Now you see what he's like. I bet you recognize him from the "good old days," as he expressed it when I entered the hall after having sweated and trembled because of my part in the play. The thought of those days seemed to calm him down. He is a very good preacher; people seem to run to church like mad when he gives the sermon. I hope it lasts; new brooms sweep the best!

It has been a long time since something has delighted me as much as what I read in yesterday's newspaper about our old friend Thorkilsen. When he gets to read this he will probably become just as bashful as we become happy.

Aunt Rosa, I don't think your headache is too bad for you to be able to calculate, or prepare the great mathematical problem: When did I last write home? You can choose addition or subtraction, or whatever arithmetic operation to solve the problem. However, if you need to, you can ask Uncle nicely to use his "Soren Matthiessen's Arithmetic." Use this tool and you will be appalled at your own … (The Almanac may also be of help.)

The evening we were at Jensen's we met Elin Bruun. She is going to be in town for some days; you know she usually stays with Pastor Bull. I hope to see her here one evening before she leaves; she's nice. She asked how you and yours are doing, but unfortunately I could not answer that question, because I…

How is Wilhelm? Send my greetings to Uncle and the small ones and Marie from me. Grandmother and Hagerup and the rest of the people also ask to be remembered by you.

I apologize, Auntie, this was too freely written, but I think you will get very mad at yourself when you think about how Grandmother longs to hear from you, and then you will remember my little speech…

Your Linka

Rangelborg[99], *December* 28, 1848

Do you think, kind Auntie, that I now dwell on the thought of my loved ones at Askevold less frequently, since you do not find letters from me that often? No, Auntie, please do not ever think, believe, or come to that conclusion. The reason for my laziness (maybe you would even call it that) when it comes to writing is that I am afraid I bore you with all my letters; all of them tend to be the same. However, when I do not write that often I urge the others to inform you of the conditions here and in the family, and there is the reason, I hope it is convincing? And even more, too?

Today is the third day of Christmas and you are home alone doing nothing; I assume Uncle is in Aafjorden. You probably have a novel and are sitting, reading quietly. Well, I promise you that you would not find it quiet if only one-fourth of the noise in here were in your nice living room. There are always many crazy people in this house, but these days two of Thaulow's crybabies are here (oh well they are quite decent), pleasing us with their presence, so the noise level is higher than normal. But if I complain, what would Grandmother say; she is sitting in the middle of all the children playing "Frans Fous" with Hanchen. She is not even well; her stomach is in great disorder, and although Aunt Loda says with certainty that Grandmother got it from the kitchen, in the meantime she's faint, and she can't do more than go for a little trip every morning. Doctor W.P.[100] has prohibited her from going out in the byre, stable, or pigsty, something she is not happy about. However, she sees the necessity of doing what the doctor tells her to, otherwise she would not have listened to him at all. Her mood suffers from all this, though, like several other things.

At this moment three couples in love are sitting next to me. I am sitting here free as a bird and making fun of all six people, three ladies and three gentlemen. They are all so, so happy, although I assume there are different degrees of happiness, too. Maybe all three couples have different feelings, like the newly engaged or those who are to get married? Like Doralise and Mathissen, they will get married sometime in 1849, but where and when? I do not know at all, and maybe they do not even know themselves. And like the two who will soon get separated, not to see each other again until they are to be united, never to part.[101]

Wednesday, January 4, W.H.[102] is leaving; you must have read in the newspapers that he is pleased with his result from Practicum. His journey will in many ways not be as unpleasant this time as his last journey; the goal of the trip is attained, and he is getting good company all the way from Voss to Bergen. W. Christie[103] is taking his exam in a while, and as soon as he is done he will start on his journey home to be home in time for his parents' 25th anniversary. Imagine what a joy for the parents, and what a joy for Hans to see his old parents so quick and fit, their happiness when he arrives, and then receive blessings from those whom he cares for. Well, maybe he does not picture it as deep and as great as is possible to one who can never, in any respect, attain that same joy.

Tomorrow Doralise and Agnes are going to Nittedalen with merchant Plato.[104] Agnes is going to stay there for fourteen days; Doralise is going just to follow her for the sake of the blessed proprieties. Kalla is staying at Jarlsberg for Christmas; the Countess didn't permit him to come here, as she badly wanted her favorite boy to stay with her and because she expects many young people for Christmas. Lillemamma was also invited (after a suggestion from Kalla), but Grandmother didn't allow her to go as she thinks she is not grown up enough. Kalla was very disappointed; he had truly been looking forward to seeing her again. He will not come here until after the New Year.

God bless you all for the coming year; may you experience many happy hours. This is a deep, hearty wish from your Linka.

Grandmother, W. Hagerup, Constance, and everybody send their greetings and wish you, Uncle, and the small ones a happy New Year. Please give my greetings and good wishes to the people at Møl, too.

Linka

Linka's Letters — 1849

January 18, 1849

Dear Uncle!

"It seems like you're emptying your entire skull this evening," Hagerup tells me when he very impertinently sticks his discourteous face inside the door. "I think I know that best myself, sir; however, it is very flattering that you miss my company when you are surrounded by so many other lovely creatures."

What W. H. said about me being emptied (regarding writing letters that is) is incontestable, for sure. I don't know what else to do in the living room; it is so incredibly boring to sit and listen to all the intelligent people discussing back and forth why we didn't consider earlier the possibility of all of us going with Hagerup to Bergen. "What is decided cannot be changed." Well, with a strong will and a lot of effort I think this could be changed. "But do it with cold blood, or better luck next time!" See, these are well-thought-through reflections, and as I am writing them down I also make sure to let my thoughts and acts reflect them. I believe I have learned them from "Peter Simple."

Your friend Elen Bruun sends her greetings to you; she has been here several times this winter, once to listen to Ole Bull. She is doing well, and she always tells me, "When writing to Askevold, please send my greetings to everyone there." Actually she has frightened me so much that I hardly dare to write to you anymore. In Bergen they had somehow heard about my political nonsense letter to you and Elen laughed and made so much fun of me that I think I'll stop teasing you with politics.

Have you read *New Year's Eve* by E. Bøgh?[105] Oh, that is a wonderful piece! Stabel gets a slap in the face just like he deserves. A man comes on stage with newspapers and petitions sticking out from every part of his body, pockets, etc, and he resembles Stabel. This is not politics! I have also seen *The Inspector* by R. Olsen; that was a dirty play and it caused such a row and chaos. I've never experienced anything like that in the theater. This is not politics!

What should I do? Hexa has stolen a march on me regarding heart robbery. Please help me figure this out, Uncle! This <u>is</u> politics.

Adieu — a New Years kiss from

Your Linka

Ronglborg, January 18, 1849
Mrs. Rosa Christie,

It seems to me as very odd to start a little conversation with you now, Auntie. It's hard to believe that I'm sitting in one of the rooms in the old Borg, as the weather outside is so windy and bad that I start thinking I'm in my room in your house. But then reality comes back to me and I am far, far away from you, my room, and from Askevold. Although a person can't always be at a beloved place, the thought is independent, it doesn't let itself be stopped by anything and stays wherever it wants. It can often be flighty, but nevertheless I would like to be like it. Imagine how wonderful it would be! In one moment I would be here and in the next I could be with you at Askevold, I would not be at a standstill for a second. I would not stay on the ground all the time, no, most of the time I would fly high, high above it; maybe I would never come down. I'm not sure if this would be obtainable, though... I guess the best is to stay patiently on this earth and wait for... Oh no, what have I been writing; I should throw this away. I hope you do not think I am totally crazy.

Today, or I should say this afternoon, many people from Askevold will visit Hagerup. It is the last day before he leaves; the big farewell takes place tomorrow morning. I wonder who of the ladies here will be saddest... you cannot start at the top, believing that the sorrow is the greatest there, you need to take steps so long, so long from there, jump over a little hill and stop by a mountain that is not made of granites or rock, no I think it will be a mountain of chalk or shale. Oh well, you never know about the farewell, the feelings between those two people are more than just normal feelings; I mean, when you are engaged it is sad to be apart like Hagerup and Constance have to be. However, I think both of them have such a strong hope of seeing each other again soon and being united forever that the separation will be less hard for them than it was two years ago. Hagerup has postponed his journey twice; the first time he was to go with Hans Christian, but as Hans Christian would have to leave in a hurry, Hagerup decided to postpone it for another eight days, even though "Møllarguten"[106] came here. Then the steamer was to be in Lærdal January 21st, and Hagerup was going to take it to Bergen, and these two reasons caused another postponement. Hagerup was not the only one here who listened to Thorgeir Audunson's music, though. Constance (who has a sore foot) and my three little sisters were the only ones home when the rest of us were among the 1,600 people who gathered one night in Logen's large hall to admire "Møllarguten" and "Han Ola,"[107] as Møllarguten called him. It was wonderful to hear Thorgeir produce the soft tones with his fiddle; it was so beautiful that I felt it deep in my bones. He didn't play any of the "Hallinger" I heard in Sonfjord, but it was almost the same kind, and I had to think of the awful squeal the other fiddlers perform. Thorgeir was a funny little man; during this night and his entire stay, he totally let himself be guided by "Ola," who led him in when he was to play and out again when he was done. When Ola played, Møllarguten first stood in the back watching, but after a while he walked all the way up to Bull and all the gentlemen around him, totally enchanted, without even noticing them. He stood there like he was dreaming; one tear came trickling down his old wrinkly face, and in the end he exclaimed: "Unbelievably extraordinary!"

While playing, Møllarguten sat on a chair that stood on a big tilted box, rocking back and forth and stamping on the tilted box so the sound echoed in the entire hall, followed by applause after each *slått*, *gangar*, etc. Then Bull, who stood by his side and looked so pleased, told him that he had to bow, and Thorgeir Audunson bowed in every direction, just like Uncle said Philip F. does. Aunt Lodviska was so fascinated by Ole Bull's person and behavior toward Møllarguten, in addition to his performance, that her heart was almost in danger. Hexa and I talked to Møllarguten, and he was funny; he said, "I'm so frightened, this seems so strange to me." He is very fond of Bull and was very depressed when he had to part from him today, but he (T.A.) longed so much for home that he had to leave. I wonder if everything seems like a dream to him... He once said, "I will be happy if I can only afford shoes and dish towels for my wife and children and a jacket for myself."

Now I'm done — this is a description á la Behrens's wedding, with the only difference that now you can't sit up on the marsh and get irritated over the long and bad way it's told. You just have to stick to your green chair, my dear Aunt Rosa. I guess I could fill up the fourth page too, but I think you are tired of me now, so adieu.

Your Linka

Ranglborg, February 15, 1849

I wonder if the last time I wrote to you, my dear Aunt Rosa, is as long ago as I think it is? No, I can't believe it is so, because it seems to me as months ago, and I'm sure it hasn't been that long. I wonder what the reason can be? Well, it's surely impossible for me to figure it out after just thinking about it, and maybe you or Uncle really is to blame? Indeed, it has been endlessly long since the last time we have heard anything from you; I hope you are well? The times are hard and everyone constantly worries for loved ones who are far away and whom they have not heard from. Oh well, this is not worth talking more about; you know where it is going. I talked about something similar in my last letter.

Do you remember when, four years ago at this time of year, you wanted some sweets at the square? What was going on at that time? I will tell you: now is the time for the market. Oh, that boring market, every house in town is involved, and here in the countryside... Oh well, here it's fine only when the young people and the children leave the house. But before that happens, they make a racket from one room to the next, and chatter away so I almost go crazy. Hanchen is the only decent one; she sits silently in a corner, looks at the others, asks for gifts from the market, and keeps quiet.

Linka, Linka! What a scribble! Your writing is as unreadable as can be! All the market stress is affecting my fingers; indeed, I can feel how it's reaching my fingertips. Oh, it's stinging so badly, Auntie, I can't stand it! Maybe the best would be if it ran down to my feet.

Some market guests are coming . . . They left again very soon, which I appreciated. But the best thing was that they brought tickets for Hexa and me for the theater this evening! Now the stress has reached my legs, so I'm leaving, adieu! But I'm going alone; I will have to find Hexa somewhere downtown.

Oh, how much fun it is to go to the theater! It's always fun but this evening I have enjoyed myself more than usual. One usually enjoys oneself during the play, but it's almost just as possible to enjoy oneself in the breaks. You, Aunt Rosa, were the reason for this, as there in the seat right opposite to me sat a lady who was so much like you that it was a pleasure to look at her. When I fell into a trance over the grandeur of the play, I would start dreaming that you were the one sitting there, and I would want to get up and walk over to you, but... Yes, the world provides stresses like that.

What I now have told you is written this evening, February 15, 1849, and not as it may seem during the time of the market, when I messed so many things up. As an attempt to make up for that, I had to do as I have done.

Monday there will again be a great ball here. I don't know whether to go with the others (Hexa and Bessa); what am I to do at such great balls? First, balls are not for me, and second, I have been sick every time there has been a great ball (once I fainted during the dance... that was painful. It caused a lot of attention that I didn't like).

February 16

It's crazy that this Aunt Lodviska starts to make a fool out of me early in the morning. Do you know why? I'm a fool because of the *Introduction to the Norwegian Language*. Lillebessa comes over to me, reads a couple of words from this letter and says: "Linka, why don't you write in Norwegian? Ha, ha!" I get a little uncomfortable at first, but suddenly very confident, I answer, "No, it's because I don't want to mix Danish with the good, old Norwegian."

I will sound like a fool when trying to tell you this, as I do not know anything about the case — I'm just guessing. Doralise and Matthiessen will presumably soon have a wedding; they are buying so much linen (tablecloths, etc.). Even better, they are looking for a home. A few days ago, they learned that old Mrs. Matthiessen passed away; thus their preparations have stopped and the wedding is postponed. These are only presumptions, Auntie, remember that, but what is true is that soon now I will have a wedding. Do you think so?[108]

The "Old One" here at Borgen is, as usual, doing a little better regarding her arthritis, but now Grandmother has a cataract on her right eye. The "adults" are doing well, although Nasa's leg is not quite well yet, Bessa has a stomachache, and I . . . (I consider myself as "old," thus I am in the wrong category and cannot write about myself). The youth are sewing shirts for Kalla until their fingers fly off, Hanchen is coughing, and the children are gone in the afternoon. During the morning they're at school, Rosa with Ms. Lofs and Agnes with

your Linka

Ranglborg, March 23, 1849

The letter I sent you on the 20th was the shortest letter I remember ever having written to Askevold. I think the reason was because it should have been and was supposed to be long; however, I will now make up for it with a real letter and real answer to your journey. I answered unclearly and incompletely in the other letter, but now I will start, my dear Auntie or Uncle.

Uncle mentions in his letter that it would be a great sacrifice for me if I were to come to Askevold for a short or longer period of time.[109] After that, he reminds me of all the balls and enjoyment and nonsense which I would have to leave. No, dear Uncle, it is nothing; those things do not attract me at all. I do not like balls and parties. I have been to enough concerts and I am as unaccustomed to comedies as if I lived far out on the countryside. However, if you could write nonsense like that before, you probably think it is incorrect if I come as soon as possible, as you have heard I would have to leave my… my… my… Well, it is quite natural that Hermann would prefer that I do not go, but Uncle, you should not be unfair and think it is wrong for me to go. I would love to come, and without having someone call it a sacrifice for me. "So, you want to leave me," my Hermann says. "Indeed, I do!" Soon Auntie, you will see me trudging the sea route with bag and suitcase, but no red-checkered cloak. Unfortunately, you are often a little ill, and this time you are allowed to be; however, you are not allowed to be very ill, as you sometimes are, before I put my foot inside the house. Now you know what rules you have to follow, dear Auntie, I hope you are pious and kind enough to have patience.

I am truly happy for an upcoming change in Agnes's civic life, which is to be a little more educated. She will attend school soon, after Easter. She is enormously excited and it does not seem as if she will follow her older sister's example, that is, to lie in bed crying the entire night before the first day of school. However, later I did quite well at school and the interest grew greater and greater over the years, and it was strongest when I graduated. That is because I have always been like "*Kjerlingen tvert imod strømmen.*"[110]

These days Lillemamma is capable of jumping through the ceiling with joy every second. The Art Society is presenting a tableau and Lillemamma is to be on stage. She is going to be a farm maid as they asked her to be, "You have to come, you have such a nice, kind face, just like a good Norwegian farm girl." I don't know if I would like seeing Lillemamma sit on stage at the public theater, but it can't harm her, the ladies and colleagues are all being nice to her and the gentlemen aren't spring cuckoos.

Have you ever seen an advertisement more inappropriate than that of jeweler Tostrup, where he says he has a supply of engagement rings? That is a joke that goes beyond all reason. People in town ask each other to marry as if they have heart troubles; there are at least two to three new engagements every day. I am glad Kalla is not in town; otherwise, it could have meant trouble in these hazardous times. Yes, I even regret that I got engaged; it is too common. On the other hand, I will make up for it by leaving. Do you think I am a little crazy? I think this would be a suitable time for W. Christie to come here; I've suggested it to him.

In each and every letter you got from me this winter all you have heard about was Grandmother's condition. She has been so-so, and unfortunately, that is also the case now. She has been in bed for three or four days; her usual pain haunts her. By the way, everything is as usual here, that is, regarding health issues. The aunts, uncles, and cousins in the whole family, at Ullern, Bærum, Jarlsberg, in Prindsens Gade, and at last here at Raglborg are well. Hanchen is allowed to go outside now when the weather is good. Well, adieu, Auntie and Uncle, everybody sends their greetings to you and the small ones.

Your *Linka*

Uncle, I am to say from Aunt Lodviska that if her eyes were better you would have received an impertinent letter from her as a reply to the impertinent letter you sent her. By the way, your birthday is coming up, Uncle; we congratulate you with our deepest wishes. You and Auntie should have birthdays more often, as we always drink you a toast in *eggedosis*[111]

I would like to greet you from Hermann, Auntie, but I do not dare to, as you do not like him!

Ranglborg, April 12, 1849

My Dear Aunt Rosa!!

At this moment, at 10 p.m., Hermann went to bed. If he weren't so tired, I would have had him keep me company for a little longer, as I intend to wait for my sister Hexa to come home. She is at a ball in "Dramatikken" tonight; you know, Auntie, young people and that kind of nonsense always go together, that's for sure. I have experienced that myself. Once upon a time I felt like going to balls or enjoying myself in similar ways, but now... no. When I enter a ballroom and the people dancing first catch my eye, I find it so strange, so unbelievably strange, that grown-ups can find it even a little enjoyable to trip around back and forth on the floor. Or even stranger, how they sit quietly by the four walls of the hall, just as elegantly and gracefully, gently and supple, as tobacco smoke that stirs up from the pipe bowl when W. Hagerup enjoys his morning pipe. It's a strange world we live in, that I experienced a long time ago. Thus I often, maybe too often, fall into deep thoughts.

Aunt Lodviska is a mean person, I have told you that before. Today she made fun of me because I have become so old, but I am too smart to let her bother me and answered quickly . . . Oh no, I changed my mind, I will not tell you what I answered, you might start to think too much of yourself or get some bad thoughts about… no, I cannot tell you more. But listen, Auntie, do you think it is correct of you and Uncle to let me wait for so long for a congratulation letter? I wait and wait every working day, but each day for nothing; there is no letter. However, I do not always get disappointed when at the post office. That would have been too bad, as my nose is big enough as it is and with a hairy mole on the tip; two working days in a row I have received letters from Bergen, first from the Governor, and then from W. Christie. The latter was somewhat expected, but I got surprised to my inner soul when finding that the letter from the Governor was for me. Oh yes, that was fun, and now, Auntie, you and Uncle are the only ones of those I care the most about who still have not sent me their wishes of happiness. If I don't get them before I come, I will have you cough them up when I see you. But it is not as nice to use the mouth compared to using the pen, right, Auntie?

I am talking about leaving, but the steamer will not start going to Bergen this year. It seems as if it has got cholera as well and has been put in a hospital. I know that fourteen days ago it was let out of the Hospital of Christiansand, quite recovered, but later it had a relapse. It has a loose screw and is now lying in Horten where it is to stay for a serious cure. It will probably be done in May. I will have to be satisfied with whatever its doctor will do; however, I would like to get on my way by the end of April, otherwise you will jump in before me, and I really do not want that. It will be fun to see all of you again, and if God is on our side that will happen soon. I am absolutely certain to come, but unforeseen obstacles can always come up. Everything is in the hand of God.

A conversation between Doralise and me: "Doralise, I will not be here for your wedding." "What are you doing then?" "You know I will leave, but tell me, what is the date of your wedding?" "Well, May 19." "That is the date I am leaving! Oh well, that is good actually, then I will not have to sew you any gift." "How mean you are, you tease!" Auntie, I think you can imagine how busy Doralise is these days; in less than one month she will be a wife. She is sewing her outfit as fast as her fingers can move, and Mathia, the seamstress, is to sew an entire set of dresses. Oh my, it is tough preparing for a wedding!

Agnes Smith has been in Nittedalen with the Sigwarts almost the entire winter. She likes being up there a lot, and Uncle, although he longs for his sweetheart, accepts that she is there, as she gets used to domestic work. Agnes is a sensible girl; I think she will be able to come down to help in her dad's house if she gets bored of it and wants to leave.

Hermann and I have spent the entire Easter holidays at Ullern. We were supposed to be at Fredrikshald, but since Hexa and not Wilhelm Preus had to come with us, we preferred Ullern, and to be honest that suited me the best. I am a little nervous around people, especially strangers.

What do I see? Four pages filled with words. Auntie, now I think you are just as tired of my nonsense as I am tired of sitting here annoying myself with this terrible steel pen. Therefore adieu!

Your *Linka*

I think Mr. Forgetful is sitting on my back, Auntie. Lodviska asked me to tell Uncle that she owes him a scolding letter, but today her headache was so bad that she was unable to write. Grandmother is quite well; she is going to attend Moer Lin's confirmation this Sunday. The rest of us are also going, to bring our wishes of happiness for Jetta on her day. Oh, I don't like it.

Give our greetings to Uncle, the small ones, and yourself! If Møl still is with you please greet her from Auntie and me.

Approaching Marriage and Immigration

(1849 - 1851)

Askevold Parsonage November 27, 1849

How calm everything is around me tonight! Outside it's silent and clear, not a breath of wind can be heard. And inside the house there is rest and sleep. Everybody is in their bed, asleep, resting with their sweet, or maybe more bitter, memories and visions. In terms of the latter, that can't be the case for those whose snoring now interrupts the earlier silence. It's the toddlers who, breathing through their noses, create one of the less pleasant concerts. However, it's quite funny to sit here listening to these little creatures' competitiveness, how one of them tries to beat the other in making the strongest, rolling, most thunder-like sound through their well-shaped nostrils.

But how is it that I'm surrounded by these little ones at night? To answer this question I have to go a long way back in time.

While the Governor was here this summer, it was decided that several people from here should make a trip to Bergen in the fall — October 12th. When the time came closer, we were very busy getting the travelers' clothes ready — Aunt Rosa, Doris, Carl, Hoffmann, and Uncle. Everything was soon ready, and on October 11th the clothes are lying in the corner room, ready to be packed, which would be done after dinner. However, Uncle, who had nothing to take care of for our journey, was walking around in the field. Auntie was busy with little Hoffmann,[112] and Maid Müller was preparing the birds for the dinner table. The toddlers were making a racket, and I was sitting in the nice green armchair by a window in the living room, sewing on the dress I was to travel in — it still needed a lot done to it. Everybody was busy doing his work. But all of a sudden the work stopped. It was as if the workers were paralyzed, and you could read the grief in their faces.

A sad message had to have arrived, but what was it? A messenger Wilhelm Christie had sent from Bergen on October 9th had given Uncle a letter while he was out walking. Pale, and with deep sorrow painted in his face, he came into the living room, saying, "Where is Rosa? Where is Rosa?" As if she knew something, she came in from the bedroom and opened the door with the words, "My dear Christie, what's the matter, is something wrong?" Uncle put his arm around her waist and led her back into the bedroom. However, Mølla came in to me, saying, "Imagine, the Governor is dead!"

I was so dismayed to hear this news that I didn't know what to say. And what was there to say? Burst out in pain? No, no, this news was so unexpected, it was hard to believe and to understand that was really true. That's probably why I exclaimed, "Is the Governor dead? How do you know that? Who brought that message?" When the messenger left the city, he was not yet dead, but the doctors said he would not live through the next day. [113]

A little while afterward, Aunt and Uncle came back into the living room. Oh, what grief! Wilhelm says that he thinks it would be better under these circumstances that there is no journey. There is no talk of the children and me going, but with still a faint hope of finding his father alive, it is decided that Uncle and Auntie would leave the next day.

It was strange, the dreams and hopes each of us had had when it came to that journey. We had just been talking about it that morning, and now to be struck with such grief. Yet, there was still a faint hope left. But a stroke for a man who'd had two already did not leave much hope of recovery.

The following morning, the twelfth, Auntie and Uncle departed. When saying good-bye, my best wish for them was that they would find the Governor still among the living.

Even without the sad circumstances, I would not at all have been sorry that my journey to Bergen had been cancelled. If I were in Bergen, I could not have avoided having to go visit people or go to parties and boring things like that, like I would have wanted to. I would have had to go where the others were going. Instead, I wanted to be on the customs boat or at the customs officer's. Now to all of this was cancelled, though, and the children and I were left at Askevold by ourselves.

The Minister and his wife were supposed to be gone about eleven days, but these eleven days seemed more like a month. What made them seem so long was the bad, stormy weather we had, that not only made it dark, wet, and uncomfortable, but also stopped our workers from getting anything done, which for me was now more important than it had been before. For example, a maid and two servant boys were supposed to go to an island some miles away from here to fetch an ox. The day they left, the weather started out beautifully, but later in the day the sea was a tempest. This weather lasted for eight days and our people had not returned, so we were worried that they might not have made it to the island safely. Finally the weather calmed down, and I went out to Søveien to look for the boat, but there was nothing to see. The storm started again. This was the fourth day after they had left, and I went back inside, pensive, not in the mood either to talk or to make jokes. It was also the day when the mail was supposed to arrive, and I waited for it, but no mail came.

Two long days passed, and I was in a rather bad mood. In the mornings, I was reading with the children, and in the afternoons I was sewing a bit and reading for the most part, as that was my only pleasure. Saturday the 20th, the weather was quite good, and — what joy — in the afternoon I saw the boat coming in at the wharf! After a while one of the boys came up to me.

"Welcome home!" I said. "You've been on a long journey now."

"Yes, you can say that again. The journey was too long, and Miss can imagine how lucky we've been. The day there was no wind, it took a little while before we got the ox down to the boat. He was so wild and such a handful, it was just too much. We had to put him in two clamps, and in the end we had to get him down and lay him down in the boat. When we were done with this, and had just pulled away from the shore, we had only taken a few strokes of the oars when the wind started blowing again, and we had to go back on the shore. And we've been there since. If the ox hadn't been such a handful, and we had gotten too far out on the fjord, then God knows if you had ever seen us again. It could've all been over."

"So the ox saved your life?"

"I'd say he did, that's for sure."

Now the mail came, too, and brought me letters from Bergen and Christiania. The one from Bergen was from Uncle and Auntie. Unfortunately they had not made it in time. At three in the morning, October 10th, their dear father passed away, calmly and in a good mood, the way he had been all his life. He lost consciousness the last night, and was unable to recognize the many who stood with bowed heads, crying as he was near his last.

The letter I got from Christiania was from my Hermann. It was very encouraging for me, even though it contained nothing about what I now started longing for — about the answer from Dietrichson[114] in America. If he answered that Hermann could fill the call, I was to leave November 2nd — not a very long time. But if not, Hermann asked me to remember my promise to return there without anything established with certainty, though I thought to myself I would not. I cannot leave Auntie here by herself this winter. Even if I would really want to be with Hermann, it is better if I stay here, and I would like that, too. If I stay I will long for him in between, but the longing will be chased away — with reasonableness, sense, and will taking its place. I am content with that exchange.

It was just as if this sunny Saturday appeared in order to show me that the weather at this time of the year also could bring out smiles. Even if it was a bit cold, it was dry and I would have had no reason to complain if it had just lasted a bit longer. Long-lasting smiles are often boring to look at, but I would still have wished that this kind of smile had been here a bit longer, as storm and rain soon reappeared. The next day also wore a stormy robe, and it had it on not only for one day, but it had to carry this heavy burden on its shoulders for several days.

My sorrow was now: "How are Auntie and Uncle going to come off the steamer if this storm lasts?" In the afternoon when it wasn't raining, I went out into the garden and gathered some apples that had fallen from the trees. I made sure that they were still edible, threw them with contempt into a basket, and continued my trip along the garden's many pathways, slaking my throat with red currants. They were hanging in some bushes, inviting me to enjoy some from the garden. I stopped and had a handful of the fruit so that I really could make the most of the fresh taste.

Down in the southern corner of the garden, I faced the wind, and the sea spray hit my face as hard as if it were rain. But I didn't have to let the sea spray imitate rain for long, because big, heavy drops soon started falling. As fast as my legs could carry me, I ran up to the door of the room facing the garden. It was closed and locked. I was afraid I'd get soaked if I took the other way out of the garden, so I called in through the living room window for Mølla to open it. In her eagerness to obey my wish she forgot to hold on to the safety hook so the wind took it and blew it toward the wall. Tinkle, Tinkle[115] — a pane broke. This did not stop me from coming as fast, but of course as gracefully, as possible through the rather small opening. The broken pane was really annoying, but I could not help but laugh a little bit at Mølla's irritated expression and bitter words because I had used the window as a door. And now I could see what an idea like this led to. Yes, the rain gave us its rather fresh greeting through the big hole the pane had left behind. I had to attempt being a glazier. With a big piece of glass, some paper, and a little paste I earned my apprenticeship in that craft; my artistic fingers did their work excellently. The rain had to stay outside, and with that the game was over, to our common satisfaction.

The next day, October 24th — nice and calm weather — as soon as possible a message to the real glaziers, since around midday the steamer would bring Aunt and Uncle. The sun was shining brightly, but during the stormy days everything had become so marked by fall, not a green leaf was to be seen anywhere. The fields and paths were covered with yellow, withered leaves, while a piece or two of this sick, dull color was still hanging in the trees.

Now a boat goes off to the steamer — a long wait — and we can see it return with the minister and his wife. Oh yes, I had missed them so, I was terribly happy to have them back home. Mølla, the children, and I, we were all down at the wharf when the boat came in with our long-awaited loved ones. Expressions of sorrow and joy were mixed on their faces; they saw their healthy children around them, as well as everything usual about the house, but what a loss for them as they once more imagine being in the living room or any other place at the custom's station! While we asked each other how we were, we made our way to the garden lounge. I helped Auntie get her travel coat off, and when this was done she stood before me like a black domino. She was dressed black as a raven — she even had a black cap. This outfit and the tears in Auntie's eyes made me cry, too, feeling the loss Uncle and Auntie had to feel for the loving father, and the thought that I should never again see the good and honorable old man who was loved by everybody who knew him, and respected by everyone, even those who didn't know him. They had left this man's bier after it had been been lowered into the ground, covered with all possible splendor — everything was marked by the grief that his death had left the city — yes, the entire country.

When the minister-couple had arranged a few things after the journey, we had a little dinner and our conversation that afternoon was mostly about their stay in the city. But as we were sitting there, Auntie suddenly said, "Oh, Linka, it might be that in eleven days, when the steamer is going south again, I'll be going back to Bergen with Christie."

"Oh, you will? "

"Yes, it is not quite certain yet, but Christie is going for sure."

Uncle: "Yes, I have to take off again, even if it conflicts with my business, there is so much about Father's papers and other things that my brother can't take care of it all, but on Thursday I'll write to N. Friis and ask if he will come here for a month or so and take over for me."

We got to bed late that evening, because there was so much to talk about. Mølla and I, however, together with the other people of the house who had been there for eight out of the eleven days that the master and mistress of the house had been gone, played rather sorry roles. But we couldn't help that. I didn't think more about this, but when I got up to my room I could not fall asleep right away like I usually do, because I was thinking. Every now and then I exclaimed, "Is Auntie going to the city again, and for such a long time! No, it won't work, we can't manage everything around the house decently!"

Finally I fell asleep, and the next morning I was the same old me. But when I said good morning to Auntie, I also said, "You are not allowed to leave us again! Yes, if you go to Bergen, you will not see me here when you return; even if it is the last steamboat going, I will find a way to get out of here!"

"Oh, you silly girl! But Linka, I didn't get a proper answer yesterday when you were asked about news from America. A couple of letters were sent to the Custom's station — Preus probably assumes you are already on your way back to Christiania. I really wanted to open them — it was around the time you could expect an answer."

"No, I still haven't received an answer. Preus only says in each letter 'I long for the day when we shall meet again.'"

"Now there is only one day with mail left before the 2nd of November when the last steamer this year passes Laugesund-Askevold, and if you still do not get an answer then, what will you do?"

"I don't really know, I'll have to wait and see what the letter says before I can give you a decent answer."

Every Thursday morning seems long to me, but never has it been as long as that Thursday. Finally it ended, that is to say, the morning ended, and the mail arrived. The red box is already in the living room and letter after letter comes out of it, but <u>nothing</u> for me. Now there is nothing for me, today when I was really impatient! The newspaper was on the edge of the sofa and I went over to look through it, and look! In between the layers was the letter for me.

"Look, I got a letter after all!"

"Oh, that's great. Hurry up and read it!"

Oh yes, they didn't have to tell me to do that. Read it I did, and I did it as fast as Hermann's nice, soft (?)[116] handwriting would permit. I ploughed through the letter far too quickly, as if it was the flattest field in the world — up one furrow, and down the next. But no answer from America, only a hope that I would go even if we did not know, hoping to get an answer regarding Dietrichson's wishes before the winter was over. But if we should do this, how was I supposed to get back to Christiania to get ready for the long, long journey? Such talk did not seem all that unreasonable in many ways, but traveling like that, not knowing, would bring so much unpleasantness with it. Besides, I was sure that if no answer — no satisfactory answer — arrived during the winter, I would often regret leaving Askevold, no matter how nice it would be to spend some time in Christiania.

That afternoon I was as undecided as I could possibly be. I could not decide what to do. Finally Auntie said, "Well, there is no answer yet, but what is Preus writing about your journey?" This question gave Auntie, Uncle, and me the opportunity to have a serious talk. It was not at all as if anybody was trying to convince me to stay here through the winter. "If — which for both your own and Preus's sake I do not wish — Preus should get a satisfactory answer — oh, no, two young people like yourselves going to America, you haven't thought that very well. I am afraid it's a rash plan — though if it's really what you want, I wouldn't wish that Preus gets an unsatisfactory answer. But may God give you strength and help you think about what Preus will have to go through over there. If an answer should arrive now, you could get ready to leave here with the first steamer. I believe that ought to be early enough, but consider this thoroughly, my dear Linka, and do not stay if you would rather leave. You know we would like to have you, but..."

"Yes, I'll have to consider it."

Later in the afternoon, Uncle and I went for a walk under Prestebakken. That was where Hermann and I spent more than one pleasant hour last summer. There Uncle and I talked about America for what must have been two whole hours. Uncle wanted to know my ideas about this distant country. He wanted to know if my thoughts were based on reason or if I was just captivated by youthful ideas. I hope he understood from what I said that this is not the case. He also explained to me what such a journey could lead to, both good and bad. But he didn't try to change my mind — on the contrary. In the course of our conversation, when we were back in the living room, or over at the big marsh where Auntie was, I silently wished, or even exclaimed, "How I'd love it if today I'd gotten a certain answer from Dietrichson, and not one that puts sad furrows in my forehead." What a mood you can get into from feelings of doubt and uncertainty like I had this evening! How much I would have given to have a conversation with Hermann, who indirectly — yes, certainly — asks me to come to him this fall, now when I've decided to stay where I am. With the firm hope that God will help me even if I don't make the best decision, I finally fell asleep. The next morning, Friday, November 1st, I greeted Auntie and Uncle, telling them that I would not leave the next day. My heart was not at ease when I said this, but I comforted myself that I was not doing anything wrong, hoping that Hermann would not be angry or sad when the steamer only brought him a letter and not his Linka. A kiss from my dear Aunt and Uncle put an end to my grief, although my conscience would not quite be silent. When Saturday came with its steamer, and Uncle went onboard, it was as if my heart was breaking, and why? Yes, my Hermann!

There was nothing more to do here, though, and silent and in my own thoughts, I went with Aunt on a little walk through her marshes, roses, and sheds. I think all I was able to say was, "I'm glad, Aunt, that you did not leave, too." Now I was completely stuck at Askevold until spring, since the only thing I could think of was for me to go overland by myself in the winter, which was not a wise thought at all. If there should be a decision about America saying that we were leaving, I would not be able to come before April, when the steamer service resumed. If I could just get a letter from Hermann telling me how he's dealing with the fact that I didn't come, a stone would fall from my heart. Although this was a heavy burden, it felt lighter when I thought of how good my staying here was for Aunt Rosa, as well as for my little students, who would not have had anyone to read with them. If you live peacefully in the country, where one day is like another, you seldom see other faces than the ones you see every day. But if some of them don't show up, and they "turn into a Swede" and leave us looking for them in every corner, they'll be missed right away. Our memory will soon tell us that the missing one is out traveling. But after all, it's wrong of us to let go of anyone, because we don't like the emptiness in our daily lives when someone has left. I did this reasoning after Uncle had left. It's true that I felt like everything was as usual, but the master of the house was gone, and at dinnertime, when I was called down together with the children, his seat on the sofa was empty. As the "honorable teacher" I sat down, but "ow, ow." One of the chairs really would have been a lot better, since the padding was so uneven. In order to more or less keep my balance, I took a pillow to sit on. It helped, and it had another advantage: it made me higher, and with that came more respect. Strangely, even as big a fan as I was of the seat in the sofa, I enjoyed it a lot more in the summer when Hermann sat by my side. Oh, that time and its joy! After dinner I visited the moss-covered bench in the summerhouse. Sitting there, old memories returned, as fresh as if that day had been today.

When I came back inside, I took my place in Aunt's green armchair while she was inside taking a nap — I wouldn't be allowed to sit there if she were in the room. I took the opportunity to sit down comfortably with a book — English? — but first a little gossiping with Mølla to keep her from taking a nap, but I still heard a strange, snoring sound from the sofa every now and then! What had my conversation been like? Mølla was sleeping! Maybe Linka should take a nap, too? But not for long, because Auntie now padded into the room, still a bit sleepy, and asked for the coffee. At first I imagined it was Uncle's snoring coming from the sofa, but a perplexed Mølla jumped up from the sofa. "Yes, coffee!" Auntie marched out. I didn't catch sight of her before supper, except for a brief moment at tea time, because she was working in the cowshed all afternoon, while Mølla and I were sewing, reading, talking, and thinking — and afterward — ? — we had to scold the toddlers a little bit, but after the candles were put on the table we played *gnav*[117] with them. It was so funny watching Carl's face when he had the opportunity to say "*kis!*" or "*hugaf!*" He was supposed to be serious so he didn't give himself away, but for him, being serious meant making the funniest faces. I had many a good laugh watching him. It didn't get too late, however, before I gave Auntie a good night kiss, and marched up here to my lovely room, which I would truly say is the nicest room in the entire house. It is so nice to come up to in the evening, at least when Marthe has lit a fire in the stove. Sometimes a nasty storm prevents me from getting it really warm in here, and then I go to bed at once. Otherwise I always stay awake for a while, reading and writing. Many a long letter has been composed up here at night. By then, my thoughts have found the peace to wander off to wherever they found a resting place that evening. In between, they've been disturbed by cats playing, wind hitting the house, and snoring from Mølla's bed, where she sweetly slumbers. Surely she has some high-flown dream in her head, since when she's "in seventh heaven," the little lady sometimes finds the joy of life. This evening I also spent quite a while saying good-bye to my room, since tomorrow will bring to it a new inhabitant — my "good-bye" for that time was sitting until late at night, writing to Hermann. The next evening I found myself in the guest room — there were memories from the summer, from 14th of July to 6th of August. Minister Friis, my teacher and friend from the first visit at Askevold, was now staying with us to take care of the parish in uncle's absence. He didn't do anything to disturb our peace, since for the most part he stayed in his room. In the evening, Auntie, Friis, and I could play some whist, and eat a spiced apple. In particular, that was when he talked with us. By the way, he came down for every meal.

During this period, I would have liked to be in a good mood myself so I could cheer up Auntie, who was rather sad, but I couldn't manage it. Each time the mail came, I sent a letter and I got a letter, but H. still expected me, and finally the letter came saying how disappointed he was. He talked about how I had not kept my promise. But you are wrong about that, my dear H. However, this will not stop us — if you get a letter from Dietrichson saying that we are leaving in the spring, I will come any way I can. A couple of mail days — the only day of the week that could bring a little bit of rebellion into our cam — had passed without any good or bad news. But this, too, was going to change.

Mail day, *November* 15th — I got no letter myself, which made me sad. After having waited for eight days, I had nothing, and now there were eight more days until the next mail day. I thought I could use the newspapers to make up for my disappointment, but Friis and I soon threw away the papers — bad news from Uncle Carl in Bergen had made Auntie cry terribly. She only pointed at the letter and told me to read — what I read shook me and my whole body went cold. But I don't want to talk any more about this awful evening and its bad message, or my conversations with Auntie. I tried to comfort Aunt in her despair as much as I could. But Auntie said, "Bertel Prestøen is going into town tomorrow morning. I'll send one of the boys over to see if I can go with him. Then I'll leave you and the toddlers tomorrow."

I couldn't make any objections to this hasty decision — I saw both the necessity and the utility of it, and I hurried to get things ready — helping to get everything in order and to pack Auntie's clothes. A few days earlier, Mølla had gotten permission to go home for a few days, so her helping hand was missing. Later on Bertel arrived, and they decided to start their journey early the next morning. Finally all the clothes and the luggage were done, and we went to bed. I went to bed downstairs with Auntie, but what a confusing lot of thoughts and feelings I had — I couldn't sleep! Sorrow, compassion, and disgust went hand—in-hand in my heart, and fought with each other for prominence. I grieved for an old friend, but detested using such an expression about a fellow human being. But all in all I was sad, and now Auntie was leaving — if only her coming would just be of some help!

The next day came with a fresh wind from north. At eight in the morning, Aunt's boat pulled away from the parsonage's wharf, where I was left with all the children, wishing the city people a safe trip. But I also thought and dreamed even more.

Now I was again quite alone as commandant of the parsonage. I was not happy about it, but with God's help I was hopeful, and I comforted myself with the belief that everything would be all right. It was the children especially, and particularly my little godson Hoffmann — he was not happy that his mother had left him in such a hurry. He was not well either, but grumpy and nagging, and I was mostly concerned about that. The nursemaid had to sit up with him the entire night. Since I have always been a night wanderer, enough to be comfortable staying awake while the snoring from the sleepers sounds like a waterfall in my ears, I decided I could take the first part of the night for my turn. So since Auntie left, I have stayed up like this until some time between twelve and two each night. Often we have had bad weather during the night, so I have not wanted to go to bed, knowing beforehand that sleep wouldn't come until early morning anyway. To make time pass, I have chosen to write really long letters to cousin Hermann, my siblings, and other relatives both in Christiania and Bergen. Or when I am bored with writing letters, I read or, like tonight, continue my little diary. Every now and then Hoffmann wakes up and I have to go to him, or sometimes

I hesitate, as it is already early morning and the maid can take the child and see to the ovens. The one who is up has to be stoker both in the lounge and here in the bedroom, where I am enthroned — well, not at the moment, but soon — in the big bed with little Camma at my left side, who with her great bear turns several somersaults down to the bedpost, usually sticking her feet in my nose, and then back up to the headboard with another roll. But this time it also involves me in one way or another. Sometimes, like last night, she turns a <u>somersault</u> from the bed down to the floor. In alarm, I jumped out of bed when the sound of her head hitting the floor awakened me. Little Camma was lying there, sobbing, with her nose and her legs up in the air. "Poor little Camma, does it hurt a lot? Come now with Linka, and we'll go lie down in the big bed again and *Titei* will tell a story about the wolf." This has an excellent effect on her crying organs — they are completely silenced.

Camma and I are back in our bed again after having awakened not only Hoffmann and Marthe with our noise, but Mølla as well. Half awake, she sits up in bed and asks, "What was that sound? It wasn't the clock again, I hope," — and with that good night! Mølla was sleeping again, but before I did the same, I had to go see what Mølla's exclamation about the clock was supposed to mean. I believe it was yesterday morning Mølla and I jumped out of our beds because we heard a smacking sound coming from the living room. As we were putting on some clothes, the maid, Marthe, came in, pale and patting her chest to calm herself down. With fright printed on her face as well as on ours, she exclaimed, "God help us, the clock fell down! The cat tore it down; it came in while I was sweeping the floors in the living room!" The clock! When I came into the living room, the pretty alabaster clock and glass were in ten thousand pieces on the floor. The clockworks were still in one piece, but what was sitting over on the bureau? It was that nuisance of a gray kitten. But all of a sudden it was gone, and we assumed it had gotten out through one of the open doors that were now full of spectators. They were expressing their compassion after the loss of the pride of the house — that was also our only guide for telling the time. Soon Minister Friis came down — yes, in the meantime we had gotten dressed — we inspected the clockworks, and Friis tested it to see if, by using a scaffold, he could make it work again, but no, it was bent by the fall and it couldn't be fixed. However, what could be done was to pick up alabaster and glass pieces — which we also did — and what did we see under the bureau? The cat! Friis chased it out with his cane, but instead of running out through the open door, it jumped up into the window frame, tinkle, tinkle, it took out a pane, and into the garden the cat went. Meanwhile, we're left in the living room, mad at that stupid cat. "The cat and I have always been adversaries, and we won't be better friends after this day" — even if I didn't say this, I still meant it. I was also thinking about how sad Uncle and Aunt would be when I wrote them and reported the accident. That will be done tomorrow, since that is when the city transport leaves. Maybe it would be a good idea to send the clockworks, too; it might just be that they can get a new case for it.

Since I've now started the list of unpleasant surprises, I'll continue in the same style — but not of the same nature: Mølla, Friis, and I were spending part of the evening eating apples, making jokes, practicing drawing caricatures and handwriting, when all of a sudden we were silent. With a degree of tension we heard a strange humming. "Oh, it's the wind in the chimney," I said, taking a candle and going into the kitchen to see to the fire. But it was not the wind. What could it be? At this point we could feel a slight trembling — "Earthquake!" we burst out — but this was hardly said before it had passed. However, for my own part — and I believe also for the two others — I had been pretty frightened. A fear overwhelmed me, made my limbs tremble. Of course I hid this, but my pale face gave away my feelings, which at the moment were not at all pleasant. Now I have seen to Hoffmann, put logs on the fire, and from the star above Haarkollenuten, I know that it is past three in the morning. We don't have any other clocks now, and some cloudy night I might stay up until dawn. Maybe "Bergen's summer" will make time pass more quickly!

Strangely enough, I found out this evening that I am a little fool — and why? — well, here I am, writing willingly, I am already at November 27th-28th — and I remember having some loose pieces of paper here in this folder, on which there are written different things, starting on November 18th. I should just add them in all their simplicity:

November 17. Now another lonely day has gone. It is past ten at night, and bedtime is coming fast. I am sitting in the green armchair in the bedroom, my hand under my cheek, and I have to ask myself: how did you spend this day? Did you do anything good and useful? The answer, I'm afraid, is questionable. It is: for the most part I've been sitting like a thoughtless, or maybe thoughtful, person, with a book between my hands, but not considering its words. No, this girl has had her mind on the staff at the custom's station and even more so, on Auntie's boat. Maybe she has made it to Bergen by now. We have to thank the Lord for the fair wind she has had — such a nice wind from the north — exactly what you call a "bridal breeze."[118] In between, I've also been thinking about how alone I am. I have nobody who could talk to me and lighten up my thoughts about an old friend's happiness in the future, though I have still found help and comfort for him, and my thoughts have wandered off to visit other places.

The loneliness has asked me, "How do you like me?" "Oh, well enough at times, though I can get too much of you when I'm sad. At times like that, there seems to be even more of you, and you make me even sadder. But how will you treat me if I go to live in America for some time? Just like I now wish that I was surrounded by the people whose company I am used to, this wish is limited to the people I am used to seeing here. In America, I will tolerate you really easily, you peaceful loneliness. Hermann will be my entire company there, and he will stay with me, but what if he has to travel because of his work? I am not alone after all — there is One up there who surely will protect me and help me!" Now my thoughts are once more in Bergen; I see the surprise at the custom's station when Auntie comes in. None of the joy there used to be — seriousness and grief. But good night!

November 18 — Here I am this evening, as I've been for the last two evenings: sitting alone in the bedroom, of course in my good friend the armchair, with five snoring toddlers around me. I'm supposed to look after them when they're awake and asleep so that nothing evil should happen to them. But I cannot do this without you Almighty God, and I call for your spirit, both for them and for everybody else!

This has been a long Sunday, but this day, as well as the other days, would have seemed longer if I had not had the duties of the lady of the house hanging over me. "Miss"[119] has become a very important person at the parsonage. I've been running in and out a lot, in the kitchen and hay barn and cowshed and boathouse, starting early — 9:30 in the morning — going until late — three in the afternoon. My first task this morning was to find somebody who could help me by mooring the yacht more securely, as it was about to be thrown ashore during the last storm. The work was done to my complete satisfaction, and because of that I can sleep soundly tonight. It will probably be the last night I am so alone, since, if the weather permits it, Friis will come back from Aafjorden tomorrow. In a way this will be good, but it is just that I have to do more with the blessed food, and I do not like that. Instead of reading my prayer book today, as I would have wanted to if I had had peace and quiet, I read a historical novel, *Thorvald the Voyager* ,[120] which has told me a lot about the old Vikings and about paganism and the introduction of Christianity on Iceland. It was fun, but now good night all! All! H.

The 19th, 10 p.m. — This afternoon there hasn't been the same peace over my house as the previous days — far from it. As I was sitting in the nice living room with my cup of coffee, thinking about the ugly weather that would stop Mølla from coming back from Aasnes, and Friis from Aafjorden, I looked out across Søveien and saw three strange creatures: three flustered women, fighting hail, rain, and wind, approaching the parsonage by leaps and bounds. A glance out across the sea told me that the church boat, with Friis aboard, was nearing the wharf. There they all were, Mølla and two women…! Instantly my coffee was set down, and out with the tray. Hello Mølla, her sister, and Margrethe Friis, sister of the Minister.

Yes, it has been a cheerful evening, and I too have been cheerful, but not really in my heart. I went with the flow, and had fun with the others. I am going to do this while my guests are here, although I won't force myself to be cheerful. But just as I start to feel cheerful, thoughts come along that make me serious and preoccupied. Neither Auntie nor Uncle is at home; they are at the customs station. I wonder how things are there? I can hardly believe what I know is true, and what consequences it must have!

The 20th — This day has passed in the joy of company. As the weather has been good, we went for a walk, but we were scared by a pig and started running at full speed! In the evening we played *Svarteper* and had a lot of fun. Jelly.

The 21st — was like yesterday, except that we had our fortunes told in cards in the evening. I'm afraid I was told that I'm fickle and Hermann is stingy, but we are still celebrating our wedding next year.

The 22nd. Today my guests have left me. I have received letters from Auntie and Hermann. He asks when I will be coming. It is too bad that we cannot agree on this. Imagine, H. cannot initiate reconciliation with Grandmother, either. I don't like it. H. has had a conversation with Uncle Wilhelm Keyser. He is good and kind, but I think it is depressing that I cannot look after myself. Uncle says it will hurt him if I do not willingly accept four Spd.[121] per month from him, which he gladly offers. Oh God, You have sent us comfort and support. We would not have had such comfort, if it had not been for your love. How good the uncles Keyser are![122] H. says he can support me too, if I do not feel that I can accept Uncle's, but let us just leave it now. H. wants me to come to Fredrikshald, but I do not <u>want</u> to go there.

The 24th of November — After I got a letter from Auntie on the 22nd, I knew there was a lady coming here in a few days, and a room had been prepared for her, but I had no idea she would come as soon as today, Saturday the 24th. It surprised me to hear that she was en route. In the morning I was upstairs in the office, cleaning up in some papers since this was to the lady's room. I was almost done with this work when Mølla comes in, saying, "Bertel Prestøen is here, and a lady is with him, they are down at the wharf." Quiet and calm — and unassuming — "Oh , is that so?" and keep cleaning up in the papers. God knows I was not calm, I shivered at the message. I thought to myself how yesterday I had wished that the boat that was taking the lady home would tip over, and no one perish but her, but that was a terrible wish and I asked God for forgiveness. Now she's almost at the wharf. "You terrible person!" I was standing for a little while, in doubt whether I should go down to receive her or not, but was awakened by Mølla's call and ran quickly downstairs with her. However, I was once more in doubt as I walked down the stairs to the wharf — should I say welcome? My mood — I'm not sure whether it came across to her as I took her hand and greeted her. I had a pitiable person before me. Now, 11 p.m. I have spent a half day with the lady, and when I think about how I judge her and how my relationship is going to be with a lady who looks so abandoned and depressed — I feel sorry for you when I look at you and talk to you. I have every intention of being friendly and good toward you and help ease your sorrow. But when you are out of sight I think of you as deception and audacity itself, full of intrigues. How then can I be good, though you, Almighty God, are her judge and not I, a sinner!

New Year's Eve, 1849, Askevold[123]

Those people who have contributed to my happiness I have to recall with the greatest thankfulness. Kind uncle, please understand my feelings! How much I have to thank you for, not only because of what you have been to me, but also for my siblings. God's blessing and mine, and the siblings' warmest thank you, have been with you in the old year, and will also be with you in the new and coming years. We are never going to be able to return your thoughtfulness, but it is our great consolation to know that sometime you will receive your compensation for this, and it will indeed be a great compensation — greater than anything here on earth can value. Yes, in this as in everything else we trust that the highest, the heavenly, the Infinite Good above, hears our prayer as we pray for you and your well-being.

I hope this has come to you when you are well and happy. This time I hope to have caught you at home. Other times, when I came to see you or talk with you, I have always been unfortunate enough to come to a closed door and meet your caretaker at the gate, greeting me by saying, "The professor just left…" I have a feeling you do not have time to talk to me more now, so therefore, adieu!

Your Linka.

January 1850

Askevold New Year's Day — 1850 —12 Midnight

I start the New Year and end the old one by appearing as my friendly self — as a night owl. Yes, I believe I am going to start and end my years in that way, sitting up, since I am reluctant to go to bed early. This evening — this night — I have written to several of my relatives and thanked them for the old and wished them well in the New Year. I have only written to the Keyser uncles once before. I greeted my sisters and reminded them of our custom at home, of seeing who could be the first one to write numbers of the New Year. I could claim to have been the first one this year, since I wrote exactly at twelve.

Everyone is now surely in bed and I'm sitting here alone talking to you without getting an answer — not even with H. do I expect to have a duet — talking, I mean — since I know well what a sound sleeper you are. But even if everybody is sleeping, there is still One who is watching over all of us. You, Heavenly Father, are not sleeping. With You I will speak. Yes, with all my heart I pray that Your spirit may guide me so that in the coming year I will do <u>something</u> good, and not only evil and wrong! My conscience is my guardian, and let it never sleep! If I am about to do something, then let me always ask you, God of mercy, if what I want to do will please you! And if I have done something that can be good, then never let me have selfish or arrogant pride in my heart. Selfishness and arrogance seem to me to be two creatures far too willing to serve — oh, help me chase them away from my soul, help me God, for Christ's sake!

January 10, 1850 — I am always glad to receive letters, but seldom have they brought me as much joy as today. In his box, the mailman had letters for me from those I am most fond of, from my sisters and from Hermann. And what doubled my joy many times was that I was thought of and sent a New Year's greeting from four different places in the same day. Little sisters at Uranienborg wrote December 26th, Ovilia and Kalla at Jarlsberg wrote December 26th, and also Hexa and Hermann at Fredrikshald remembered me December 26th. Imagine the noise and the mess there would have been if we had all been together. Maybe I would have been even happier than than I am now. However, I have been cheating a bit — the letter from my little sisters was from New Year's Eve, but it arrived with the same mail. It has made me happy for a long time, and it will make me happy every time I think about it, that I am not the only one thinking about those whom I don't see, but that other people are also thinking about me. Even a dear uncle, an old minister and bachelor at Bjelland, sent me a few lines on Christmas Eve, which I received today. Aunt Rosa has enjoyed my letters today as always, that is to say, she has been allowed to read the ones she wants, but that naturally does not include Hermann's. An old rule says that I keep them to myself.

January 23, 1850 — Oh, that seductive skating ice! Yesterday it was raining so much you'd think the Heavens were opening. However, a strong wind from the North appeared, chased the rain away, and brought back cold so that the big pond by the church would freeze. Flattering myself by saying the ice would be kind to my light figure, this afternoon I took my skates and went down to the ice, followed by all the toddlers. I put on my skates and got ready, but it seemed as if the blank mirror could very well decide to be unkind, as only the closest part is strong enough to support any skating. Oh, now I'm too far out — that time I almost fell flat on my face. Oh ice, you obviously can't take any skating farther out, but can you take it if I just skim quickly across your surface? "Listen, Doris and you little boys, now you shall see that I dare run right across the pond even though it is creaking!" Now I started — I almost reached the other end when … oh no!…… creak, crack. My skates went through the ice and there was Linka, flat on her face in the water, crawling with both arms and legs to get up, which was not easy as there was a slippery layer of ice underneath me. When I finally made it back up, wet as a crow, and their surprise had passed, the children greeted me back on the mainland roaring with laughter, a laughter which lasted as they came with me up to my room. But would you imagine that they wouldn't tell anyone such a funny story as their teacher falling into the pond? Now they are running downstairs and I can already hear them calling "Mom — no, Marthe, listen" — I guess they found her first — "Linka fell into the pond!" This little accident will still not keep me from using the skating ice if it gets some more frost. It is so refreshing to enjoy oneself like that at dusk. I usually take a walk at Søveien for my twilight exercise, but I don't like that as much. True, it's been several years since last I was tempted by that pleasure, but since I now have let youth re-enter my legs, they shall have this joy.

February 1850

February 16, 1850 — This very moment I received a letter from Hermann in which he informs me that an answer from Dietrichson has arrived. Finally the long-expected answer has come, and not too late! It says that A. Preus[124] has been accepted as a minister over there, though it also says that if Hermann doesn't get the call after Dietrichson, the likelihood is that a congregation can be formed for him.

The answer has arrived, the long-awaited answer is here, but it's not satisfactory — so indeterminate, I don't know whether to be happy or sad about it. If H. had gotten the call, I would have been happy, but something this indeterminate is not something I like. Now we should listen more to the voices that do not predict a good journey for me, and therefore are only reluctant to give it their approval. Aunt Rosa is against it, which I do not like, and I am tempted to say that if the entire family is as much against it as she is, then I <u>cannot</u> leave, and H., if he still feels called, will have to leave alone, and I will be left alone, longing for him — that will be my fate.

Uncle speaks more for than against the journey, and tells Auntie that she should not speak to me about how I shouldn't undertake it.

Hermann says I should not write to anybody about Dietrichson's answer, but I will not obey him in that. Right away I'll write to Uncle Wilhelm Keyser and ask him, without regard to Hermann's and my wishes, to say straight out how he feels about the journey, and if he thinks that my departed parents would have been against it. Yes, this is what I will do, and H. won't know about this letter right away. I'll ask Uncle not to speak to him before I get his answer. Hermann, you know I am afraid that your eloquence could make Uncle change his mind. Now I want to hear what his opinion is before he changes it, if that should happen, because of what he hears from you.

That the mail today would bring me some odd news has troubled me. If I should take superstition into consideration — like the old women do — then my dreams have brought me news to make me both happy and sad.

February 26 — Today I sent Hermann a fine drawing, plus a mile-long letter, even though the letter was not as long as its intention was <u>good</u>!

A few days ago the skating ice said good-bye to the world, and wind and rain came and took it away from us. Both the children and I are happy that it stayed for such a long time; the farmers' children are, too. When I have been there one or two hours with the children, after the toddlers have left because they were cold, the farmers have also left little by little, and I have been left alone on the pond in the lovely, starry nights. When the moon is up then, casting its glow onto the churchyard below and the dark church, then these surroundings have comforted me, and after grave conversations with my heart, I have left the ice. During that time I have covered the ice with many letters, and especially this sign: H., H. I've played "tag"[125] with the children on the ice — or else I have had to pull them. I've taught the farm boys that they should not bend their knees so much, and they have really gotten a lot better.

April 1850

April 1 — The way my life has been the last few months has been curious, different. Before she left, when I complained that I didn't dare be mistress of the house, Aunt Rosa told me, "Oh, don't worry about that. It will be good for you, my child!" With that, the case was settled.

It was the 10th of March. In very nasty weather, Auntie went over to Saugesund to wait for the steamer that was scheduled come there and go to Bergen the same day. But one, two, and then three days passed, and the weather was so bad that Auntie could not come over to us: to her husband, children, and Linka. In the storm and rain, she, little Hoffmann, and the maid had to seek shelter in a hole of a house in which the windowpanes were missing and the chimney was clogged. In order not to freeze to death, they had to make a fire in the bad stove, and the smoke went out through the window frame.

Finally an armistice was declared between the weather and wind. The ocean was calm again, and Uncle went across to Auntie in his well-manned boat. The conversation between the two was to make the important decision: was the journey to Bergen necessary or not, since the auction which was the reason for the journey had most likely been held during the days Auntie had been in Saugesund. While this was being discussed, a rumble and a roar could be heard, then a shout: "The steamer is coming!" The levelheaded marital discussion was interrupted, and Auntie was soon onboard and in Bergen by the evening. My face fell when Uncle returned without Auntie. Away she had gone, and now she is ill in Bergen, and so is little Hoffmann, too. Both were in danger, but God was with them to help — as always!

However, all the duties of a housewife have rested on my young shoulders. In the beginning, I thought it was very troublesome, but now the work is going smoothly and well, as if I had been keeping house for years. Food was especially troublesome for me, and the entire Monday was spent only thinking about food for that week. In my difficulties I had to slaughter a calf a few days ago, but I gave proof to the proverb "the trolls are slaughtered at the wrong time." The slaughtering was hardly even done before Uncle was presented with a quarter of an ox's shoulder. The same day we got a load of big flounders and some lobsters. Have you ever seen such a thing? If the meat and the fish had come two and a half hours earlier, everything would have been well, but now I had to salt something, either calf or ox, and we have plenty of salted food. I wanted to get Uncle something fresh, since he likes that best. Now I deserved a scolding from Auntie because her pretty calf was no longer in the cowshed.

The housekeeping was not the only thing; I was also a teacher and had to look to my duties concerning the teaching. Unfortunately, though, our reading and so on weren't going too well. The lessons couldn't always be held at the set time, and that made everything a mess. I was used to having the woman around who had been here since last October, but I was silently annoyed with many features of her behavior. I don't think she is reserved enough, and she always has to go around things, even in the smallest matter; she can never get straight to the point, and I don't like that. She is sailing her ship and I am sailing mine, and I hope we will not end up on the same latitude and longitude together. When it comes to that, I have a repulsive magnetic pole, with which I can keep intruders away. Nothing is so bad it cannot be used for something! Thursdays are my free days; then I send and receive letters from friends!

April 10 — Tonight I'm a foot[126] taller than usual, and what's the reason for this? Spring is coming closer and closer, the trees are already starting to put forth buds ready to burst. Yes, the gooseberry bush is already green. All the fresh green growing in the garden reminded me of the herbs in the meat soup — "Oh, you're housekeeping personified!" How refreshing the green decoration is, both for the eyes and the palate. We will have to get something like that ready! Uncle — what will you do with the hotbed? We will have to fix that right away. I, Miss Important, have arranged it, and the hotbed is now done.

N.B. If it will get warm, in a few days we can sow it. It has actually been quite amusing, commanding two men today, though what if it will not warm? Then I will be just as embarrassed as I was confident the first time I was here, when Auntie wanted to teach me to make a hotbed. I can recall very well how unwillingly I stood next to Auntie and watched how it was done. I do not understand what came over me then, for I usually like doing things outside a lot better than working in the house.

April 11 — Today I've written two certificates that Uncle dictated for people who intend to go to America. They were for Arne Sætre and his wife, children, and maid. Maybe I will see them again in America. But who else but you, my God, is to decide that? The thought of America and the journey to America is with me wherever I go. It slips away in between, but it quickly finds the way both to my head and my heart, sometimes with light, and other times with darker colors.

April 28 — Promises are honorable, but keeping them is difficult! For fourteen days I have been promising the children some eggnog, but something always got in the way. And what got in the way was their own behavior. They had to behave themselves for a whole week if they were to get eggnog on Sunday. Today was their happy day. Having poured the eggnog into a big cup, I took the entire bunch up to Prestebakken this morning, where we enjoyed the warmth and the happy light of the spring sun. We were to greet it with the delicious drink I had already poured into the cup. Faithfully holding a cup each, the kids surrounded me on green. "Yes, I can see that you have cups, but do you want to eat with your fingers?" "No, Linka (some giggling). You'll have to get spoons for us, because we weren't allowed to bring them with us." With my knife and a twig it was easy to make superb spoons. And mmm...... what a great treat!

I am very fond of the toddlers here. When I was sitting up there with them I felt that they were closely tied to my heart. From the children's point of view, what tied me to them at the moment, was probably the cup of eggnog! With smiling, roguish faces, one after another they looked into my cup and then down into their own. The sound of their wooden sticks scraping against the bottom of their cups got louder and louder. I was mean enough to keep them on the rack a little bit longer — little children need some self-control. "Come now, and you will get more!" and they did not hesitate. There was the sound of their eating — "Now we have to go back home." I gave each of them a kiss and left. I got a feeling I would not have fun with the children like this too often.

May 1850

May 7 — Today, like almost every Thursday, I have received a letter from Hermann. This time his writings put me in a bad mood. Hermann does not like that I have not gone in with one of the first steamers. But what use is there for me to leave here now, rather than later, when there will be no trip to America this year, and when I cannot be as useful in Christiania as I can here while Auntie is gone. In the letter I got today, Hermann very clearly shows me that he is not at all pleased with my plans, since he tells me that he will go to Fredrikshald either the 27th, 28th or 29th of June, and spend the vacation there. In several letters I've told him that I'll come to Christiania on the 30th, so what kind of talk is that? Talk is what I call it, but I might as well say prattle, as I am sure Hermann has written this in anger. However, I won't say any more about it — maybe ask when I should expect him at the wharf in Christiania? Time will probably help in this matter, so no use fussing about it now.

May 18 — Happily I have now returned the management of the housekeeping to Auntie, and I was more than a little proud when I could present to her two big tubs of butter, churned during her absence. The thanks I got were a kiss and the same words as when she left: "Being alone has been good for you." I did not get more praise, but since I did not get any complaints, I live in the hope of not getting any later either. Oh, it is such a joy, being able to be a comfort and delight to such good and kind people as Auntie and Uncle. I think I am just that, as I have daily proof of how much they love me. When I think about my sisters, I consider myself fortunate. There is something so maternal in the way Auntie treats me. Both Auntie and Uncle act as my parents, and how attractive, how extremely attractive this is for an orphan. If my sisters could just have the same feeling where they are — but they do not, because despite Grandmother's good, loving heart, she's too strict. She doesn't have that mild seriousness that can do so much more than strictness.

May 26 — At this exact moment — at five-thirty in the afternoon — I am coming back from church. I have been godmother for little Olaf,[127] the parsonage's temporary inhabitant. God knows what the future of this child is going to be! My best wishes be with him. Auntie, Uncle, and Mons were the other godparents.

May[128] — At this moment I hear Mother and Father[129] having a little marital dispute. As a result, I start to wonder whether H. and I will argue so gently. I do not exactly like arguments between people, especially not among siblings and married couples, not to mention between children and parents, which must never take place. But I guess that is how it is in all marriages; they have little disagreements like this in between: "Yes, I will pull you by the hair if you are not a good man, so keep your promise!!" Character-wise, we are both as stubborn as two billy goats, but there is still hope for us to become nice people. May our hearts host a conversation between stubbornness and humility — oh, what a more beautiful language the latter has than the former. Isn't it so that in other circumstances or things in this world, that our mind sticks to the most beautiful? So why should it not do so in this case?

I found an envelope in my folder showing that the letter inside it had twice been prevented from being sent, but it finally went on the April 19th. It contained some wormwood for Hermann. I can't say anything to excuse the bitterness in that letter, since it is bad of me to be bitter because Hermann was bitter toward me.

June 1850

Sunday, June 16 — There has been a row of busy days since the last time I wrote, because Auntie and little Doris are coming with me to Xiania.[130]

Only a few hours left, and I will say good-bye to you, dear Askevold, where many a happy hour has been spent, both in my childhood and after I have reached a more mature age. God's blessing always rest over your roof. Isn't that the best wish I can leave you with!!

A while ago I came from a wedding at the neighbor's, Ole Askevold. There I had the chance to see and say good-bye to many of the farmers I have gotten to know and grown fond of. I had tears in my eyes when we parted. Good-bye Uncle! Good-bye Auntie! Good-bye children! Good-bye all of you servants! The boat put away from the shore and a shot from the wedding house ended the leave-taking. Oh, that was truly hard, even though I was leaving to see my loved one.

June 17 — Bergen — Now my travel has started again, and on the exact day a year after I came from the South and arrived in Bergen. I came back the night between the 16th and 17th. The 16th is my Hermann's birthday. It is strange how I have greeted Bergen twice on this day. I would rather it had been Hermann.

What a change in a year! The custom's station made a sad impression, though, as I looked up at its windows where there was nothing to see besides the naked windows, bearing witness to emptiness. A year ago I went up there to greet a dear old man, whose body has returned to Mother Earth. He was himself happy in life, and his family was happy with him. Now the man — Governor Christie — was gone and his family split. His son and my old friend, Wilhelm Christie, met us. He was sad and his head was bowed, but he cheered up after a little bit having seen Auntie and me again. He offered to let us stay with him while we were in Bergen. This afternoon we took a ride to say hello to old friends. Governor Hagerup's, at Landaas, was our first visit, since we are like the cows — we eat the best things first. After that, we went down Fridalen to one of the loveliest families I have ever known — yes, I am quite charmed with Custom's Officer Christie, his wife and his thirteen children,[131] of whom the oldest, Wilhelm, is a friend of mine from childhood. I was very happy to see them again. Happiness and contentment seemed to be in their hearts. The second oldest of the children, Hans, was especially happy. He had been a law candidate last year and was now back at his parents' home, and had a favorable post in the city. I can never think about Hans's return home without being touched in my heart, and in that see a convincing proof of God's loving reward to good children who spend their time wisely. Without his parents' knowing about it, and sooner than what they had expected, he took his Honors degree, achieving a top grade. Despite the poor winter travel conditions, he went straight home. I doubt that anyone has ever left the wharf in Christiania as happy as he was — such a childlike, true joy was to be read in his eyes. It was close to Christmas now, and Hans's parents' anniversary; and this year they were celebrating their silver wedding. That day many guests, family and old friends, gathered at Christie's. All the children were there except Hans, lovingly gathered around their parents. Even though the parents would have liked to see all their children around them, they were happy and comforted knowing that Hans was well and safe in Christiania. It was not possible for him to leave Christiania, since he would be taking his exam in the spring. But they would have him here in the summer!

The party was joyful and happy, when Wilhelm came in and in a moving voice asked his parents to step outside. For a moment there was silence. The guests were wondering: fear that an accident had occurred chilled the atmosphere, but that was only so that they could feel real joy later. His parents came back in, their faces shining with happiness. Deeply touched and serious, and surely with a tear in each eye, the customs officer and his wife entered the room with their Hans between them, and presented him to the guest and the others. Whose joy was the greatest, the child's or the parents'? In their delight, none of them forgot the Father who had sent them this encouragement from above! Happily knowing that he had done his duty, and by this returning some of the care his parents had given him, the son rushed to his parents' embrace, where.... No, I cannot find words to express the feelings in these three happy hearts, therefore I shall be silent and continue with what I can express.

June 19, the steamer — The stay in Bergen was short, but long enough to say good day and best wishes to the people I care about there. Old Aunt Thrine, Wilhelm (the elder), and all of the customs officers were hard to bid adieu. I had to think about my journey to America and so on. From the customs officer I got a nice present — one butter and one cheese server in silver, which were followed by a couple of words about how they should decorate my breakfast table in America and later. Even though Auntie is with me, I am terribly bored on the steamer — I talk to nobody and mope and draw and read. "You're as sour as a bottle of vinegar,"[132] says Auntie, who is talking to different people. She is smiling and friendly, so people dare approach her. "Don't come near me," is what the expression on my face says. It looks like we're going to get bad weather tonight. It is a bit inconvenient since we will be passing Jeddren. We'll be in Stavanger soon. The drizzling rain is changing into bigger drops, which will more serious with more wind.

June 20 — Soon I'll be leaving the "Prince Carl," on board which I amused myself tonight quite a bit. I will go backward and start with the last thing that happened. The captain onboard — Herman Smith — has an assignment, since he will get to Christiania before me. He's to ask my sisters to have a bridesmaid's dress ready for me, since presumably I'm going to be Constance's bridesmaid. He didn't want loose messages, but wanted to know how many shirts should be starched, how many not starched, and so on. Auntie took care of the dictation, as I don't like dealing with details like that.

We had quite a sea passing Lindesnes. Almost all the passengers were sick; both men and women went to bed. We had no bed — the lounge was our bed — and that is where we sat, leaning our heads toward the wall. "*The Constitution* ahead!" was called out. Auntie and I had to see the funny sight of two steamers passing each other, too, and we stood on each side of the helm outside of the lounge. However, this movement was not good for us, oh, oh , oh, soon we were feeding the crabs, in honor of *The Constitution,* not them.

The night we passed Jæren was merry, in seasickness that is. In Stavanger, I talked to Momma's old friend Hanne Holfeldt, who in her old age had married Pastor Gjør. It was fun seeing her again, but the stop there was so short, because the steamer soon took off again. While we were there, a few merry young women had come onboard. They boasted of being sea heroes, and with much laughter and chattering, they made themselves a bed on the floor in the lounge, where Auntie's, Doris's, and my bed were, but in a corner — Smith took such good care of us. The young ladies kept making noise with no consideration for the other passengers sharing the room with them. It made no difference to me, since I couldn't sleep on the steamer anyway, but they should have had consideration for an old lady with whom they shared seats. In the end, though, this lady lost her patience. With sharp words, she let them know how she felt, and told them in a rather hostile way to keep their mouths shut and stop eating all that cake, since that would make them seasick. This angry outburst only made matters worse until Mother Seasickness came and seriously punished the inconsiderate. Because of this, the neighborhood was unbearable for the old lady, even though she may have been a bit glad. "How disgusting! I can't stand it!" With these words she stood up. She didn't look very pretty as she stood there with her angry face and her hair in a mess around her face. It was already getting to be early morning, and I had been lying in a kind of dreaming or traveling sleep all night. At this time of the year the night is lovely and short. I was smiling to myself at the old woman and the ladies, but I almost laughed out loud when I saw the old woman standing there, fat as she was, hurrying down to the women's cabin where her bed was, calling her maid as she threw herself into bed: "Nicoline, get me some sandwiches!" The movements were bad for her, as she was soon suffering from the same evil as those she had just left, but when that was over, she had some of Nicoline's sandwiches and turned over to go to sleep. The steamer entered calm waters. The rest of the ladies in the cabin had been awakened when she called for Nicoline, and now they started talking about the weather and so on. This left the old, angry woman in a bad mood again; she felt it too. Breathing heavily, she sat up so quickly she hit her head, "Oh, it's impossible to get any rest here!"

But I have been going north while the steamer has been going south, and stops — we are in Mandal! "Auntie, there is Uncle Hoffmann to meet us." The greetings are postponed until we get to the hotel in Mandal.

June 21 — We'll be leaving Mandal tomorrow. Uncle drove Auntie; I went with Doris, in a cariole. We drove quite a ways up the very deep, sandy road. It had many beautiful views along the way. But that didn't last long, before my horse shied and jumped to the side, and there the cariole, Doris, and I were, lying in a ditch!

It's very pretty here at Bjelland, a lot prettier than I thought it would be. But how empty …… that's probably because there is no wife here. Uncle should get himself one, but he only wants a young and pretty one, and that is too much to ask for a man who is more than forty-two years old and not very attractive <u>for those who do not know him.</u>

This visit has only lasted a few days..

June 23 — We leave here to go to Christiansand, where I have some old friends at Pastor Lasson's. I don't like Daniel Isaksen; the last time I saw him he looked like a dandy and was putting on airs.[133]

June 25 — on board the "Gyller" — The stay in Christiansand lasted only one and a half days. I did not have a good time because memories from my past were hard to bear. I would have liked to be at Tveid — oh Tveid! Will I ever see you again? There, where Pappa and Momma lived their happiest days. I remember you as a wonderful place, where I would prefer to be while I'm here on earth. Grandfather Keyser's portrait was hanging in the sacristy in the Christiansand church[134]. There were many features in that face that are similar to those of Father's, whose image will always remain in my heart.

It doesn't look like we'll have to fight for space aboard this boat, either with young women or old, since we're the only passengers. It's nice here; the captain and the mate are really nice.

We could have easily played a great trick on ourselves. Having arrived in Arendal at three in the afternoon, and believing we were spending the night there, Auntie and I discussed whether or not we should go ashore. Something one of the crew said made us go ask Capt. Knap, "What time are we leaving here?" "In a little while" he answered. Auntie and I looked at each other and laughed. We told Knap about our mistake. We'll be traveling tonight until we reach Sandsjøsund, where the steamer "Christiania" will meet us. We'll board it and take it to the capital, where we'll be tomorrow evening.

June 28, on board the "Christiania" — It's night, between 2 and 3 a.m. We're now on board a ship which is going a lot better than those we were on before, and when I think about how it will bring me to my darling before sunset, I'm almost fond of it. There will be a lot of people on the pier to meet us, some to meet Auntie, and some to meet me. And Hermann — my <u>beloved</u> — if you are not there, my other <u>loved ones</u> will be there. Oh, how excited I am to see all of you again. Sun, you who now let me see your first rays of light, may our Lord let this newborn day be a day of joy for me and others before you let your light disappear behind the high mountains. Oh, shine today long and beautifully. Oh, my God in the high heavens and everywhere — let not your sun set without my yearning having been satisfied. It can only happen at Your will, and if it does not happen, then that too is by your will, and best for me! I will now take a little nap and dream about Hermann and my sisters and everything dear!

Oh, what a godforsaken, ungrateful soul I would have been if I had not turned to God with thanks in this silent nighttime. Today he fulfilled a wish I have had for a long time — to see and talk to those to whom my heart is strongly tied! Also a surprise You granted me, which took away all the bitterness from my heart!

"At five this morning, a gentleman came on board who asked me to deliver these flowers to you when you woke up." Holding a bouquet of wonderful roses before me, that was what the maid said, as I got out of my bed about seven or eight this morning. "What was his name, the one you got the flowers from?" "He said you were not allowed to know the name, but he is up on deck, walking and waiting for you." It is a gentleman! It has to be either Hermann or Kalla.... I was quickly dressed, and then out the door. I glanced at the lounge; in the door right above stands — Hermann! Then, we could only shake hands and greet each other, saying "good day, dear." But later today, our reunion kiss was solidly placed on our lips. Now I've spent some delightful hours. Arm in arm, Hermann and I walked up and down the deck, looking at the beautiful nature surrounding us and talking about new things and old. What I especially had to know about was Hermann's relationship with Grandmother. A letter I got as a pleasant surprise while I was in Christiansand told me that a reconciliation scene had taken place out in the open, in the midst of lightning flashes, thunder, and pouring rain. Nature was roaring to subdue their anger. The tension had been there since before I left Christiania a year ago, and I mostly blame myself, since I don't wear the robe of humility; after that, Grandmother and Hermann are equally guilty. I'm glad the disagreement is settled, and I hope to spend yet a few pleasant hours with H. at the old fortress.

At ten the anchor was dropped at Xiania wharf. Oh, what confusion and what joy! Old Grandmother in her little wagon right away demanded the attention of the travelers. However, I gave way for kind Aunt Lodviska, who probably would get more out of sitting next to Aunt Rosa than I would. Aunt Rosa was followed by a big crowd, but I was left with those I really wanted to be with: my sisters and Hermann. The march from the wharf did not go very quickly, since there was no reason to hurry. I greeted the entire family at the wharf, and now I wanted to talk to those who were with me. But as I walked through town, fewer and fewer were left of my crowd — Kalla had that errand to run, Hexa that, Lillemamma that, Rosa that, Høna had one, and little Agnes was going to Hoppa to buy herself a pencil, because the kitten had chewed her last one to pieces. That was how H. and I were left alone again. We all planned to meet at the fortress at the same time, but after we thought it over, we decided to meet at the Palace Hill. H. and I went to the cemetery; I was glad to once again stand by the graves of the departed. An hour later, the entire company of siblings met again at the arranged place, and we decided to start going up the hill. It seemed to me as if an unspeakable joy surrounded us. For the moment we were so carefree and walked happily together. I could not help but think a thought that came hastily to my soul, which I later came to see was sinful and ugly. Was it not pure desire I felt when I said, in my heart, "Oh, if we all could fly up to you, parents, who now in all your glory are looking down at your children's happiness!" God forgive me my rushing desire and ungratefulness, that let such a thought come into my breast without regard to the exhortation You gave us through your apostle: "Let us with steadfastness live through our destiny (the destiny given to us), as we look to Jesus, the beginning and completion of our faith, who for the joy that was set before him, endured the cross, despising the scorn, and is now sitting at the right side of God's throne."

When supper was over and the wagon for Ullern was ready to leave, I suddenly started thinking about where to go. I did not really have a home — no, that would have made my joy too great. It would not be good for me; it is good when a little bit of grief can make its way to my heart; it subdues my haughtiness. It wasn't necessary to talk to Hermann about this now; I will later, though. But to the two aunts who have my confidence, I spoke — to Aunt Maren and Aunt Rosa. "Should I come with you tonight, Aunt Maren, or should I share your bed, Aunt Rosa, until after the wedding?" We agreed on the last option, and here I am, surrounded by Aunt Rosa's and Doris's travel-snoring.

June 29 — The day before the wedding is a curious one. The only duty the bridesmaids and groomsmen have on this day is to get the principals to drink a toast at their party. I like being a bridesmaid when we do this, but I would not like being a bride. As bridesmaids, Agnes Smith, Hexa, Høna, and I invited guests to Borgen[135] to have wine and chocolate in the evening. Hagerup went with the men, and things were probably more serious there than with us. The bridesmaids gave such lovely speeches(?), the bride was really touched, and we had a great time. Early at night, it was already quiet in the bride's house(?). It's midnight and I'm not yet quiet.[136]

June 30, Ullern — Good afternoon guest room! You, who have now been assigned as my chamber. Many memories from a childhood long gone are coming to me as I'm sitting here with you in the silence of the night. Your walls have often witnessed much noise and laughter from my sisters and me when, free from school during vacations, we came up here, rather than be in the city with father. Out of school and free as birds, we could run around like wildcats up here with our aunt and uncle. And after a day's work — that is to say, after whittling in the woodshed, walking on stilts, sitting high in the branches of the cherry tree, etc., etc., and finally after each having taken our horse and ridden out in the fields — then, after all this useful work, we turned to you to rest our tired bodies in your comfortable beds. How much we then fought and kicked each other because we all wanted more room in the bed. Oh, what crazy kids we were! It is not with such a happy heart that I now see you again. Happiness is not found in my soul as simply as it was then. Where I'm sitting now, you seem sad and desolate to me. I can't help that my eyes are filled with tears. The happy days of childhood are gone!

July 1850

July 1 — It's strange how you change your environment and often get different characters around you. But that's not really new to me anymore.

July 2 — It's my birthday! Today I've entered my 22nd year. Why have I been so sad and discouraged the entire day? Why have I had tears in my eyes when I received congratulations from the good people of the house: from Aunt Rosa, from my siblings who came to see me, and from Hermann, who didn't stay away, either? Yes, overwhelmed with anxiety, I was up here crying for a while this afternoon! I've been a puzzle to myself today, and I can't solve it tonight, either. There's a sincere dissatisfaction with myself when I now look back on the twenty-one years, of which the last three or four have been as an orphaned girl — it's as if my heart is breaking because I cannot say, "You, Linka, you have spent your time quite well," but have to call out with my conscience that I have not spent the time God gave me at all well. I should have taken care of the siblings, I should have taken care of myself, but I did neither, as a disobedient, incapable child. Oh, can I count myself as Your child, can I call You Father? I stand before You, begging for forgiveness, good, merciful Father!

July 19 — H. and I have been talking a lot recently about a trip to Fredrikshald. The fact that I don't wish to go on another trip right now is quite natural, but a man's will is a man's heaven, according to an old proverb. I have been obedient, and we are leaving tomorrow. I don't like leaving Aunt Rosa. She is leaving Xiania soon, and when will I see her again?

July 20 — This morning at seven, I left Christiania on the *Hardy*. It has been a boring trip down the fjord; the *Hardy* is an ugly, unappealing ship! Theodora Egidius has been my company. This would have been excellent if I had only been in the mood myself. Hermann gave me little joy. He stayed inside the cabin, preferring to stay down there in the sickening air instead of out on the deck where I, and everybody else, found it most comfortable. I had expected Hermann to spend some more time with me — I think he came up once, that is all. At eight-thirty this evening we arrived in Halden. Old Uncle Preus was waiting at the wharf, holding Arthur Breder under one arm, and leaning on his cane with the other. From that perspective, he looked like a frail old man. Jørgen Breder wanted to take care of our belongings as soon as he saw us, and we were soon in a boat that took us up to Remmen, where the rest of the family was gathered. When Ludvig Breder[137] came to meet me — us — I exclaimed, "It's an alluring route up here to Remmen, but such a steep trail!" He took my arm, led me to the house, and introduced me to his wife, mother, sister, cousins, etc. I found the whole scene terribly boring. Hermann was happy to be at home with his father, sisters, and family; he was cheerful and contented. I felt strange, because the family was serious and unaffectionate. I was happy to see my three Keyser cousins: Marie, Jane, and Hilda. And Pauline? Where is she? In "Strømstad," at a health spa. Elise was funny; round as a rolling pin, she was making sure everyone got food. The *Hardy* had served rotten flounder for dinner, so the dried meat tasted very good to me now.

The evening went, and so did the guests. I was once again standing there listening to a discussion between Jørgen and Ludvig Breder about where I should stay. "Tonight here, and later with you," said Ludvig, and with that it was settled. In the meantime, Hermann had disappeared with his uncle. Good night! And with that, I close.

July 21 — The morning was spent chatting nicely with Elise. I did not give Hermann's not being there a thought until Elise bursts out, "H. is really a strange fellow; he said he would be here for dinner!" The afternoon passed and Hermann did not come. "Do whatever you want," I thought and went to Glende, where I got to know three honorable people — old Mrs. Breder and her two daughters, Louise and Alette. Then we went over to Rød to visit the garden. We thought no one was at home and went right in, and there sat old Anker with several gentlemen, all strangers to me. I had not been visiting there, and was so embarrassed, yes, even more embarrassed than Anker himself. As soon as I could, I went out in the garden and told off Louise, who had fooled me so. But she laughed at me, saying, "You're such a clown!" Excuse me for being informal, [138] but, oh well. I knew you so well before, and Hexa has said that I should suggest being informal right away. "Yes, please do," and that was it.

July 25 — I'm really tired these days, since walking from the city to Remmen, to Glende, and then to the city again is a daily habit. I'm also looking at different scenic places; they really take great pride in nature around here! And Fredrikshald — how Norwegian and wonderful!

Hermann isn't being very friendly down here. He really amazes me, and I don't understand his reasons. I often go out with the rest of the family members, but without him. The other day there was a party at Remmen. Hermann didn't want to go — I had to go by myself. Hermann: I was angry with you, your behavior hurt me, but why should I show you how hurt I was? No, I will remain quite indifferent, if Hermann keeps on acting like this. He's only been nice one afternoon. That was at Glende. We were with the entire family. Wonderful party! Wonderful weather! Wonderful garden! Wonderful black cherries and flowers! How could we not have a good time? Engaged couples especially seemed to enjoy the garden; no fewer than four couples were walking there at one time. They attacked the flowers. Hermann and I have never given each other such nice bouquets as we did that day. When I came to Glende by myself, everybody was very amazed at Hermann. I answered indifferently, and "Linka, you're a strange person"[139] could be heard from different parts of the room.

After we ate, I took Marie's arm, and we went out to a haystack and we talked back and forth about our future. I tried to make Marie leave the place where she's staying in Christiania, but unfortunately, my work was in vain. She didn't have the heart to leave an unreasonable housemistress. It seems to me a crazy weakness: an orphan girl cannot, should not, ignore her own health the way Marie does as long as she lives there. It's a beautiful thing for Marie to do — she knows the old woman does not want to lose her. I, however, reason like this: "How can the old one be fond of you, when her love isn't great enough to keep her from hurting you for the sake of her own selfish bad moods. Since she doesn't recognize your education or value your knowledge, I'm sure that if you left, she would be able to find a person whom she would feel for the same way she feels for you. After you were gone for two weeks, you'd be forgotten. The old woman should find a maid who is more suited to take her unreasonableness, who knows how to ignore it. Meanwhile, Marie, you could stay in Halden until you had brushed up your partly forgotten knowledge, and then later, make more with your tutoring than you used to." My speech, however, was in vain.

Wednesday, *July* 31 - At seven this morning I said good-bye to the friends in Halden. Many of them came down to the wharf, and Elise Breder gave me some beautiful flowers as a good-bye present. With Marie Keyser at my side, while she is in pleasant conversation with the other passengers, I'm sitting here thinking about how the last days in Halden were spent. I'm especially thinking about a trip Jørgen Breder, Hermann, and I took to Strømstad just to visit Pauline, as if a trip abroad had nothing interesting to offer. The trip in itself was fun, though. Jørgen, happy because he was going to see his wife again, was cheerful, making jokes and laughing the entire trip. He was especially magnificent when we went to a Swedish farmer to have dinner. I can't remember anything of his Swedish except for "*Telebonke med gredda på flødebøtte!*" That was what we had for dinner. We went past a great manor, "Blommesholm." There was a big field with flax, such a pretty sight — the beautiful, fresh green, with blooming blue flowers. I simply burst out, "I wish I had that flax when it's ready, then I would spin and weave!" A couple of miles from this place, we left our horses to go into the woods to look at an old "*tingplass,*" a little plain with a big stone in the middle, surrounded by some smaller stones. All three of us climbed the presumed speaker-stone. As enthusiastic as we always get when we think about our ancestors and their activities, we each gave a speech in honor of the old age of paganism.[140] After we left this place, we came to a similar one, but here the stones had been placed deeper into the soil, creating the image of a ship, with the speaker-stone by the rudder.

Pauline shared our great joy when we saw each other. The visit was a really short one, though. It lasted only a few hours; when it got dark we had to leave her, because we were staying at the Faye farm that night. The next day was Uncle's birthday. To honor him, we stayed in the city until evening, then we went to Glende. I was alone with H. at his old uncle's that day. I'd finished reading my book, and found my embroidery boring, so I started playing "top" with the top I got from H. a few days ago. It was his first piece of art from the lathe. I didn't display any great talent, which was why Uncle had to teach me. I was then his pupil, and we acted like we were in school. It really was the opposite of what you'd expect. The old teacher in mathematics, and the young student of ordinary subjects, had now left their studies to let passion drive a poor top, which was dancing carefully under the whip.

Yesterday I went riding up through Tistedalen, which is well known for its beauty. When you consider Fredriksten as part of Fredrikshald, it's the great pride of the area.[141] Yes, if I were from around here, I'd have been proud, too, since it's not only beautiful, but it's also marked by art, industry, and creativity. The proud old fortress creates a background for the fjord below, which is teeming with ships.

August 1 — Now I'm at Ullern again. When H. and I came up here this afternoon, I enjoyed the usual reception I always get. It was quite a test of my will when I said good-bye to Aunt Rosa and my sisters today, but I promised to come down to see them again soon. A kiss from them, and I went with my H. up to people who also have a greater place in my heart than most people. Nobody met us at the wharf yesterday. We visited the Preuses and the Breders first to deliver some letters, and when we got to Uranienborg, nobody was home except Grandmother. She was in a good mood and her face looked quite pleased with her children's and grandchildren's childishness when she told us that they were at Ladegårdsøen to watch the royalty. H. and I went to meet them, and make fun of them for having forgotten our return because of the royalty. I was quite downhearted when I came here and saw Ørager in ruins; while I was gone there had been a devastating fire.

August 3 — A little visit to Rosemette — her birthday . God bless you! Hexa and Hermann came up with me today. After that hot march, Hexa and I had to go have a shower in the bathing house. "Oh no!" Hexa cried when the shower was about to pour down on her back. "Hey, I can't stop it!" It was beyond my power to stop it, too. It had to be left on, and, afraid of getting a thorough soaking, we ran quickly with our clothes on up to the mill to tell what had happened to us.

H. went back tonight, a little bit grumpy because I didn't want to come with him to the city, instead of to Bærumsbakken. After visiting yesterday, the new private tutor, Mr. Hvoslef[142] moved up here today. I was traveling with him from Fredrikstad on my way back from Halden, but I did not know who he was; otherwise we would have talked to each other. I'm actually surprised at my unwillingness to talk when I am on the steamer. I don't bother to become acquainted with anyone. It was sad to walk among Ørager's ruins. Only two chimneys were left, they stood there, sticking high up above the devastated walls like two ghosts.

August 6 — I've been in the city since Sunday, to go to church and to keep Hexa company before she leaves. That way, too, we could all be together the way Aunt Rosa really wanted. In the morning when we came on board with Hexa, we sisters walked along, carrying a hatbox between us, quite cheerfully. Separations and travels have become a habit, and we've learned to hide our pain behind smooth faces. When we were at the quay, we looked up the street and saw a sleepy -ooking person who was approaching us. It was Hermann. Now it's ringing onboard the steamer — Johan, who is going along, isn't here yet. It's ringing for the second time — Hexa can't go without him. There he is — he hops in a boat. It's ringing for the third time — the music has started playing on board. The captain sees the boat coming, and waits for a bit. Very appropriately for their position, the two cousins climb onboard while their relatives wave to them, wishing them all well from the wharf, though not truly from the heart.

Auntie was going to the theater tonight; I would have liked to come with, but . . . After a little discussion with Hermann, he came up here with me and can stay here tomorrow, too. Little Bya is up here; she has a lot of fun together with little Waleska, especially when they are allowed to milk the cows. She walked with such light steps to the cowshed this evening after Auntie had given her permission to milk, on the one condition that she change all of her clothes when she came back in. "Oh no, we will wipe everything off before we come in again" and off they went. Happy childhood! I do not want you back, though.

August 12 — Today I started tutoring Waleska. She hasn't come very far along yet, but she can read, and I hope that learning by heart will not be too hard for her. It's hard to teach only one pupil. I think I'll go get my needlework, because when she is writing or doing math . . . I liked my study group at Askevold better — it was a good number of students.

I should stay around here more. I've been at Uranienborg a lot. That won't improve until Aunt Rosa leaves, though, since I want to enjoy her company as much as I can. When I think about her leaving me in a few days, my heart beats with a sad melancholy whose presence in a motherless, orphaned creature only can be compared to separation from a motherly friend.

August 26 — I didn't keep my promise to myself, and giving in to Aunt Maren's constant wishes for more than a couple of days, I went to Borgen to stay there for the last days Auntie is in the city. She has left now — I said good-bye to her today. I make it sound as if her departure took a long time, but no, I did a few errands in town for her that she had to do before she left. She was supposed to be at the wharf at 11 a.m. Maybe a tear was blinking in my eye after having said good morning to Auntie. As I ran down the stairs to the garden, I grabbed my handkerchief, and when I passed Lilleløkken, maybe I recalled that I needed it higher up than the tip of my nose. It was almost 11:30. By leaps and bounds, I ran down to the wharf where I was expected. Saying good-byes at wharfs is not something I enjoy. Auntie had already given me my instructions, and soon she, Uncle Hoffmann, and little Doris were on board, and I was in Uncle Carl's lovely wagon with Hermann, on my way to Ullern. Hermann did come with up here with me, but then he had to go read with Nissen. I could see that he would have liked to be with me today more than other times, because he knew — I could see in his eyes that he felt how sad I was at the thought that I might have seen Auntie for the last time. Forgive me, my God! If we are good we shall meet with You in heaven!

August 31 — H. told me today that Dietrichson has arrived in Stavanger. Maybe Auntie has talked to him there, and her thoughts about America are more positive. She is probably in Bergen now, just in time for old Wilhelm to get my letter of congratulations on his birthday.

September 1850

September 2 — Now, between four and five in the afternoon, I assume Auntie has arrived at Askevold — to her home, her husband, and her children. I can picture them running toward their good wife and loving mother to welcome her home. I almost want to be there among you! May the Lord delight you with His spirit! Tomorrow I'll start taking English lessons from Hvoslef, hoping Dietrichson will bring good news.

September 8 — To our joy, Aunt Maren outdid herself today, and proved to everyone that she is now well. She went to church with Hermann and me; Wexels gave the sermon. Auntie and I had dinner at Uranienborg, and Hermann came up in the afternoon. Then we all gathered nuts in the garden. We often enjoy this at Ullern, too, when Hermann comes for a short visit, or when Auntie and I go for our afternoon walks. These days the walks have gotten longer; we go up to Moer'lin at the nail factory.

Around this time last year I was at Askevold, and Auntie and I often went to the nut grove at Ask. I climbed up in the trees and bent down the thick branches, while Auntie, who was standing below me, pulled them down with the nut hook. There, she caught the branch, and with a face showing her great delight, she robbed it of its tasty fruit. I got a letter from her today; she wrote that she arrived on September 4, the date of her and Uncle's wedding anniversary.

Dietrichson has now arrived.

September 9 — The entire day I have had America, Hermann, and D. in my head — how full it has been, it is strange it did not burst. Have H. and D. talked together today? I have a strange feeling of uncertainty. It is as if I think simultaneously that we are and are not going to leave, though my hope is for the better. It is with You, God and Father, who only want good for us, and who strengthen our hearts with your spirit so that our efforts to fulfill our wishes are not in vain. And if they are, that, too, is Your wise decision; then it would not be good for us to go to America. Now I am not at all anxious about the journey — on the contrary, I am excited about it. I have not been disturbed in my reflections today, since Auntie and Uncle are at Stabæk at Ring's, and Hvoslef, my English teacher, is in the city. I just remembered my homework for tomorrow.

September 15 — Last night, H. came up here just as I was having my English lesson. However, I would not let myself be disturbed. But when I was done, we enjoyed each other's company. Among other things, I learned that we're going to Dietrichson's tomorrow. He will grant us an audience with him, just like a king. Oh well, I'm going along. I brought a letter from A.C.[143] to read in bed. His description of America entertained me until 12:30, and when it was time to turn off the lights, I was too awake to sleep, and I couldn't sleep the entire night. Finally it was morning, 6 a.m., and I got up. At 10 a.m. H. and I were at Dietrichson's. We spoke to both him and his wife. H. stayed with the former; the latter had a conversation with me. Everything would have been all right over there if it had not been for the servants. The maids were allowed to use fans and were all dressed up — copycats. Many times when the lady of the house told her maid to do something, she answered, "Do it yourself," took her fan, and sat down with it. When I said I was going to bring a maid from here, Mrs. Dietrichson advised me not to, but I am not so sure I'll follow her advice in this matter. "The maids — nobody — cares about contracts in America." Oh well.

While we were talking about housekeeping, D. and H. had gotten into quite a discussion. The former was so ardent and uncontrolled I was amazed, the latter so calm and formal I was proud. The subject was a theological question, and they could not agree, but by the time we left, D.'s anger had passed. Mrs. Dietrichson paid me some compliments, and I promised to write her if it should be my fate to go over to her. D. could not give any answer to the application until November. Still two or three months from now, then my expectations will be over with. It was around this time last year I was at Askevold, waiting for a decision about America to come with every mail, and when I did not get any, I decided to spend the winter there. A wise decision! This year we are also talking about a journey, to Fredrikshald, but I cannot go, because if we are going to America, how much will have to be done, and then how can I then go on traveling and traveling? If I'm in this house, I ought to start thinking about doing something useful, and not only be a bother. It's strange how H. can't understand me when it comes to this; it hurts me that he gets mad every time we discuss it. My conviction in this matter cannot be wrong, however, and it must remain the same. H. got mad at me because of this today, too, and he did not want to walk me up here, not likely to come to Klingenberg with a lot of us. Silent as two mummies we walked up to Ullern. Hermann stayed for half an hour and then down to the city again. Now you are at home, H., and you must be lying in your bed, dreaming of the one you love. God bless you and look after you for your Linka.

I have not seen any of my sisters today. I met Kalla after the service and sent with him the greeting, "may God be with you!" Today has given me a great deal to think about. I am not happy. That is probably because H. was grumpy when we parted. From here on he should tell me what is wrong with him; if he does not I am always kind of anxious inside, if not on the outside. Besides, he looked pale and sick. He is playing with his health, he should be more careful. Good night my Hermann!

September 17 — Right now, I'm lying in my bed, but only a moment ago I arrived from the city. I went for a little ride in the lovely moonlight to fetch Auntie and to congratulate my cousin, Doralise. On our way back up, I started pondering how different people's thoughts, meanings, and feelings can be. What if everybody thought that the little ride I went for tonight was <u>foolish</u>? Just like when Auntie left, I had talked about a birthday visit to Doralise, and then I remembered my English lesson and never did it. One thing is for sure, Auntie did not like the trip, and I won't take any more trips like that. Also I have been wondering if it could be possible that I went to town every other Sunday, did my errands on Monday, and walked back afterward. One thing is that I would get to see the siblings a lot less, but if I am going to America, I would rather visit them and our parents' grave less often than be so restless — oh, if I could keep this promise! But even though I think this is a good idea tonight, tomorrow may change my reasoning altogether. Good night all, all! God be with us all!

Tuesday, September 24 — Friday I ran downtown to pay my debts to Olsen, the jeweler, and Jordan, the comb maker. Hvoslef accompanied me, but we separated at the market. After finishing our errands, we would meet again at Uranienborg and walk up. My bills were not exactly considerable, but having them paid was like having a stone lifted from my heart, and I promised myself I would avoid owing money. If only I can keep this promise, it is good as gold.

My walk turned toward the cemetery, until I stood by the graves of my dear departed ones. So many happy memories and melancholy thoughts arise in my soul every time I visit this place, which conserve the remains of what was — is — to me the dearest. Still, I would not wish them back with us; they must be joyful up in the eternal salvation with our heavenly Father, freed from the world and its sorrows. Oh, how much better off you must be there! And would I want to wish you back again? No, no, I would not, but I will look forward to when we will gather in Heaven, and ask for God's blessing over us.

I removed the yellow, dried-up leaves that had fallen on the graves from the surrounding trees. I straightened the mignonettes and the white flowers that are planted in the hay, but oh, how glad I was when I saw that the cuttings I had planted by the head of each grave on my previous visit to the cemetery were healthy and had sprouted! I had taken a cutting from the myrtle by Papa's grave and put it on Momma's, and a cutting from the fuchsia by Momma's grave and put on Pappa's. These are thriving; I've never been able to make any cutting thrive. "This is another good omen for my future," I exclaimed as I saw it. Indeed, Momma and Papa will pray for me in Heaven with the Almighty. For the sake of Christ, He will strengthen me with His Spirit so that I am enlightened to follow His path, and He will bless me when I do what is right.

I do not know how long I was standing there dwelling on these thoughts, but they were interrupted by a man with a watering can who came and sprinkled the flowers. Sprinkling, or rain, freshens them up, just as being here today gave me joy.

Soon I was at Uranienborg, where four sisters greeted me first. I can't believe I'll rarely spend time with them, and will perhaps soon be separated from them for a long time, and from brother and another sister, Hexa, at Halden!

After I had rested for a while, Hvoslef came, and we walked back up here together. I was quite ill that evening, since I had barely sat down since I left. I could not be with Hermann!

After returning here, I had a little laugh, but I wasn't in the mood for much more. We were sitting by the dining table when the big, chubby cook carefully put her red-cheeked face in the door, and whispered: "Master! There are thieves in the Ørager garden!" "Well, then, tell the boy and the maids to bring something in their hands and follow me. Come, Hvoslef, bring your cane and give me the mop. Come on, everybody, now they'll get a smack; not that I think there are any. One, two, three, everybody go." Aunt Maren and I sat in the bedroom in excited expectation. Soon we heard laughter and the entire party with the little boys in front returned, disappointed.

Now the thieves can come, as we had a great apple harvest today. Everybody has been busy with the apples; oh, we'll have a lovely time this winter! That is, if the rats don't fill themselves up before that. This evening I've taught Uncle how to make furniture stuffing out of rye straw, after a recipe from my *Huuslige Allehaandebog*,[144] in which many unusual things can be found. I wonder when I'll be able to use it in my own house.

Saturday, September 21st, Hermann came. He still was as crabby and sulky as a rat on sour cheese, but I soon managed to cheer him up again, and he told me what he had done since the last time I saw him. Most important to me was his view on a question regarding theology that did not agree with Dietrichson's.[145] The consequences might even lead to a cancellation of our journey. Then my quiet suspicions may come true, and my hopes and dreams will go up in smoke! However, God directs everything for our best! I dream of pastors and disputes every night; America is always in the background, both night and day. Now good night, everyone!

October 1850

October 7, Wednesday — Today I should have gone to town, but for two reasons I am where I am. One: Tomorrow Hermann is to take his catechist test; apparently it is best for him if I don't come and disturb him. Two: Soon it is November 15th and by that day I would like to have finished my linen sewing that I'm working on now, so I don't have time; thus I'll have to suppress my desire to talk to my Hermann. Good luck for tomorrow! And always! Good night to you and to everyone. Today we received precious accounts from Voss. I long to hear from Askevold.

October 9 — Oh dear! I haven't laughed the way I laughed tonight for a long time. Today Auntie and I spent the afternoon at the nail factory with Mother Tullin, a perfectly nice lady. About 8:30 p.m., "Dutta" came with a boy and lantern to fetch us. We were supposed to go home by daylight. "No child, you cannot walk home under such conditions! Not at all! .... go tell my boy to get the wagon ready!" "He won't." Aunt said, "in that case, it would be better if Carlsen does what he promised <u>not</u> to, namely, keep the gig in the city, and my boy goes home to get the milk wagon." The boy walked home again.

The waterfall was beautiful today. I had to go down a few times to look at it, and it was already pretty dark the last time, but it still looked really beautiful. When I was standing on the bridge, I saw the wonderful light from the forge below the waterfall. The sparks from the hot iron on the anvils were flying all over, shining through the fine, drizzling rain from the waterfall. I couldn't help saying "if someone could just paint this!"

Well, the milk wagon came at ten. Auntie and I ride on two sacks of hay in the back, Dutta sits as coachman in the driver's seat up front, and the boy walks next to the wagon with the lantern. Off we go. Because of the dark, every time we hit a stone, the sacks — and us — are in danger of falling out. The horse finds its load of milk heavy to pull and stops after every twenty steps — it's Dutta's horse. She thinks it has too heavy a load, and jumps off. In the beginning, I found our situation very comic, and we all laughed a lot — it's just that it's so slow! The Vakkerød-hill takes forever! I'm starting to get bored, get a stitch in my side from all the bumping, start thinking about the lovely starry sky — but — for a long time a man has been walking behind the wagon; what if he grabs me by the shoulder and oops, there goes Linka. Oh no, the man was more decent than my thoughts, I got to Ullern in one piece and now I am in my bed, wishing everybody a good night, praying heaven's blessing may be with them!

October 18[146] — The other day, I heard Ola Bull's delicious[147] violin!! Yesterday Hermann came. He had dinner here, and spent the entire day in my room working on his sermon.

October 19 — Because of sister Ovidia's birthday, I spent the 10th of October at Borgen. We drove down there in the afternoon; it was nice there. At teatime, Agnes S. and Tr. came, too. Hermann came, but . . . to invite me to a party at Breders'. How could he think I would leave my sister today? No. Hermann was rejected, but I got just as honorable a "no" from him when I asked if he would stay with me and the siblings tonight. Sister O. and Hals played. That is my moment of pleasure since I so seldom hear music. Agnes and I walked up and down the billiard room, talking about how couples ought to treat each other. During this conversation I often found myself thinking "Agnes, you are engaged, why don't you tell me right away instead of going around, getting at it indirectly?" But I guess you have a reason.

I spent the night at Uranienborg, and went to town in the morning — boring shopping — had dinner at Preuses'. In the afternoon I went back to Borgen to see if anyone had come to get me, but no one had come. I walked back, played whist with the older folks and Hermann in the evening. It reminded me of the whist at Askevold.

At eight in the morning I said good morning to Hermann before he went to the war academy. Oh my, how he looked tired, that sleepy-head! Well, if you ever become my husband, you'll get straightened out!

The Preuses do not know what to do with me whenever I am down there. They make so much out of it, as if they were really, really fond of me — I wonder if they are? I was there a long time and went to the cemetery afterward, but it was closed. Today, October 12th — five years after my confirmation — I could stand next to the grave and pray to God. At three in the afternoon I went to Borgen, where Hermann met me to walk me part of the way. He brought me an invitation to a party and came a bit late because of that. He should have walked me all the way, but H. preferred the party. He walked me to Frogner. H. did something to me which he often has given me long lectures about, describing it as ugly as anything: not keeping one's word — which should not happen at all — not even if insignificant.

I made it up here all right on my own. I saw my little cuttings in H.'s room —fearing the frost, I had asked H. to take them home to his place.

October 21 — Just now, at 11 p.m., I came from Borgen. Before I turn the lights out, however, I have to write down how I spent my day — Sunday. I went to church this morning. Every time I enter God's house it is a moving experience, but today it was more so than usual, not because I was in the prison church, but because Hermann was having his examination sermon[148] today. No wonder I was more emotional than usual. I soon felt calm again, though. I sent a warm and sincere prayer to the dear Lord God that His word would always be preached purely and truthfully by Hermann. If that is so, then You are with him dear God, as it is your spirit working through his heart. Dear God in heaven, let it happen for Christ's sake! Then his speech would both honor you, and benefit and deeply comfort fellow human beings. If this should happen and Hermann becomes your faithful Christian servant, would we not both early and late turn in gratefulness to You our dear Lord!

During his entire sermon, Hermann exuded great tranquility. I don't know anything about how to evaluate a sermon, but I do believe that everything he discussed was made quite clear from the context, and that the flow and the arrangement of the sermon were good.

Several times during his sermon I sat wide-eyed. Hermann had written his sermon at Ullern, where I also read it. I noticed several times that he deviated from what he had written, but he didn't get off track at all; he only paused a few times. Afternoon, dinner and evening were spent at Borgen. Good Night!

October 23 — This evening I got the sad news that Mrs. Thaulow, who used to live at Borgen, is dead. Her husband died three weeks ago — oh, they are probably a lot better off where they are now than what they were when they were here! But the poor little children they left — six little orphaned children — dear Lord God, father and savior of widows and orphans — be with these little ones whose destiny is so hard to bear. From now on they will live with strangers, they will be split up, sent to different places. Oh, let them not experience the painful feeling it is to feel like a burden to other people — let them not be in too much pain when they miss their own home! You guide everything in the right direction, God. Still, I have to write down what I have so often been thinking: There should be some sort of foundation for orphans, some sort of institution taking care of their upbringing. There should probably be such a foundation in every house, but how often is it not the case that even if the heart is in favor of such a help to your neighbor, other duties will not allow you to follow through with it. The children should be assured of a good, beautiful upbringing, Christian and virtuous, in order that they gain the knowledge that will enable them to take care of themselves when they grow up — both girls and boys. Yes, I know well how I would have organized such an institution, and if I'd had some of Rothschild's money, it would have been arranged. But since I am not that lucky, God does not find that good for me; the state or some rich bigwig should start something like that for children of officeholders. Craftsmen have such an arrangement for their sons, but for the girls?

November 1850

November 1 — Tonight I've returned to my room after being away from it for two days. Wednesday, I drove down with sister Ovidia — Lillemamma — she was here for two days, helping me with my coat. We got it done, and had two really fun days — she played the piano for me — us — of course. It hurt me to see sister Ovidia depressed when she was sitting in the "Red Room" once again. I would really, really like her to be happy where she lives. Maybe she is — maybe I'm wrong!? How can I be content when I know my siblings are not always happy in their daily life? Oh, how I long for the day when my H. and I could offer them a home. Yes — a home — how often it's missed by those who do not have a real home! But I hope and trust in better days to come!

Since Wednesday, I've lived with the Preuses. It's so nice there, and they are so friendly — plus my Hermann lives there with his uncle and he comes in when he has time. He was really surprised to see me there Wednesday evening. I had taken the key to his room, and he had to come present himself to me appropriately when he got home. We played cards with the two old folks, and after they had said good night, we spent a happy hour together. Thursday was spent in the same way, until the afternoon. Then I went up with Aunt Maren, whom I met at Uncle Smith's. I feel so sad tonight; I feel bad! My God, give me strength!! You know my longing, you know what is bothering me. Oh, what an ungrateful creature I am! Forgive! Forgive!

But look! Auntie hung up my bookshelf. She is so good! For some little reasons — maybe foolishness on my part — I hadn't hung it up. The little attention surprises me, makes me happy — yes, it helps to put me in a better mood. It doesn't take more than that. Oh, Auntie and Uncle, that you care about me as much as I care about you! Now I think this place looks twice as pretty as when I came in here this evening! Good night all! All! God bless you!

November 7 — I should have been downtown today, but I cancelled the trip for two good reasons. 1.) Hermann is having his catechism test for the bishop tomorrow, and it would not be good if I came down there and disturbed him. 2.) The 15th of November is coming up soon, and I'm supposed to have my linens done by then, so I don't have time. Therefore I can't obey my wish to be with you today, my H., it's better for you to be alone! Good luck tomorrow my friend! The Lord be with you always! I miss Askevold — today I got good news from Voss. Good night all!

November 10 — Now it is Sunday at 10 p.m. and I am ready to go to bed. Before this can happen, and before I say good night to fellow beings, commending everyone to God, I need to write down a description of how I spent my day.

Sunday, November 10[149] — It's now ten and I'm ready to go to bed, but before this can take place and before I wish my fellow humans good night, I would like to write down an account of how I spent the day and what it was like. I first woke up at seven-fifteen, but everything was still quiet. This seemed very strange to me; I thus assumed that I'd slept through all the noise from when the girls and the boys left their rooms. To be certain in this matter I jumped out of bed and went over to feel if the stove was warm; oh my, cold as ice. The maid had not been in here yet. Then I went over to the windows and opened the drapes, oh no! Last night when I went to bed, the stars were out and it was frosty, and now what a contrast! A thick, thick snowfall, and the ground all white; the beautiful spruce trees in the Øragerlund elegantly dressed for Sunday in their winter coat for the first time this year. No, still it was not time to get up, back in bed again. The maid lit a fire in the stove; after staying in bed, thinking philosophically for an hour, I got up. By the breakfast table, I found Auntie and brother Kalla; he came up here last evening with Hermann, which I found enjoyable, as I miss my siblings a lot, and I don't see them here very often. Fourteen days ago, sister Ovidia came up here for three days. Since I haven't seen any of them until today, and it probably will be a while until I see any of them again, therefore I'm excited every time I see them, as they aren't as serious as I am, but happy and joyful. Hermann soon entered, and after finishing breakfast, Auntie and Kalla went for a ride — inaugurating the sled by going to try out the winter conditions. Hermann and I were alone in the living room — Uncle's Sunday enjoyment. We read for a while in our books, but soon it was eleven and H. left, and that pleasure was over. Before H. left, he told me that I'm one-sided because I don't want to come to Thald to spend time in the house, and because of my reasons for that. Most of the day I read Theremin's diary; Kalla read a piece by Kierkegaard. Since dark, I've been alone; Auntie and Uncle went to Stabæk, and Kalla and Hvoslef went to town. I fantasized a little on the piano in the twilight, then I got a light and played cards with the children, drew a little, and then Hvoslef came back from town. Evening food — a little conversation — good night — and now it's ten-forty-five and therefore good night, everyone!

November 11, 1850 — Today I was tempted by the wonderful conditions to take a trip down to Uranienborg. This morning Uncle and Auntie drove down in the big sleigh, and this afternoon, Hvoslef (my driver with my old friend the sledge[150], exactly like it was in my memories from the summer of '47 up here). I saw my sisters at Borgen, but I had to go downtown to talk to Hermann. He had his catechism test in Oslo Church with the bishop today, and I had to see how it went. I got a look at his happy face, which I think says a lot. Bang and sister Mette came with me into town at dusk. I met up with Hermann, and together we walked to Borgen, where we spent the evening together. We were taking off at nine-thirty. I found my place in the sledge and the trip back up was just as comfortable as it had been on the way down, hearing the jingle of bells was a joy to my ears — the big sleigh — it is my first sleigh ride this year! Good night ...

November 15 - My destiny is making a state visit tonight: good evening my dear Linka. Before you went to bed now, you probably blew your nose and found it to be unusually long.[151] You have probably noticed this change in your looks without being able to explain it, but you will get to know this reason very shortly: While I was doing my round today I also happened to have a conversation with your pet, memory. It was sitting silently in the innermost chamber of your heart. When I asked why it looked so sad, it answered accusingly, "Oh, my cousin, ask, although you already know, since it's your fault. Have you forgotten that today is the 15th of November, the day my ruler, or owner, was expecting a decision about whether or not her boyfriend will receive a call to be a minister in America? But you have been so harsh, you have not wanted it to be that way. She has been working at the slaughter table all day, she put me in here so that she would not forget herself while working with the meat. Only now does she let me have life, since she is alone in her room, in her bed at ten — but good night, we have to part for a while. I want to fly away!"

November 16 - Let me see — it was a year ago today when Auntie left me and Askevold, her children and her home, to go to Bergen to her husband and friends. Today, as we were making sausages, I have often thought back a year in time and compared then and now. How different are not only my feelings, but also my position? Tonight, I'm in a depressed mood. Everything! Everything seems so sad and hard to find in this life, but how do I dare say that? Do I dare hope for a better life when I do not take the life the Lord offers me down here, without being impatient? Oh, my God, do not let this happen, but strengthen me and help me with your spirit so that I will never stray from the path You have put me on!

I was very busy working in the house today, but at the point when I was most useful, I fainted — when I woke up Auntie was calling to Gunnar Greve.

Now I hope to sleep myself well. Good night!

Sleep has wandered away from me already It's 4:30 in the morning — it's too early to start lying here, pondering. I have lit my candle, and will now read or draw until I get sleepy again — it's now the 17th of November — Saturday morning.

November 18 — I went to church with H. today and heard a wonderful sermon by Wexels[152], had dinner in town, and in the afternoon I went to Borgen where I found everyone extremely content around a cheerful table of Boston, and the smaller siblings were competing in needlework. I was driven back up here in pouring rain this evening. I guess the sleighing conditions we've had for fourteen days now will be all gone tomorrow. Good night! Hermann did not come up to Borgen tonight, but was at a party at Preuses' — earlier home correcting essays.

November 27 — Hvoslef is knocking on the front door right now. Oh, if only he is bringing a few lines from Herm. I wrote him some words today, and to get rid of some tension that has been bothering me today, I'd like to get some words from H. No letter now. *Think*[153] will have to comfort me tonight, too! Good night.

— [154]The rest of the accounts of the aforementioned Sunday should follow here, of course, but there will be none, as the loose sheets on which they were written, and even the notes from the Christmas spent at Fredrikshald, are either left at Halden in sister Hexa's folder, or have disappeared. Well, the loss is not great. I had fun this Christmas, and during the roundtrip to Halden with Lillemamma and Hermann there were several funny scenes, such as: Lillemamma tipping out of the cariole in the middle of the muddy country road five kilometers outside of Halden. There she was on the ground. It was dark; we had left early in the morning to be in Christiania in the evening. We did not come further than to   [155]; then Lillemamma and I were so tired of the cart bouncing us around that we preferred the bed. The bed was not very inviting, however, because the sheets were dirty. I asked for clean ones, but before they came Lillemamma had already gone to bed, telling me, "oh, Linka, how picky you are. Isn't the person who lay here in this bed one of your fellow human beings? Well, what if it was 'Dirty Roll'[156] who had lain here, then…" She didn't get any further as sleep caught her. I lifted her gently and put the clean sheets on the bed.

The late morning of New Year's Day Hermann received his letter of call from Spring Prairie Congregation. What a New Year's greeting to Hermann and me from our Lord! We arrived in Christiania already on January 9th; how badly I wanted my sister Hexa with me, but that was not possible as Pauline was in a poor condition and it is not too many months until I will be coming back. So now I am at Ullern, and have left a big gap in my diary.

On the evening of February 16, 1851, I walked up here with Hermann in lovely, clear moonlight. I spent the entire day, until 4 or 5 p.m., in town. I joined Hermann and Mrs. Breder for evening prayer, and we listened to Wexels. How hard it is for me to see old Wexels exert himself like that; for a short moment he completely lost his voice. How lovely he preaches. After church, Hermann and I started to walk back here, but first we stopped by Borgen, where we just made a very short visit, and soon continued our walk together with Kalla. He wanted to follow us a little bit for a serious talk. We talked about yesterday's party at Marie Rasch's, but mostly about a trip to Christiania that Hexa wants to take to visit us. She wants to spend more time with me now that I'm about to leave. Hermann had many doubts, about which he had written to Kalla, and Kalla was now going to give his advice. He couldn't ask me, as I have a biased point of view.

December 1850

December 1, Sunday — I was visiting at Stabek this evening, a little afternoon visit in honor of Madam Ring's birthday. I walked up here from Borgen this morning after having spent Saturday in town, and said good-bye to them this morning. H. came with me to Sjølyst — after H. had left me I thought about what we had been talking about — and the result? H. scolded me for not wearing anything around my neck when I had a cold, and still do, although this was said in few words, just like my answer — that I was wearing enough. But what was it supposed to mean, both of us being of few words? Next time I'd rather go on a walk with Hermann's cane. I'm going to tell him that. Now good night!

December 2 — Oh Linka! You're such a patient girl: for more than half an hour you've been making kindling, blowing on flames, and nursing that cold oven to get a fire going in it. Oh my, the wet logs did not catch fire earlier this evening. It was really cold in here — now, however, it's burning brightly in the heating stove. Patience makes the difference — and now, accompanied by the pleasant roar of the fire, I can rest on my laurels. Good night!

December 6 — Friday. Today, in the morning, I drove downtown in a sleigh with Uncle — spent the day at Preuses' where I was with H., with whom I spent several pleasant hours today. It kind of made up for the very unpleasant Tuesday I spent with him. Then, in spite of Hermann's wishes, I didn't want to stay in town, because Uncle had come down with the gig just for my sake. I ended up staying until Wednesday after all, but at one point I was so mad I didn't even think about the application H. had written and was going to send to D. But I have thought about it now, that's for sure. Walking back and forth between Smith's and Mathiesen's. The maid's secret about Agnes. The drunken man when I walked up here Wednesday afternoon. Well, I didn't walk today, but drove a sleigh on bare pine. Uncle walked in front the entire way — my conversation with the boy every time I asked him to stop so that I could get down from the sleigh, because it was so hard on the horse. Now good night!

December 12 — Thursday. I can really feel how Christmas is coming up soon now. The last days I've been as busy as a mouse, etc., and what is worse, I have this feeling that no matter how fast my fingers work, I still won't get done. It's not only knitting and needlework that takes up my time; I also do dyeing, and that went really well today, I must say. But I'm not surprised, with the help I had, even though it was the first time — it has to be called <u>first</u> time since the yarn from Askevold was the one I tried unsuccessfully to dye a few days ago, and today we did it over. It was already dark when we were doing the dyeing — I had to have light when the cook yelled, "Miss, the water is boiling!" "Yes, hurry up now, Hvoslef, and you'll see how strange it looks when the color hits the water." Yes, what a wonderful color! "Oh, it's boiling fast now, I have to skim off the top." With that I was down on my knees, into the chimney with a candle in my one hand and the ladle in the other, my eyes running, and coughing because of the smoke — hey — maid, the yarn is on the bench — the water is hardly boiling now — that's wrong — however, when the yarn had made it into the kettle and was boiling as it had been earlier, I had to laugh together with all of my helpers. Hvoslef stood there, he had taken the candle from me, the cook was standing behind me holding a bundle, and finally the maid and I on all fours in the chimney, she with a long stick and I with the ladle. Now it was done — beautiful! Congratulations dye-girl, soon a skillful dye-er!

However, underneath all this, my mind has not been at ease. Hermann was up here yesterday. He started writing his application up here and continued it downtown today, and according to his own words he was going to hand it in afterward. He could not receive the position on the terms Dietrichson had set up, so he had to make his own terms in the application, and now it is all up to Dietrichson, what he wants and what he can do. But You, God, who knows everything, You also know this, and what will be to our best, and we shall be satisfied with that. Now good night!

December 13 — Sunday. Yesterday I drove across the ice into town. It was hard to drive, as the ice was bad — the bay — the boy complained all the way across the ice. I spent the night at Uncle Smith's and I met there with Carl With for the first time since Agnes's engagement was announced — that was only three or four days ago. He was not well, and soon left. Hermann came later, and we spent yesterday evening together, but we have not paid attention to each other at all today. H. was correcting essays and going to church this morning, and I could not come along since it was impossible for H. to walk me up here in the afternoon, and I had to go while it was still light out. There are several reasons for me to think that H. behaved less than nicely toward me in this matter — if he had wanted to, he could have walked me up today, just as well, as he didn't go to church — I heard that from Kalla. It's strange how we always argue whenever I come to town — H. never complies with my decisions and what I ask him to do. Oh well, ... good night — I can flatter you that because of you I dream about pulling you by the hair. I drove up here with Ben's horse, as I stayed at Rangelborg until it got dark, when Ben offered me a horse. It was pouring when I was driving — one could drown.

December 19 — Thursday. Today has been what I would call a good day for me — this afternoon I finished my sweater. I also got several letters, from Auntie and Uncle and little Carl at Askevold — they scolded me for not writing enough, and little Carl repeated a verse I composed for my pupils over there.

Little children here with me
Quiet must you be
Nicely on a chair must you sit
Or else you will be hit
On your back
Smack![157]

It's a short verse, however, it made me really happy to know that they still remember me. From Hexa, who also scolds, and finally from Hermann, who tells we that it's been decided that we won't have communion tomorrow, since no communion service is scheduled.

It's now 10 p.m. I'm staying up to finish my slippers so Hexa can get them for Christmas, and I'm taking them to the shoemaker tomorrow.

Yes, now the slippers are done, but what time is it? 1:30 in the morning, December 20. Oh, how late, but now they're coming to Halden — how sister Hexa's eyes will shine when she sees Lillemamma, Hermann, and Linka coming to her. Now good night! — Morning —

December 21 — Was censor at the examination of Dutta and Bassen. They were good. I was a strict grader.

December 23 — Monday. I am at Skjeberg now — came here this evening at nine-fifteen — I didn't like dropping in on them so late like that. The description of it was — the nice room — and now I am in my bed, tired of all the traveling this day. That stupid boy — Ovidia and the boy on the rattletrap cart[158] — several little scenes from the journey we started on at six this morning when we left Breders' where I slept last night. Good night![159]

December 24 — Tuesday — Christmas Eve. Tonight I'm down here in Halden — however, every Christmas Eve I have to repeat my old saying "never as nice as at home! — the blessed years of childhood!" Two sisters plus Hermann have been with me, but still? — There was a lot to be missed. We spent the evening at Ludv. Breder's where the entire Breder family was gathered. Tonight I am at Jørgen's where we went this morning. How excellent it was, watching Hexa being surprised when we came, but even more so after half an hour, when sister Ovidia came. Our arranging of the trip from Skjeberg — meeting up with the horses that came to get us from town — and then sister Ovidia in the cariole behind us so that Hexa would be surprised —

Part Two — 1849-1851 • 173

which she was too! Now good night! I wonder where I will be next Christmas Eve? How are my little sisters tonight?

Christmas Day — Not at church — bad weather — spent the day at Glende, and am now ready to go to bed. G.N!

New Years Eve — Good-bye old year, accept my thank you for what you have been to me. The last eight days of you have been a bit noisy, with parties, visits, and balls — I have only been to one ball, but that was enough for me. I sent my sisters to one more. I have also been irritated for a couple of days down here — regrets, reconciliation! Good-bye, good-bye! Thank you my God!

January 1851

New Year's Day — Now at three in the morning, January 2nd, I've returned from a ball at Rød, where I only danced a little bit since I did not feel good. I just had a little dance with Hermann before I left, long before everybody else thought about leaving. I believe the ball was fun, but I was in no shape to go over there today. This New Year's Day was too important to me — why this one more than other New Year's Days? I went to church this morning, and when I got back here, H. read a funeral sermon by Kierkegaard. During the reading, a letter arrived for H., but he and everybody else would not be disturbed by that — apparently I should say that as far as H. and I were concerned, we were both kind of disturbed, the letter being of great importance to us. Finally the speech ended, H. and I grabbed the letter, and oh, what a New Year's present from the Great Giver! In a few lines from Dietrichson, H. was called to be minister where he had applied — Spring Prairie. It is impossible to write down all the thoughts that have run through H.'s and my heads since we were told this around midday. Only you, Father, know our thoughts and our prayers, and as always when we are good, you will listen. So now, this, our sincere prayer, has been answered. Thank you, God, and help us!

January 7 — Wrote letters to America, Hermann to Clausen and Preus, and I to the latter's wife. I asked her about what H. and I should bring over there. I also sent a drawing for our house and a plan for the interior. If our house can be like that, we shall be content with it, although I am hoping more than really believing, since I am wondering whether or not the farmers will pay attention to my drawing? It has been a lot of fun, planning our house, showing it to Hermann and talking to him about it. Soon it was done, and has now been sent, my best wishes be with you, letter and drawing, on your journey — come back with an answer soon! Good night!

The 12th of January from Halden — the accident — several incidents on the road — the night at Melbye and here to Christiania Monday, January 13th.

January 14 — To Ullern — nice room. Habit is half of man's nature — Auntie ill and in bed when I arrived.

Letter

Ullern, January 30, 1851[160] — Yes, my Hermann, you are right that Linka cares about you; you are her "*Knort*"[161]! She does so more than she is able to show with words or actions. Her comfort is that Hermann still is convinced that he is in possession of, and that he is the first owner of, the strangest little jumping, beating creature that calls itself her heart. In return, the heart says, "My owner is good, I could never be so happy with anyone else. The Lord will strengthen my love for him so it gets as solid as Dovre[162]." Oh, I could keep sitting like this talking to you all night and forget both about sleep and that it is one-fifteen in the morning. Yes, I really could, and I dare tell you that. My conscience is clear; today I casually walked around outside.

Now about your little epistle from today, thank you for that. So what if Gislesen delivers a sermon at Haslum on Sunday? I still know nothing about that, but then another three weeks will pass. In any case, it is probably best if you come up here Saturday, unless the weather gets too bad. Then you can have me come down on Sunday, I think. Oh dear, again that terrible hat problem. I mean I'll get ... oh, I don't know, but I have to shout, "Oh the dress, the dress!" It is better to enter the American forest with, etc. Arup must be a strange man, I imagine going over to him and putting a hat on him like this drawing.[163] P.S., when I get a hat, all visits can take place. The Market is coming up. Is it possible for you, Hermann, to buy me velvet and then go to that lady and ask her to sew me the same hat as Mrs. Tinne made for Elise Dietrichson? No, darling, I assume you cannot, I think I can have it done on Monday.

Good night! In my evening prayer I send prayers to our Father above. Oh help us both, be with us, you Mighty Spirit! Maybe you are dreaming about your

Linka

February 1851

February 7 — Today I bought linen and lining cloth. My God! You — Father of the fatherless — help me and strengthen me, I feel so sad tonight. And surely it is the man who was supposed to be my best friend who has put me in this depressed state of mind. But I guess I'm no better than he is. I feel I'm proud and arrogant — how disgusting must I be, standing before You, oh God — still I dare to call you by the dear name of Father, still I dare beg you for mercy! Mercy for my numerous sins. Oh, Lord, break my arrogant heart, let me feel like what I am, small and insignificant. And it is this arrogance, this self-confidence I have found to such an extent in H., today I got another proof of his great confidence in himself. How often, like today, after having stated his opinion or made a decision doesn't he think like this, "What I say and what I do must be right." Can this self-confidence please you, oh God? Can you forgive it? Yes, you forgive it for the sake of Jesus Christ, and let Him set a clear and living example for us — so we can learn humility from it!

February 16 — Tonight Hermann and I have walked up here from town, in clear weather and wonderful moonlight. I spent the entire day, until four or five in the afternoon, in town. I went to evening service with H. and Mrs.B.[164] and heard Wexels. It hurt me to hear and see how he strained his lungs—and even so, at times I couldn't hear what he was saying. After church, Hermann and I started on the trip up here, but we stopped by Uranienborg for a short visit, just to say hello — then we continued on our way. This time Kalla came along, too; he needed to talk seriously with us. Our conversation was partly about the party at Marie Rasch's yesterday, but mostly about a trip Hexa really wants to make down here. However, she had so many doubts, which had been presented to Kalla. He was supposed to consider them, and then advise her. Hexa couldn't ask me, because I looked at the matter from one perspective only; that I wanted her to come. Oh well, we managed to put together a letter to Hexa on our way — and I'll be very happy if she comes in here after she gets that, but if she doesn't, she'll have to wait until I come to her.

We parted at Langeløkken, and Hermann and I walked arm in arm along the country road with long, long steps, as if we were in a terrible hurry. But I was actually in no hurry at all. It was as if a voice was telling me, "This is the last time you will walk alone on this road with

Hermann." The thought made me sad. I thought about old and more recent days, and I remembered how often, both in good and bad moods, I had walked on this road. Now, with very mixed feelings, I once again traveled it on my trip to dear Ullern. I clearly remembered the days when my siblings and I still had our blessed home, which we have now dearly missed for five or six years. The days when we left that home to spend summer and Christmas vacations up here — the happy days that left us, never to come back — when we more ran than walked downtown to see Papa and to take lessons with N.P. Tharo — Anna. Those days, summer by summer, winter by winter, stood before me. Every journey I've been on since losing our home stood clearly before me, and in the last ones — the last one — I've generally had Hermann by my side, though I have often been without his company, too — but the reasons for this? Childish tricks most of the time. However, what people cannot see, especially not Hermann, is that these tricks have been very annoying to me. Several times I have wanted to meet Hermann here when he made his usual trip up here on Saturdays, but I've always ended up disappointed. All this, my memory reminded me of tonight. I said my good-byes to the road, although I guess I will still walk on it several times. However, it will be easier if nature, as well as my reflection, is always as calm and peaceful as it was tonight.

Sometimes H. and I talked a little, but soon the conversation was at a standstill. Now we were at Vækkerø-bakken, where the noise from people sledding drew our attention. We kept on walking, and soon we found ourselves leading an entire company of boys and girls, and an equal number of sleds. The company followed right behind us and, eager to play tricks on us, they started singing a song about a couple in love, traveling far away from their home; but the young fellow died, and where his wife or his girl went I could not hear. Well, I guess this could be seen as a reminder for me, but I have been thinking — and my hopes and beliefs have been strengthened by You, oh Father in Heaven!

Now we bent in under the gate to *Furulunden*[165], and walking through the lovely avenue we talked about Arup[166] and H.'s ordination the entire time — how he can't get Arup to officiate the ordination, etc., which forces H. to go to Xiansand[167].

Coming into the living room we were surprised at the sight of Auntie, who hadn't been in there since the Saint Anthony's Fire.[168] Now H. and I have said a verbal good night to each other, and I'm also writing it down — maybe that can make up for having been a bit grumpy toward him. But that was because I was tired. Now it seems like I can't sleep because I am too tired. Adieu, all, all!

Linka.

Letter — *Ullern, February* 17, 1851

My dear Hermann!

I am very english this evening / nigth, for I have just now written an exercise, which was surely excellent.[169]

Today I received a party invitation from Marie Rasch for tomorrow evening at six-thirty. Are you invited, Hermann? And if you are, will you go? Then I will not be able to see my "Knort" up here tomorrow! I will be down in the town if I go to the party, which I will not if you are not invited. Sunday to church, and if you would like, a visit to Hall. In the afternoon, in town or at Uranienborg, as I want to go to Tellander Monday, otherwise my tooth may be offended and get lost. For that reason, my dear, could you please go to Tellander tomorrow, Saturday, and ask him if I could come see him Monday morning? He himself should know how long it might take to have a tooth filled.

I don't like at all that I'm going to town. It causes such a restlessness, which I can't stand, especially now in what are busy times for both of us. Oh, if only we were done with everything and were on the ship, giving the people we will leave behind our lifelong farewell! Since I just wished that, I have to include that our wallet should not be too full with our purchases here as well. I feel rather bad when thinking that the cost of what we have bought was fifty-four Spd. We wanted to be tightfisted, but my dear Hermann, what will happen to us?

The future appears to me now as a smiling, friendly face, and every dark thought ought to fly away, right? And you, Hermann, walk next to the gentle, waving future. May the Lord hold his hand upon us. Let us pray to Him, pray together, and He will help us!

Goodnight, goodnight! Now I want to sleep and dream about you, and then in your dreams, you will think about your

Linka

February 18 — On this day eleven years ago, Momma's corpse was taken to the grave and down into the black earth to which it belonged. It was taken away from us to be hidden in the grave, and once again become earth. But if the corpse has dissolved, the spirit — the immortal — is still alive, and by God's mercy and eternal love, it is living with the greatest, most powerful, most fair, but still the mildest and most caring of all spirits. Yes, up there with Him is where you are, Momma. Papa is with you — for the sake of Jesus Christ, the God of Love has, by his neverending mercy, let his Spirit go where you also are. Oh, how wonderful it must be where you are! If our loss down here is great, if we, seven siblings, feel abandoned and depressed by the loss of our dear parents, we still do not wish for you to come back down here to us. God our Father is looking after us with his fatherly hand — with support from his Spirit we will walk down here, pleasing Him and you. Your spirit will surround us, and if we do what is right, He will be happy with us for this, and you will pray for us, that God might help us and strengthen us in what is good! If we do this, we shall sometime be with you again — oh, what enormous joy! Thank you, thank you, spirit's loving God, for your mercy!

February 20 — This evening at six-thirty, I walked up here with Hermann, but across the ice. I had been at the dentist's to have a tooth filled.

Letter — *Ullern, February* 28, 1851

In a little while, in about an hour, I will leave with Uncle. Should we meet at Breders' for dinner? I will go straight to Uranienborg, leave from there around eleven or twelve, I think, and then I will probably do a short stop at your place. Adieu, my Hermann! Your

Linka.

March 1851

March 9, Sunday — Yesterday afternoon Wilhelm Breder drove me up here after I had been in town since Tuesday, almost eight days. I drove down with Hermann on Tuesday, and since it had been decided that he was going to Fredrikshald on Friday, I wanted to be in town with him until that day, not only to enjoy myself in his company, but also to get my friend, Anders Monsen,[170] the artist from Askevold, to paint Hermann's room. I managed to have him do that. One of my greatest amusements during my stay in town has been to watch Anders paint the room. By the way, I have been in my part of town and Hermann in his the entire day, except for meals, when we were together at Breder's or at Preus'. We have also been at Uranienborg every day, and on the 7th, Aunt Lodviska's birthday, I stayed there for the night. Hermann went to a very cheerful party at Pharoe Pettersen's that night. Several of Hermann's good friends — some of his schoolmates here in town — plus Wilhelm Wesselberg and Kalla, my brother, said their good-byes to him as a bachelor that night. How strange, this was probably Hermann's last party with his fellow students before he gets married! This was the 7th of March — Friday — the day Hermann was going to leave. Obviously, it didn't come to anything that day, but on Monday he was leaving. He couldn't get ready before then; what took him the most time was packing and taking care of his books, as well as the ones that had been sent to him from the various bookstores as contributions to a public library for the congregation over in America. All these books were lying in his room, and I could not deny myself the pleasure of looking through them, seeing what kind of books the people had been given. Therefore, I started looking through them in the order in which they were lying. I had probably looked through half a score or so of books — just the titles — at least I had only been looking at the books for a short time, and several times Hermann said to me in a very irritated voice, "oh, Linka, now you're making a mess in my books again." "I'm putting them back in the same order they were in," I answered. H. was still on pins and needles on account of his books. Soon he leapt off the sofa and came over to me with such a disgusted and suspicious look that I was offended by it. I left the books and went over to Anders to watch him paint. I watched for a while, and then left the room. I was angry, and it hurt me that on several occasions H. has had so little confidence in me.

Yesterday — Saturday — I came up here as I said, early in the afternoon. I had a horse so that H. and I could come to Haslum church to hear Gislesen[171] on Sunday. Hermann didn't come until ten last night, and we started arguing about a trip my sisters are taking to Fredrikshald for our wedding. I said that I did not care for them to come — obviously because I had no money to give them and therefore had to forego the great joy of their coming. Hermann wanted to bring at least one, two, or three, if not all four. "Well, either all or none," I answered, "otherwise I'll be sad and not at all happy, but now I do not want to talk more about it." At eleven-thirty we said good night. We had made our last night together as engaged as long as possible, sitting in the sofa in the living room. We've spent so many pleasant hours in it; should we now, this last time, argue?

Today — Sunday — Hvoslef, Hermann and I went to Haslum church where we heard Gislesen preach, which was beautiful—really a joy and pleasure to the soul. He expounded upon the gospel about Christ's temptation so beautifully. How he warned us against the temptations of this world, and how many prayers he prayed for us. Oh, if we could only avoid the state of apathy or drowsiness of spirit, in which we are so often tempted — for, as Gislesen said, they lack the sting which can wake you up from your lethargy! Yes, that sermon will be useful for me for a long time — the 1st Sunday of Lent. Last Sunday — Shrovetide Sunday — Hermann and I were at Tanum where Gislesen also preached beautifully about baptism, etc. After the sermon there was a wedding ceremony which H. and I also had to attend since we wanted to find Thorkildsen, an old friend who also attended church. After we had found him, and as we were talking to him, Gislesen also came over to talk and to invite us to his home for dinner. Gislesen is such a nice man, his manner and way of — we were sorry to say we were unable to come. He knew we were going to America, and that made him twice as eager to have us come home with him. But since we were unable to, we bid each other farewell and left, happy to have gotten to know — at least a little bit — such a pious man. Oh, Hermann, if you could only achieve such a way of preaching, that will be as comforting for the members of your congregations as my soul has been comforted by this man's preaching! My prayers for you are heartfelt and warm!

H. left this afternoon at six-thirty, and we shall not see each other again until after he has been ordained. Uncle, Hvoslef, and I came with him part of the way downtown. I kind of think, though, that Hermann should not have to go to Christansand to be ordained. If he doesn't act something like what I think in this matter, I'll counsel my Hermann, saying that he has been arrogant — and that is bad — Hermann, do you realize this? Well, time will show what you decide, and I will be very pleased to take my words back. Now goodnight, you and all! God be with you! You are now in town, I'm here at Ullern, and tomorrow you are leaving! Go with God!

Letter — *Ullern, March* 9, 1851

Here I am without you again, my Hermann! Just like poor Peer Eriksen. In an hour you are leaving; that is, an hour from when you read these words and not from now, Sunday night at ten-thirty.

I don't have anything to tell you except for everything my love for you can form into beautiful words on paper. However, as you certainly can feel what that might be, I find it best to skip that part this evening. Instead, I would like to say a prayer for us to Him, who looks down on us with his fatherly eye, and helps us believe that our path is right although it might be small and narrow! Go toward God, my best friend in this life! May God help and guide you to do what is right! Without indiscretion or obstinacy, my Hermann will and wants to remember to do what his gentle mind tells him is the most appropriate for a young man, and destroy the bad sprout of pride that has gained entry in almost every human being, like you and me.

Hermann, we want to ask the heavenly spirit to pick this terrible weed out of our souls!

Adieu, adieu, your, *your Linka*

March 10 — This morning at about eleven, Hermann left town — I was up here and only in my heart could I wish him good luck on his journey, and thank him for the time we have spent together here as a happy couple. We will not be together here again until we are man and wife. I guess you will be spending the night at some station along the way. Sleep calmly and well!

Letter — *Ullern, March* 10, 1851, at 10:40 p.m.[172]

Where are you this evening, my Hermann? You didn't tell me anything about your trip, naturally because you didn't know anything about it yourself. I really hope you aren't staying at Bønnefjorden again, and thus I tell you as a comfort, "Good night," hoping that you are at a place as nice as this place, all set for bed in a nice, cozy room, and ready to lie down in a well-made, sumptuous bed. Ever since eleven this morning my thoughts have been at the country road, and before that at the last farm on the left-hand side of Revier Street when coming from Bank Square. Why did my thoughts go in those specific directions at those specific times? It was because I felt how my Hermann was doing and how much he had to do before leaving today, which I later heard did not take place until around eleven. That was actually good, because if you had left on time at nine you would not have gotten your English books that came with the messenger. What would have happened to your English then?

Thank you, my dear, for the words that I received from you today, you are and will always be my Hermann! I truly and fully believe that we will be happy when the two of us are alone over in the West. Hermann, I feel that your company is more than enough for me and I do not need any other travel companions. Except one, who will be the first and the last companion on our journey, our God! Now we will not see each other here at Ullern again, until we are tied even closer together with an even stronger and, in this life, everlasting bond.

Today Ottesen[173] left for Drammen. He catechized today and received the mark "Laud," both for his preaching as well as for the catechizing. He is embarrassingly doubtful about whether or not to *submit his application; his girlfriend and her family are so much against it, especially since they have heard that Rock River is so unhealthy. Ottesen has not been able to get a clear message from Dietrichson either, which he thinks is Brandt's fault. I feel bad for Ottesen and cannot understand how his girlfriend can make him so doubtful. He has to carry an understandably embarrassing doubt, which we thank God we are without!*

Now I will say goodnight, my Hermann! You include me in your prayer as I include you in my nightly prayer. Sleep well! Have a safe trip tomorrow! Adieu,

your Linka.

March 12, at 11 p.m.

My Hermann! This evening I can't be as virtuous as I was last night and go to bed without saying goodnight to you on paper. Last night I got ready for bed so late that I didn't dare to start a little conversation with you. I assume that my watch goes too fast and thus I do not really trust it, now I expect some scolding since I went to bed some minutes later than the time we decided. I could use a little more of the night, so I guess I regret that I made that promise and would like to ask you for permission to stay up until midnight. That bedtime has already worked for me for many years, and I do not think it will do me any harm now.

I assume you arrived in Thale around 6 or 7 p.m. Will I soon get a little journey report from you? If only I knew what day the mail arrives where you are. You'd better address your letters to Breder, as I then might get them with the milk delivery. I go for a nice walk every afternoon, but still no morning walk. The weather needs to be rather appealing when that happens, which it hasn't been at all. It has not been unpleasant, however; I guess it has been quite good for traveling, compared to what it was when we last traveled together.

Shame on you, Hermann, I didn't think you would have been such a troublemaker. Maybe you would like to put the blame on me, but no, my dear, I won't let you do that, not even if you do not let go of your old habit and protest. Am I acting cruel when I say that you often or regularly contradict me? No, you might say, as I assume you will feel little stings in your conscience because more than once you have been less than good to me. However, don't think that I tell you this in an accusing way, not at all; it is more an opportunity for me to blame myself. I admit that several times I have been difficult and not as obedient as would have been the most appropriate. Therefore, you have wanted to punish me but you did so in a wrong way. Instead of somehow trying to make me improve by softening my stubbornness; you have hardened it by being hard yourself. See, Hermann, this is something I can write to you, but I do not think I could ever tell you when we once will sit down and talk. What kind of characteristic behavior is that? With me, you would never obtain anything by repelling force with force, which I guess you have had to learn and experience. If you can make me soft and obedient, my dear, it would not be against my will, as my heart and soul would be saved from many fights. I think I have already come far regarding meekness as I now ask your permission to be up late at night. Actually, I think I could have advised myself in this regard. It is the feeling of being in a dependent relationship with you that contradicts this idea. Nevertheless, whoever I might be, the feeling of love with which my heart beats for you is the predominant feeling, the one that often makes me sad and happy, friendly and peevish, attractive and repellent.

Thank you, my dear Hermann, because several times you have forgiven my strange, peevish, and cranky characteristics. Unhappiness with myself, and nobody else, mostly causes these moods. Always, always, I see myself as a useless human being, because I have had to count on other people's help after becoming an orphan! I wanted to be proud, but as I did not have anything to be proud of, I became bitter, and this bitterness developed into peevishness, which affected you. Why do I let it affect me so much that I have to turn to others? This will be my destiny for the rest of my life. Oh, I have to go through a total change if I want to love life, which I must to become happy. The change may not be that hard; repeatedly I praise my love for you; it will cause great things for me!

Good night! May the Lord protect you and everyone. Finally, my *Knort* will get a k… from his *Linka*.

March 13, 1851

Now I have to hurry to say good night to my *Knort*, as my candle is burning out and down on the plate, not caring that it is no more than ten-fifteen at night. It is surely a result of last night's late bedtime. This morning, however, I slept so late that I got my seven or eight hours in total. Oh yes, I am a good girl! There, I got to praise myself a little, something nobody else cares to do. I feel like doing that today, as opposed to last night when I talked to you; in the entire conversation I was putting all my dark sides on view. In fact, I regret that; why would I want to be so open? Why would I want to tell you how I am, then to be left in front of you completely bare, exposing all of my dark sides and so few of my sunny sides? No, Linka, you behaved foolishly yesterday; you should almost throw this letter away, as the tone of the entire letter gives the impression of a hurtful dissatisfaction with you. However, I mean what I say, and therefore my Hermann should bother himself for a little while and read it. In fact, I was a little sad the previous evenings as well, but today I have been good and energized. If you could come to me now, you would see me smiling and without tears, either in my heart or in my eyes. I can well imagine how you are doing, but are you staying with the merchant or the head clerk? If you are at the latter's, you are probably wearing your nice student suit, sitting with your legs crossed and writing something, maybe even a couple of words to the one who is thinking of you right now, with hands, fingers, and heart. If you are writing, you cannot really move your leg, but if you are reading…. Oh my! Then there will definitely be movement in your legs. When they move the fastest, you remember your Linka and for a moment your feet get a break. Now the candle tells me goodnight. God be with you, my Hermann, my good dear *Knort*. Your *Linka*

March 14, 1851

This morning I received your letter of March 10th. Did you mean March 11th? Thank you for that, my *Knort*, again I think it is fun to see real letters from you. Actually the letter I got today was far from real, because it was too short. However, the "Nose-fish"[174] never is good, and today that is my comfort. Tomorrow I will have this entire long epistle sent, perhaps reading or skimming through it will be your Sunday enjoyment. I assume you have little time and wish that it were somewhat shorter, but do not feel bad about that; next letter and those that follow will not be as lengthy.

You might preach this Sunday; the Lord seems to be with you! And He is with you every time you preach His words, also this Sunday. I will not be able to hear you, but I can read your sermon, whether you want to send it to me, or I wait until we meet. Sunday morning I plan to ride to town with Jacob. If Wexels delivers the sermon I will listen to that, otherwise I would like to hear Jensen. I imagine that he and Gislesen are so opposite of each other that for once it may be rather appealing to hear and see him. By the way, I plan to spend the day at Uranienborg after a short visit to Breder's.

How could you lodge at Askim Parsonage? Who is the pastor?

You have to pass my thanks to Elise for the cloth. It seems to be very good, and it looks nice, too. I think we should keep both the twenty-four ells and the bolt of thirty-four ells, my dear, as it's good quality and it's a very good deal. Will we need as many towels as can be made from thirty-four ells of cloth? Don't you also think we need that? If only we had some more money we could get ahold of a little more, that is, by being modest and not excessive. Saying this, it's in my opinion that you should buy more. Yes, cash is a good gift; you probably need more of that. In your next letter you should tell me a little more of how sister Hexa is doing, you didn't mention her in the letter I received today. Adieu, my dear! A k... from your *Linka*

March 14 — Today I received the first letter from H. since he left. It's quite fun to get letters again. Tomorrow I will send.

March 15, 1851, Ullern — I always feel this need to congratulate people I am fond of whenever something good happens to them. Today was the same way. My dear, good Uncle, today you've had the pleasure of seeing your wife enter the honorable thirty-seventh year in good spirits, healthy and content,. You've been happy to have her by your side for eleven or twelve years already, and to have been the person with the greatest contribution to her happiness. You have prayed to heaven that she might stay with you and your children for many more years, and you have felt happy hoping that your prayers will be answered. In your prayers and in that happy hope, a person far away from you is taking part, but not too far for our prayers to be joined together.

Soon it will also be the 28th of March — your birthday. Uncle — you're turning forty, aren't you? Aren't you happy, looking back at the days that have passed, although you don't wish for them to come back — your spirit wants to go on, hoping to have it just as good as you have it in your daily life here, where you feel happy — and your feelings are true! You have told me, "Every day brings us one step closer to our grave" — we have to keep that in mind, not to frighten ourselves, but as a light to us, like our happy days here on earth when we have been and are good human beings. But since we now are happy down here, and have many people we love and care about, then it is natural to want to be with them for a long time and pray to God about this — and receive fulfillment of our prayers when they are answered.

Letter — *Ullern, Sat. evening, March* 15, 1851
Just now I was standing in the hallway with Kalla and Hvoslef, telling them goodnight. It was quite different from eight days ago when I was with a cousin of mine named *Knort*. It was quite strange being able to stand so peacefully and quietly holding my candle. Nobody disturbed me, either in my soul or body. I wonder if the latter was that calm. I almost believe, honestly, that it seemed like it missed something or someone. Its heart beat a little faster; I will let my Hermann decide whether it was caused by yearning or tiredness. Let me hear what you say.

Should I imagine you at the pulpit tomorrow? God be with you! I will not go to Osloe [sic] as the conditions prevent me. However, I intend to go to Evensong to hear Vexels.[175]

It is late. Good night, my H. Your

Linka

Did you remember that two years ago today we . . . yes, now you remember the rest! Good night!

The 21st

You can't imagine what wonderful weather we've had today. It was so wonderful and beautiful to take a walk this afternoon that if I'd had my Hermann with me and put my arm in his, it would have been a happy hour.

You'll still just get a good night k… from me because I've written letters to both Uncle Hoffmann and Uncle Christie, the two other worthy pastors, so now I can't give you, who deserves it, more than this in addition to a handshake that is as truthful and solid as a *Knort* who is squeezed onto a stump. When both the *Knort* and the stump are well, they aren't easily parted by others. The *Knort* tells the stump that Hermann is not to have a cold. So let God take care of you, for your *Linka*.

March 29, Ullern, Saturday evening

Since the last time I had my hands on this piece of paper, you've received a long letter from me that I wrote in town; furthermore, I also received a reply on Tuesday, and besides the few words for me, I read a long letter from you for Breder today. Thank you for everything! I don't want to talk at all about the bishop's case now; I know Jensen, Breder, and Johan wrote to you in that regard, but how? I'll talk to Breder about that on Monday, when I go to town.

This whole week, sister Ovidia has been with me and we have sewed like our fingers are running wild, even if it is Saturday evening. Concerning Ovid's sleep, I have often pulled her out of it and over to the piano. I've heard her play so rarely this year, so the time I have left I need to use my ears for the pleasure they can bring to my mood, and delight to my heart. If my fingers always stay by the needlework, it's a sheer drudgery, what boring work, but the thought can travel wherever it wishes and always seek conversation with whomever it would like; if the conversation gets really visual, the needle work falls for a little while, down in my lap. Soon the stitch becomes so big that I need to take a small pause and have a look, then I discover that the needle is stuck. But it's no big crisis; now I'm upstairs with my work and am sure of finishing in a decent time. Every afternoon Sister and I have gone for a long walk in the snowstorm, for one hour, or two hours and a quarter or a half. Today it's not snowing any more, but we staggered ahead in high snow, delighted by the lovely newly fallen winter suit that dresses the trees into their Sunday outfit. It makes the ground as even and shiny as a still ocean surface on a hot summer day when a whitish fog rushes across it. Also, "Blokka" provided four- to six-foot-high snowdrifts. On the way we sang "*Til Saeters drage Ovid og jeg,*"[176] the song sometimes interrupted by serious conversation.

When, as I mentioned, I drifted into thought while I was doing my needlework, what did I think about? Most often I talked to my *Knort*, but not until this evening have I <u>wanted</u> to write down my thoughts and ideas. The first I just gave you; the last, my dear, you can easily imagine. Therefore, I'll now say goodnight, as it's three minutes to twelve, soon midnight. Tomorrow Hvoslef, Ovid, and I will go to Haslum; I'm looking forward to that, but if you were there it would be even better! But now, adieu! Your *Linka*. You might be sitting and thinking about a sermon right now. You are my Hermann!

April 1

Have you been an April Fool today, my Hermann? I haven't yet, but perhaps I will tomorrow when we go to town to hear the account from you at Breder's, the way I expect and want to hear it. The mail is here today. I won't be straightforward, I'm telling you, Hermann — tomorrow I'll be an April Fool.

Sister Ovid will walk down with me tomorrow; she's been here since Sunday, and for eight days now, a long visit. Yesterday I was in town, but I couldn't access your things as the stairs were gone and the door nailed shut with wedges. Anyway, your things are sealed and in that regard I don't have to worry. Goodnight!

Letter — Christiania, March 21, 1851 — At Breder's

I just received your letter of Monday evening at seven, no date. You are not and have not been well, dear, since you came to Halden. After your first letter, I reasoned you were a little tired from the trip, but now I can see it is a little more serious. I pray to God that He again has made you recover.

Right away I will share with you a conversation I just had with W. Breder: B: "You've received a letter from H. Does he say anything about coming here to be ordained? Because now I can tell you that I have written Arthur (?) that after a conversation I had with Pastor Jensen, I think I understood that he and Arup regretted their vague reply to H., and would be willing to do him the favor. However, as I wrote to him, H. might have reasoned that without doing anything he could expect the Bishop to send him a request."

"Yes, from H.'s letter today I can see that he might have expected such."

"Well, so he does talk about it. I will write Arthur and immediately correct what I wrote before, as it could not be expected of the Bishop to send H. a request although he wanted to ordain him, when H. doesn't want to resubmit his request. I think he should do so, especially since in his conversation with the Bishop, he did not propose his application as if he were asking a favor, but more as if it were something he could demand."

My dear! When I now include a conversation Uncle Ullern had with Ottesen, where Ottesen told him that Arup has stated his willingness to ordain him without any other objections, must I now find it necessary to repeat for you what I told you one evening in the sofa at Ullern? "I think you have been a little arrogant in your conversation with Arup." Yes, my *Knort*, I know you so well and I could read from your heart that you felt disappointed in how Arup behaved toward you, that you felt offended. Because of that, and because you felt you supported a somewhat Christian and fair case, you did not want to rephrase your request to be more prayerlike. But what did you achieve by doing this? You achieved nothing, my dear, but you have lost some of the satisfaction with yourself that you previously had when you always succeeded in your projects. Should you not ask yourself, "What important things have I done in the previous years that did not succeed?"

You probably have to admit that you have been unusually lucky. And you do, my Hermann, I know that every day you have sent thankful prayers to Him who gave you everything good! Don't you have to admit that you have become a little spoiled from what luck has done for you? With Arup's answer, you faced a small, offensive rock. Immediately you interpreted it as a great insult and do not want to talk more about it to the man who offended you. Think about it. You must know it best yourself. Could you not have shown a little more humility, if I may say so, toward the Bishop? Could you not have proposed your request without begging or being a flatterer or a hypocrite, but presenting your request a little more beseechingly? And would this have been shameful for you? No, it would not. When now admitting this, you might write to Arup and again ask him to do you the favor of ordaining you when Ottesen is being ordained. You are thinking that it will be a little hard to do that, your pride says no and refuses, and you come up with many reasons why you should not do this. Let this feeling and temptation be, chase them away, Hermann, and renew your request to the Bishop! Soon you surely will be happy for what I wrote.

Linka, you have been terribly long-winded writing this to me, you are saying, my Hermann. I know you are thinking that, but I wanted to tell you, I have been going around for several days wondering if I should talk more about this with you. My thoughts and the bad mood concluded that I blame Hermann if he does not...etc. Now I want to see how he acts, whether he wants to be good or stubborn, which I really did not want you to be, but no more about this. You can be stubborn with me sometimes, but in this case you are really stubborn to yourself. Today I went to town again and wiped out some money. I think we need lots of that, but it seems like you do not think I share your opinion that we need to be modest with our belongings. The closest example of this is that of Elise and the towels. From the sixty-eight-foot[177] piece of cloth, twenty-four towels will be made, which does not seem to me to be too much. We have to limit ourselves to those on the ship, and also until we get everything somewhat settled at the parsonage. On the other hand, I don't care to get nicer ones; our faces are so pretty that we can put up with a little dirt. No, I will not buy any linen, woman, never that!

But listen, my dear. I can't have the pleasure of writing or talking to you anymore, as I have some business to take care of. Today I bought my bride's veil and walked around with my purse like I always do. I also got a sample of the pastor's collar and now I'm going to order four of those from Lomse.

Farewell, my friend! God bless you!

Your Linka

Johan sends his greetings, and thanks Uncle for the letter. Adieu

Thank you for the one Spd. Yes, I like going to comedies, but I think I'll spend the money on a big sketchbook I would like and which I later will bequeath you, my dear!

Thanks you, too, for the signet. I have one that I like to use that C.N.K. gave me. Old memories honor my loved ones!   Greeting

April 1851

Letter — April 3

Hermann, I never thought you had such a cold heart that you wanted to fool me on April 1st the way you did. You say I deserved it, well thanks a lot, and no more about that.

Half a second later: yesterday I was in town — I followed sister Ovidia. She has provided us with so much play up here; when sitting she often had to run up and play for me. I have no more time left to hear music. At Breder's I met Pastor Norgaard, he asked me to give his best greetings to you; he really wanted to see you before the departure, but that can't happen. I had dinner at Preuses', went to Uranienborg in the afternoon where I stayed for the night, went downtown this morning and took care of my affairs, and visited Uncle Rudolph to tell him you intend to write Arup about your ordination. For that he was very content and said, "I think this affair has been so unpleasant that it is hard to describe, but I imagined there had to be a misunderstanding." We talked a little about the future, and afterward I walked up here across the ice. The conditions were bad; I walked in snow and water. Yesterday, when I walked with Ovidia, I often had to stop; so we also walked across the ice, and the conditions were just as bad, so sister was upset. Before we got to town, we stopped at Holmen where we visited Kalla. I looked through the catalogue of the books from the book auction. Kalla says you got a few useful books for almost nothing, but then I saw Rudelback's magazine among Messel's books. Kalla wanted that himself, so I told him he should not give it to you — that is, if he got his bid accepted at the auction. It is aggravating that this magazine has been sold for almost nothing, but I guess there is no point telling you that.

Yesterday I received a letter from Askevold; the people there are all doing well. We can't get Marthe, so we will have to be satisfied if we can find someone when we get there, or manage without one. On our trip there, Marthe would not have been at any help for us, though; she would probably have been sick right away, as I know she's not a naval hero. I asked Johan to order the chairs. Yesterday I read a letter at Preus's from A. Preus to the daughter of G. Dietrichson, from Koshkonung, January 14. He still does not know if we are coming, and thus he says, "I am waiting for a message about whether or not Hermann is coming here." They elected him superintendent at the church meeting, but he suggested Clausen,[178] as he felt unfamiliar with the proceedings and had too much to do to undertake this. Furthermore, he conveys from the congregation that Dietrichson should not be angry if the pastor's residence is not done when he gets over there; they will still provide a temporary house for him. The same will probably be the case for us. I do not know if Ottesen has submitted his application. I have told Hvoslef to ask him that, but he has not been able to get in touch with anyone. If I knew where Pastor Steensrud or Steenstrup (?) lived, I would have gone there, but where would I go? Consequently, I have no message to give you.

Whew, it really is windy today! If only it came from the south so the ice would sing its last verse. The other day I visited Marie Keyser, who is really affected by Hilda breaking the engagement. Yes, she and Resner had known each other for a long time before they got engaged; I blame her for a great part of it, almost a lot. You are my Hermann and I am

your Linka.

Letter — *Ullern, April* 3[179]

This evening I have written a letter for you, my best friend, and it is so short and petite that you might reproach me for it and not like me. That is up to you, however; I like you anyway, since you have been my clever, reasonable, non-stubborn Hermann, and want to write the Bishop. Thank you! You will never regret doing that. If only you were well again. I do not think your ordination can take place before Easter. Thus we might not be together for the holidays, but we should not be sad about that. Soon, soon, we will see each other every day. I have my confirmation certificate, but if Landestad cannot use it to marry us, I intend to write Pastor Larson in Christiansand next Monday, and ask him for a baptism certificate. But now good night, Hermann! I will not mention any of this in the letter I am sending with Jacob to town tomorrow, because I think I want to be a little mad at you. However, I do not mean it as bad as you think, thus I will still send you, if not black on white, a k... from your *Linka.*

Sunday, April 6, 1851

My Hermann,

This morning I received a letter from you of April 2nd. Does it have to be four days in the mail? Thank you for sending me some words, but mostly for the letter to Arup, which I hope is the way I would like it to be. I cannot come to town to read it, no matter how much I want to. But now good night, my friend. Dream of me and I will dream of you.

Now, at four in the morning, I am home from *Dramatikken*. More about that another time, as the mail leaves in a few hours. However, I have to tell my Hermann that I have been to a ball, but I acted like an old lady and did not dance. Breder had promised to come and bring Arup's letter, but he did not show up. Nothing is decided about Sister's journey; Johan is waiting for good weather. By the way, you know what I told you, I did not want to say a word for or against in that regard. I have to write Pastor Larson for the baptism certificate. Kalla wants to be my bridesman. If Landestad will marry us using my Confirmation certificate, I will attach it in my next letter. Now adieu, my Hermann!

Your Linka

Letter — *Uranienborg, April* 11, 1851

Is this the first time you've gotten a letter from me written from this place? I have been here since Wednesday afternoon. Both yesterday and today I have been down at Breder's, and both times I received the unpleasant news that a letter from you has been sent to Ullern. When I was down there yesterday, I told them that I would probably go to Ullern that same afternoon, but a heavy rainshower prevented me. Now I am weather-bound here, but it doesn't do me any harm, as I am done with most things, and thus I should not be so scared as I am nowadays. I have almost finished all the sewing, and I am waiting for some burlap that is to come to town, so that I can sew covers for our mattresses out of that. Yes, my dear, time passes by and our journey, etc. is getting closer every day. The Lord is helping us! After what I can read from your letters to Breder, you will be coming here. What your mind is thinking, however, I don't know. But even worse, I can't answer your letter to Arup, which I also read when I was in town. Breder and Johan have written to you about this, when they predicted its outcome, more orally actually. If you want to know what I think — don't worry about it anymore.

Today I read from the newspapers that Brandt[180] has been chosen as pastor for Pine Lake. It surprised me, as I had heard from what I considered a secure source that Ottesen applied for the mission and wanted to go there alone, without his girlfriend. It hurts me that Ottesen's wish did not come true. However, he seemed so happy when he decided on his journey. If only his girlfriend had answered straight out, Ottesen would probably have been on his way and started his spiritual work, without having to struggle through the lessons.

If God gives us health, my Hermann, I pray that we will be fine, and that everything will turn out well for us over there and we will be truly happy. I can only answer for myself, but when I have my Hermann and even a rather lousy house, I will be happy and content with life. If the congregation would care about us, too, I would be even happier. However, no matter how happy I might be, I would never forget Him who created everything that is good. When we thank Him, oh, how weak and empty our prayers of thankfulness are. We really have to bow to the ground before such greatness!

Tell me now, Hermann, do you really have enough trust in me to let me take care of your house? You have always expressed such distrust in me, more than anyone has. When I say this I do not want you to believe that I am angry in any way; no, I reason like this: Hermann must know me better than I do and everybody else does. It is difficult to really learn to know oneself, and no matter how much I trouble myself to achieve this, I never dare to believe myself, even when dreaming. One can't always judge one's conscience for one's self, and therefore, I let you be my judge in this case. I don't know if my character and the dignity of wifehood fit together; however, you should say whatever you believe, feel, mean, and think about me, whether you do it orally or in writing. You will not hear more about this from me, so you will have to "take me as I am." I have my own thoughts about you, which can be a little sharp, but you should not feel bad about that; I have great trust in you. The last part should not be taken very seriously; no darling, do not do that. We'll discuss it more later.

Some time ago my old friend Wilhelm Christie, the customs collector's son, ran in the door as if he were shot out of a cannon. "Are you on your way already?" I asked. No, he came to town to ask to be hired by the railway. If he can get a good position with the railway, he will not go to New York at all. Everyone is doing well in Bergen. Today I got a letter from Uncle Hoffmann; he asks me to greet you. It was a congratulation letter, a little too early… But now adieu, my Hermann. See you soon! Farewell,

Your Linka.

Monday, *April* 14 — The Summer Day — It is all snow and ground frost here in the eastern parts, while the western parts — at least Bergen county — are experiencing the first, fresh green sprouts of spring. At Askevold, for example, the bushes in the garden are already green, and if we walk out in the fields, we can find spring's first messenger, the blue anemone, under some bushes, smiling friendlily at us, giving us nature's first spring greeting. On each farm, husbands, wives, and their hands have started working their land — everything has been given new life in the life of these quiet harbor folk. But how long does this life last? After fourteen days or so, when the grain and crops are in the soil, see the man with his unusually slow calmness put his boat on the water to go out on the fjord for a good catch of fish for his house. His women and men — the latter who have been sitting by the herring seine all day, mending holes on it, while the constant whirl from the spinning wheel below bears witness to the women's industry and energy.

It is different here — the snow has still not left our fields, ground frost is still deep and ice has still not left either fjord or ponds — everything is still winter. However, a beautiful sign of spring has been given; some blue anemones have been found here too. There is also a bad sign of spring, the terrible driving conditions on the roads. This and rainshowers have kept me in town since Wednesday evening. I have stayed at Uranienborg with my sisters, and from there I have been visiting different houses in town. Friday evening Sister Ovid and I went to a concert, together with Wilhelm Christie, who just came from Bergen. It was fun, I especially found a boy from Valdres very amusing. A lady was talking to him for a while, but in the end she said, "You are such a funny billy goat!" "Well, then you are a goat!" said the boy and ran away, laughing.

Yesterday I went to church and heard a beautiful sermon by Wexels. I had arranged it so I was spending the night at Smith's, but because of rats, I spent the entire night beating on the floor with a big cane. The afternoon was spent at Uranienborg with all the siblings except Hexa — the more I see them all around me, the harder the separation from them appears, but God give me strength, both spirit and body! Yesterday morning I bumped my way up here in a cariole — oh my, what driving conditions! Now good night — all!

Letter — *Ullern, April* 14, 1851

Now, my Hermann, I have the honor of sending you my confirmation certificate. I got it from Askevold a long time ago, but when I heard it was not enough, which I actually found strange, I first had to ask Landestad through you if he could use it. Here is the reason why you have not received it earlier: I have answered my question on time. First I have to write for a communion certificate, but I will get it from Pastor Holmedahl, as I went there the last time I received communion. As I cannot walk down the aisle with you anyway, I think Lillemamma, Kalla, and I will go Maundy Thursday, if I have my wish. Now, adieu, my friend! You are deeply thanked for your two last letters, one of March 30th and the other with no date.

Your Linka, my *Knort*

Letter — *Ullern, April* 16, 1851

As this is the last letter my Hermann will receive from Linka while we still are sweethearts, I would like to do it a little differently than usual. Well, we will always remain "sweethearts" and later even more than what we are now, but soon, oh how strange, we will receive the blessing of the church. We will see our love being tied together in a bond, which with the help of God will not break until death, the interrupter of the temporary life's joy, captures one of us. Then, although one is dead and gone, the one who is left behind has not turned off the delightful, passionate feelings that tied them together. Instead, a bed of goldilocks and forget-me-nots are preserved in the heart, and are braided to a wreath around our heads when we again meet in eternity!

Strange…how could I write down what I just said? I was not myself when writing it. Lately, it has often happened that I am like a stranger to myself; it seems like there is a revolution growing inside of me, but what will the result be? Thank you, my *Knort*, for all the letters you have sent me, both this time when we are apart and when I was at Askevold. Every time I receive and read your precious writing, it is the happiest time of the day. You have always been kind to write often, with the exception of the first three to four weeks at Askevold when you had me wait from the moment I arrived. You have no idea of how angry and sad I was then, to the degree that these emotions can be combined. I wonder if divine providence has planned for us to be that far apart again. It's useless to wonder about the future, but that you will always be my Hermann, my *Knort*, my Arminius; that's for sure!

Now, answers to your three last letters. I can remember that in my last letter I said March 30th, but that was wrong; that time you had not dated your letter. I received your last letter of April 13th yesterday. I guess I was in a bad mood when you last received a letter from me, as I wrote about your trust in me. But H., you must not say that your trust is not, and will not forever be, strong and solid. Yes, God help you in that. I am pleased if you have now finished a nice letter to Arup. Welcome when you come! How did you feel when Landstad read the blessings for us? Don't you agree that they ended in a singular, warm prayer to the Lord? I guess I will see your sermon when you come. No, H., your anger at my answers to your letters is unnecessary. How can Uncle Christie have knowledge of my having been close to anybody else? I have bought linen for four sheets; I think that will be enough as you have some and I have two. If we take linen at Ludvig's, we will have to pay for it later. I have received four Spd. from Kalla; he has not told me how much the Tønsberg Book costs. No, I am never up later than until midnight; well, now I see that it is that late, but it is not a working day tomorrow and thus I can sleep in tomorrow. Imagine, H., our chairs are going to cost four Spd a piece, terribly expensive. When Johan told me that, I figured it best to only get one, but they have started making both of them. I have not wanted to order the box for my dresser as I thought it would be better if you do it when you come here; that way everything will be done the next time we come here. I did not know where to keep the printed materials if they had been done.

Now I want to give you a one, two, three k... for all new and old letters, and a faithful handshake as well.

Your Linka

Letter — [No date or place indicated]

I haven't been able come to you in town, my dear; nobody has been here to take care of Auntie, who is still ill. When you come tomorrow, I want to walk all the way down the country road to meet you. If you want to wait until eight at night, you can come with the horse that brings the doctor here. Please answer me on this matter. If you are not home now, you can send a few words to the Waitzen House, and ask them if the messenger from here can bring it for you tomorrow. Do you feel like giving Auntie a bottle of Eau de Cologne? I don't dare give her mine, as I remember what you said at Halden.

Deliver the attached letter to the Post Office today.

Now adieu, my Hermann! Welcome tomorrow, walking? — riding? That is up to the waiting *Linka*.

Is my hat done so I can go to church on Sunday?

Maundy Thursday, April 17 — There is a lively conversation here in my room tonight. My little sister Agnes came to visit me, and now she's my bedmate. To keep her company, Waleska has moved up here too, and it's these two kittens who are now talking. They're not tired at all, and since I don't want to go to bed until they're asleep, I'll probably have to wait for a while. We had storm and rain today, which is not nice weather at all; however, it's been good enough for us to go outside and get some fresh air between showers. There is more activity than usual here these days; W. Christie has come back here to apply for a job at the railroad. If he gets the job, he has to cancel his trip to America. I sent letters to Askevold and to Hermann today. My letter to the latter was a little bit different both on the inside and the outside, since I guess it will be the last letter I send to him while we are still engaged. I got a letter from H. on Tuesday, in which he writes that he is probably coming here on the first or second day of Easter. He is still telling me about how our banns of marriage were published for the first time 15th of April — Palm Sunday. I find it rather strange, this custom of publishing the banns from the pulpit — what's the purpose of it? I can't find any other reason than that it informs the congregation about our plans so that they can make objections if they have anything to say. This is also confirmed by what the pastor says: "If anyone has any objections to this union, speak now or be silent ever after." But I think this lecture could be given from the chancel after the service has ended. Then those who wanted to could stay and listen and the others could leave. Maybe I will be a wife in three weeks. Oh, I have good intentions — at least as far as I have the knowledge to judge them — help me to carry them through, my God! The word "intentions" reminds me of a sermon about intentions by Kierkegaard which I read today — about patience to preserve one's soul, and that intentions coming from such a soul will be accomplished by it. I didn't get to go to church today, and probably not tomorrow either. Driving conditions are so bad I don't want to ask for a horse. Did you preach today H.? Good night!

Good Friday Morning — April 18, 1851 — I just received a letter from Hermann. He says he's coming here on the second day of Easter. I'll have to go down to meet him then. He's probably on the pulpit right now — help him with Your spirit, oh God!

Easter Eve [*April* 20] — Presumably the last holiday for a very long time I'll be spending in my country of birth. I spent the entire day up here; in the morning I tidied up in my letters. For the most part I studied English. I also wrote a letter for H., but when I had sealed it and it was all done, I remembered it was Saturday — and Friday is mail day — my work was in vain. In the afternoon I was sewing until dusk, and then I went for my walk, entertained by W. Christie, who had just come from town. We were happy to hear his good news: he had been hired at the railroad here. That means I will not meet up with him in New York, as we had planned before. After supper, at which Lomse and the little maniac Agnes were present, I played whist with Uncle and both of the Wilhelms. Was this holiday evening spent in the way I wanted to? I would have preferred to have my siblings and Hermann here with me, and then spend the time in the same way as we spent the nice holidays at home, my parents' home. Next Easter I will, with God's help, be in my second home with my Hermann, but far away from my siblings. But you, God, will see to it that we have not spent the last holiday together. Good night!

L.K.

Tuesday, April 22 — Tonight, I want to start with a little description of yesterday. At nine-fifteen Auntie, Uncle, Wilhelm Christie, Dutta, and I went to town in the big wagon. Everybody but me was going to church. The reason I couldn't go to God's house yesterday, the second day of Easter, was that Hermann has written me that he was taking a trip here, arriving with the steamer *Christiania* at ten in the morning. I arrived in town precisely at that time, and walked down to the wharfs where the boat had just anchored. I was walking around quite by myself among all the people there, without knowing anyone. Now the boats started coming from the steamer and something told me Hermann would be in the first boat. It's at the wharf now; I see one person after the other coming up from the boat, but no Hermann. The second, third, fourth, and last boat all come, but none of them brings H. I had gotten a *[sketch of a nose]* and with that I turned around and started walking up to Breder's. There we agreed that H. must have overslept, that he missed the steamer in Moss, and had to go by land. This would be fair reasoning, since H.'s a sleepyhead, and it's happened before when he is traveling, that he was late because he overslept. I was more annoyed than distressed that H. had tricked me, since I want to be able to trust him unreservedly when H. says something. But how am I supposed to do that when decisions are ignored time and again? If H. had now overslept, that was too bad. I wasn't really sure how to meet him if he arrived in the afternoon, as I presumed he would. I left after a couple of hours, to go up to Uranienborg to see how they were. Shortly after that I went to Uncle Smith's to have dinner. The entire group that had accompanied me from Ullern was there, except for W.C. who was going somewhere else. Hvoslef, Brother Kalla, and C. With were also there. Just as we were done eating, the bell rang for Evensong. I went with several others to church, where we heard a beautiful sermon by Bruun. It's the first time I've heard that man; his speech appealed to me, it was beautiful, although I would have liked to see him a bit calmer. Calmness suits the pulpit better. There has to be some life, of course, but it easily becomes too lively. I went from church down to Breder's to see if H. had come yet, but no. I started walking down the street again to go to Smith's, and at the square I met Breder and his wife, and Sister Ovid who happily showed me a ticket to a comedy. I wanted to go to the theatre, but could I leave the party at Smith's? We'd have to talk to Uncle about it — we went up — he was sleeping — we went down the street and came back up — he was sleeping — well, now we could not wait any longer, we had been fooling around in the streets long enough, so we went down again, although Sister and I first stopped by Morelin where nobody was at home. However, we broke in and found her sewing things, needle and a thread, and soon my gloves were one piece again. After having played around a little bit at Morelin — Mrs. Tallin's — we left and soon I was sitting in the theatre for the second time this winter.

The play was *Cæsar de Bazan*.[181] It was early and I was lost in thought, without being disturbed by the play or the music. My thoughts were about a change of thoughts, feelings and actions within me, as I now found myself sitting in the theatre. An hour earlier, I was walking from Breder's up Grendegaten. Feeling depressed and angry, I was going to go to the cemetery to my parents' grave to ease my troubled heart. And now I was in the theatre? Strange character, strange feelings! How could a sudden desire to see a comedy make me change my mind about going to the cemetery? I do not know how to figure that out, but I know one thing, and with that my thinking was over — if I had gone to the cemetery and stood by my parents' grave for the first time this year, with sorrow and happiness mixed together, knowing how good it is for them where they are now, pondered over old memories and asked for comfort from above to strengthen my soul, I would have felt happier than I was now.

The play started, it went well — little by little I cheered up. I was in quite a good mood when I once again sat at the supper table at Smith's. I spent the night there and made a racket for the rats.

Sometime in the morning a horse came for me. I hurried up into the gig, but just as I climbed in, a letter from H. was handed to me — up again — I read the letter. H. didn't give me any explanation for not coming yesterday. He says that Arup will ordain him the 30th of the month, and that he will come here on Wednesday — tomorrow. Also, plus our traveling plans have to be changed so that we leave here on the 2nd of May, that we will have our wedding the 5th or 6th, and then, because H.. prefers to spend the last days with <u>his</u> dear ones down at Halden, and because he can get guidance from Landstad, we are spending the last days there, and then go to Kragerø, which means we are not coming back up here to <u>my</u> loved ones?! H. does say that we are bringing our friends down there with us; although I've told him that this can't be done, he doesn't understand that. What will he end up doing in that matter when he comes here now? All of <u>my</u> loved ones here are not accompanying us, not even the <u>dearest</u> — all my siblings! And I shall not see them again and give them the pleasure of seeing me as a wife, and what hurts me even more is that I will miss a daguerreotype I was supposed to be in, when all of us siblings — all seven — were going to be together. How strange that H. cannot realize that I have more people here that I am actually closer to than I am to any of his family — they're basically strangers to me! Why can't he understand that as much as he wants to spend the last days with his family, I do not want to be at Frederikshald for fourteen days, and then not see any of my people?! Why can't he think like this: we're going to Moss anyway, no Sunday will be lost, as the steamer to Moss comes on Monday — Sunday afternoon we leave there and then up to Christiania, where we can stay for one or two days before we take the steamer to Kragerø! Within that time we can say adieu and also get the daguerreotype. Why couldn't he say this and not change our old traveling route? It must be because Hermann is so lost in his own family that he thinks I will praise them to the heavens just as much as he does — yes, they are kind enough, but they are just not my dearest and H. should be able to understand that much about how I feel. But, my friend, do what you like. Even if you do not seem to think about how you hurt me in doing this, you do well in other things, and I will not accuse you or say anything to you about this matter.

This afternoon I said good-bye to Wilhelm Christie; he has been hired at the railroad — my best wishes go with him! I am fond of him as a friend! May God guide you! I got a wedding present from him, a carafe and glasses. Good night all!

May 1851 — Xiania, 1851

May 1 — Although the last few days have been occupied with farewells to beloved friends and dear places, none has been as hard and painful as that of this evening. I just came back from Uranienborg, a place of many memories, painful and pleasant, serious and joyful. There I saw my little sisters for the last time for many years, and gave them a good-bye kiss. When I turned to Grandmother and Aunt Lodviska, my feelings changed; I knew that I could not expect to see them again in this life. I thanked them for the kindness they have always shown me, and went again in to my little sisters, took their hands in mine, and hurried out into the street. I prayed in my heart that the Heavenly God brings us together again, and if that is not supposed to be, then sustain us by His Spirit so that at last we may stand before You, O God, without fear and trembling, but in sheer joy!

I also exchanged a farewell with the kind people at Ullern, and with Lomse, who had been called to Uranienborg this evening. Earlier he had told me that he wanted to come with us to the wedding, but now he told me that he was unable to do so. I spent only a short time at Uranienborg this evening; I was so busy packing and visiting that it was nine-thirty when Hermann and I got there. The last person we visited was Pastor Steensrud, where we also met three other pastors: Wexels, Stockflet, and Bruun. They wished us happiness, played for us beautifully, and blessed us. God's blessing be upon us! When is the next time we will be in this area? Tomorrow we are off, but first, we'll go to the place where my dear beloved ones' remains rest in the shelter of the earth. God be with you, my dear siblings! Always choose His path and you will be happy. We were also visiting Uncle Wilhelm and Uncle Rudolph today. The wishes of happiness from these dear people follow us as well. Oh, please be with us, Heavenly Father!

May 2 — Today I arrived at Halden. I did not travel from Xiania alone; Attorney[182] Breder with his wife and son, my cousin Johan Preus, Brother Kalla, and Sister Ovidia were my traveling companions. Wasn't that an impressive wedding party? After not being able to see Xiania and the beloved surroundings anymore, after having said farewell to everything in that area that is dear to me, I joined the conversation of my fellow travelers and shared their cheerfulness, though I was not as cheerful on the inside. My siblings and the churchyard occupied my thoughts. Before my departure this morning, Hermann and I went up to my parents' graves, where my heart was uplifted in a fervent prayer. Oh, how calm and comforted I felt afterward. Thank You for giving me peace of mind! Parents intercede for us, so that we can pray as we are supposed to.

We arrived here at eight in the evening. The trip went well. However, at Horten our hearts beat a little faster, as we were close to running aground. It would not have been so bad to go up for a little while and have a look at the new town with all its new arrangements, but destiny was good to us — or the steamer *Hardy* — and we cleared the shore. Funny — when the trip was over, the master of the ship started to scold the coxswain, despite the fact that it was his fault alone. These things always happen in the world.

When passing Næsodden I wrote a letter for Hvoslef, asking him to accept a copy of Kierkegaard's *Works of Love* as a remembrance of me and my English lessons. By the way, the time on the steamer was spent in conversation, knitting, and reading. Fredrikke Breder (the attorney's wife) seems to be a strange, quiet, and introverted person when you first meet her. Now, however, after getting to know her, I really like her. She is a very kind and loving wife. Her whole family at Halden came to the pier to meet us, and it was a great surprise for Hexa to see Ovidia and Kalla. Her eyes were as big as planets on each side of her forehead. From the pier we first went up to Ludvig Breder, where we went through a whole lot of effort to get everything organized, but finally everyone went to their rooms with their own bundle of beddings. Ovidia, Hermann, and I went with Hexa, while Kalla and Johan stayed at Ludvig's. The attorney, his wife, niece (Marie Breder), and son went up to Glende. After settling down for the night, Hermann and I had a little discussion. It appeared that for several months, I had been offended because of a remark he once made, and for that he scolded me. But now, good night to all!

204 · *Linka's Diary*

May 3 — Tonight I am nearly exhausted, because I was at a party at Glende, and we trudged out of there in the rain and wind at eleven or twelve at night. We hiked up our skirts, and how we laughed — everyone is fresh after the trip. Now good night.

May 4, 1851 — This evening I am to say "farewell" and "thank you for good companionship" to my girlhood. I know what you have been to me and what you have brought me, but I do not have any clue of what wifehood will regale me with. But You, my Lord, will be with me and everything will be fine; that hope keeps me looking toward the future without fear. Adieu, girlhood, we have always been good friends. I cannot remember any day that I have been bored with you, and still I will part from you. Certainly, wifehood must be somehow appealing, since I have decided to join it, but what is it really? Tell me, my cousin Independence, will I enjoy you more as a wife than as a girl? "No, as a wife you'll just be a slave." Oh, now I do not dare to marry! "Oh yes, I believe you should, as you may not even notice your slavery as a wife. Rather, you will think of what a woman's mission is, and your love and common sense will teach you to follow its voice. Then you will remember me, your cousin Independence, no more, which will do you good, as I really belong to the man."

"Should I forget about you, whom I care for so much? Well, then I will also part from you this evening, convinced that you are not bitter, even though as a girl I made you my companion. I do not doubt that there will always be a spark of affection for you in my heart, but since it has come to a point where it has to be cowed, please help me, Father, to get it away. However, I am too stubborn to agree with You that the woman shall not think about independence. The human being is an independent creature, and I will recommend every woman to consider that; I insist that a girl should and must do that. She can, of course, be in a relationship where she will not gain much from it, but if she combines it with high-mindedness and cleverness, it will seldom cause any harm." No, I must not do that; this determination has frequently caused me distress throughout my girlhood years.

I find myself writing an entire dissertation, which might not even make any sense. Well, that is because saying "farewell and thank you, maidenhood," touches me; I think you will understand. What stronger proof of my friendship can I give you than when parting I will say, "Although as a wife I will achieve the greatest degree of earthly happiness, I will never forget my days as a girl. Every happy hour I will spend as a wife I will weigh against those I experienced as a girl, and the same goes if sorrow is the case. When admitting human beings' need for sorrow, I would like to say: may wifehood never suffer in comparison with girlhood!"

As a girl, I have had a hectic life, traveled a lot, with long and short breaks. I was born in Christiansand in 1829. Papa, Christian Nicolai Keyser, and Momma, Agnes Louise Carlsen. In 1830 my home became Tved's beautiful parsonage. Occasionally we made short visits to Uncle Preus in Christiansand; his wife was father's half sister. At that time Hermann and I were already good friends. In 1837 we moved to Christiania, where Father got a job as a professor. Mother died in 1840 and one year later, during the Christmas break, I went with my brother and sister Waleska to visit Pastor Randers at Skjeberg Parsonage. We enjoyed ourselves the short time the break lasted, until New Year and then January 10th came, and we went back home. This was in 1841-1842, the year after Mother's death. In 1844 I went from Xiania to Pastor Christie at Askevold Parsonage, which is situated right by the ocean. There I was confirmed in 1845, and some time later I took the steamer to Bergen, where I stayed for five weeks. Then back to Askevold. In the summer of 1846, I went back to Xiania with the steamer, around Lindesnes. When I got back, Father had become a pastor at Aker. The ministry did not last for long; he died one month after my arrival. After his death, I stayed at the parsonage for a month or two, and thereafter my sisters and I moved to Uranienborg. Kalla went to stay with Uncle Wilhelm Keyser. In 1849 I went to Askevold again and stayed there until the summer of 1850. Then I went back to Christiania, but this time not to Uranienborg. Instead, I went to stay at Ullern, the beautiful place. One month after my arrival, Hermann took me to Fredrikshald, where his father and married sisters live. We stayed there for fourteen days, and after a little trip to Strømstad we went back and relaxed until Christmas, when we again went to Fredrikshald. New Year's Eve of 1851, Hermann received a letter of call to become pastor of Spring Prairie congregation. This rushed our departure. January 12, 1851, we went back to Ullern; May 2nd to Halden, and then my journeys as a young girl are history. There have been enough of them, though, and besides, I have forgotten to include the little trip to Ringerike, as well as that to Sørum Parsonage. I guess I have spent much money for travels in my girlhood, and I assume wifehood will not offer less. What about my long journey to America? Oh my, that will be expensive! Farewell, girlhood!

Oh, what a sight! Those crazy sisters! Here they are; the sisters in negligees, one of them giggling and roaring with laughter so that I have to laugh as well. Ovidia jumped out of bed and ran right over to the hatbox; now she is standing in front of the mirror wearing her new straw hat, to show Hexa that it really is new. She is being wild this evening, and does this only to make me laugh until I cry. Lillemamma is trying to do the same; I know she has put an entire armful of wood in my bed. Oh, I am going to draw this amusing scene. But now it is time to say good night! Good night, little sisters in Xiania!

May 5 — Today has been — no — today is an odd and significant day. I am about to dress up as a graceful bride to walk down the aisle for my Hermann!

I am a wife now, about to begin a new chapter of my life. How strange! Hermann, with the blessing of God and the Church, by our union we will go out in the world as one. May God be with us!

Here I stand, still wearing my entire wedding outfit. It is so touching. The table in front of me is filled with presents from family and friends. Every one of them has shown that they remember us, how kind! The wreath and the veil are being removed by the bridesmaids, Hexa and Ovidia — Lillemamma. What did I really feel when it was being put on? I had so many serious feelings that a shiver came over me; my eyes were filled with tears. I remember what Tholuck says about the woman and her bridal veil: "The bridal veil must be delicate, shimmering and transparent. It is to be placed over the crown of your head and shall extend to the floor; it is a symbol of your will at your husband's side."

This is certainly not the first time I've thought of this. Many a time before, I asked myself if I am suitable for being a wife, and I have often dwelt on this question. Once I even told Hermann. "I have second thoughts about becoming your wife; I do not think I can become the wife I am expected to be." Hermann then comforted me for a long time, so it is really his own fault if he gets a wife who cannot make him happy. Right?

All the presents have been chosen with our long journey in mind. That is, there are mostly transportable things like silver, embroidery, and table linen. I assume I should describe the wedding, too. At two-forty-five, I went to church in a carriage with the groom and the bridesmaids. The whole family was waiting in church. Kalla "gave me away." Landestad gave an appropriately beautiful wedding sermon; he joined us at Breder's after the ceremony, where the family had gathered, and where everyone was joyful — some danced, some played cards in the evening. An annoying tradition at Halden is that the bride and the groom are expected to show themselves to the people gathered outside, which Hermann and I did. The crowd was unusually quiet and calm; it was said it was because we were such an august pastor couple.

But Linka, why are you writing now what should have been said in the beginning? While I was still in my good bed this morning, flowers were brought in to me, and this continued throughout the late morning, yes, even when I was getting dressed with the help of my bridal attendant Louise Breder, flowers arrived. Yesterday afternoon flowers were also delivered to me. We had such a collection of the loveliest flowers. There was myrtle in every bouquet, and I took a little from each one for my wreath, which was made by my bridesmaids and my bridal attendant. See, it was very encouraging for me — a stranger at Halden getting so many fresh flowers, particularly in a season when the buds of spring do not yet bring any flowers. I had violets, like my little sisters in Christiania had requested me to use today, and therefore I put one in my belt. So where did the flowers come from? From the windows. Strangers had decided to give up their own joy of seeing the flowers in order to delight the bride, and they did make me happy.

My bridesmaids were Elise Breder (Preus) and Fredrikke Breder. It feels empty not to have any parents today, but may God ease the pain with the joys of the moment, and thank You for that and for so many other things!

May 7 — The last days have been a fuss without end. Ever since Friday the 2nd· and until today we have been to family parties, and yesterday to a big party at Anker's in Rød. However, this should be the end of these huge parties, as today our guests have left, with the exception of Fredrikke B. Today I said "live well" to brother Kalla; it came straight from the heart with a prayer to the Lord for luck for his future and his upcoming exam, which is in a few days. The wedding was at an inconvenient time for him; he was kind to come. He made me happy by bringing a daguerreotype of the four youngest sisters.

May 9 — Today I took Communion; sisters Hexa and Lillemamma, Uncle Preus, J. Breder and wife, L. Breder and wife, and Hermann were also at God's table.

May 14 — When one becomes a wife, one is not allowed to do what one wants, and thus I haven't had a chance to write anything these days about the excitement down here, despite the bad weather — about our songs in the evening, especially at Elise's, about the sisters' joyfulness, about my writing Grandmother a secret, wifely (not childlike) letter of apology because sister Ovidia is going to stay here longer than she planned (which is good for Hexa, but sad for Henny Penny at Uranienborg), and about Hermann's and my being busy with letter writing and packing.

I just came from Glende, where I sketched the little place, and said good-bye to the loving old wife of the pastor, Aunt Breder. She stood by the stone fence and waved.

May 15 — After rattling along in a cart, H. and I are now sitting here at the Customs in Moss, waiting for the steamer to come. It's expected to arrive soon, but we wanted to shorten the wait by walking around in the big town, and now that little trip is over. My impression of the people here is that they're like people in every other town: extremely curious and likely to stare at people they've never seen before. But now the steamer is here; we board after three hours of waiting. I have to add that we stopped by the old Pastor Randers at Skjeberg to say farewell, and stayed there for an hour.

We left Halden at seven in the morning. "God be with you, sisters!" were the last words in my heart. The whole family is dear to me, but my sisters were the last ones in my prayer for all of their well-being. God knows if old Uncle's eyes will ever see us here again.

The weather was beautiful that morning; the sun was shining and above our heads a little happy skylark trilled its song in the gentle morning sunshine, cheering our spirits that were saddened by the departure. I heard the cuckoo for the second time that morning; the first was when I was drawing Glende.

Hurray! Now the steamer is underway! Waiting here for so long has galled me regarding Moss, and I'm tempted to be naughty toward it in my sketchbook!

May 16 — After a bad night, I was out of the bed at four-thirty in the morning. Between nine and ten last night the *Constitution,* with us on board, arrived in Sandøsund, where we met the *Nordcap.* The steamers lay side by side for half an hour so the passengers could visit each other. Our travel companions were some very joyful Englishmen. One of them was especially joyful; she was a strange creature, who behaved completely like a man. When I went to bed sometime between ten and eleven, she sat down in the lounge. Earlier she had been sitting outside on deck with the gentlemen, but now the whole company moved inside. The lady had a toddy with them, and a pipe, and sang and drank with them. At one o'clock in the morning, she came back to the cabin, where she was loud and kept the door open while talking to the gentlemen. When she finally closed the door she turned to her chambermaid and the stewardess, who could not at all understand what she was saying. That I can prove with a funny example: when the lady went to bed she said in her awkward way of speaking that she wanted to be awakened at six o'clock in the morning. "Very well," the maid answered, "you will get your water; it will be placed on the table." What nonsense, I thought and laughed to myself, although I was irritated that I was unable go to sleep. By then, we had arrived at Fredriksvern and the steamer stopped. At five we'll continue on our journey, in nice and beautiful weather.

We arrived at Brevig at seven, where H. and I got a pleasant surprise. Pastor Nielsen and wife[183] came out in a boat to talk to us and they lay alongside the steamer for a little while. The conversation was short, and soon we had to say farewell.

Now, at eleven, I am sitting aboard *Columbus*, in the cabin that is to be my living room for the coming weeks. A strange, melancholy feeling arose in my heart when I saw *Columbus* for the first time in Langesund, and Captain Hagerup shouted at me, "There, madam, is the ship that will take you to America! The flag and the banners are put up for you." I was standing next to Hermann, who also seemed a little melancholy. Our only acquaintances on board are a couple of ladies, one of whom is the Master's wife, and the Master of the ship himself. In addition, our traveling companion, a student named Ziiølner,[184] introduced himself to us in Moss.

Farewell! Now we have left the steamer; Mr. Duus[185] brought us over in his boat and took us directly to the emigration ship. There we got most of our things in order, including my dresser. Our cabin is large and beyond all expectations. Thereafter we went ashore to enjoy our dinner at Consul Duus's, the ship owner. Both he and his family, his daughter and son, seem to be nice, courteous people. This afternoon we went for a walk to see Kragerø's beautiful natural surroundings. And indeed, it was more beautiful than I could ever imagine. The view was especially pretty, and so should it be, as the path leading to it is called "Lover's Lane." We then took little trip back to the ship to get settled, and Duus sent a maid to help me out. I found bed linen for her, and she made her bed. When we left the Duuses' this evening, they apologized that they could not offer us lodging due to illness, but we are welcome to have every meal with them. "Yes, thank you!" Now I will go to bed aboard *Columbus*. Good night!

May 17 — After having thanked my bed and my beddings for being so nice and contributing to a fairly good night, and after breakfast and dinner at Duus's, H. and I came back on board to take care of our mail. I was interrupted by a visitor, however; because H. and the visitor took over the lounge. I tiptoed into our cabin, and organized the contents of the drawers and the books. H. was just about to open a box that is standing in here; Ziiølner brought it from Xiania. We did not know anything about the contents, but I had a feeling it would be something extraordinary. As a result, they called me in to be there when the lid was taken off. Guess what it was? What a surprise! A painting of a dear and loved place: Uranienborg! It was a present from Hermann's friends in Xiania, how kind of them. A tear visited my eyes at that moment, and I wonder what really caused it. Old memories? Melancholy for the beloved ones who are or have been there? Little sisters, who now may be walking among the beautiful chestnut trees lining the avenue, the trees that now probably are wearing their lovely, blossoming spring outfit. Yes, I think so. More tears wanted to visit me, but I managed to chase them away; I don't like them any more than I like any other inconvenient visits. I retired to my own little bedroom and let the gentlemen be alone with their pipes and wine, and stayed by myself with my own thoughts.

After two hours we again went ashore and spent the evening with Duuses, and went for the same walk as yesterday. Today the road swarmed with people. People had gathered near the beautiful path mentioned earlier, and put up tents in honor of the day. There were sailors and city girls, emigrants and farmers with wives and daughters.

Several fiddlers struck up a tune, and people were dancing and drinking. One fiddler was especially good; he called himself "Ole Bull" as he claimed to be a friend of the fiddle master. He did the most unusual steps while striking up a waltz, a quadrille or a *Halling*.

Here I am sitting and writing, after having made the bed for the first time; it will not be the last. My hope is that we will be able to sleep well in it, and that tomorrow the immigrants from Telemark will have arrived, so that we can be on our way. I had a feeling that we would be leaving on the 17th, but no.

I am going to bed now. Father, into your hands we commend all those who are thinking of us and longing to be with us, and for us to be with them — and ourselves as well.

May 18, Sunday — After breakfast, which we need every day just like we need sleep, everybody left Duus's house to go to church. Pastor Barth spoke so rapidly that I feared he was expecting a catastrophe and wanted to get done with the sermon before it hit us.

To my delight I woke up this morning to a humming sound and noises on board; what could it be? I had a good feeling that the farmers from Telemark had arrived, and with that in mind, I let myself fall back to sleep. Later I learned the truth, and my expectation was confirmed. However, two loads were expected, and this was only one of them, a group of sixty people.

Later, after a good dinner and dessert, I sat down to write some letters. Again I was interrupted, but I soon forgave the interrupter, as his news was nice and pleasant: the second group of farmers had arrived. So now they are all here.[186] If God contributes with wind and weather, we'll soon be on our way.

Two other emigration ships have arrived, also with the purpose of getting supplies. But poor people! We should be happy for all the space we have in our ship. I'm not speaking of our nice cabin and lounge — the farmers' room is also airy and spacious, with a high ceiling, so they can stand upright wearing a hat if they desire.[187] In contrast, the farmers on one of the other ships have to bend down to walk in their room, which I think is quite inexcusable. They visited our ship to look around, and that only made things worse. Now they're dissatisfied, and have been crying bitterly because of their bad conditions. The entire ship is so poorly equipped that the deckhouse, filled with people and food chests, crashed down and fell into the room below, which was also filled with people and chests. That's how the story is told, but since only two people were hurt, it was probably not that serious.

We had an enjoyable evening and did not leave the mainland until 10:30 p.m., when we went back to the ship. The rain was pouring down outside as we went to bed in our "house," which lies as beautiful as a swan at the pier in the Kragerø fjord. The bed is now made; I will read for a little while, and then good night!

May 19 — We're so lazy here on the ship that it's a shame. Today we got out of bed as late as nine-fifteen. Coming up on deck, we had the pleasure of seeing both passengers and crew stow away chests and boxes. The latter were filled with flatbread, meat, butter, and more. Others contained different kinds of cheese, including *gammelost*[188]. Finally, there were kegs filled with salt herring. These, however, Duus hopes to get away, as the odor of the rest of the provisions is bad enough.

Again the day was to be spent at Duus's, but we received an invitation from Doctor Homann, and went there instead at one-forty-five, after writing onboard ship. In the afternoon, we went for a walk in a light shower, which did not bother us. Later, I enjoyed myself by looking out from my seat at the window; I was watching two ships weighing anchor and getting ready to leave. One was going to the Faeroe Islands — thus I watched it with a lot of interest. I imagined the Faeroes' joy when the ship arrives, and then I remembered my own long journey that is about to take place.

We had a good laugh when one of the sailors pretended to be sick, due to nervousness for the journey. Still, he had to go. Before we left the Homanns', the gracious madam of the house gave me a beautiful bouquet, which now is standing in front of me, decorating the coffee table. We left with an invitation to visit them again.

Arriving at the pier, I was surprised by the sight that met me. *Columbus* was packed with people, standing on the deck and hanging on the ropes, and there was a lot of noise. Someone played the fiddle, and people danced *Halling*. When we entered the ship they were staring at us, and we could perceive some annoyance, because custom required the visitors to leave. The ship's residents, however, enjoyed looking down at us in the lounge, where we talked, wrote, arranged flowers, smoked tobacco, and sealed letters. Duus will take care of the letters in the morning before we get out of bed. Now it's bedtime, and H. has already gone to bed, but unfortunately, I'm not sleepy. We made our living room, the lounge, very cozy today, by adding a wastebasket and a sofa pillow. Among the letters I wrote, there was one for my sister Hanchen, in which I tell her that the quilt she wanted to give me for my wedding, as well as the slippers, has not appeared. Good night, everyone!

May 20 — Today we had a visit on board from the Duus family. The wind is good so we hope to get going tomorrow. We went for the same walk as usual, and this evening there was music and beautiful singing. Now it is eleven-forty-five and a suitable bedtime. Good night! Kalla, my thoughts have often been with you there, as you sit by the examination table. May the Lord grant my prayers for you!

May 21 — The last day before departure that I spent in Norway. How has it been, from beginning to end? At eight-thirty out of bed, nine-forty-five ashore to Duus's after getting an invitation from Doctor Homann on the way there, an invitation we turned down as it was our last day. However, we stopped to see him this morning, and again this evening, since we didn't find the lovable old doctor at home the first time. Today I again received flowers from the lady: a rose and a pink carnation, how beautiful. Both this morning and in the afternoon I wrote letters and posted the mail on time. We were all over at D.'s country house in Bærøen; how very beautiful it is there, a well-arranged garden. As a memento of Kragerø, I drew a little picture of one of the views there.

Then it was evening; wine at the table and a large number of toasts: to the travelers, to the remaining, to the ship. Thank you for D.'s hospitality, etc. After supper, when we were about to say our good-byes, the champagne came in, once again a lot of toasts, but the last toast we drank in the lively, bubbling champagne, was "good luck to our beloved fatherland! Good luck to Norway!" It was a toast I drank to from the bottom of my heart, and I assume that was also the case for Hermann, who proposed it. After this came the parting, but the entire family wanted to see us well on board. This was a last proof of their kindness toward us. They have been so kind and welcoming the entire time we have been here, and we are very grateful. In half an hour we raise anchor to leave Norway, Europe!

Oh, my dear Father, we are always in Your care, and You are our protector — oh, hold Your hand over us also on this journey, and let whatever happens be Your will! Lord! I am now surrounded by strangers

— only — well, I should not say only, as there are many — You my Father, and Hermann are here with me. Will You never leave me, my God? No, no, You will not, as long as I stay with You — and — God, I will do that, I will pray to You every day that I must not be lost, that I must walk on Your roads here in this world, that I may be a good wife, so that H. finds in me the woman he believed could make him happy. I will also pray that Hermann receives power by Your spirit, gentle Father, to manage the vocation to which he has been called as Your servant. The strength and the help we need comes from You — send it to him, send it to him, then! Hand in hand we walk out into the world! Be with us always, we will always need Your help — You, almighty Father. Hear my prayers for the sake of Jesus Christ!

I am going to bed now; the ship is still lying still in the harbor. Shall it be the last night I sleep in Norway? Only You up there know the answer to that, only You know if my eyes will ever again rest on Norway's mountains. And it would not be good for me to look into the future, no, no — big changes can happen before that, and would it be good for me to know these? Oh, no! Good night siblings, all you dear ones! May the Lord hold His hand over you!! Farewell! You will remember your Linka.

May 24 — Today I feel well enough to write a little bit. In the last two days I have been far too sick to use the pen. I could hardly think, so my memory will have to be good enough for the previous days:

May 22 — At two or three in the morning the sounds of the crew preparing the ship for departure could be heard. The anchor was raised, the noise from the chains could be heard all the way into our bedroom, and carried with it a message that we would leave soon. At four or five, H. and I got up to greet Kragerø as we headed out of the harbor. The captain's command sounded and the sails were hoisted and in a gentle breeze we slid out between the skerries. None of our friends in Kragerø were at the wharf, but two female figures became visible on a high crest. "Look, there are my wife and daughter," the captain said to us. Even though he is an old salt (not in a dishonorable meaning), there had to be some pain inside of him, and a wish to stay home. After having been home for only two or three months he once again left his wife, children, and a good home. What a sad life, being a sailor — it might work if you are not married; if you look at it from the opposite side, how sad it must be to be married to a sailor!

H. and I were too sleepy to start the day that early. We stayed up a bit longer to enjoy the sight of the beautiful light from the morning sun, but then we went to bed and slept until twelve when the Captain put his head inside the door to say that if we had any letters we wanted to send, the pilot was leaving. We said no thanks. Some strange suspicion I got while I was down in the cabin made me get dressed in a hurry and take a quick walk up on deck. I asked the captain, and the way he was shaking his head told me that the wind was <u>contrary</u> — we had to tack. The later in the day it was, the stronger the wind blew, and the heavier the sea got. I felt tired and in the afternoon I went down to rest — but Linka, why did you do that? If you had known the consequences, you would have been smarter. I was stupid when I left the deck, as I did not get up there again that day — oh my, how terrible it was to be seasick, although I occasionally got a little laughter down there. There were scenes — I was lying there all by myself, but every time I was about to throw up, good fortune sent me help, either Capt., Ziiølner, or Hermann. Yes, Hermann was the first one to help me, but he paid for his helpfulness. The crabs were calling him — yes, their calling was so intense that in the end he had to hurry up on deck, and sheltered by the ship he offered the greedy animals whatever the day had brought his storeroom. I, however, was lying there, eating some ship's biscuits, but soon I started over again — the ship was moving so much, it rose and fell back down on the waves of Skagerak. Nobody was with me, I could not fight it anymore, but there is someone — it was Z. I don't know him at all, but I wanted to save my carpets. I was embarrassed, he was shy, but still — now thank you Z. I'm done for now — disgusting! Johan, come take it out!

For a long time now I felt quite good. I lay quite still, laughing at Z. and myself. It was starting to get dark and my bed had to be made. I got up and, oh no, I got sick again, pretty bad, too. The captain, who had been sent to help me this time, held his hand on my forehead, saying "poor you" more than once. When I was done, he offered to make our bed. I thought it was a shame, but I was in no condition to do it myself, so I accepted and lay down on the sofa. At ten H. came in, and with the best wishes of a good night, the cabin passengers, Z. and ourselves, went to bed. That was how the first day on board ended; it had not been pleasant. God see to it that the following days will be better!

May 23 — I was rather well. In the morning, that is to say at between eleven and noon, I made our bed right away and then hurried up into the fresh air. The wind had not changed, we were tacking between Jomfruland and Kragerø (?). There were big waves and a cold wind coming from west. We tucked in and found a place in the middle of the ship, to windward. I had my dinner there — gryngrøt[189] with a glass of Madeira. Rather strange food, but if you do it yourself, it's well done.[191] The food was good, and we sat there quite comfortably. However, we were going to be disturbed. Just as if the stirred-up sea was envious of our peace, it decided to end it by sending quite a squirt of water over our heads. We had to laugh when we stood there, all wet, but it was really annoying, being disturbed like that. It was not long before I asked the captain "isn't this a storm?" "Far from it! You said yourself that you only got a little squirt of water on you, in a storm there will be big waves." I was satisfied with this comfort and sat down on the henhouse, inside of which our three hens were cackling a bit against the weather, but apart from that they just behaved as if they wanted to get back ashore.

Moody, and not feeling quite well, I sat there the entire day, amusing myself by every now and then talking to some emigrants courageous enough to come up from their room. They all said that there was a lot of sickness among the people — "they're really sick!" But with that, our conversation was over, as the person I was talking to had to go to leeward to say "Ulk" etc. etc. I have all my meals out in open air, even supper, but oh no, I got sick again, and over to leeward with me too. However, after this one time, food tasted good.

We went to bed after a few hours. I was looking back on my day like I always do in the evenings, when I exclaimed in my heart, "Today I have been fonder of Hermann than ever before." Why? O heart, you are so strange. You keep beating, but don't say anything. A prayer from us to our Father, in whose arms we rest!

May 24 — I've been well today, had good appetite and felt good in every way. What a weakling I'd have been otherwise, since the weather has been beautiful. Until dinnertime it was almost completely still. The children were playing on the deck, the little boys were playing "train," the little girls were rolling peas and grain. Afterward they invited the boys to help them pick up, and right away it went into the mouth as soon as it came into their hands. The adult men and women gathered little by little on deck, everybody smiling, greeting the good weather — the dear sun. I wonder if, in their hearts, they didn't send a grateful prayer to its Giver? There is more wind now; we're sailing before full sails. We have had more wind since this calm. For three days now, we've been tacking, so we have not even lost sight of Trumlingene, three mountain peaks between Risør and Arendal. We've seen a church and a lighthouse today. The names? Now we could say "Farewell" and thank you for good companionship to you, good friends, maybe we will reach Lindesnes tomorrow, and then it will be farewell to all Norwegian mountains. It is up to You, our God! Well, good night everyone, both on land and sea —not those who are on watch, though.

The 26th of *May*, Monday — Let me see whether or not I can perform my art now; the ship is going fast, near gale, one splash of sea after the other says hello to us onboard here. The ship is tilting so much to one side that I'm almost sitting on my nose, and those who are up walking would stumble around if carefulness didn't make them hold on to something.

Yesterday, Sunday the 25th of May — We also had quite some wind, but it was not too strong for us to have a service. Hermann preached, and I believe that most passengers came up for it. Hymns were sung; it sounded so strange when our tunes were mixed with the sound of the wind. The entire service built me up, and it touched me in the depth of my soul; if only everyone who participated in this two-hour-long devotion felt his soul being touched like I did! H. really had to make an effort with his lungs, and he used his bass well. The wonderful clear sky is part of the reason why we did not go to bed until eleven at night. Sitting in pleasant conversation between the two of us, or letting our thoughts fly, either to our past or our future, we watched the stars. One star after the other looked down at us with its clear light. The pipes had been smoked. Throwing our glances at the mountains of our fatherland for the last time — we assumed that the next day would not allow us to do so again — we left the deck. Take care of them, oh God, those who are still in Norway to whom we are dear!

Our assumption was right. Nothing but sky and sea has been visible today. On the reef here, we've seen a number of fishing boats, and we find ourselves longing for fresh fish. We've caught up again with a schooner that had impertinently passed us earlier, but the wind is getting stronger — reef the sails — the wind is whistling in the sails and the North Sea is roaring. God, hold your hand over us!

Tuesday, May 27 — What a change from yesterday when I was writing! Yesterday spray from the sea washed the deck, while the dark clouds of a squall were hovering threateningly above our heads. Little by little we got to feel their masses of water, stronger and stronger, while the wind, as if showing its joy because of the rain, grew stronger. To me, used to being on land, there was such buzzing and roaring and noise here, I was unable to read decently. I stayed in the so-called chamber the entire day, where I had to get a good grip not to fall on my nose, even though I was sitting down. I didn't want to follow <u>my husband's</u> example in this — he took a dive forward, to the great amusement of the farmer he was talking to, and also to others standing around them.

It was strange, sitting at dusk, watching the big waves that really showed me their white teeth. Hermann had been at supper for a long time, and I scolded him a bit when he came back up, for not having come up to me sooner. He should have known that I wanted to share the pleasure of watching the waves with him. "I've made our bed," was the answer he gave me, and I was happy again, as this is not a very pleasant job when the ship is moving so much all the time. That's why H. often helps me. One night I had to laugh. We were both trying to make the bed; H. was at the head and I was at the foot. I found our situation so strange I had to burst out, "If only our family had a mirror to show them how we are working here."

Yesterday evening we also witnessed a very funny scene in our bedchamber, but of a different type. We were sitting in the captain's cabin until eleven, but then it really was time to got to bed. But oh my, how our bedroom smelled! The doors to both Z's and our cabins had to be opened, because a smell had made its way in there from the emigrant room — it smelled of tobacco mixed with camphor, and it was terrible! The worst smell was at Z.'s, something his puffing, complaining, and swearing told us, and finally some "ouch" because the movement of the ship had made him hit the wall. There are curtains in front of our door, so we couldn't see him, but we still had to laugh, and we just laughed more when Z. exclaimed, "I can't stand this without something to strengthen my heart!" With that he jumped out of bed — at the same moment the ship tilted to our side, and Z., falling over, managed to grab something on the wall so he did not come in to us. The ship tilted again and Z. made it over to the basket of wine. "Some port, pastor and wife? Do you want a glass of port — the weather is so bad, we need something for our hearts!?" "Yes, please." The ship tilted again and again and again before Z. got a hold of some glasses in the cupboard — how H. and I laughed lying there, imagining this creature in his underwear. When he had finally got the bottle and some glasses in his hands, he stumbled from one side of the lounge to the other, trying to gain his balance so that he could fill the glasses and bring them to us. Hey, there he is, stumbling over here, but the glass is empty, the good port was poured out on the way. "Hold the glass, Pastor, and I'll fill it up while I can hold myself steady by the wall." So, now we'd gotten our port, I emptied my glass quite nicely as I was lying there behind the curtains. Oh, he still tumbled around from wall to wall in the lounge, laughing and screaming because he hit himself, but finally it got quiet!

Today there has been no such noise. With all sails crowded — mainsail, topsail topgallant, jib, flying jib, foresail, stern top, stern topgallant, lee, jib, and staysails — we're sliding calmly over the surface of the sea. The emigrants are gathering up here, to enjoy themselves in the sun after an anxious night. The children are playing, the women have found a place in the sun to sit down, working eagerly on their needlework (knitting), while the men, leaning toward the rail, conversing, are smoking their pipes. The young boys have got ahold of their guns, and gunshot after gunshot is heard. The generosity of the farmers toward their minister is also visible here; today we got a mysost[195] and a white cheese from a woman. That led nicely to a conversation about the three nice boys she has, whom we'll probably get to know better later.

May 28 — Today the same beautiful weather as yesterday. The surface is calm, even calmer than yesterday, when there was still some movement from the earlier wind. How strange it is to experience these calm, nice days on the sea, within some wooden boards and logs put together. How grateful must we not be that You, our Father in Heaven, are leading us and saving us from fear — yes, I do know that when I am led by Your fatherly hand, I should never fear, but forgive me my weakness. I will not stop thinking that nothing worse than death can happen to us, which will only lead us to life with You, dear Lord! And is that bad!? No, coming to You would be nothing but joyful, but I guess it is the sight of the roaring sea and the sound of the wind sweeping over us that makes me fear — but Lord, strengthen me with Your spirit so that I do not fear, as I know and admit there is no reason to!

Both fish and people seem to be enjoying the sun. Also today there is the same life on deck as yesterday. Children, women, and men are passing the time in the same way, but every now and then the game, work, or conversation is disturbed by a "look, look" from the lips of a spectator who encourages people to look at the dolphins gathering around the ship, either in waltz or gallop — they are going fast, that is for sure. There is life in our camp. Z. and H. have gotten hold of their fishing lines and want to try their luck on these banks we're passing — Doggers Bank. I can hear a "hurray!" It's H. who's caught a whiting. He had not planned on fishing today, but stumbled his way up the stairs when he heard that Z. had caught a fish. They might have better luck today than yesterday, when the fishermen took their book and pipe and just sat there with the lines hanging after the ship; they did not bother to pull them up. Finally the first mate pulls up one of the lines, and has a gurnard — my good friends from Askevold are greeting me here, far south in the North Sea.

What we did not get of fish yesterday, we got today. Besides the four whiting our fishermen caught, we also got hold of four flounders. An English fishing boat came up to our side and we soon started exchanging goods with him. The capt. got four flounders for a bottle of brandy. "It's water," Z. told the Englishman, who with a surprised face set the bottle to his lips, but his face soon returned to normal. The farmers climbed up the rigging and on the deckhouse to look at the English, as if they were strange animals, and by offering tobacco plugs and liquor, the farmers also got fish. The ocean has been swarming with English and Dutch fishermen today. The sea lane is getting narrower now that we're coming in between the countries and approaching the Channel. It's no wonder that it's seemed so crowded here today; we've gotten a new passenger since we left Kragerø. I don't know whether it's a boy or a girl, but the baby was born a couple of hours ago.[192] It's been quite funny watching many of the farmers today. Every time we've passed a fishing boat, they've asked the same thing: "This'll have to be *Alert*, now, won't it?" Far from it! *Alert* is the second emigrant ship that left from Kragerø, and we think that we saw it outside of eastern Risør!

May 29, Ascension Day — I started this day earlier than usual. At <u>ten in the morning</u> the captain came down to us. He suggested we wake up, since H. was having a service. It got to be one o'clock before we had breakfast and got ready, and that was when we, as we said, went to church. When we arrived, the congregation was gathered. Everyone was wearing his best Sunday clothes, even the crew, and in between them you could spot the little cook, now clean, but usually so dirty. I say honor those who should be honored. The ship's dignitaries, the captain, mate, second mate, Z., the minister and finally his wife found their places in chairs in the front. For a long time, even during the singing, my eyes were pleased at the sight of the congregation who were now sitting in two rows on the deck — the men on one side and the women on the other. The entire group was gaily illuminated by the sun, which was shining in all its splendor above our heads. Both the men's and the women's bright buttons and filigree brooches competed with the beautiful borders and white linen sleeves that decorated the dark clothes, to see which would shine more, and have the most radiant light. But now their heads were uncovered, and with a beautiful little prayer, H. started our little period of devotion. We were done about three, and I was surprised that we had been sitting there for two hours — it seemed like such a short time, although my heart was filled with joy. The singing went quite well; everyone opened his beak and sang with power from the heart and the lungs.

Just as if we had really exerted ourselves, the entire group of dignitaries went down to drink port and eat cake, although the captain and the mate had to hurry up, as the wind had turned during the service and came from north again, which was good. May it follow the old saying, "Where the wind goes during the sermon, that's where it goes the rest of the week." We had flags flying during the service, too, and an American took that in honor of himself, and raised his flag and greeted us. We found our binoculars — it was another emigrant ship!

I spent my time until dinner at five- or six-thirty studying a theological journal. I read about "The Legality of Divorce." It hurt me to admit that I had not taken any standpoint whatsoever in this matter before I got married. But I'm just as smart now as I was before, since the journal says the same as I have always believed, namely that one should not remarry if a husband and wife don't like each other anymore and leave each other or get a proper divorce. I hope I won't be in any danger of it coming to this. What am I saying — is it irresponsible? Why should it? My hope is in earnest!

Every now and then I've been interrupted; I've been called out to look at all the fishing boats surrounding us, both close up and farther away. I was more seriously interrupted when the mate came down to me, saying "The coast of England is now in sight, Madam." Far away, shrouded in fog, this strange land could be seen. But what was floating just a little bit off the coast? It looked like a three-masted vessel, but it was not, as there were no sails, ropes, or tackle. On the other hand there were three masts on the hull with a ball in each top. It's a light ship floating on a shallow off of North Foreland. Now a scaffolding *[here Linka made a small sketch of scaffolding]*, that's how it looked to me. It was a so-called Rescue Tower, on which there are iron chests filled with food and water for any sailors unlucky enough to be wrecked or run aground in these difficult sea lanes. We could see the shoreline quite clearly now, and I saw another lighthouse on the shore this time. It was South Foreland Hill. These two, North and South Foreland Hills, were the first my eyes caught sight of after four days with nothing but sky and sea. However, the eye did not rest only on the land to the southwest, it also wandered toward the east — also there it could see land — France — France and England next to each other, so close we could have them both in sight! We were at the entrance of the English Channel, which I so often have read about in geography, not knowing that I should get to see it with my own eyes. The good wind and strong current soon brought us closer to the steep white cliffs of South Foreland. Their white slopes showed clearly toward the North Sea. There is a peak, and another one; now there are many, but they are English. We kept to the English side, moved farther and farther away from the French coast, and soon we could no longer see it at all.

I did not derive much joy from seeing all these mountains. I sent a grateful prayer from the bottom of my soul to our faithful, heavenly pathfinder, who has led us quickly and safely across the North Sea — but still — there would have been a different joy if this were ten years from now, and it was the Norwegian mountains rising on both sides of Xianiafjorden, just like the French and English mountains are greeting us now. I tried my best to make a sketch of the entrance, but it still turned out wrong, as it was impossible to look at both the French and the British coast at the same time. As we approached Dover, this lively little town also got its place in my sketchbook, with help from our binoculars. Big, flat-roofed houses, a tower — I assume it was the church — and on the promontory near the city lay Dover Castle. It looked to me like a little fortress. It made quite a lively impression on me, looking over this city.

In its harbor are several ships and two big steamers, while numerous smaller boats, fishing boats and bigger ships that had kept us company for quite some time, setting their course in there — but what is that? There is steam coming from the mountains — oh, I should have taken a better look, it was the train on its way between the mountains. We saw some people, but very unclearly; maybe it was animals running around on the beach. Up at the castle there were sentries; we could see the guardhouse, too, but it is the sentries that form the picture in my imagination, as well as the flag on the fortress' flagstaff. A long ridge formed the background; on it green meadows and luxuriant tilled fields seemed to bathe in the last rays of the evening sun. A boat is approaching us, and the crew asks if we have any mail to bring ashore. "It wouldn't have been a bad idea to have some letters ready now," I thought, but I had no regrets when the captain said that it had been reported that *Columbus* had passed the straits of Dover.

While I was busy with the coast and my drawings, our farmers had other pleasures in mind. The fiddler had taken his fiddle up on deck, and the lively dance had started. The ball was opened by two crewmen, but they soon got a hold of a girl each. The farm girls were <u>too shy</u> to feel comfortable with these in waltz and gallop, so some women from Larvik had to take over. Some started talking about *Halling* and *springdans* or *gangar*. So the fiddler had to play, and the farmers danced, to the city people's great amusement. They could easily be heard, with their laughter and cheering.

I now remembered what the Mate had said to me as we approached the entrance of the channel: "When Madam comes to the entrance, you have to pay a toll,"which means that those who have not been here before should provide treats or entertainment. I suggested we drink wine, but the farmers are paying the toll with their dancing, so we have to watch them. I kept one eye on the dancers, and the other on the coast. The binoculars were often used, and I satisfied the farmers' curiosity every now and then, by letting them look through the glasses. But I think they fooled both themselves and me saying, "Look at all those strange things, look, Gro or Birgit."

"But Kari Kraagnes and Tarje, her brother, are dancing, it's a *springdans* — it's so much fun watching them, step out the way, so the minister and his wife get to see our best dancers!!" It went really well, too, *hutsch*! The boy did a somersault with one hand on the ground, and

Tarje Kraagnes

Kari Kraagnes

landed safely, still a part of the dance, while the girl was spinning round and round like a spinning wheel — spin, spin, now they are spinning round together, and then the dance was over. A forty-year-old woman came forward to step a *Halling*.

It was a curiosity, but it was not such a pleasant sight for a woman. The crewmen had a lot of fun with the farm girls. In particular, there was one quite cheerful fellow. He had his clay pipe in his mouth; wore his hat on the top of his three hairs; had a red shirt; white pants, poorly kept up — almost alarmingly — by a leather strap, from which there hung an enormous sheath knife. That made a good appearance — he was a real sailor. It got dark, and with darkness the fun came to an end.

There was now room on the deck for me to have my usual evening stroll. While I was walking, I sought to understand why there is this strange feature about my personality that almost always makes me sad when I'm surrounded by joy and cheerfulness. I've often — certainly — tried to break this stream of feelings, and I've also often succeeded in appearing cheerful, and a few times — it had felt so good — I've defeated the seriousness, been happy with the happy — no, I don't want to say happy, I'm often happy, even though I'm serious. I would rather say cheerful with the cheerful. I didn't come to any conclusions in my night of pondering, which was interrupted by a desire to see the Dogger lighthouse.

It's gotten late while I've been sitting here writing. I'm going up on deck one more time to see if I can see anything unusual — it's so dark, though. I came up just in time to see something really strange — we were close to sailing our bow right into another ship. Lanterns out, we had been really close, but luckily it all went well. The gaslights from the town of Hastings got my mind on something else. Our ancestors, our old Norse giants, fought quite a tough battle there. Yes, I do remember you, old graybeards! However, I'm a little mad at you for having burned down the woods on the west coast of our fatherland!

Now, good night, those who are far away!! and those here with me!

Part Two — 1849-1851 • 225

June 1851

Sunday, June 1 — At ten o'clock this morning we passed the last English point, Cape Lizard. The journey through the channel has been good, but the last days it has been so foggy that it has been dripping from sails and lines. The coast has been hidden to us, and our eyes have not had the pleasure of catching as much as a little glimpse of the Isle of Wight's loveliness. We've proceeded nicely and calmly through the channel in the fog — our only amusement has been to look at all the lighthouses in the evenings. Every second there's a light blinking toward us, and we fear sailing on ships in dark nights, which is why the lanterns are well used. Z. and H. have tried fishing again, but with no luck. We went to church again today — our church is great, now and forever. There is room enough for millions of souls — my only wish is that they seek it truthfully!

Lovely weather the entire day. There has been dancing here tonight too, and a lot of cheerful people. Just like last time, the dancing ended when darkness came, and the deck was left to us. It was a strange sight looking at the streak of light in the water behind the ship. Sometimes it seemed like a million stars, other times it seemed as if the stars were fused together and it was like fire. I guess this is phosphorescence, and even if it's only insects, it was an amazing sight. However, our eyes deserted this to greet the very last sight of Europe — it is ten in the evening — a lighthouse east of us. It is St. Agnes on the Isles of Scilly — now it is gone — farewell, everyone in Europe, until we meet again. The last place name was similar to my youngest sister's name. Farewell, you, the siblings, all!

June 6 — The Atlantic has proved to be very capricious since we entered it. One day still, one day the wind is rising a bit, then near gale, then storm, and the wind comes from all the world's different corners. Although it has had its calm periods, the ocean has been strange. Even though we have not exactly seen the greatest waves possible, the ocean is in a way working harder and lurching more now than in a storm, when the sails contribute support to the ship, making it lurch less on its way across the sea. In particular, the farmers have had a hard time, but if there has been a calmer period in between, they've taken the opportunity to get up on deck. But until they have the chance to grab a rope or something to hold on to, they reel about like drunkards, and frequently hit the deck, nose first. The men are having such a terrible time. Still, some of them have to do service as kitchen maids, and, carrying their pots of porridge, their coffeepots, and frying pans, they've been quite a comic sight. Their fear of falling has been great. But despite his fear and carefulness, and the good iron heels which he stamped onto the deck that was made slippery by the fog, there was one man who fell right on his nose during some powerful lurching. Ouch! The man was lying facedown, his pan was overturned, and his beautiful fried pork was everywhere. With a look of despair on his face, he joined in his friends' laughter, a laughter that became louder as the unlucky fellow started picking up his pieces of pork.

June 7, Whit Saturday (Pentecost Eve) — Writing is difficult work tonight, because we've had near gale the entire day, and it's coming against us, too. But God still lets us proceed by tacking; however, we feel the sea so much more then. While I'm writing, I have to hold on to the table with one hand and set the inkpot in the corner of the sofa to make it stand. The men are sitting upstairs with their glass of grog and pipe, in cheerful conversation about humorous anecdotes from the old days. It's raining and blowing more and more. Soon the servant, "Sooty Johan"[193] will come down with his tureen of porridge to set the table. Even though we are at sea, we will remember and celebrate this solemn day with porridge. But you, at home in Norway, have probably said to yourself tonight, "Well, Linka and Hermann are not having porridge tonight." You've probably gone to bed now, as it's twelve-thirty where you are, and only ten here. You're running away from us, that's how it is. However, don't think that we are standing still. Well, I can't say that with complete certainty; this morning, even though we did not exactly go backward, we did not move forward either, but turned around in a circle twice with our ship. Not the slightest breath of wind came through the air; there was no rippling at all on the big wave that rose slowly around us. It rose into its unyielding arch to receive the next one. Still, there does not seem to be any unity in their movement. It seems like the distant winds, coming from all directions, have made such a jumble with the currents that the ship is unable to stick to the right course, but has been turned around twice.

For a while, there was silence onboard, but when two big whales showed up close to us, squirting water, all of a sudden there was life. A farmer said to his closest neighbor, "Oh no, look at that — it's bigger than a large cow!"

We've seen the Leach's petrel (storm petrel) today, too, like we have the previous days. I don't like it, as it is a harbinger of bad weather. This was also the case today, after dinner — rain and fierce wind. My dear little sisters and all relatives, this is the first holiday since I was married. Until I can expect to get my own home, I will be away from you. God grant that one day I will experience the great joy of seeing you in Hermann's and my home for a holiday — we would spend it just like we did when all of us were still at home, in the dear home of our parents. And if this should not happen, there will still come a solemn day more joyful than any we have ever had together down here — we will look forward to that and pray to God our Father to send us His spirit to live in our hearts and guide us so that we are prepared to take part in the joy on this great solemn day! Good night!

June 9, Second Pentecost Day — It is so sad with this terrible weather we've had during Pentecost. It's been so stormy, it's been hard to gather our thoughts around the celebration of it — having a service with our farmers has been impossible. Today the sun broke through the thick, rainy clouds that opened up to us yesterday so that their heavy, wet vapor could pour down on us. All the farmers have been out in the sun today, and the children have been playing about on four legs; using just two legs is luckily not such a big issue for them. The hens that are everybody's favorites, because their clucking reminds us of land, have chosen the children as their company. The children are chewing on sandwiches and throwing some to the hens. Oh, you ungrateful rooster! He takes a whole sandwich from a little girl, oh how she's screaming! The rooster is so surprised at this, it gives her back the crust. Times are uncertain, however. We were hit by a great wave, squirting on young and old — oh my, how wet they were! After a while of just looking at each other, they started shaking off the water from their dresses and shirts. But a heartfelt laughter was heard throughout the big boat, where a lovely farm girl was lying on top of some fur robes. "So why are you lying there?" "I'm watching the bedcovers, so they don't take off." "Oh yeah, so do they have so many legs that you're afraid they'll walk off?" "You bet, I'm afraid they will! Ha, ha!" The girl was probably not thinking about the same legs that we were, but we laughed, and the girl laughed, too. But now it's time to make the bed. And good night!

June 10 — Morning: good weather. Afternoon: serious (little) storm from contrary wind — reef in the sails. Mainsail and Mizzen in!

Oh my, I'm almost scared — but even though my heart is beating fast, I had a good lung-exercise at supper tonight, as the ship moved so much we could not leave our teacups on the table, where knives, cheese, and bread were all over. Meanwhile, the cabin boy was standing with his back to the door, bracing himself with one foot against the sofa, holding the teapot and the pitcher of water in his hands. We sat on the sofa, and we couldn't help sliding toward each other all the time. The capt. and both mates slid across the floor on their chairs. "I prefer standing," the mate finally said, and he balanced himself so well, it was a joy to watch him. But ouch, a sudden, powerful roll came, and the mate hit the wall, and we fell over on the sofa. We shrieked because we had skillfully saved our teacups. But on the floor, our last jar of the preserved cream[194] from Glende was rolling about — that was a shame! Laughter is a good thing, but now over to more serious work, as I will probably fall over when I try to make our bed. It was not pleasant down there, and it had been dripping a bit down in our bed too, but there was not really any more moisture than there usually is. The entire job consisted of shaking the headboard. The farmers are in their room, singing hymns with all their might. They seek comfort in their fear — just don't forget to thank the comforter and helper when the fear is gone!

Sunday June 15 — Nice weather today, after several days with rain and (storm) near gale yesterday, up to storm from the west — still contrary wind — we traveled with <u>shortened sails</u>. But I didn't notice the storm much because of a several-days-long inconvenience — a cold — it has made me keep my bed. I haven't been up at all, only today, to look at the big waves. They came as if they were going to swallow us, but *Columbus* rose above the waves like a swan. We have been living in what I would describe as "domestic comfort." H., Z., and the captain (the last one only once in awhile) have been down here with me. We have been entertained; we solved riddles, performed tricks, and so on. It was midnight before we went to bed. Today the weather was so nice we were able to have a service onboard. But the waves were so big, and the ship moved around so much that the pastor's wife almost fell on her nose twice while the pastor was preaching. I was more than just a little bit scared that the farmers might see me smiling during the service, since that might have upset them. It's already late, I'm tired, and since we're now sitting in pleasant conversation, as we were yesterday, I guess we aren't going to bed until sometime between midnight and one o'clock in the morning.

June 16, Monday — This morning we woke up at 11 a.m. when Z. and the captain came to our cabin, wishing H. happy birthday and presenting a beer glass of eggnog (I've never had so much eggnog at one time). Then we, together with the two congratulants who had a similar portion, drank to H.'s health. Our guests left when we had emptied our glasses, and soon we heard two gunshots from the cannon and a burst of rifle fire, one at a time, though. The rifles belonged to the farmers, but I'm not sure if they fired in honor of the minister or if it was to get rid of the thick fog, since when they asked the mate why he cleaned the cannons, he answered, "We're going to shoot away this thick fog we have today." I'm afraid they may have believed him. The fog was so thick, it fell like rain; it was so damp and wet and sticky on deck that we mostly kept to the lounge today, too. All of a sudden, we were in motion. "A big whale right by the ship! Everybody up." And as we stood by the rail, the whale, as if to honor us, rose up over the surface so that we could clearly see the monstrous gray creature. "Would you look at that! It really is bigger than a cow!" a farmer exclaimed — their usual object of comparison.

To honor Hermann, I went over to the galley to make curry for a canned goose. Well, now it is out of the box we brought. At dinner, we christened our traveler's case, and in the evening, with a glass of toddy, H.'s cup. We haven't used all this before, because I wanted to wash them myself, and it until the last week I have not felt well enough to get up and do things like that. However, we've gotten used to the tin utensils belonging to the ship, and they do not make the food taste differently. I also think it would look strange if we ate with silver utensils and everybody else with tin. H. and Z. are playing cards tonight. I've been doing some needlework, but a little while ago I was drawing our parsonage, including a lot of different creatures belonging to it, for the captain. It's time to go to bed now; it's between midnight and one in the morning. Good night all! This is the first birthday in many years H. is with me or I with him. One year ago today, I left Askevold; how are you my little Askevold-children? If only I could see you right now! Good night!

June 17 — Get up quickly, Linka! A ship is hailing us! I ran upstairs just in time to see a brig lying at our side. We were going in opposite directions — the brig close-hauled — so we did not spend much time together, but it was enough for a little conversation in the middle of the Atlantic. They had written their longitude observations on a board, and our captain hurried up and wrote his with a piece of chalk on the ship's side — how close they were! There was only a difference of two miles. This put the captain in an excellent mood, and the English were again greeted with a flag when they waved at us with hats and aprons (the English mate's), and soon we were far, far away from each other.

We continued with our tacking, wishing to be able to sail as well as those we had our little sea conversation with — short but cheerful and encouraging! Once again we directed our course toward Greenland — a while ago we were going toward the Madeira Islands, we prefer the wine there to the whale and cod-liver oil on Greenland. But God will soon give us good weather and wind so that we will get to where we are going.

June 19 — Yesterday we had thick fog, pouring rain, and no wind, but today we have perfect wind and weather. We have four hundred miles left before we reach our destination. You, our guardian, have led us this far, You will also be with us further! The sun is gilding the sails; it wants to say good-bye for today! I wanted to go up to look at it. How beautiful it was, seeing this queen of the sky, sinking down into the bosom of the sea, concealing itself little by little — now it is gone, but it is still gilding the light clouds of the western horizon. The captain tells me, "See, this is a good-weather sun, red and clear as it sets." Well, welcome back, sun, give my best to wherever you are going on your way to the Orient!

June 20 — We're such night owls! We're still working here, and it's 11:55 p.m. Our work consists of, as far as the men are concerned, playing cards, which they have been doing both today and yesterday, and I'm reading *Aals Erindringer*.[195] This morning it was so still, the rudder was tied fast; since then we've had a light, favorable wind. During the still period, the entire ocean lay completely still around us, only in a few places could you spot a little bit of a current, rippling the sea a little bit, but the ship lay so still that we lowered a one-hundred-fathom-long fishing line into the sea, and it fell straight down — but the bottom? The Atlantic is probably deeper than one hundred fathoms, but it is full of banks and we thought we might be above one of those, but we weren't. We still wanted to fish, though, and we made a device that allowed us to catch strange sea creatures on the surface, and during this still period, that's what the men amused themselves with. I sat with the captain's magnifying glass, studying all the beautiful rarities they brought me, wishing that W. Christie or a better zoologist, L.O. Rasch, had been there. Some animals will be bottled in alcohol, because we think they're unusual. It's now two-thirty in Xiania — good morning! Good afternoon! We're going to bed now, at two o'clock in the morning.

June 23 — I've never been as scared as I was last night, so I have to write down the reason, even though I was quite angry with myself for being afraid, as I wanted fear to be unknown to me. The weather was cold, but it was still enough for us to have church yesterday. The north wind turned our noses red and our hands a bit blue, but what could we expect from the Arctic Ocean or Greenland? With its lustrous setting, the sun broke through the clouds and created, on the opposite horizon, a beautiful rainbow, and around the horizon it brought with it — horizon clouds[196] in sailor's language — the fresh crimson clouds, which had chosen dark gray, almost black, hats as headdresses. The entire sky was lit, and it had to seem wonderful and astonishing to the spectators, of which there were not few. Wide-eyed and with mouths wide open, we watched nature, and it was not until the sun said good-bye and bowed under to report our arrival in Wisconsin that we had something to talk about again. But describing this scene has taken more time than it lasted. "Oh, this sky means bad weather, Captain!" "Not at all — it's only eastern wind." It got to be midnight and we still had not gone to bed. Z. and H. were playing cards, with grog and their pipes, while the Captain and I were performing tricks, and I was quite an eager student. Then but all of a sudden we were disturbed in our peace. "What's that sound?! Oh no" Capt.: "The sails are slatting!'" and with that he got up in a hurry. The mate opened the hatch and called in a frightened voice, "Captain, the wind is on the port side!" I got up from my seat too; "no, Linka, where are you going?" I thought, and hit myself on the forehead for being scared, and sat down again to draw, but I was shivering, since we could hear the calling and commands from the deck. H. was pale because I was scared, and he and Z. threw away the cards and ran upstairs. At two thirty, three, four the captain was downstairs again, the weather was once again good — we had gotten a good wind, and the bad weather with rain and western wind had passed. How fast the weather changes, so that mischief itself (that is what it is to us now) could come and disturb our voyage. Now — at 4 in the morning — I went to bed. The men were still playing cards for a while, and at 7 a.m. they went to bed after having been up smoking their pipes and fishing, but without finding bottom and no biting at all. 3 p.m. —had breakfast. That is the life we lead. Oh, how lazy! It is now 6 p.m., in the middle of the day for us, in Xiania it is around nine — what noise and feasting there is there tonight, midsummer. I hope the Atlantic will not make any noise, and not present any icebergs to us when we are lying quite still with flapping sails. We are in the middle of the currents the icebergs usually follow — their course. Yes, I'm praying, and I believe God can hear my prayer, He will forgive me my weakness and fear for the sake of Christ.

June 26 — At four o'clock this morning I heard someone calling on the deck. It sounded joyful in my ears and it came from right above my bed — it was "the bottom!" Both yesterday and the day before that, we have been taking soundings to find the banks of Newfoundland, and today we finally found them. It made me feel so much closer to America. We hailed an Englishman yesterday. The same ceremonies as last time, writing down the longitudes, but this time there was a difference of eleven miles in the observations of longitude. However, since the Englishman had just passed the bank and surely had a chronometer onboard, we adjusted to his observation, and that later proved to be a good choice. Apart from flags, we said good-bye to each other by swinging our hats, and I used my handkerchief — too bad it was a bit gray!

In spite of pouring rain and quite a bit of a wind at night, it got better this morning. We got up a bit earlier than usual since great fisheries were to take place today. I guess it was around ten-thirty when we came up on deck, and just as we came up, the captain pulled up the first cod. I had just made it to the stairs when the mate opened the hatch and said, "Come on, the first fish is already lying on deck!" I streaked over to where I expected to find the captain, but both he and the fish were gone, that is to say, they were hidden in the crowd. Now the fishing got really lively. There were soon three lines in use, and one fish after the other was pulled up. They were big, fat codfish, three or four feet and fat as — well, I have a person in mind, but I do not think is appropriate to compare this person with a gaping cod. Hermann was standing amidships and I was standing by his side to watch both the man and the fish, and sometimes I tried to pull, but it was wasted energy, as I got tired after a few tugs — that cod was a strong fighter! I soon gave room for the farmers who surrounded us — I couldn't help it, I had to tell them that they must not stand on top of me! I sat, reading, down in the living room for a little while, but then I had to go back up to see if the fish were still stupid enough to let themselves be caught, but I'm sure they were having a nap, as the fishermen were standing, sleepy, with their lines in the water and no biting to liven them up. The farmers had gone to have their dinner, later than usual, but they soon sprang to their feet again, as the fish started biting. The farmer from the mountains had never seen so many fish, he said, "And there's no trout as big as he was!" "The captain can't fish with this one and a little bit more," some highly educated farmer said to the captain, showing him a _ _ _ !¹⁹⁷ "How many fathoms would you say that line there is?" the capt. said. "Oh, it's a couple of fathoms, and then I've got another one here that's ten fathoms" "There are thirty-four fathoms to the bottom here," the captain said, "so you would have to make at least twice as much before you can use it, but by then we'll probably have sailed." The farmer immediately started making a new line out of sail thread and he got his line finished incredibly fast, and soon bait and jig were on and the line was in the water, and to the great joy of the emigrants, another fisherman soon joined in. It was getting very wet and slippery to windward where they were standing, so I went for a walk on the lee side. Every now and then I found myself watching all the funny expressions when a big fish was thrown onto the deck. But what is that? Both long faces on the spectators and a little laughter — affected obviously — from the fisherman, a cry, "Oh no! This must have been the biggest fish we've seen, and then it fell off again!" A big, beautiful cod had taken off again just as it was pulled out of the water, and it had taken half of the gear in its escape.

After having watched the faces for a bit, I went back downstairs again, bringing with me a pretty farmer girl, Margit,¹⁹⁸ whom H. and I had thought about taking as our maid. I spoke to her and then I engaged a maid — for the very first time — if only I am lucky with this one! I pretended not to know too much about her, but I said that I knew she was alone and that she did not have anyone to support her, and if I could do her a favor by engaging her, then I would do it. "Thank you so much" — we talked to each other for a little bit, and then that case was settled.

The fishery lasted until about 5 p.m., when the sails were hoisted and we had dinner. I guess it was envy speaking when I had my walk on deck, when a man said, "I think we should be sailing soon. That would be a lot better!" "Well, I don't really think so, the little wind we have is contrary, so we can still lie to for a while yet!"

The fish tasted really good for dinner, but then we haven't had fresh fish since we were at Doggersbanken and had a big, dry flounder, which didn't taste as good as the cod did today. But then today it's been an entire month since the last time we had fresh fish. Back then, our mouths had only been without this delicacy for eight days. Catching sixty-nine big fish in five hours has to be considered a successful fishery.

June 27 — We salted the fish today, and even though the farmers were given twenty-four fish, we still had one and a half barrels salted, proof of how big the catch was. Our fishermen, especially Z. and H., naturally, still have marks in their hands from the heavy fish they pulled up. H. has even gotten an infection in both of his forefingers, and he has bandages on them. They tried fishing today as well, as the still weather is lasting, but the ship has left the good fishing spot and the attempts were not met with success.

July 1851

July 1[199] — This has been quite a lively start of the month, at least as far as the weather and wind are concerned. After several days of still weather, we got several days with near gale from the west, contrary to our course, and today we have near gale coming from the northeast. With all sails filled we went out of the two-hundred-mile radius from New York, and now we're 170-180 miles away from the same place, according to our observations. We have said good-bye to the fishing banks and also to our ocean friends, the whales. "Good-bye!" The last ones are seldom found in the areas we are now entering, and we won't be followed any more by the daring dolphins that have been playing around *Columbus*, on board which the fishermen have not been few — some even used their guns to tease them a little. They couldn't do anything else.

While we had the breeze from the west on the 27th, I was sitting down here, busy with my needlework (which I have not worked much on at all) and all of a sudden I heard cries and noise from the deck. I thought there was an iceberg in sight and ran upstairs, but I was surprised to see live fire! However, there was no danger. The cabin chimney was burning, but with a lot of sweeping and a few buckets of water, the fire was soon out and the pipe swept. Yesterday, the 30th, was Grandmother's birthday, and I guess the family was gathered at Uranienborg, assuming that we would be in New York. It was my guess; before we left I guessed that we would have arrived on that day. Dinner ma'am? After the meal was over — I have to add that today we ate caraway soup with fried eggs!! Not two hundred miles from New York, and getting this food from Norwegian sources — not canned, I should say, that is worth noting! It was good, and could it be the last greenery from Norway we will see in a very long time. We still have a grouse and fish cakes left, but canned.

July 2 — So, today I'm spending my birthday on the Atlantic Ocean. Certainly this day — this morning — has not been without joy for me, but I don't have time to write now. I'm going upstairs to see the flags being run up in my honor! I have been visiting my siblings today; their portraits are greeting me, just like Agnes's and Anne Marie's.

July 3 — Because of close-hauled wind, we have to keep a SW course — bad wind, in other words — whereas we had both good wind and beautiful weather yesterday, and warm — the warmest day of our entire journey so far. The sun was shining and there were a lot of other strange things taking place that in a moment will be written down so that I can remember them in my old days, God willing. I guess it was about six o'clock in the morning yesterday, when, after having slept quite peacefully all night, I opened my eyes — wide awake. I was certain that it had to be late, as there was no sleep in my eyes, and the friendly light from the sun made its way through the little round window above my head. But since everybody else was so quiet and I could hear the distinct snoring from my neighbors, I didn't want to get up, and took out my usual morning book on the ship — the New Testament. I brought it out from beneath the headboard and read the last chapters of Luke. I thought a little bit about what I had read, about the birthday, etc., when H. woke up and gave me a birthday kiss. We took a little nap again, but we were awakened by a loud crack — and another one — it was the cannon. Now we were encouraged to get up, we dressed quickly and went in to the living room — two more shots — so powerful that two of the windows in the hatch fell down on the table! This, however, did not interrupt Z.'s and the captain's congratulations, while the two fiddlers were playing lively *Halling* tunes on the deck, where the farmers flocked around them, looking down at us, as we had each our glass of eggnog to our mouths. H. and I had the Norwegian flag draped above our heads like a curtain, and they drank toasts to me with their eggnog. And just as if the fiddlers knew about my patriotic mind, they started playing "*Hvor herlig er mitt fødeland.*"[200] I was really touched by all this fuss, but I was embarrassed when I went up on deck to thank the fiddlers and saw four flags above my head, and heard the lot of farmers giving me a three–times-three "hurrah." They seemed as embarrassed as I did, nodding to them. I guess we were thinking the same thing, that I did not deserve any hurrah. After talking a little bit with a few of them I went down to fix my clothes and my hair a bit, but mostly my thoughts, as they were a bit messy after all this fuss. That was when I went to visit my siblings, who probably cannot imagine that I could get such a cheerful morning greeting as the one I got today at 10 a.m. in the middle of the Atlantic. I have never had such a greeting before, and will never get it again, but both past and future have and hopefully will contribute to a more content heart.

When I came back on deck after a while, I saw the flags still waving in the fresh wind, and I had to tell the captain that "you have been honoring me for too long now!" — he claimed that he had not, and let them hang there until late afternoon, when nobody would be on deck until sunset. The evening was spent in pleasant conversation, cards, grog and, for my part, sketching the room, until ten-thirty, when I thanked the captain and Ziiølner for their nice preparations and surprises. It really made me happy, because it was a proof that they had nothing against me; otherwise they would not have gone out of their way to be so nice to me. I said good night with a faithful handshake. I have to add that H. wanted to serve me grouse, but the man who canned it had given us an inedible bird, and H. had to serve green peas and meat patties, plus some good wine. Z. gave me *Aal's Memoirs.* I expected to get *Birkedal's Sermons* from H., but I ended up with a long nose, and I didn't get the book I really wanted, but I guess H. will give it to me when he is done with it.

I guess it was around midnight, when we were all interrupted in our usual pleasant conversation down here. The Captain was called up on deck, there was a humming sound heard astern. Everyone, Linka too, out of the lounge; I almost tripped on the steep stairs. The captain's trained ears immediately recognized the humming: "It's a steamer." It was not good news, though — with the darkness and thick fog. Out with the bullhorn and the flare. The strange but clear sound from the bullhorn, and the bright light from the flare, served their purpose, and soon we heard a bell ringing. It was a signal from the steamer. There was silence for a while now — we could hear the sound coming closer, but there was nothing to see, the fog made sure of that. We weren't so sure that the flare could be seen, but it was still lit once more, and the captain stood on the deckhouse, waving it, while the mate sounded our harmonious instrument. Now the humming was at our side, and now it was in front of us, not the slightest breath of wind in our sails, so it didn't take the steamer long to pass us. Just for fun, the Mate sounded the bullhorn in the air pipe to the farmers' room, which of course disturbed their snoring and started a discussion down there about what this could be. Now, at 1 or 2 a.m., we're going to bed.

July 5, Saturday — I'm barely able to scribble down a few words today. Yesterday it was completely impossible because of the storm; nothing was possible except reefing in our sails. Yesterday evening, however, I was able to get up on deck where the new moon shone beautifully and lit up the different groups of people who had come out of their rooms, chased out by the heat. I don't think it could have been any better for them out there, though, as the wind was humid and warm and not refreshing at all. I was standing with my face toward the wind, watching the sea, the dark, green-black sea. One single strip was lit by the moon and the stars above my head, and the cloudy horizon was illuminated by lightning flashes in quick succession. I have never seen anything like that ever, but even though it was beautiful, I still prayed to God that the lightning would keep its distance. I went to bed around midnight, with the thought of being awakened by fire from lightning and thunder in my head. I was not feeling well, though, so I blamed the humid air for my condition.

This is the warmest day we have had since we left Norway. America's sun is greeting us now, which is good, but it did not have to bring the wind along. We have had so much contrary wind on our journey that we would really like to have some good wind at the end, but it doesn't seem like we're going to get it — God is trying our patience and punishing our impatience. According to our own observations, we are seventy or eighty miles away from New York. We tried to make sure of this by signaling to a ship headed toward us that we wanted to come on board. The ship ran up its flag. It was English, but it didn't bother to meet us, which was why we complained about it, saying, "It's really unusual to give a signal of hailing and not be accepted; but when it happens it's usually such a big …… Englishman that's to blame!" I am amazed that they aren't too ashamed to show us their flag.

July 6, Sunday — The loveliest weather in the world, but the little wind we had was contrary. It was so warm and humid that I had to find my cotton stockings. After the service we had a baptism. Our church was large, with a wonderful azure vault, but our congregation was small; however, there were enough witnesses for little Anne Olafsdatter's baptism. She was the little one born only a few days after our departure, and as we are approaching a land where there is such a great confusion as to religions, I do not believe this was an irresponsible way to officiate a baptism. I had the great honor of carrying the child. The minister's wife has already begun her mission. Little Anne got a Mexican silver coin as a present. Her parents were so happy that I wanted to carry their little screamer, but I really thought it was a lot of fun, and I was so happy that they asked me to do this. H. was wearing a cassock today. The water is 21.5 degrees; it was only 18 degrees in the shade, but it was 26 degrees in the sun. A big flag stretched out above our heads served as a parasol today.[201]

July 8 — The loveliest weather in the world and <u>GOOD WIND</u>, but, afraid that it might change, we have not dared to talk about it. Six — six sailing ships have been sighted today. There is dancing on board tonight. Yesterday we had terrible weather and contrary wind — bad showers, and lightning last night. All preparations for storm were made onboard, and we were sailing with our sails reefed, but the good God spared us from the storm. I was sitting down here in the sofa with my sketchbook and a light in front of me — the men were upstairs. During a powerful shower, the sails were slatted, but there was no danger since the wind was only a light breeze and only the smaller sails were hoisted. I prayed to God and felt very calm, but when I opened my eyes after being in deep thought and a bright zig-zag of lightning was flashing toward me, I got this strange feeling — almost sad. I kept on drawing and went to bed at about eleven or twelve at night. The weather was still not stormy, and tonight we never got a storm, either. We sounded yesterday, and after two unsuccessful attempts, we hit the bottom. However, our calculations seem to put us ahead of where we really are, as by our estimations, we should have about fifty miles left, but there is probably more than that. I wish we could hail someone!

How beautiful the Atlantic can be, and such beautiful evenings it has to offer! I just came down from the deck, which was lit by the clear but melancholy and pale light from the moon. However, the atmosphere was anything but melancholy — they're dancing *Halling* and *gangar* up there, the fiddle has sounded cheerfully for a couple of hours. Now there are other figures in the moonlight: six couples, girls, are dancing *Springdans* — I watch them — dream myself away to Norwegian mountains where I sit down to rest on a little rock, the dancers dancing on a green meadow in front of me. But no, away with all dreams — the captain's words, "Full sails, mate!" soon wake me up and the real world has no Norwegian mountains, no green spots. I can see nothing but the ship, the sky, and the sea. The dancers no longer amuse me. I come down here, thinking about my Norway and all the dear ones there.

July 9, Momma's birthday — We got a pilot on board between eleven and noon today, which proved that our estimates are not wrong, as assumed yesterday. We are not astern of them, and according to the pilot we have about forty Norwegian miles[202] left — which means that our journey is soon over. Good God, you have led us all this way across the sea, be our guide also on this last part! But the pilot — is that what Americans are like, so arrogant and pompous? The pilot came on board more like dandy than a real sea dog, like I think they ought to be. That is how I have seen them in my country, and I like them better when they come with their simple clothes and shirts than as a man dressed in fancy clothes, with — oh well, the clothes should not really matter, I don't want to judge all Americans based on their clothes. The pilot might be a good man, especially if he brings good wind with him, so that we'll be in New York by dinnertime tomorrow. Our poultry was slaughtered today. I really wanted to bring them with me to Spring Prairie, but I could not, so now I guess I will have to try to get a Norwegian egg hatched, an egg the hen gave us after her death.

July 10, Thursday — Today, exactly seven weeks after we left Norway, we're approaching New Y. by leaps and bounds. We only have a few miles left, and if the wind doesn't shift and the fog doesn't get any thicker, we might be there in a few hours. Several pilot boats have hailed us, and they have been so close we were able to watch the people on board, among them a black cook — a Negro. The farmers took him for the devil himself — "he isn't really black either — he looks like a cat that's not really clean" — their comparisons. We have seen land since seven o'clock this morning. I am not looking forward to going ashore, although I shall be glad to have solid ground beneath my feet again. I have had a strange anxiety about me yesterday and today, and I don't know what to do about it.

July 16 — I already feel like an inhabitant of New York — and what have I been doing since the last time I wrote? It was in the afternoon, around four or five, on the 10th of July. We anchored off Staten Island, after tacking in toward the harbor through storm, thunder, and lightning. We didn't see such squalls during the entire journey as the ones America greeted us with. In one moment, all sails were down, still the ship tilted terribly to one side. Thunder and lightning and terrible showers — it was awful, but we didn't have time to get scared. We could see land, and that took all of our attention! Seeing land again after seven weeks had to make us happy, and we thanked our Heavenly God from the bottom of our hearts for having led us to land and brought us safely across the sea. What would we do without You, my God, sinful creatures as we are!

It was not a warm welcome America gave us. It was as if the wind from the west, which has bothered us far too often on our way, and the mighty storm were America's way of showing her strength to see if we could resist it, as if she wanted to push us away from her. It didn't matter that Norway gave us wind from the South as soon as we raised anchor; we didn't turn back, even if she hated to let us go. It didn't matter that America gave us wind from the west; she couldn't push us away — no, nothing is as strong as Your will, God Father! When You are with us, what can be against us? You, great, good ruler and creator of the world, without whose will a leaf does not fall to the ground! All our gratitude goes to You, who has led all of us — 169 people[203] — back to land, our thanks to You are sincere and of a grateful heart. Oh, are we such evil creatures that this word, "sincere," might be false? Oh no, no, we cannot be that selfish — our hearts are moved, they stammer out a grateful prayer to You. Oh, hear it, oh Father, out of your mercy for Christ's sake!

It was surprising — amazing — to watch the numerous ships sailing out of and tacking into the harbor, all sails were furled in a hurry, and there we were like plucked chickens; soon a shower was over, one or two sails were hoisted, just to be furled again when the next shower came, but the country! It was beautiful, a really pretty seaward approach, but how surprised I was — the field was cut, and in only a few places were the haystacks still there. In other places, they had been taken in; how the animals there must enjoy themselves! The farmers were feeling a bit better after every shower, and were gathered together with us to observe and wonder about all the new things. Now the anchor is dropped. "Captain, thank you, thank you for having brought us safely ashore!" I said to him, taking his hand to a trusty handshake. Our pilot was sitting in an armchair, commanding. I did not like him. He left the deck with the custom's officer who had come on board, and I did not say good-bye to him. We were not allowed to go ashore, just as nobody was allowed to come to us, but an emigrant swindler still sneaked onboard, trying to talk the captain into becoming an accomplice, but in that he failed. <u>Falkenberg</u>, our captain, is not a man to accept such injustice; with contempt, the swindler was shown off the ship.

Now the doctor came, and from him, we got permission to go ashore. The captain, Z., Hermann, and I rowed to Staten Island to look around for a while. As we came ashore, the doctor gave us oranges, which he presented to me through his window as we passed his house. The captain had told him I was a minister's wife; that was nice of the man. When we were going back on board, we were delayed by thunder, lightning, and showers for an hour and a half, so it was midnight before we were able to get back onboard. That night three crewmen ran away, and they stole *Columbus*'s best boat — such rabble! Since that night, the captain and the mate have relieved each other on watch to make sure nobody else runs away. Still, there have been several attempts. On Friday the 11th, we took a steamer to New York after having gone in one of the rowboats to Staten Island. The captain was immediately surrounded by agents from different offices. Soon we were standing on the wharf in New Y. But how empty and sad!, in spite of the crowd and the noise surrounding us on all sides, making it impossible to breathe. Empty and sad because there was not a single face I knew, not one single person except for shouting peddlers and salesmen, who, breathing heavily, exhausted from business, found their place in an omnibus which would take them to the office as fast as possible. I went to the exchange and consul's offices today, too, where I met several countrymen. We had a "table d'haute" dinner at some Danes'. But, oh my, was I tired and dizzy when we got back to *Columbus* in the evening! My traveling companions got a description of New Y. from me, which was not very flattering. One of the farmers who had come ashore with a bunch of the other farmers, helped me in my description as he exclaimed, "And you should have seen their horses — big, black beasts they are, but do you know what? They have white and red covers on their ears!" By this he meant — I guess I could also call it a cover — a net into which the entire horse had been put, with finery and fringes, protecting the horse from flies — horseflies. Working horses and equipage horses used this; some had straps across their back and tassels by their ears. We were used to life on the ship, being together with common farmers, whose only noise consisted of singing, dancing, and a bit of chatting as they crossed the deck with their pails of food and frying pans on their way from the galley to their room. So after having heard nothing but these sounds, together with the roaring sea, the whistling of the wind, the pipe, and the words of command on the ship for seven weeks, no wonder I was glad to be back on *Columbus* after experiencing the noise from uncountable carriages, horses, and people creating an incredible racket, crossing all the streets and everything. Sometimes we had to wait at corners fifteen minutes to be able to cross the street. And if we wanted to spend that time talking to each other, we had to yell at the top of our lungs, and still we could seldom hear what the other one said.

In the harbor you can find traces of the same rush that the city is so marked by. Numerous smaller and bigger steamers are in the rush of business, going back and forth between Staten Island and New York, yes, from several of the surrounding islands — Hoboken, Jersey, Long Island. Several transported people only, of which there were plenty, even though a ship would arrive at the same harbor every half hour, others had gotten hold of ships with crews which they directed in or out of the harbor. Ships are sailing in and out day and night, and many neatly built sloops, schooners, brigs, etc. passed us daily when we were living on *Columbus* in the harbor. Emigrant ships anchored up right at our side, and driven by flood tide and ebb tide, we greeted each other.

Just as out in the harbor there is a lot of confusion, the same describes the city's trains, omnibuses, carriages, and wagons. Having seen all this, I am not surprised that people who live their daily lives in this noise and mess look like they suffer from tuberculosis — yes, to me it is striking how unhealthy everybody looks. The women look like china dolls that would fall over if you breathed on them, and the men are long, pale creatures, whose fragile pelican legs threaten to break off at every step they take, and what will happen to them when they bend down to help a woman? For when they get the chance, the American shows himself as a gentleman; the women are highly regarded and have great power.

On Sunday, July 13, we went to a remarkably pretty church, where the lovely tunes from the choir, and the singers' beautiful hymns, made a very pleasant impression, but the service was in English, and the ceremonies the Episcopal church's own, so I was not edified any more than I understood them. Sometimes there was a strange humming in the church — it was the congregation repeating the last lines of a prayer spoken from the pulpit. Many people were sleeping, by the way.

All emigrants, ourselves included, had to leave the ship on Monday the 14th. Our last greeting was a "hurray" as an answer to that of the crew. I was quite moved when the steamer took us away from the now-so-dear ship and crew — a tear tried to make its way out, but away with you, you traitor of the heart! There was such a racket when we arrived at the wharf where the steamer lay that was to take our farmers to Albany. Quarrelling, noise, and fuss! I took a bunch of loose things and started walking through rows of dockworkers, men in shirts, horses, and wagons, leaving H. with one of our big chests that was broken, and Z. arguing with a swindler who demanded half a dollar ($) for having lifted our little suitcase onto a wagon. I walked through several streets, searching everywhere for the name of our hotel — finally "Scandinavia Hotel" — I went inside and went our rooms and then Z. came with the wagon. Another quarrel — the man did not want to leave the wagon until he had gotten twice what it was supposed to cost, but the captain and Z. protested, and the swindler was disappointed this time.

It's awful here, though. I don't trust a single person here, except for a few. It's awful having to be so suspicious all the time, although it is necessary. This is New York and the way they do it here, showing strangers hospitality by fooling them. We have once more been out on *Columbus*, spent the night there, and now said good-bye to both the ship and its crew. The captain and both mates got a little something to remember us by, and when I came up here, there was a *platmenage*[204] waiting, a present from the Captain for H. and me. I got a mustard spoon from Ziiølner. I was very embarrassed, and the captain, who came ashore with us, was embarrassed, too, but soon he had to leave us, and we were all quite emotional when we bid each other farewell. I had gotten to know the captain — he had a loveable character. I was fond of him, and when he now said good-bye to us, I felt farther away than ever from everyone I had left behind, as I saw him and our ship leave us. He had, by his obliging manner, saved H. and me from all kinds of the journey's inconveniences, which we did not notice at all, and he brought us safely across, away from everything dear. As one person, H. and I watched him leave. Norway had seemed closer as long as we were surrounded by familiar faces and traveling companions, but now we turned around and saw nobody, nobody, except for strangers. Ziiølner stood by our side, our faithful traveling companion and friend; he also wanted to stay with us now.

July 28, Monday, Muskego parsonage — At 7 a.m. last Monday, July 21, we traveled by steamer to Albany. The trip through the Hudson River was hot, but pretty. The scenery on both sides of the river was beautiful, but monotonous. In the end I got bored, and when we went ashore at five in the afternoon, I was relieved to get away from the extreme luxury and the formality of the American aristocracy. I walked with H. and Z. behind the cart that was to bring both our luggage and us to the railroad. Soon we were rolling away in the steam-driven wagon, but this speed scared me a little bit at the start, and it annoyed me too, as sparks came in through the windows, burning holes in our clothes. We traveled the entire night, sleeping a little bit in spite of the shaking, scraping, and squeaking, and arrived at Buffalo at 9:30 a.m. We put in at the "Niagara Hotel," where we had our two broken chests repaired. Maybe they were broken because they were angry about being separated from the rest of our things, which had been sent on the canal with our maid, Margit, in the care of her and the rest of the farmers. We had breakfast, and took the noon train to Niagara Falls! It was big and beautiful, yes, but it did not make such a great impression on me as I wanted this famous attraction to make.[205] We were by the waterfall for one, two, or three hours, drank of its sunburned water, went down again on the railroad and got tickets for the steamer. The three of us walked around for a bit — strangers in this city as in all cities here — to find the ticket office — there it is! — lucky — we have tickets. We had been onboard the steamer and gotten a cabin. At seven, it was back onboard; we were to leave at eight, but it got to be eight, nine, ten, and eleven before the steamer left. It had gotten a telegram saying that it had to wait for some train passengers — it was so boring to wait, and several times I exclaimed, "The steamers in Norway were never so unpunctual!"

Through the entire night, morning and part of the afternoon we steamed away on the big lake, and at 5 or 6 p.m., we reached Detroit. I bought some lemonade in a bar — H. was with me. The bartender tried to cheat us, but we had gotten so good at speaking English and at math, so he had a long nose — then quick, to the train. It's already moving —

Part Two — 1849-1851 · 245

oh, now I'm in my seat with H. at my side and Z. right across from us. We just made it! The entire night on the train — 4 a.m. at New Buffalo. Once more on a steamer, steaming away, 10 a.m. in Chicago! Now we followed the coastline the entire day, stopped in several smaller places and at 9 p.m., in terrible lightning, we arrived in Milwaukee! Now we had reached the second goal of our journey. Here, as in New York, we were received by terrible thunder and lightning. We were glad to go ashore, but what kind of joy was that — surrounded by strangers, not one familiar face to spot, not one familiar voice to hear, but — that's a Norwegian! Yes, there are two, three, four; soon we were at the hotel, having a long talk with the Norwegians we'd met, who had come to the wharf to meet us. Night came and good night! H. and I threw suspicious looks at our bed as we crawled into it — are we really going to have a good night in this? It looks so alive! Trusting our tiredness from the journey to help us fall asleep, we went to bed, but the light by the bedside often crackled when we put a variety of bugs into it. It got to be three in the morning, and even though we had been killing seven different kinds of insects, our bed seemed more and more alive. We were disgusted and preferred to get up. We each spent the rest of the night on our chairs, but our legs were often covered with strange, brown dots.

It was a terrible night, and I was happy in the morning when we found ourselves in a buggy — a type of wagon — which would help bring us to Muskego parsonage, to Pastor Stub's.[206] We drove a few English miles the wrong way, so we didn't get there until six in the evening. But it was nice and cozy there, just like I had imagined a little parsonage in America, maybe even a little nicer. The pastor's wife received us with a happy face, a bit embarrassed, though. The minister was not at home. They had not gotten H.'s letter in which we thanked them for the invitation and said that Z. would come along. I asked her if she had room for all of us, and her smiling answer lifted a stone from my heart. I went out into the little garden, picked a mignonette, and gave one to H. It was the first flower taken and enjoyed in America — it cheered us up. God, let this joy from the flowers in the fields be a good sign for joy in our hearts later!

On Sunday Hermann preached here[207] — we went to church. It is the smallest church I have ever been to: no steeple, no clock, no altarpiece, no chasuble. But otherwise, the service was like services in Norway. I was annoyed at the farm girls — well, some of them were dressed like ladies. Seeing them sitting there with their fans, I did not look over at them, but I could still see it. Still, some of them had some of the good old Norwegian stuff in them. Among those I would place the one who came over to H. and me with a trustworthy face and offered a solid handshake, welcoming us to America. There was also something at church that made us angry — we met some Norwegians who were members of the <u>Frankean-Lutheran Congregation Sect</u>.[208] They were going to their school to hear one of their elected pastors. Poor, blindfolded people! How can you let yourselves be deceived like this, leaving your childhood religion, that so clearly bears witness of the truth!

Hermann went into town today to see if Margit and the rest of our luggage had arrived, and to get some things for our house. Hermann — how sad you made me today! You can no longer remember what you promised me — not to leave me like this until we had reached our home at Spring Prairie. How could you forget what you promised me? How can you, who do not understand anything about what a household needs, go to town to shop? When you, in an impatient voice, ask me about each little thing I have written down that we need, if this is really necessary, and one time you even said that I do not consider the amount of money we have. This has made me sad. H. has shown me distrust I didn't expect, and he has made me indifferent as to what he does and doesn't do. He can buy whatever he wants and what he finds necessary. My Hermann! My conscience tells me that I have not written down or asked for more than things that even you have to realize are completely necessary. And if you had told me that we should wait until times get better for this and that, you could have chosen a better way of letting me know. You have achieved nothing by doing what you have done. You have shown no love, only a great self-confidence — God forgive me if I am wrong in this!

Linka's trip to Niagara Falls

There are four extant pages describing this trip. The first page begins "2 /" and the last page ends in mid-sentence.

Here one easily gets dizzy. It is hard to believe that these two great waterfalls fall down in different directions; I wonder where the river ends. "That is more than I would know," I said, but our guide reminded us that the flood splits and each arm falls down to a waterfall. There the eastern arm has seen a little more, thus the little arm stole Iris's nose and out of that made a little beautiful island, Luna. This arm falls down from the same height as the two others. The first fall has the poetic name — yes?? — the two large falls are called "Horseshoe" and "Hog's Tail" / "Hog's Back," or was it "Bull's Head?" The names are not important, though; one can picture them from their descriptions.

However, we were standing there in awe, staring at the waterfalls the same way as the immigrants nowadays stare at the red-panted Zouaves who walk around in the streets.[209] We have to be polite and not stand here for too long, remembering that there is another large group of people who wants to take the same trip as we are on. Thus, we soon started marching again, along the dock, and up a steep hill. When we reached the top, Papa took out two glasses of wine and what is better: cake. So, we had cake and wine in front of us,  Niagara with mountains and forest in the background, and young and old, beautiful and less beautiful people around us. All of them were dressed elegantly, some sitting in a tent, talking cheerily, drinking wine and eating — cake, grapes, peaches, pears and apples — while others were continuously parading along, breathing heavily and waving, talking more seriously. Some were scrambling or jumping enthusiastically to and from the tower. With all this around us, how good the refreshments tasted! Now, when picturing this image in my mind, I instantly feel more awake and alert.

It's four o'clock, and time for a quick visit to "Luna." A few fifty stairs down through the mountain led us to a little stream, over which there is a narrow (only room for two people next to each other) bridge to "Luna." There is a view almost like in the moonlight here on this charming island, with small beds of flowers, benches, and a grove. Maybe not, since the sun is shining too brightly, and we have to find a place in the shade to get some rest. Dulliz does not have much time; if we want to take the Canada path, we'd better get going. Again we cross the bridge. Imagine this: a husband and wife are crossing the bridge with their child. The husband lifts the child up and lightheartedly holds it over the railing. God punishes the lighthearted man severely; he loses the grip of the child's clothes, the waterfall is right there and envelops the child. The father jumps after it in despair. I can't recall if the mother jumped, too. How terrible.

Afterward, we had a remarkable trip. We wanted to get down under the waterfall. A tower is built right by the rock wall, and long, long, winding stairs take us down. We are standing almost under the waterfall now; how it roars, it is almost impossible to hear what another person says. We have to move away a little so we don't get soaking wet. Oh, how beautiful, how tremendous! The depression in the wall is so deep, created by the dust, rain, and splatter of the water that continuously hit the rock. It's possible to go in there, but first you have to go up to the house of the old man who sits by the foot of the tower. There you can rent rain clothes for a couple of dollars, and thus go under the waterfall into the depression and out on the other side. However, the walk is considered risky, and we did not do that. We would not have seen more anyway. The waterfall is only little Bull's Head plunging down between Iris and Luna, but from down here it seems so big. Hog's Back is also here next to it; they both make a deafening noise and an overwhelming impression. There is a story about an Indian who was a traveler's guide. He also came to this place, where he got so excited that he threw his dearest belonging, his pipe, in the waterfall, shouting, "The Great Spirit who created this, to you I sacrifice my pipe." What nonsense.

Time flies — we have to go up the stairs again. If it weren't five o'clock soon, I would have told you about all the beautiful views from …

July 29 — The little lake right outside the house allows us to go rowing quite often. Today we went to a little island, which was so overgrown and bushy that I can't imagine there have been other human beings there before, except for an Indian or two.

In the afternoon we went to visit a farmer. It was quite fun. They served us coffee and cake (good). These were decent people, but then it is the most decent family Stub knows among all the Norwegians here, and all the ministers like them. They were happy to have us, and they congratulated us for having made it here. I left them hoping that I would find families like theirs in Spring Prairie.

The Spring Prairie parsonage

Part Three

A New Life in America

(1851 – 1864)

Linka's sketch of the Spring Prairie parsonage

August 1851

Koshkonong Parsonage[210] — *August* 9,
Saturday — The first thought that came to my mind when I wrote down the date above was that tomorrow is Kalla's birthday, and a few days ago, the 3rd, it was little Rosa's. God bless you — stay with Him, our faithful support and guide, and you shall be happy!!

This morning Hermann left for Spring Prairie; he is giving his installation sermon there tomorrow, and then in the three sister parishes[211] Monday and Tuesday. I'm not worried about him, and why is that? It's not that I have such a great faith in his knowledge, but I have faith in You, God. I come to You with prayer that Your spirit may live in him, that he may speak Your word with frankness and joy in his heart and on his tongue! I believe You have heard my prayer, O Father in Heaven, therefore I am calm, and my heart is filled with true gratefulness for being able to pray and talk with You. Yes, Lord Christ, your love is eternal, let me truthfully feel how good you are to me and let me show my gratitude in thoughts, words and action!

So, now Hermann is at our parsonage, or not exactly there — as it is not done yet, he's in a neighboring house where we'll stay until our own is done. But he has seen our parsonage, seen our home. I long to get there, and get things settled; I'm excited about the day when our belongings that have been brought from Milwaukee with four oxen will arrive—in five or six days, I guess. I've been kind of annoyed lately, because we couldn't get all our things up there earlier. I've been angry with my husband and told him that he has not exactly gone out of his way to get everything up there as soon as possible. He didn't seem to care when we would arrive at our home — a week sooner or later didn't matter to him. But there is more than one reason for me to long for it, and I can't be indifferent about it. The main reason for this is that our present hostess, Mrs. Engel Preus[212] is ill, and would prefer not to have strangers in her house right now. I can't stand being a burden to other people, and I will thank God when I will say good-bye to Koshkonong for now. When Mrs. Engel gets well, we would like to gather here again, maybe for a godparent's feast!

We left Muskego on Friday, August 1, and at about nine-thirty in the evening went into an American — a "Yankee" — tavern. Our maid, Margit, was with us, and her simplemindedness resulted in many a good laugh that evening, especially when we were having supper. She was eating at our table; it was really enjoyable, even though Margit might have preferred to eat by herself. For the Yankees, watching a farm girl from Telemark in her national costume was like seeing a clown. She was not used to knife and fork, but used her fingers, and helped herself to food without being ashamed. She also participated in the conversation, saying that she "spoke American" knowing that "*ja*" means "yes" and "*nei*" means "nix."[213] There was nothing impertinent or arrogant about her; she only had these faithful, mountain-girl manners, making both us and herself laugh. She, Ziiølner, H., and I spent the night there, in the same room — the night which was only a few hours long, as we got up early to continue our journey.

We arrived here at Koshkonong about 6 or 7 p.m., in rainy weather. We were unexpected and it was a dismal <u>first</u> impression, but the weather was dismal too. I met a third minister's wife here, Mrs. Dietrichson.[214] She, her husband, and four children came here this summer too. They have gone to their parsonage now, Rock Prairie[215] — she seems nice. We bought a big, beautiful brindle cow, my favorite color of cows, for ten dollars ($). It is the first living part of our household we have ever bought. I hope that our next purchase of the same thing will not be as old. Because it's my first cow, and because my little sister Agnes loves cows, it shall be named Agnes.

How are you now, dear siblings? I long to hear from you <u>about everyone!</u> How harsh you are, having me wait this long! I've written letters twice, and one of them has probably arrived now. During my stay here, I've had to admit the truth in the old saying, "Even the worst is good for something." Even though I don't like staying here for this long, it allows Margit to learn a little bit by helping a new maid who works here. They're both new, so neither embarrasses the other. Still, Margit is learning a little bit from the trained city girl.

I wrote to our captain on *Columbus* today — Falkenberg. Both H. and Z. were supposed to write, but then they didn'; they both caught the procrastinator virus. H. did not like what I wrote; he said he would write on Tuesday, though I did not dare to trust this. I know H. too well when it comes to letter writing, so I sent my letter to St. John's. It is now midnight on this hemisphere or on this point of the earth, but not in Norway, where it already is six in the morning. You are going to work now, strollers are enjoying the beautiful summer morning — but it is

Sunday, so there are also workers among all the people strolling along the roads, as they flee from the city to replace the city air with pure country air, spending their Sunday with relatives in the country. Later on, different roads and streets will be definitely more crowded than usual, as people are going to church to hear God's word! As I am now going to bed, I say good morning to you and good night to myself! H.: good night to you! You have not been away from me for this long since we were married.

August 11, Monday — What an evening! After Mrs. Engel and I had ended our evening walk out on the porch, watching the sunset, the moonrise, the stars being lit, and the moths above our heads, we went into the living room to make the last evening hours pass quickly with needlework and chatting. But we didn't sit at the table for very long! — Cockroaches and spiders kept falling from the ceiling and walls, attracted by the lights on the table. How are we going to get rid of them? We put our chairs in the middle of the floor and sat down, making sure our skirts weren't touching the floor, but ouch, there's one falling, and another one and yet another one from the walls! I have to get up to kill! My legs have never been as vicious killers as they were tonight, but it is so awful with all these insects, I shudder every time I kill one, but... I wish I were a dear friend of theirs!![216]

September 1851

September ?, 1851, Thursday[217]

Living room — Spring Prairie Parsonage.

These are the first lines I am writing in my diary since I arrived here, the destination of the journey from Norway — from home to home! What an important name — home — we use it so often during our life in this world, but do we have a home? Is there any place here where we shall always live, from which we shall not be moved, from which moving would be impossible? No, no, this place does not exist on earth. The place where we pitiful human beings, who should be considered wandering workers, travelers in complete darkness who are only waiting for the light so that we can take the right way, here chose to call home, is not really such, it is merely a temporary place of residence. But our home — our righteous, true home — oh, happy creatures we are, children of mercy! It is in heaven we shall see the light — where in our wandering we shall see only light and blessed radiance, and never, never twilight!

September 7, Sunday, Spring Prairie — Almost a month has passed since I last wrote in my book. That's not really a long time, but there has been a considerable change in my life since then. I am now sitting here writing, with my feet under my own table, as an old saying goes. I have a house and a home to manage, and am done with traveling. My husband and I are really enjoying ourselves in our humble home. So far we have one room to call ours — we are staying with Lars Møen, closest neighbor to the parsonage. Because the parsonage is still nothing but a basement filled with water, we can't live there. We came here on August 18th.[218] The unfinished parsonage was a depressing sight. Perhaps a tear hid my house-to-be from me, from seeing it the way it will look when it is done, with a nice interior, sometime in the future. The carriage had passed it, and my eyes saw nothing but oaks and hazel, but we soon reached Lars Møen's and the carriage stopped. Then we had to get our boxes and chests out. Ziiølner was a great help, and I also did my duty as a carpenter. Before we were unpacked, the utensils we needed for supper were done — a wooden spoon for each of us. After three days of hard work, we were finally somewhat settled. In a room of about twelve feet[219] square we have a bed, which takes up an entire wall along its side, and half a wall at the head, a painted, red table, and a sofa at its side (the sofa consists of two chests filled with clothes, and on top of these we put the pillows from my old sofa). There's a dresser at the end of the sofa, which has a cupboard on top of it. The cupboard reaches all the way to the ceiling, and all this takes up one wall. The cupboard serves as pantry, milk storage, etc., etc. Two armchairs (my treasures), a dresser, and a storage chest under the bed completes our furniture. Along the walls the bookshelf, the button case, and between those, guns, tin articles, iron, duster, paintings, steel utensils, etc., etc. We can't forget tools, etc., for the room to be full. And full it is, two people can hardly pass each other in there. We left Koshkonong on Sunday the 17th of August.[220] We made it up here in one piece, but not without incident. We took the wrong way and went from Herod to Pilate. We didn't make it to Norway Grove, where H. was giving his installation sermon at the parish, until the afternoon. In spite of this, the farmers were still gathered when we came. That made me happy, as did seeing several national costumes, so I had to break out, "Some of the old Norwegian faithfulness is still alive here in America!" We stayed with parishioners, and told them about our mishap on the way there. Our horses and carriage fell into a ditch and I had to be carried ashore. Our horses were close to sinking, but God helped us in our need, and the next day we were here at Spring Prairie.[221] Hermann and I thank the Lord. Our merciful, caring Father who has led us here is great!

October 1851[222]

October 5 — Oh, what a great few hours I've had! I've read the first letters I have gotten since I came to America. I can't say received, as I got them a couple of days ago, but I wasn't at home at the time, and I wanted to wait to read them when I could enjoy the letters from family, friends, and siblings in peace and quiet. The waiting paid off, too. Not a sound could be heard except for the melancholy sighing of the trees. This morning, after Hermann had left to visit one of the parishes — Bonnet Prairie — I sat down in my living room with a big package with letters on the table in front of me. My heart was not throbbing with curiosity or the desire to know what the letters would say, but I quite calmly opened the package, and letters, as well as some songs, shone toward me. From what was written on the envelopes, I could soon tell which Norwegian souls had shown their generosity. Even though time was valuable to me, I took the time to find the ultimate comfortable position in my armchair — and — now I was no longer at Spring Prairie, I was in Norway, wandering about between aunts and uncles, cousins and siblings, speaking seriously with them, and joking with them, hearing a lot of good things, and, thank God, very few bad things. The letters were written only a month after I left, so there was not a lot of news. But what songs had they sent? They were songs of honor, used by Scandinavian students who had been gathered in Xiania during Pentecost, when we were fighting storms in the Atlantic. They had amused young and old, but most of all themselves. If only I had a quarter of the wine those people have drunk, then my newly dug cellar would not stand empty, and every Sunday my husband would be served a glass with his meal. The glass would be filled with grape juice, though, and I suppose I would have a little myself. [223]

All my siblings have written letters to me. I have walked with them to the cemetery and laid a garland on Momma and Papa's grave. In covering their grave with flowers, we celebrate their birthday, our blessed parents, and children of our common Father! In my mind I often put flowers on their resting place, but looking up at the sky, the comforting spirit tells us — You can see us! You can see us from your home in heaven, and <u>there</u> you pray to our merciful Father for your children. My heart joins in on what my siblings are writing. What a comfort it is, knowing that the same God that guards sinful people in Norway also lets his merciful arms reach out across the world!

November 1851

November 4 — Oh my, I'm so cold! My feet are cold! These lines of the old children's song bring out memories from a time when we sang these lines each evening. It was dark outside and we sat hand-in-hand around the lively fireplace where dry spruce logs were burning and the light from the fire lit up different corners of the room. Father was walking across the floor with the youngest of us in his arms, keeping time — oh, those were wonderful days! I sang about the cold, but I think I felt just as little cold then as I feel heat now. It makes sense too — at that time an oven took care of the heating and maybe the cold was not as harsh as it is today. My walking kept me in motion, and laughter and jokes warmed a child's blood.

Here I am now, an old woman — twenty-two years old — with a serious expression on my face, sitting calmly on a chest with a pillow from a sofa on top of it, which is why we call the chest our sofa; now I let my fingers march across the sheet while the legs stay calm underneath the table, now my eyes are searching every corner of my living room, looking for an oven, but in vain. Greedy, filled with envy, they glance through a crack in the door — in there, in another living room, there is an oven, it is burning so lively — hear, hear it hum! Should I open the door? No, the people in there are talking so much, the children are crying and making noise, even though I still hear all this noise, there is a bad atmosphere coming from a room like that — cats and dogs and even a stove — no, I prefer being cold. These kind people daily encourage me to keep the door open, but I always give an evasive answer — because of the cupboard it is impossible to open it more than a little bit, and there are several cracks in the walls leading out to the yard, through which the heat would disappear, so a little opening in the door would not help all that much anyway. I'm looking forward to getting my own living room in my own house; then I'll have a fire going all the time. I've already made a plan which makes me feel less guilty about being so lazy these days, especially when it comes to sleeping late in the morning. I'm sorry about that — when I get a heated bedroom I will get up between five and six every morning, take my spinning wheel, and start spinning. Margit — my maid — will come into the same habit, and I hope to be a hardworking and decent housewife.

I think quite often about all the intellectual advantages men have as opposed to women. I'm not saying that they are more intellectual than women by nature, but that knowledge has developed their intellect to a much greater extent than what is the case with women. When she seeks to develop her intellect it is viewed as a sort of secondary matter, something useless that could never serve the world in any way — when these thoughts come to mind, I often get bitter because I find it unfair. When I feel that nature has been just as generous toward us, why should we not be allowed to develop our abilities without limitations? Nature did not give them to us only so that we could use them to salt the food and mend socks. Surely our Lord wants us to develop our abilities, though most of all to be good housewives. After all, that is our calling, and we shall and should prepare ourselves to meet this request with good conscience, piety, order, love, humility, and eagerness as our principles. I said that the development of our intellect is like a sort of secondary matter. Well, considering the turn my thoughts have taken, I come to the result that this is how it really is, too — for example, what does it take for a woman to enjoy the good reputation "she is a sensible housewife?" What we are told is to "love God and fellow human beings." Her piety must be the foundation of her entire housekeeping. In that case, it can only be good, and her role has been filled; her consciousness bears witness of that, and with a light, <u>humble</u> heart, her spirit, soul, and heart thank the Lord because He is "with her all days."

But this is like saying that our intellect is not good for anything — which is not true! When we have learned to know and love our God, and through that have gained the knowledge necessary for the formation of our spirit, which is the most important for all human beings, and through this we have also learned what our duties and life are, and acknowledged the necessity of striving to meet these expectations. Will there never be a time in one's life when it is useful to know which way the wind blows beyond our range of vision? Won't it be useful for a woman to know something about the world, its past and present history, about human beings, their customs through different times, etc., etc.?

Of course, I'm not speaking about those honorable creatures you seldom find in this world, who have given their entire life to the heavenly, and are totally beyond this earth, although they live on it. No, my thoughts relate to ordinary people, taking myself as an example. I'm sitting here, in a part of the world I don't know, among unknown people.

More than once I've been grateful that my parents let me go to school, where I learned quite a bit besides my religion. I can't claim to be such an honorable woman that I don't care about other books as long as I have my Bible. I'm afraid it happens quite often that I pick up the novel instead of the Bible, and leave the latter on the table in front of me.

I'm so old-fashioned that I have Walter Scott and Ingemann as friends, and they seem like decent people to me. I guess I can make friends with different authors, but I prefer those who stick to the true history of the world. A little bit of love can be added to some characters, like ginger or mustard. When I have one of these novels in front of me, and, with the knowledge of history I have, I'm able to put what I read into a context, I read it with much greater interest than if what I read is entirely new to me. And if I've forgotten some of the history I learned in my childhood, which occurs quite often, I'm afraid, I take a graceful step to the bookshelf and pick out Lasson's Historie, which reminds me of what I've forgotten. This might also be the case with geography and the little I know about languages.

Since I was married, I haven't had the greatest household to care for; it started here, and it doesn't take all of my time to look after one maid, one room, cook for three people, and take care of our clothes, none of which needs mending. The only task is to mend socks and iron clothes — what terrible work! Especially the shirts. I have a lot of extra time, and why shouldn't I take a book or draw away with a pencil in my sketchbook? I will not agree that it would be more useful for me to take to my needlework, or that it would be far more entertaining, rather the opposite — but the world prefers to see a woman busy with this type of work. I wonder if the majority of people seeing me with a novel wouldn't go away saying, "She takes good care of her household — we saw her reading a novel!" What if, on the other hand, they had caught me with needlework that might have been lying in my lap for hours. As I heard footsteps approaching I felt obliged to start working the thread — there might not even be a needle to it, and as the door opened I was so busy I did not even look up. My visitors would come over to me, saying, "What a contrast! Here is the personification of diligence. Even in the little time she has left over, she sits down with her needlework; while the other example we saw today was reading a novel, she probably walks around the house with it in her pocket. The love story makes her burn her porridge and forget the gravy." You terrible, back-biting world!

November 24 — As bad as you might be, "Breihøn," you got me butter today. It was the first time you've given me anything, so I'll comfort myself with the same saying as fishermen use.[224] Since it was the minister's wife herself who churned it, with a paddle she whittled herself, I hope that you'll give half a pound next time, since you only gave half that much today. I have to do some domestic work around here, so yesterday I made sacks for Ziiølner. He'll need them tomorrow, when he's taking a yoke of oxen to Koshkonong to get some rye for me.

December 1851

December 7 — What a beautiful painting I've had before my eyes now, in complete darkness — but how can I say I've had it before my eyes when I've been sitting in darkness? I guess I have to say that my imagination has visited my soul today and cheered it up with a visit to Norway, this mountainous home of mine. It led me into my newly married sister's and my brother-in-law's house, where love and happiness have found their place.[225] While the party people of Christiania are ignorant of the value of enjoying oneself in one's own home, you're sitting in peace and quiet in your living room, envious of no one, just content and happy. So how are you? In the rather simple living room, there's a sofa and an armchair, as well as a pianoforte — this may be a luxury, but acceptable. Then you have a table, and a chest with a nice clock. So when I think about it, your living room will be anything but simple, sister and brother-in-law. Be that as it may, the chairs and walls are cheered up by paintings and engravings here and there, which complete the inanimate objects. But now we get to the living parts — the interesting parts.

Let's see — are you interesting, you that I called living creatures? You're all sitting there, dreaming away, in deep thoughts, sprawling in the corner of the sofa, in an armchair. The corner by the heating stove might be where you, sister Bya[226], have found a comfortable place for your thoughts — for, flying around as they are, you had better stop them with darkness, or bring them to silence by whispering them to your playmate "Vildrian" which you undoubtedly brought with you in your school bag. Lillemamma is probably the only one awake, or at least her fingers are. She is incredibly happy to be in a sister's home playing her own piano, all her fingers, *Tommelstott, Slikkerntott, Langemand, Ildebrand,* and *Lille Petter Jensen*[227], are dancing across the keys. Helped by the humming of the fire and the clear light from the moon coming in through the windows, they feed the dreams of everyone there. The pianist's own dreams seem very learned and serious. She is playing melodies that are all new to me — but what now? What now?? Light — *"Kørner's battle prayer."* I know that one. Now the dreams are waking up — now they are singing — gone — quiet once again. What now — I recognize this — the *Overture to Norma*, *The Marseillaise*, *The Parisienne*, etc. Songs from *Til Sæters* — beautiful melodies from home — let me join in:

"*Nu har jeg laget dravle og mysse og nu*" [228] etc.

The song is livelier and livelier, and suddenly, they start singing "*Hvor herligt er mitt fødeland!*"[229] etc.

There's a knock at the door — "Good evening, cousin Johan, my dear," Agnes calls, crawling from her shelter under the table with her Vildrian, jumping up to hug the little doctor, who gets a singing "good evening" from the rest of the assembly. Little Rosemette sees a letter in Johan's hand; quick as a *nisse*[230] she runs over and grabs it right out of his hand and then back to the light from the heating stove to see what's written on the envelope. "Letters from Hermann and Linka, I can see it on the envelope!" Letters! "Hey, bring some light over here, stop dreaming!" Soon everybody has gathered around the table and the letter is opened. Johan: "Here's one for you, Kalla! Here's one for you, Hexa, sister-in-law! Here for you, Ovid! For you Henny-Penny! And even one for our *nisse* and Bya too! The envelope and this sheet here are for Wilhelm and me!" See what my imagination is dreaming up. I seem to think that a few lines from us here in America will create all this fuss. Even worse, I think that I was disturbing your thoughts as I sat here dreaming, since some of you, maybe all of you, have been thinking, "If only Hermann and Linka were here!"

I have been with you — God has let my thoughts be calm and sweet. My Hermann and I have been with you and seen that you are happy and content. Even if the Atlantic separates us, there is even more that unites us. Our strongest union is in our daily prayers to the Heavenly God, and we are all tied so firmly, so firmly together by the bonds of love!

December 13 — We've had real winter today: minus seventeen degrees and a biting wind from the North, as is if it were in the wind's power to let our limbs shiver as if it were twenty-five below zero.[231] Truly, that is how it has seemed, but what should we expect from the northern sea of ice, from which cold winds can blow straight down on us, unhindered by any mountains.

I've been haughty enough to allow myself to gloat. I've been thinking back on some discussions we had in Norway — about winters over here. Everybody said I didn't have to worry about bringing winter clothes, but in this case my stubbornness was no disadvantage. I'm glad to have every single piece of clothing I brought, whether it belongs to summer or winter wardrobe, whether it is for myself or for my house, because everything — except for cotton cloth — is so expensive here, and we've been out of money since our journey ended. All in all, it turned out more expensive than we ever thought it would. And in addition, the farmers here have wheat instead of money. But wheat is so cheap that going to the nearest town to sell it brings more expenses than income. I have reason to be happy about everything I have, and even more so, about the fact that there is nothing I don't have that I can't live without.

At the top of my list of problems I've had until now is my table linen. Half of it is completely rotten, and I can't use it at all. Some of Hermann's books have been ruined, although not completely, and, oh, several clothes have been damaged, although that could have been avoided if they had been sent up here earlier, since it happened in Milwaukee. Shamelessly enough it was the evil person, oh no, how can I talk like that, as if we had no part in this, just gossiping about what happened. We have to blame ourselves for not checking around when we left the boxes with a man who promised to store our clothes under a roof, but instead left them outside in rain and humidity. So there is no reason to be mad, you get what you deserve, my good wife! You have to think — and be careful. Be satisfied with little, Linka — yes — do you have a lot? No. Do you keep servants? Yes. You should not. But I have both a maid and a young boy. What do you need them for? I have two cows, three pigs, one calf, and one dog; Hermann, Ziiølner and myself. And you can't take care of this yourself, especially since you don't live in a big house, but in one single room? Well, I guess I <u>could</u> take care of all this myself, but that would be to make life worse than duty warrants; my conscience is not as tough with me as its questions suggest. I can't hear any voice suggesting that I should turn myself into a slave. Neither does my conscience blame me for being lazy, or not very productive, as I'm not always very productive, for example when I'm drawing. I'm not being productive, but the hours I spend doing this bring me so much joy that it makes me better at everything else I do. When I'm done with my duties, drawing is my reward. What about reading and writing? Reading is necessary, and writing, for example in this book, I also believe to be useful, as I get to know myself a lot better. I strive not to lie to myself — yes, I <u>strive</u> not to, but can I trust myself not to make this error? I'm afraid not — that dark selfishness, the one it seems like I can never suppress — oh God, forgive! Forgive! — is in my way here too.

Still, I don't quite understand you, you say that you don't really need servants, but you still have them? — If I were to do all the work myself, I would be working like a dog all day, no peace or rest, and not being used to hard work, I would be bad at it, and maybe in the end I would get sick, and what good would that be me — us? Hermann would have a terrible time. We would be able to pay back <u>good friends</u> some money a bit sooner, but there is no rush. It doesn't matter whether H.'s brother or Father Preus[232] gets their money this year or next year. I make an effort to be content with as little as possible when it comes to the household — we must have food, but our food is simple. I could use some more pots and pans and other equipment in the kitchen, but I can do without it. I would rather do without that than without a maid — the only reason for me not to keep a maid would be to be able to pay back our debt sooner, but I'm not about to ruin my good health to do so. Keeping her doesn't make me feel guilty in any way, and neither does she contribute to any greater debt.

As far as the boy is concerned, he'll be confirmed in a year or so, God willing, and since he works for his food only, I believe we are saving more money by having him here than what he costs us. He has only been here for a few days. His parents are good people, and he has enjoyed a better upbringing than is the case for most of the farmers from the mountains — more like the people around the towns here. I'm especially thinking about their sense of cleanliness — religious knowledge seems to be the same with one group or the other. Margit, my maid, has eaten with the people we are staying with since she came here. Christian, the boy, is supposed to be in our room. This room is so small that when four people are in here, it's overcrowded. When we're sitting at the table, one of us has to sit on the bed. This has become my place, both when we are eating and at other times, too — for example, today and yesterday when the wind blew its way through the windows.

264 · *Linka's Diary*

Hermann left his place and came over here to sit. It's really cold here; everything is so open, and it's blowing in through windows, walls, door, and roof. We've finally gotten an oven in here, but since its pipe is also the chimney, and does not lead all the way out but stops in the attic, we haven't really used it as much as we could, fearing sparks and heat. I'm kind of worried, even though we've checked the attic tonight.

But God, You are the best guardian, looking after all of us, You will save us! I thought I was uncomfortable before, but it has gotten worse with one more man around. I have to get substantial food for the boy. He needs it, going to work every day — earlier, when Z. and H. were gone, I didn't think of food for myself other than sandwiches and coffee for dinner, and otherwise tea. I sat here so quietly in my little room, but it's not like that anymore. I'm not really pleased with these changes; I wanted to manage without a boy as long as we are staying here, but it has not done much good to tell H. my reasons why I think the boy should wait until we got settled in our new house. Then he would have something to do if H. and Z. didn't have the time. They've managed to get firewood for us so far, and I believe they could have managed for a little while longer, too. It's been a while since H. and I discussed this, and then he <u>seemed</u> to agree with me. When Christian arrived, he told me that he didn't think we could just send him back — I was very serious when I answered him that he should do whatever he felt like. The boy stayed, and Hermann does not seem to have thought about how this <u>one</u> inconvenience for him would create several inconveniences for me — still, "take life as it comes to you." But thoughtless shouldn't come into play. That proverb can also be true in serious matters.

𝒟𝑒𝑐𝑒𝑚𝑏𝑒𝑟 30 — This evening I came home from a Christmas visit down in Koshkonong, where we had a good time. But if we had a good time while we were there, we didn't enjoy ourselves quite that much during the journey. Traveling across the prairie, I seriously thought my pointy nose, my hands, and my feet were going to freeze. It's strange how biting, how piercing the wind is, blowing across these Great Plains all winter. And you can read in letters to Norway, "it is not cold here." It must be people still bothered by the summer heat who write things like that. Isn't twenty-three or twenty-five degrees below zero,[233] in the middle of the day when the sun is shining, enough to make you shiver? It was very strange to go across the prairie in moonlight like we did tonight, even though it was a little bit cloudy. This time it didn't remind me of the ocean, like it usually does. Due to two days of mild weather, the hilltops were bare, while the hollows were filled with snow and small puddles, frozen because of the cold the last twenty-four hours. Cutting through this ice, the wagon and the horses made such noise that I sometimes had to raise my head, which I had bent into the wind. Staring out across the fields, my eyes were entertained by ice, soil, mountains, woods, and (the sound of a threshing machine — distant jingle bells) imagination, pure imagination — America doesn't have as beautiful a landscape to offer as you imagine, Linka, so bow your head again and be silent.

January 1852

The 18th of *July*[234] — Daguerreotype — At the market, in baths, fierce thunder and lightning in the evening, letter writing to Norway.

It's already morning of New Year's Day [1852] with you, while we are still sitting here, celebrating the last hours of the old year, talking to and about our friends in Norway. Since the names of Uncle Wilhelm and Uncle Rudolph have often been mentioned and thought of, before I go to bed I have to send you a heartfelt, sincere handshake, which is meant to tell you how fond I am of you — it would only please me if it was firmer than my strength allows me to shake a hand — it can never be too firm. Thank you, thank you! for the year that is about to leave us. Tomorrow we'll see — if God wants — if the New Year will bring greetings from you, just like I now wave good-bye from the old one.

Good evening Aunt Rosa. Thank you for everything Uncle and you did in the year about to ebb.

Dear siblings — 1852 — I was the first person with last year! God be with you!

January 14, 1852, the Parsonage — The first lines I write in my diary in the first days of the newly begun year will be a conversation with my God and Father. Conversation — how dare I use that word, how dare I raise my voice to the level of Yours, You forever and always raised above me, Your fair judgment should crush every limb of my body, should forever condemn me, should punish me for my great sinfulness with condemnation and torture until the end of time — oh Father — You Lord of love! How can I be bold enough to approach you like a child calling You by the blessed name of Father? It is your eternal love that makes it possible for me to do this, to come to you without the fear of being pushed away — yes, in Christ's name I dare call you Father, in His name, He who suffered a terrible death for all of us, for me — yes even for me! How my devastated soul bends down into the dust, knowing how your innocent and always just Son was tortured. I should, together with Mary and John, always be lying by the cross, mourning, eyes filled with tears, though I have to admit, I do not. Oh, boundless ungratefulness — yet, is it right to show my appreciation by praising You, my God, in joyful hymns, instead of feeling the pain of guilt in my heart, the guilt for which You sacrificed your Son? I am guilty of more and greater sins than Mary and John, but I do not feel the same humbleness in my heart as these, far, far from it. Yes, Lord, this shall always be my prayer to You, that Your spirit may live in my heart, making my haughty soul more humble — give me strength to do this. My will is ready, but my limbs are so weak — so that both in joy and pain can sing with Mary and John. Oh, how I trust You; You are a forgiving God, mild Father. Your endless mercy awakes a strong hope in me, so that I safely dare coming to You, safely dare to pray, safely dare to talk to You. Because of Christ, you will not push me away, but in your fatherly love you will look down on us all, on the siblings, on Hermann and on me, in mercy!

Thank You, Father God, for having given us a good house. This will be the first night we spend under the new parsonage roof. The last two days, we've been busy moving. Yesterday we were mostly busy talking, but today all of our furniture was moved, pulled by two huge oxen — I believe something big was needed. We have quite a few things, even though it didn't seem like much because it could all fit into the one room we lived in. But back there, it was stacked up so well that a quick glance did not do our wealth justice — yes, great wealth, because we're smiling with satisfaction as we look over everything we own — but, alas, not with humble gratefulness!

It will be fun, taking care of my <u>own house.</u>

January 29, 1852 — Tonight, I'm sitting here alone with the boy and the maid. H. and Z. went down to "Musquigo,"[235] where the synod of Norwegian congregations in Wisconsin will meet. It was quite a load of meat going down there on a big wagon: eight or nine men were going. They were representatives and alternates from H.'s congregations. Some of the travelers went down more to enjoy themselves than because of their great interest in the cause. I would have liked to be a part of the last group. It would have been so much fun, on Monday when the synod is gathering, to sit down in a corner of the church to observe and listen. In my heart I would pray to God that a bond of love in Christ's name might bind together the congregations that sent representatives to this meeting, with their spiritual advisors leading the way, that they may agree on useful laws.[236] But even if, in solemn moments, I turned in prayer to Him who knows their hearts, I would still find something funny, and I would probably not be able to keep myself from smiling.

I guess that everybody, speakers included, will both speak and act a bit shyly, but little by little, courage will come to the speakers' tongues, and they'll be waving their arms vehemently. And sitting there, I would see the young pastors stand like fighters — fighting each other with a certain dignity, though. In the beginning, dignity and seriousness would make the young men, barely thirty years old, look like old men. Each face they set up would be marked by the strange mark of age, but the process in which their self-control is forgotten and their young temperament becomes visible would make me smile quite a bit. Watching how the farmers always defend their minister's opinion as the correct and better one, and if he has to admit to his opponent that he was wrong, watching the farmers follow him like a flock of sheep — that would really be a lot of fun. I'm not saying that our farmers are unable to form an opinion themselves; I'm merely giving them praise for their faith in their minister. I almost said *han fa'r,*[237] as they used to call their spiritual leader at home, but this lovely expression has been abandoned by the Norwegian since he became an American. He finds himself too clever to talk so simply and beautifully. Now it is only: Pastor, Minister, or Preus. Oh, world, you know how to give us funny ideas, don't you?

You've had bad weather today, Hermann, you and your traveling companions. Rain and wind — yesterday sunshine and lovely spring weather — how strange it is. We can get good weather tomorrow — a powerful hand is to decide. May He hold his hand over you, over all, over us here at home!

February 1852

February 1, Sunday — How did I spend this day? It's night, and it's quite natural for me to ask myself this question. It might seem to me as if it has been spent in a good way, although I know that the judge of all our actions is saying, "you committed one sin after the other today."

Well, I do admit. I humiliate myself before You, just judge, exclaiming "selfishness will quickly tear me away from You, Lord, tear me away from my sinful, corrupt soul!"

Today, I had Margit and Christian in here; I read them a sermon and sang for them. I am still not used to being a lecturer and lead singer. It doesn't allow me to focus entirely on the contents and what the song or the sermon teaches us, but I guess it will get better with time, since I want, every evening and Sunday morning when there is no service or when H. is away, to read God's word with the people working for me, as long as I am not ill or anything. I learned a lot in Kierkegaard's *Works of Love*[238] today. I don't understand half of what he is saying, but I understand enough to know that I am very interested in his book. I understand some parts in between, and these parts stay locked in my brain. I compare myself to a stirring stick, stirring *smørgrøt*[239]. When it's pulled out, there's still some butter sticking to it.

March 1852

March 22 — Up and down, in and out, back and forth, is what the weather has been like lately. I wonder if in Norway, the country situated far, far to the north, they're saying, "Our friends in Wisconsin are probably experiencing full spring now, while we're still having winter." You're fooling yourselves, dear friends. Even though we're some latitudes south of you, I do believe it's still colder here than where you are. When the sun shines down on us in all its splendor, it might give us some heat through our windows, but if we step outside, an absolutely freezing wind greets us, forcing us to get back inside as quickly as possible. About a month ago, we thought that spring — summer — had come to stay. We had really mild, almost hot and humid weather for a couple of days, then we got one of the fierce thunderstorms they have around here. We've been spared these for the entire winter, and now it came so suddenly that out of pure astonishment, I didn't even get as scared as I usually get in thunderstorms. I really wish I could suppress this fear I get — it's so silly! Even if I'm shivering during what I consider unusually powerful lightning flashes, I want to watch them and pretend that I don't care at all, since I know that God is looking after me and everybody! The foot of snow we got one night about two weeks ago is gone, and the weather seems a bit milder today. The wild geese and ducks that showed up during the aforementioned days fooled us just like they fooled themselves. As the frost came back, they went back south in flocks. This time these dear messengers of spring were too early — I saw a flock going south today too. "Welcome back," I shouted at them, as they flew in typical goose formation above my head, high up toward the clouds.

Now I can sing along with the dairymaid "*Nu har jeg lavet dravle og myse.*"[240] Well, I had to rewrite it to "I've now churned and made *gammelost*[241] — curdled *surprim*[242] and put everything on the shelf — etc." I actually made *gammelost*. I wonder how it will turn out. I made it in a new way — it's supposed to be done in fourteen days, when it's rotten and ready to be eaten — it all depends on that. I think I'll make myself a *mysost*,[243] and H. can have the other to himself.

March 28 — My wish to have all of my things made of beautiful wood is really being satisfied here. Today, I got four milk bowls made of cedar. I'm thinking about the feeling I had when I heard about the "cedars of Lebanon." I didn't know that these trees existed other places than there, and thought they were a rarity. But they're not rare here; they're a very beautiful tree. At home, I've seen people sowing bushes in their gardens, but it never occurred to me that they were cedars. Here they look like big, rugged oaks. I had imagined the proud cedar more like a huge spruce, straight and rigid, but that's not the way they look around here. The smell of them is just like that of our juniper, but the color is brownish red. I also have bowls made of dark wood — walnut and cherry.

April 1852

April 7 — No, this is too funny not to be written down. For the past few days, I've basically had to be "Margit," since she's been sick. This has given me the opportunity to spend more time in my own kitchen than I usually do. I've done the dishes, etc., and all in all I've been paying more attention to whatever is in corners and cupboards than usual. So today I made a discovery that makes a great example of the luxurious vegetation America has. My kitchen table is made of a box — the same box we used to carry the painting of Uranienborg with us from Norway. Now we've turned it over — and as legs we took four pieces of an aspen that was standing in the woods right outside our door, which had been beautifully turned and polished by nature. It was frozen and raw, to be sure, but what difference does that make? It only contributes to fertility — to my great joy I discovered that the legs are putting forth leaves — beautiful, green little branches, covered with green leaves. Look how our good God lets the summer thrive in our house while it is still winter outside. One of the green branches will be sent to Norway in a letter — "this grew on the legs of my kitchen table!" That will surely make them laugh, and maybe there will be a comment like, "Linka doesn't wash the legs of her tables!" Yes I do, but not up in the corners by the tabletop. Besides, if it had been the case that I didn't wash them, I would argue that the beautiful polish would be damaged if I cleaned it too much!

May **1852**

May 25 — Lovely heat and summer! How wonderful spring is — it doesn't matter whether you're in America or Norway! Nature is so full of life, with all the green, and the smells! Everything is so encouraging, for eyes, heart, and nose! In the last eight days, my eyes have really been enjoying themselves, watching the green sprouts growing rapidly on trees and ground, so that each day has something new to show me, always more wonderful, always more beautiful. But soon the growth of spring will be completed and nature will reach the peak of its splendor, exposed to the burning rays of the sun.

My nose, what does it have to do with nature? As the eye leads the feet around fields and woods, there is an exhilarating scent streaming toward the subtle smelling organ, which inhales it with the greatest desire. The hand reaches for the nearest flower, leading it up to the fastidious nose, but soon the flower is viewed with disappointment — although beautiful, it has no smell! Oh "Violet," how beautiful you are in all your modest simplicity! Also here in this western home, I can find you, but what did you do to your scent, that you so willingly offered back in my old Norway? Lilies — lilies of the valley, you and the violets are my favorite flowers! Are you no longer standing side by side? My eyes have sought, but cannot find you, lily of the valley. Please do not hide from me; I'm so fond of you! I want to plant you and the violets in my garden. You shall stand there in peace and quiet, do not fear disturbance! Please grow and bloom in my garden pavilion! I will care for you! But where do the lovely smells come from that the light breeze is bringing us? It must be the grateful breath each young sprout sends to the giver of the life in which they are thriving. My heart is also rising in grateful prayers to You, our good Lord and Father, who has arranged our stay down here so perfectly and wonderfully! If only our lives down here would please You, but our thoughts and actions are full of sins and mistakes! Our souls are filled with ungratefulness and haughtiness. Your Spirit, oh Father, if only Your Spirit could fill our minds so that our conscience really could feel when You, with love and mercy, warningly knock on the door to our hearts. Be merciful for the sake of Christ! And, oh, we are begging for mercy, we, who contaminated with great sins, stand before You in prayer. Yes, in the name of Jesus we dare to do this — oh, if only I could repent like I should, if I could only feel my great misery!!

The birds do not sing as cheerfully to my ear here as they did at home in Norway. Dressed with beautiful, multicolored feathers, it seems like the birds here are more of a pleasure to the eye than what they bring to the heart through the ear. It just occurred to me that the birds here might be model of the Yankee — the outside is shining brightly, but seldom — often not at all — does one ask what is inside.

May 30, Pentecost[244] — What a wonderful time of the year! What a wonderful day for celebration! Nature is so wonderfully decorated! If only our hearts could be only half as beautifully adorned before You, dear Father, as You now present nature to our eyes! Yesterday, the day after Pentecost, there was a service here. Since no church has been built yet, a schoolhouse built of oak had to do; it is far from pretty. At home you seldom see a cowshed as ugly as this house is on the outside. It is a little bit better on the inside. The floor is decent, and along the walls there are two rows of benches. At one end there's a bench and a table; at the other end there are windows on each of the walls where there is no door. During the service, the table is used as altar, and the farmers have been kind enough to leave four seats on the bench for the minister and his wife. Saying the liturgy, the minister — Hermann — is standing in front of the table, on which the minister's wife, on special days or at communion, has placed a nice, white tablecloth. After having sung the liturgy, he takes his seat again — one step to the side and then one backward and he is there, by my side. Hymns for the morning service are sung as well as in any farmer's church, and during the last verse, Hermann stands up, and now the table is used as a pulpit. The congregation is eager to come to services. During the winter, when it was cold and terrible, fewer people came, I guess. Crossing the prairie in that awful wind probably made people stay home in their warm houses, even though upon arriving at the church, they would find the oven we have placed in the middle of the room well heated, almost red. I won't claim that the entire room was heated accordingly; it's impossible because of broken windows, and openings in roof, floor, and walls. But still, there are usually more people than there is room for on the benches. Also, once a week H. holds "Edifying Meetings," when he reads and explains a story from the Bible, plus he reads an edifying story about the missionaries or something like that; a lot of people attend. When it is too dark, or bad weather, it's mostly neighbors, but on moonlit nights, people from more distant farms show up. These edifying meetings are usually held in the evenings, looking back on a day of hard work. If the weather is nice and we expect more people, then Marthe Møen goes down to the schoolhouse with her candles, and Margit carries my papers. The candles in the windows take care of the light of the eyes, while Hermann, with God's help, awakens the light of the Spirit in our souls.

As the year is proceeding and springtime has entered the air, more and more people gather at services. They also come from the sister congregations. There isn't enough room for everybody in a building as small as the schoolhouse; there are even a lot of people standing along the walls on the outside. I haven't dared to go into the overcrowded, stuffy room, since I caused a great disturbance on Easter Sunday, when, in the middle of H.'s speech, I fainted — "lost my senses" as the farmers say — causing him to stop preaching and see me well out the door. Instead, I bring a chair from home, which I place by the window, in the shadow of the house, where I actually like it better than inside. On Ascension Day, H. held his first confirmation — good Father be with him — be with us all with His Spirit! There were even more people than usual here that day; I was joined by many in my pew outside. We had the clear blue sky as ceiling and the blooming trees as walls. NB: In by the wall, there are only half-rotten splinters.

Yesterday I sat in my usual place, but on the other side of the house, since the service was held in the afternoon. H. had been preaching in Norway Grove in the morning. I don't understand why people prefer to sit in the sun — well — I was sitting by myself, and just as if the beautiful animals felt sorry for me, they did their best to lead my thoughts onto something else: The one poor gander we have had followed me down there, and it was standing by my chair. The only bird I have heard singing some nice tunes since I came here sat in a tree, whistling the entire time. Still, I do believe I paid attention; I tried to see if I remembered the course of H.'s speech, but I'm afraid I did not know the sermon hymn, unless I wanted to guess from the gospel. This can be a proof either way, but one thing is certain, I didn't look around a lot — I don't approve of that kind of fussing around. I didn't even get the pleasure of watching a pretty little bunny that came running out of some bushes, sat down on his tail and looked at me for a long time. Ziiølner made me aware of it too late. These animals are not rare around here, though. I often see them around the house, and they aren't afraid of looking out from underneath some bush when we're out walking.

July 1852

July 5 — A couple of days ago, I got back home after having been down at Rock Prairie, at the Dietrichsons' with Hermann. All the ministers' wives and the ministers were there, the latter to dedicate two churches; the first ones were just coming along. But we really enjoyed ourselves for the ten days set aside for the gathering.

It so happened that the last day of the gathering, when we all parted, was my birthday. Nobody except Hermann knew that it was a special day for me. I easily get emotional these days, and I always start crying. That was why I did not want any congratulations from the only close people I have in America. I tried to act indifferently, and I succeeded.

It was quite fun how this day turned out to be a different day for the others, too. Dietrichson and his wife came with us to Janesville, quite a big town, considering it is in Wisconsin. It's situated so that both the Stubs and the [A.C.] Preuses, plus ourselves, have to pass through there on our way home. Arriving in four buggies, one for each family, we landed at a very nice hotel. The best thing about the staff there, though, is that they play the pianoforte so cheerfully. Mrs. D. had to play for us, and we all sang. It was nice to hear some music; none of us had since we left home. Time passed too fast and we had to part from the Stubs and Dietrichsons, as we were going with the Koshkonong people to their home. We got home the next day. Our first job after having greeted Ziiølner, Margit, and our three dogs, who all came out to the buggy as we arrived, was to have a look at all the little chickens that had hatched while we had been away. In Janesville, several animals were on exhibition; we went to have a look at them. It was interesting; there were lions, elephants, tigers — what big animals! You can't really imagine what an elephant looks like before you have seen one — it is an inflexible, clumsy machine, though — what beauty can you find in it? That would have to be the trunk — and what would it do without it? It reached its trunk out to the audience and people put candy in the bowl of it. The candy was then brought to the animal's mouth, and then it was gone, it must have been like a drop of water in the ocean.

You just had to be amazed at the lions' heads, and their beautiful tails with their rapid movements — that is what I liked the best. It was their thick mane surrounding their heads that made their forequarters seem so big, although I thought it was also well proportioned to their hind quarters. The lioness with her cubs was also funny, but none of these had a mane or a tail like their Mr. Papa. What beautiful skins the tiger and the leopard had, and what an expression in their faces! The hyena frightened me, but the zebra is a beautiful animal; I've seen mules their size. The rhino — oh my! It was in the same class as the elephant and the stuffed hippo. The llama and the camel looked pious, but ugly. The golden pheasant and the bird of paradise(?) were beautiful, they looked so proud and grand with all their feathers, but I do think the pheasant was prettier. There was a terrible smell and it was really hot in the circus tent where it all took place, so we were in a hurry to get out of there.

I had to laugh at the funny animals in the last half of the circus. "Yankee ladies" were sitting on the rows of bench seats. They had fans and parasols, and were breathing heavily from the heat, and many of them were pale as porcelain dolls. What taste! So much for the Yankee fashion. I don't care for it!

August 1852

This book has been resting in my drawer or on my bookshelf since 1846, without my ever using it or writing a single word in it. I have used it, though; I have read through the lines on the first pages more than once, and more than one tear has come to my eyes — because of the memories they bring. But I'm not saying they are tears of grief — they are tears of joy and of gratitude, as always joined by tears of sorrow and longing, making their course cheerful and easy, not hard and bitter.

The book itself is a gift from Hermann. An old promise obligates him to fulfill the work he began of writing down the poems and speeches that were written after Father's death and read at his grave. To honor him? Wasn't it to ease the worried hearts of those left behind?! But it has been so long now, I've given up hope of having Hermann write anything more from those days — that goes for myself too, as that work consists of copying, and where would we get the originals from? I'll have to let it go and be pleased with what I have — thank my Hermann for what he has given me. The gift is very dear to me, but if the promise had been fulfilled, it would have been even dearer.

In the beginning of the book I will write down some hymns we found that Father left, hymns he either translated or wrote himself. In the latter part here, I will start notes that belong to the diary I've kept for several years now, from 1844 to 18-. I haven't written every day, and that won't be the case from now on, either.

Spring Prairie Parsonage, August 11, 1852
— It occurred to me that there is one thing that I haven't discussed at all in my diary, and I find that rather strange, especially since this one thing has seldom been off my mind. It's quite a while ago now, but there was a period of about two or three months that I was a mystery to myself. I had a feeling I was going through a change, but I wasn't sure. However, I've been sure for a long time now, and being sure includes admitting that there are sinful aspects to this thing, if not exactly in my mind, then elsewhere. In the aforementioned period of doubt and uncertainty, I reminded myself, as I still do and always will, of how I so often claimed in a mocking way that I would never have children, I would see to that! It took me a long time to realize that no <u>Christian</u> can ever say anything like that, but I thank your Spirit, God our Father, for educating my heart, for letting me see how wrong I was to speak and act like I did, and for making me pray to you for forgiveness. And You, oh God, heard my prayer! You forgave me — yes, I do believe so — and what joy for me, and delight because of our forgiveness also, when I with certainty could proclaim that next winter Hermann and I will not sit by ourselves in our house, if it is God's will that everything goes well!

People usually say that women in my condition are often bothered by bad moods. This has not been the case with me, as far as I can tell. In the beginning, I found myself more cheerful than I have been during the last few years. Lately, I've been more marked by seriousness, but not melancholy seriousness. I thank God for being so good to me — us — and that He lets us, by His good will only, have such a good life as we have. We don't deserve it at all — if only this could be said with my heart's sincere humility!

A couple of days ago immigrants brought us letters and packages from home. It is such a relief hearing nothing but "Everything is well! Everything is like it always has been!" But since there are two old people, both rather weak, in our family, I guess we should expect bad news in the not very distant future. To the eye it looks as if they are not far away from the grave, but it might be that younger people are even closer to their resting place. Thy will be done, oh God! Hold your hand over young and old — and let your peace live in our hearts so that when you call on us, whoever it is, we may leave this world as one of God's children! But who deserves this glorious name? Nobody! Nobody! Mercy in Christ's Father, our God!!

It's quite a celebration for us every time we get letters and packages, and although we've gotten some letters before, these were really the first packages since we came. And everything was nicely shared between us. Hermann got books, which is a useful garment, if only for the spirit — the body needs something too, something more substantial; therefore he also got a pair of big, wadded traveling boots, so I hope he will not be as cold on his travels this winter as he was last winter.

For me — nothing for my spirit — oh, how can I say something like that? Of course I did, I got a watercolor book and a cake recipe. No, the mother of the house needs to think about the body — not only her own, but others' too. Besides a dress — black — and some smaller things, I got two pairs of cards for making wool. I had asked for all this, but I was really surprised when an uncle of mine — Lomse — sent me a waffle iron and an iron for making *Gode råd* ("good advice") waffles[245] — he said the two of them had to follow one another, because, as he says, "Good advice is of no use unless it is followed by warm waffles." However, since you can get tired of these after a while, he's also sending me a *krumkake* iron. This is wise reasoning, Lomse, I wish everybody who sends us packages would learn from you and be as thorough. We had written and asked for the other things we got, and gifts are something quite different. Two of my sisters have thought the same, so from little Rosemette I got a collar she has sewn, and Lillemamma sent me an ivory tea set. I asked her about that before I left, but did not get it. Now, though, she says she felt so bad she decided to send it to me, but I wish she had not; now I feel bad for taking something like that from my sisters. There are several little things that I brought with me over here that I now would have wanted my sisters to have. It's a shame that the box for the tea set was broken, though; it made me really sad. Thank you, all of you, for being so kind to us!

There's one more funny thing about all this. My dress was nicely wrapped in a <u>beautiful</u> old linen pillowcase — that has turned out really useful! I have made seven little caps out of it, and will use the rest for something else — if you'd known that, it would have made you laugh for sure!

August 28 — In general, my feelings for America are quite cold and indifferent. I find everything that has to do with home a lot better. But that's not really true. Being impartial, I have to admit that several things are a lot better here. The most important advantage of this country is the soil, which is a lot more fertile. Combined with the heat, it creates a far better environment for growth than what you find in wonderful Norway!

The reason I make these comments now is that there are a few acres of fallow land outside our house, and on part of this land we have planted "pomkins" and "watermills."[246] Well, I should have used the Norwegian names, I like them better — *Græskar* and *Vandmeloner*. What you do when you sow the seeds of these fruits is actually a lot of fun. After you are done plowing, the furrows are quite straight and even — what you do is that you walk behind an ox, taking every second furrow, and for each yard you dig a hole in the turned turf, put the seed in the hole, and bury it again. You sow potatoes and corn the same way. The fallow soil is very nutritious, and fruits like these seem to thrive in this new soil. We've had evidence of this: our pumpkins are really big. I believe the biggest one we've had so far was big enough for a bushel basket, and it might be that we will see more of that size as more pumpkins ripen. The watermelon is delicious; I ate a piece of it a little while ago. I've never seen watermelons this size at home, but I think they had a fresher taste.

We often put on comedies in several acts to keep the pigs away from this piece of land with the aforementioned fruits. Only three-fourths of our land is fenced yet, so all kinds of animals have pretty much free access here. It's a good thing that we have three dogs. Like most dogs, they should be trained to be good <u>shepherds</u>, but I guess they haven't been very well raised, since old Jak savages pigs and cattle if we send him after them. "Norge[247] is probably a bit too young; he may become very good, but he's not smart enough yet, and he's too easily discouraged. My little Lurv[248] is a lot of trouble and a little coward, so you just have to laugh at him. So in a way, each of our dogs has its faults, and if we want the pigs out of our field, we have to join in ourselves to get them going. When the big momma[249] comes out in the field with Norge and Lurv, Norge runs after the pigs, and I follow behind him to encourage him, while Lurv is tangled in my legs, biting my slippers, and amusing himself the best he can with those. Whenever Hermann or Ziiølner goes out there, they get impatient, and old Jak is brought out, but then he starts his savaging and the two good men have to sprint through field and bushes to get Jak back.

October — December 1852

October 5 — I was wrong when I wrote the 5th of October; that's tomorrow and who knows if I'll live to see tomorrow? "Who knows how close I am to my end," the hymn says, and that's true — death may strike us every moment. It's all in God's hands. And we are content that it is in God's hands, because God is good to us. "Everything is for the better for those who truly love God." So if death should tear me away before tomorrow — away from this earthly home — oh, I say that would be for the better for me! But how! If God calls me I will account for every useless word I've ever spoken — I will stand before the throne of the just judge. How am I supposed to pass this test — I will have to sink deep, deep, for what good, what useful things have I ever done? I should tremble at the thought of death — at the thought of that moment being close when I shall face my final test, and still I claim that if God would let me die now, that would be the best, because God is good, He only does what is best for me. But does He only do what is best for those who truly love Him? Do I then truly love my God? Well, I do think I love my God — I often say to myself, "How good God is to you, how many good things He gives you," but is that loving Him? No, and if I still say that God's love for me is great — yes, enormous. If my love could only be a hundredth of His for me! Is this showing that I love God? No, no! I can make several good promises, I pray to God that His spirit may give me the strength to keep them, because I feel that it would please Him if I did this or the other — oh no! How true! How true!

"The spirit is willing but the flesh is weak," says the apostle. Temptation is walking around like a roaring lion, coming toward me, smirking, nice, and flattering. Selfishness and haughtiness are again leading my steps — and can these ever do what pleases God? No! No! No in all matters!

So what is left for me now? Nothing, except for the recognition of myself as a poor, evil creature, who should be severely punished by God eternally, instead of being an object of his love. And if only these words had come from a truly repenting heart! I do say to myself, "You really are an evil creature, Linka!" but do I really feel the pain of being what I am? No — I guess I do not. In that case humility would take root in me, the bitter tears of regret would run down my cheeks and I would share the attitudes of the publican who found himself unworthy to lift his head toward the sky, but with bent neck called out, "God, have mercy with me, poor sinner!" "God, have mercy with me, poor sinner!" I call out to you, oh God, now and often, but not with a heart acknowledging my sins, the only heart that could ever please you! O God Father, this is how I do nothing! Nothing that You may find good, like I should if I love You, and still I claim that I love You! Help me, Lord Christ, so that I shall not be thrown into the eternal flames! It is my comfort and hope that You, who suffered death on the cross — also for me — You will not leave me, but stand by my side as I stand before the throne of judgment, and for Your sake, my neverending, countless sins will be forgiven, and because of You only, I can pass my judgment, "for God so loved the world, that he gave his only begotten Son, that whosoever believes in him should not perish, but have everlasting life." Therefore I can face death without fear.

Here I am — making up my own accounts for how death may strike me, and the consequences it may have. Everything is only good and from the good. But Linka, sit back and imagine vividly: someone comes to you and says, "I am an angel of death, sent by God to fetch you, take you away from this earth, and bring you before his throne and judgment." Would I, with a content, calm, and dedicated mind, with Christ's name on my lips and in my heart, follow God's messenger without looking back on all my earthly possessions, my Hermann, my siblings, and everything the good Lord has given me? Oh yes, I sincerely ask you my God, whatever time and place you call on me, let me be prepared to stand before You. Let me not be like the five virgins who had no oil left for their lamps when the bridegroom came! Let me love everything You have given me here on earth, but nothing, nothing like I love You — once more — "the spirit is willing but the flesh is weak." I wish I were able to love You with a sincere heart — oh Father — Your Spirit strengthen and help my spirit to do that in the name of Christ! Against the devil and all his evil — You can eliminate him — and neither do You let the temptations I face be greater than what I can bear. But everything, everything with the help of your spirit! — for Christ's sake!

December 7 — Only a few lines in this evening hour. I'm feeling better than I have for a long time — and what has been wrong with me since the last time I wrote? Oh, good Lord, you put me in a light sickbed for a while, and it has done me so much good! Weaknesses of the flesh awaken the spirit — if only I had been awakened to the righteous supplication and to humbleness in front of You, my Lord! Oh strengthen my faith, secure my confidence in You — my prayer is just as heartfelt as my gratefulness, dear Father, for the gift You gave Hermann and me on October 13th this year.[250] He is almost two months old now, and on Sunday — the second Sunday of Advent — he was baptized. He is now included in the body of Christ — and if only he will be a child of God! Me, a mother — oh what a responsibility, what a dear, dear responsibility I have resting in my heart now. I really wish that my little Christian Keyser will be a child of God — that is his father's and that is his mother's heartfelt wish, but we cannot fulfill this wish ourselves — no, God in heaven help us — Your children — oh happiness! — to achieve wisdom in our hearts for the upbringing of our child, so that he may please You, so that without anger You can look down on our little family — Hermann, Linka, and our dear little son, Christian Keyser. Hold your hand over my siblings, over all people dear to us, over us and our house! And now good night, in the blessed name of Christ!

New Year's Day 1853 — I just put my little Keyser to sleep. I've had him in my arms the entire day. I have a maid, yes, but she got a few days off to go home for Christmas. It's a very strange situation for me now; I'm no longer master of my own time, for when Christian calls, I have to go. I haven't gotten any work done the past three months — I haven't done anything in my house. I've been around the house a little bit the past few days — everywhere I go, my eyes meet the most terrible mess. I would really like to do some serious tidying up, in the kitchen, basement, and attic. But stop! The wound in my right breast is still open, and great precautions should be taken. But no wonder this house is messy! I've changed maids no less than three times while I have been ill. Strangers have been taking care of the house — there has been no guidance at all. I thank You once again, my God, for having made me well — I hope it is Your intention that I shall soon recover completely so I can walk around like I used to. Still, if that is not what You have intended for me, then Thy will be done! It is for the best!

Every day I make good promises, but oh — God help us — how poorly they are kept. Today, on the first day of the year, I have promised You a lot, oh God, and all my promises are nothing but what You tell me to do — and I say I want to — so help me to do so with your Spirit — help me to become a good person. To the siblings, to all dear ones, to all people, I ask You, however little we deserve your good will — hear my prayer, for Christ's sake! Amen!

It's the holiday season, and old memories have been more frequent visitors in my soul than what they usually are. Days of childhood when we spent our happiest days with father and mother, every Christmas Eve when we flocked around the Christmas tree, picking candy and presents — those were wonderful days! We are far from each other, siblings, but I do believe that in these times we have greeted each other more often than usual, both in our prayers for the others' well-being, and in the thoughts of times past, that with all the memories they bring with them, still they are not wished back by any of us.

I assume you received the letter telling you that we had a little baby boy, right before Christmas — oh, how you must be smiling and laughing, imagining me as a mother of my little *Kvitebjørn*[251]! Well, I really, really love him, and Hermann no less. As proof of this, I note that every time I change his clothes, H. comes in to help me — yesterday he went as far as starting to undo Christian's diaper, but in the end his fingers were too fine to continue. I kept him on the rack for a while, though. When I have C.K. all the time, like today, I get exhausted, and tired of him, but it's strange — if somebody takes him away from me, I haven't been away from him five minutes before I start longing for him. Is it maternal love? O God, help me so that I will not be a weak mother!

H. came home from church (?) unusually early today — a house at some farmer's — when will we get a church here?? Since then, he and Ziiølner have done nothing but eat Christmas treats — dinner first of course — smoking tobacco and drinking beer.[252] This has been nourishment for the body; as to their spiritual nourishment, they've been telling stories from the past, and to make sure all this is well digested, they've been stretching out on Ziiølner's bed, which has its place in the living room. Now, at 9:15 p.m. H. is snoring in his own bed — Z. is writing home and I'm at sitting here, but I'm also going to bed now, for the "nightly disturbance" will hardly be nice tonight.

There's no point in saying that I was the first among the siblings to write 1853 this year—you get the day six or seven hours before I do, but I remember well when we were home and early, early on New Year's Day morning, when we sprang up in nothing but our underwear to scribble down the year. Lying with the table in front of my bed — the old horse-hair sofa — I had pencil and paper ready from the night before, and I was more than just slightly annoyed if anyone had sneaked up in the middle of the night and, under the light from the lamp and half asleep, had scribbled down the year. God bless you and us all! He will arrange it so that when we get old, we can look back on past years with the same joy — and if only all of them may be lived to please You, God our Father!

February 7 — Alone! Alone! I'm alone today, and will be so for fourteen days. Hermann has gone to our synod meeting[253] — oh, Linka! How can you say you are alone? Your God is with you, is He not? He foremost, and then there is your little son and then your servants. No, God be praised, I am not alone — and I hope I shall never be so unhappy that I find myself alone and abandoned in this world. It might very well be that I will be alone, seen with earthly eyes, but with spiritual? How desperate I would be if I were ever abandoned by my God.

The other day I read an article by Paul Gerhard — I have to recite a few words in which he describes us, and the life here on earth. My thoughts have often been occupied with this matter, but I have never been able to find the words to express my feelings. However, Gerhard is a man who knows how to describe the matter truthfully: <u>what is a human being?</u> <u>A slave of death</u>, a wanderer passing by; he is more fleeting than a water bubble, more transient than the blink of an eye, more vain than a picture, more disappearing than a sound, more fragile than glass, more changing than the wind, more unsteady than the shadow, more deceitful than a dream.

<u>What is life?</u> <u>A waiting for death</u>, a scene for an empty and vain play, an ocean filled with lamentation and misery, a vein about to burst at the first light stroke, or about to be infected at the slightest sign of fever.

Our lifetime is a labyrinth which we enter right from our mother's bosom and which we leave on the threshold of death. We are but dust, and like smoke, dust is nothing; therefore, we ourselves are nothing. Viewed from the outside, this life seems to be an honorable kernel of need, but if you open it with the knife of truth, you will see that on the inside it is nothing but worms and rottenness. If you compare the incredibly short time granted us in this life to eternity, which does not know any limit or end, you will understand how foolish it is to be occupied with this transient life without concern for the eternal. Use the world, but do not let your heart attach to it. You can very well be careful with work and actions of this life, but do not let your soul be spellbound to this life. Our fatherland is in heaven, this world is merely a shelter, so do not enjoy yourself so much in this shelter that you forget your heavenly fatherland. The safest is to expect one's passing away at every hour, and with earnest repentance, prepare oneself for the same. Oh Lord, silence all our heart's love for this world, but ignite in us an intense longing for the heavenly kingdom!

I have written down more of this article than I originally planned to, but I found it so true and solid that I would not mind recording all of it instead of just the main ideas. And I will end with this little verse that Gerhard uses in his introduction:

Like ships on the sea,
Like a waterfall from raging cliffs,
Our lives will quickly pass,
From the cradle to the grave.
NB: It is Johan Gerhard, and not Paul G., who wrote this.

February 20 — "Sorrow and happiness walk together." That is surely true, oh good God! And I have often reminded myself of this little phrase of truth, but seldom, very seldom, is it pronounced with such a happy heart as just now at this moment. I was sitting with my little Christian Keyser at my breast, thanking God for having given me such a fine, healthy little boy. Oh, my joy and gratitude to God were and are always great, but how insignificant they are, compared to the love and goodness of the good God! I was sitting there, looking at my little C.K. when suddenly I was aware of a little flaw which I know is very dangerous — oh my Lord God, You know the feeling of grief and fear running through a mother's heart at times like that, and You know just as well the indescribable joy I felt and still feel when I realized that I had been frightening myself. Yes, God is our good guardian! I say that today as I said it yesterday, when I was close to being pinned between the horns of my cow and the big oak in our yard. It was my Father in heaven, using our neighbor, Niels, as his tool, who saved me, but how I was trembling when the danger was over, and then went inside to find C.K.! When I am holding him, feeling his hands in mine, it feels so right and so incredibly good to pray, and when Hermann comes, and we're sitting together, all three of us, so happy and content — Lord God how good You are to us, we ungrateful — we sinners — but Lord, we know, for Christ's sake, for the sake of Christ's suffering and death, yes — eternal love and compassion — for His sake alone, alone.

May–June 1853

May 23 — It's been a long time since my head has been as full of all kinds of things as is right now. For a long time, I've been expecting letters from Norway, without getting any, but yesterday evening, mail arrived, and it was so thick and closely written and from so many family members and friends that I didn't finish it until today. I had to smile last night, when I put away some of the letters without having read them, for little C.K. was to blame for this, and it has never happened to me before. More than once I have stayed awake until two or three in the morning, to amuse myself with newly arrived letters from home. O God, every day You send us so much good, one thing better than the other. Today, You let us get letters from our dear ones, and how blessed — none of what our earthly eye would call bad news. We have been here for two years, and the news from home is still "by the way, everything is like it used to be!" This "by the way" is put in because two other pieces of news are reported: that sister Hexa soon, yes, with God's help it is already over, will be confined, and that sister Lillemamma (Ovidia) was engaged to Christian Kaurin on the 9th of February. I knew him as a child, a little bit as a youth, and talked to him every now and then. He told me in his letter that L. told him that I thought he was conceited — oh well, I can't deny it. The man had just taken his first two exams when I spoke to him, and he had done well. Show me the youngster in the same situation who would not — like Ch. Kaurin — have thought himself quite a fellow, whose person and speech were both worth noticing. There are very few exceptions. God bless your love, and I wish you to be happy, now and forever.

June 20 — Yesterday I took yet another long trip with my little Christian Keyser. It's so much fun, having him on my lap when I am driving! NB: when he is being nice. It's so much fun to bring him when he is not a crybaby, but it's tiresome when he is. I have tried both, especially when I took the long trip to Koshkonong on the 13th of May. To tell you the truth, I was against going at all, because a woman can stay home when she has small children, when she is <u>thicker</u> than what she would normally be, and yes, a wife does best to always stay at her house. But I would be fooling myself if I said that if it had not been to please Hermann, I would have preferred to stay home. Sometimes I think it would be fun to talk to Engel or others, but then I always want to invite them up here, and right now I can't offer them the same comfort as they have at their homes. Therefore I'm reluctant to invite them — and I don't really suffer any great privation, being alone with H., C.K., my maids, and my house.

Oh Lord, whenever I am away from home, I feel like I'm unable to organize my thoughts in a sincere prayer; it seems as if I'm wandering about the entire day, <u>forgetting You, Good God</u>, only occupied with what belongs to the world — yes, surely, surely! There's too much when I am home, but even more when I am away. All this is evil and sinful, and a consequence of this is sometimes I'm talking frivolous nonsense, that I should have left unsaid. And if I hear anything that makes me angry or annoyed, though I think that it is mainly when I am hurt by what is said, then I keep quiet, try to pretend like I don't care; but I don't forget. I don't know whether this is an advantage or disadvantage for me, but why am I such a fool to let myself be annoyed by people living on the same, lousy, pitiful earth as myself, to <u>once</u> stand before the great, just, powerful Judge, who will account for each word we have ever spoken — yes, why do you, Linka? Yes, you're <u>proud</u> and <u>ambitious</u> — you're <u>selfish</u>. You want people to notice your words, your work, you think you do everything in a proper and correct way — and then, if anyone comes who does not care about you, who considers your speech foolish and unworthy of an answer, who finds one or more of your actions ludicrous, then I think that people have been cruel to me. I feel like I've suffered injustice, that I have a reason to be exasperated, for I am not humble. If only I could have a tiny bit of the blessed humility, then I wouldn't think like I do, but rather, I would think that I am a bad person, and that everything I do is wrong! Then I would think that I deserve everything people do to me. I would thank them for good advice or because they are laughing at me, and let go of the inconvenience it is to be mad. If I — because I'm stupid enough to let myself be mad — could be driven to humility, then it would be an advantage to me. And for that reason, I shouldn't avoid company. But I get angry at home, too, and I could very well learn to keep my tongue at home as well.

So traveling is no necessity. What is necessary is to pray to God, and ask that He, in the name of Christ, by His Holy Spirit, will help me day by day to become a better person! Please do so, Lord God, for the sake of Jesus Christ. I often say, "take the world as it comes," and have said so through the years, and sought to carry through with it in my heart, but what has it led to, has it brought me any further? No — since I'm as described above, the world is still too dear to me.

August — September 1853

August 10 — Today is my brother Kalla's birthday. I've celebrated your birthday by, in my solitude, eating *Rødgrød og Fløg*[254], and as far as work, I've painted two spinning wheels (my own and my maid's). The work has been done to my complete satisfaction — I believe I'm a lot better as spinning-wheel painter than as genre painter, for I find no faults in my mastery of the former, but if I look to the other one, I cry out my hopelessness. I left the master too early. However, I appreciate the little drawing I know. I've spent many an enjoyable hour drawing, and I've fulfilled a dream I had as a child, watching Wilhelm Christie — he could draw all kinds of <u>strange things</u> — and Momma, who hardly drew anything but flowers, and I didn't find them all that artistic. (My dear Momma! In my home, I still have your favorite drawing flower, the "bear's ear" primrose; not many days passed after you drew that one before God called you to Him.) When they painted for me, I thought, "I wish I could draw like — yes just like you, Momma." (I don't think Papa ever drew anything — oh, yes, he drew horses, and then he had all his seven children walk behind the horse with long whips, urging him on.) Oh well, I think I'm better than all of you, I draw both horses and flowers, and all kinds of strange things, and I'm really good!!

Kalla! This is how I'm thinking as I'm sitting here, by myself — H. went to Kosconong [sic] today. It's probably different where you are. Wasn't the big family reunion supposed to be held at Uranienborg this summer? The people at Askevold (my <u>dear</u> minister-family), everybody from Voss, and the minister at Bjelland (the kind bachelor) were going to come see their old mother. This would be around the time for the gathering — joy and happiness for both mother and siblings, and my own siblings are also taking part in this joy, since both aunts and uncles like them. I will pray to God that He may give you joyful days — you pray to Him as well! And we shall meet — oh, how good, how wonderful — we shall meet, then we are also a part of the gathering. Thank You, thank You for this, my Lord. Make each one of us better every day — and a prayer for Kalla, who turns twenty-five today — he hopes to be a minister soon. Let your Spirit enlighten his soul and give it power, so that in the name of Jesus he may stand before a congregation with your words on his lips, with your Spirit in his heart, to give him courage and strength — so that he is worthy of preaching the wonderful, glorious word — to honor You and to guide and bless the listeners and himself — to guide — to bless, encouragement, faith, hope, love!

September 1 — The situation has changed quite a bit since the last time I wrote a few lines in this book of mine. Brother's birthday was probably not as joyful and happy as I had imagined — surely it was not. It was Monday, the 21st of August; Hermann and I came from the post office, happy and cheerful. With no second thoughts, we opened the letter we had received from home, but already at first glance, we knew it would bring us grief. Kalla had written, "Dear sister and brother. Pray to God that you may have the strength to read this news from home with tranquility and devotion." Exclaiming, "Sister Hex or old uncle Preus must be dead!" I took my Christian Keyser in my arms and started walking back and forth across the floor in the living room, my heart beating rapidly, while Hermann was reading Brother's letter aloud to me. I was right. Sister had passed away on the 28th of June and was buried on the 2nd of July (my birthday, when I was sitting here alone, having no idea about the sorrow you were experiencing at home).

A few weeks have passed since I received this message of grief — thank You, God, for so caringly having let my sorrow be mild and calm. Yes, thank You again and again for letting me go through this. I hope the experience will bear fruit, for me, for the siblings, for brother Wilhelm, her widowed husband. Thank You, God, for taking Sister home to You. Yes, I am so very glad that during the last days I have reached the point where I do not feel dishonest when I say, "Thank You, God, for calling Sister home to you!" In the first days after I received the news of Hexa's death, I was crying. Yes, I cried and worried — I prayed — I praised Him and honored Him, He who gives and takes, but no matter how I strove to let these words cross my lips with a sincerely devoted heart, nothing seemed to help the first days. My grief gave way for a few moments at a time, but then I kept hearing, "Eska is dead." Eska — if I ever return to Norway, I will never find my sister Hex there! But thanks to the wonderful word — Father! I read, I sang; I read about Israel's wandering in the desert — Israel's grumbling, its ungratefulness, its hardheartedness. I thought of myself, I was grumbling, too, how disgusting, how sinful! I read about Mary at Christ's cross, her silent grief, her devotedness, her humility — what an example she sets, if you would only follow that example, you foolish heart! I reminded myself of Jesus's words to the captain: "She is not dead, she is sleeping!" Yes, it is true! Glory to God! Hex is not dead, she is only sleeping for a little while, to wake up in the wonderful halls of heaven, where she shall see God and all the glories! I sang this wonderful hymn by Gerhard:

> In heaven is our true domain,
> There shall we dwell forever,
> And smile at earthly loss or pain
> Mild joys that perish never.

> There is the Father's house on high
> With many mansions glorious.
> There we with angels of the sky
> Shall sing the song victorious.

> And may we there as angels go
> All robed in radiant whiteness,
> In vestment pure as Yuletide snow
> And wings of shining brightness."

Yes, becoming that, yes, that is something I wish for. And how wrong, how selfish to want Sister back. No, I do not want that, no sister, you are happy where you are. And those you left behind, your husband and your child, your little two-month-old (when her mother died) Agnes Waleska Rosine Cathrine, your siblings and all those dear to you — God help us that we may wander down here in humility, patience, and devotion, filling the role given to us by God, and that when we are called by God, we may happily follow his command! Amen, in Jesus Christ's name!

October — December 1853

October 13 — Many, many times today I've thought about what took place on this day a year ago. That was when the good Lord gave me my little Christian Keyser — Oh my good Lord! You have given me so much good, and every day I get new proof of your merciful goodness toward me. But Lord, when You gave me my little son, You gave me one of my life's greatest signs of Your fatherly care for me. You have let me be worthy of having one of your children to protect and care for, to guide through life — through this peculiar, false, tempting, seducing world! Help me, God, so that as long as You let us travel together down here, I may lead him to You, oh God, that he may rejoice at walking in Your presence always, yes always! Help Hermann and me by Your Spirit so that we can raise Christian to please Your fatherly, caring eye!

Yes, watch over all of us — siblings and everybody, help us to watch! Amen — yes Amen in the name of Jesus Christ.

October 19 — Good God! What delightful days You have let us have recently — yes — nights too! It's already far into fall, and it's still as nice and warm as any summer morning — this so-called "Indian summer," or late summer, is such a wonderful time. It was often quite cold in August and September; many a morning the fields were white with rime, and the water puddle by the well was frozen over. In the morning our maid walked around in the kitchen with blue cheeks before she got some heat on the stove. Then she pulled off her sweater, took an old wooden shoe, put some embers in it, and added a couple of dry logs to get some heat in the stove in our room, so that we would not be cold when our lazy bodies got up. But now none of us is cold, neither she nor us. Now it's so warm that we leave our windows open during the day, and what is really good is that the cold killed the mosquitoes, the bedbugs, and all these disgusting vermin and animals, so that we can really enjoy this delightful time of the year.

Hermann is on his long journey north — we shall thank God that he has such good, mild weather. The previous two winters we have spent here, we only heard people talking about this "Indian summer;" we have never experienced it. Quite the contrary, actually, we have had snow and cold weather, or humid, raw air, with fog and rain. That is probably what the weather is like home in Norway. October is no beautiful month there. Still, I've often come to think about Norway when I go for my walks here, and when I stand on the top of the prairie, looking around me. At the edge of the prairie, the hardwood forest is really pretty with all its shifting colors, that are even more wonderful to look at in the beautiful light of the sunset, and it makes me think about Norway, with its glorious nature. I turn around and my eye seeks the wild prairie-ocean, whose fertile green color has now been replaced by yellow, whose flowers have withered, and soon it shall all turn into ashes, because if I'm not mistaken, the billowing cloud I see on the horizon comes from the prairie fire coming closer to us — oh, if only it will not cause any damage.

I have been poetic tonight — I guess it is because of the clear moonlight, shining down on me through the window, but now good night all! Thank You, good God, for everything this day has brought — give us a peaceful night, in Jesus's name!!

December 10 — How annoying — or wearisome — it is for a housewife when she's expecting guests and they don't come. I find myself in that situation right now. Ever since dinner was done, I've peeked out through the windows to look for our buggy, bringing Hermann, Pastor Koren, and his wife. Now it's night and dark, so Mom has tidied up herself and her house for nothing — although still they might come. At least my night owl Hermann ought to come, but I was stupid to put on my nice dress so early, and even more stupid not to go to bed. I guess I have a bad cold; every time I swallow, my throat says "ouch." I'm glad I didn't set the dinner table. There is chicken fricassee ready on the stove; they can have it for supper.

I got a new tray for my house the other day; I was and am happy about it. Just out of curiosity, I arranged my coffee set on it: cups, coffee sugar, and cream, plus some cookies. Right now it's in the living room, and I say it stays there until I bother to get up. All in all, my house is a bit nicer now than what it used to be. Last year about this time, I got curtains, plus six chairs, and we moved the chests, the log seat, and the firkin. This summer, Joachim Fleischer gave me a tablecloth, and now I finally got a tray, so that I won't have to carry cups and dishes one by one — when we're having guests and I need more cups and saucers than usual. When we're alone, I'll spare the treasure since it's poorly made and incredibly expensive — at home it probably costs about a half *daler*, but here it costs one and a half — terrible! I also have a dozen soup plates and a dozen ordinary plates. So yes, I'm developing my home. Some time ago we had a church council meeting here. H. is one of the three ministers of the council. The other two are A. Preus and G. Dietrichson. Then there are three laymen, too. I left the living room completely to the council and enjoyed myself down here in the office with Elise Bruun,[255] who has now been with me for a quarter of a year. I only informed the chairman that I wanted my living room when it was time to eat, and sometimes I got it, other times I had to wait — what a shame!?

Isn't it strange, how every time ministers visit each other, it's because of business — good enough, but when their business has been discussed and debated, why are they always in such a hurry to get home? Why are they always saying, as they are discussing something, that "oh, time flies, let's get done and agree, let's stick to the matter, otherwise we'll have to stay here a day longer!" Wouldn't it be nice for the ministers to spend a day or more together just to enjoy themselves? That they are not doing that here is fair enough, since all the ministers are accustomed to a higher standard than what we have here, but when the meetings are at Koshkonong or at Rock Prairie (nobody else has had meetings yet — oh, yes, at Stub's in Muskego), it's the same there. I guess they have things to do at home, but if they really wanted to stay….?! It's a blessing, though, that they all care so much for their home. That is something we have to remember and thank God for, but I think these gentlemen should arrange everything a bit differently. They should find a place somewhere halfway between them, and discuss their business there. Then they could visit each other for their own pleasure when they feel like it or there is an occasion — that would be a lot nicer and a lot more fun.

All this minister talk makes me forget the important change in my house; next to the kitchen I've gotten a guest room, and I got the bed out of the living room, which was really good!!

December 11 — A few hours ago I received letters from home — they brought a message of grief this time, too. Our good cousin and brother Johan[256] died September 13th. Weak as he was after his recent pneumonia, his eagerness and conscientiousness made him start working with his business too early, which was often doubled because of the cholera epidemic sweeping over Xiania right now. That fearful guest is raging at home, and among the numerous victims there are several family members who have already been called by God, but the loss of Johan has been the most painful so far. But — dear brother, you are, after all, up there with the good Lord, with your mother and brother, and there everything is good, very good, then all of us down here, those you left behind, do not wish for your return — peace be with you, dear lovely brother! Oh, so many people miss you, but God strengthen all of us!

I want to add what *Christianiaposten* says about Johan after it has written about the doctors and the efforts they are going through in times like this. It also praises them for conscientiously fulfilling their duties, and says that they should all be kept alive in the grateful memory of Christiania's inhabitants: "Unfortunately, the efforts have caused illness among those in whom, besides God, we place our trust. The epidemic has also crowned one of them with compassion's martyr crown, when Johan Keyser Jacob Preus passed away on the night of September 13th. The victim it found belonged in all ways to the most noble. Even though he only lived to be forty years old, his particular good humor and kindness would have made him a man of many friends and the dearest member of his family. Because of his clear eye for detail, his serious study and his conscious care for others in a long service as a doctor, dedicated to promote good health among so many, his ashes were accompanied to the grave by the blessings of many men, women, and children. There rests yet another life, lived and dedicated to the well-being of humanity."

January — March 1854

January 21, 1854 — I'm surprised to see that the lines I'm writing in my diary tonight are the first of the New Year. I was so sure that I wrote on New Year's Day, but I've been confused by the fact that I've already written to, and received letters from, Norway twice in the New Year. My appreciation and gratefulness for the goodness and love that You showed me in the past year is nothing compared to what it ought to be. Oh, I am not cold and dead —You — how good and caring You are, all-good Father. Lord, grant me a more loving heart, a more humble mind — by Your sacred Spirit in the name of Jesus Christ — for Hermann and the siblings, for family and friends, I call on you for the sake of everybody, in the name of Jesus, Amen!

3rd Sunday after Epiphany.[257] It's been terribly cold for three days now. It was impossible to get the living room heated, so we moved in here to the office/bedroom. Yesterday, Hermann was supposed to have been at Bonnet Prairie, but since it was twenty-two degrees below zero[262], he figured that none of the confirmands with whom he was supposed to read would be there, so he didn't go until today. We made it really cozy in here instead — if we constantly made sure that the oven was red-hot, it was possible to keep the air in here warm, but our poor feet! The wind came from the East, and no paneling or molding around the floors can keep such an intrusive guest away. Hermann placed his feet on the stove, which made them nice and warm. I was sitting by my spinning wheel, spinning with all my might, but it didn't help — my feet were cold, and of course, my toothache wouldn't go away. Hermann knew what to do; he went out and came back in with our buffalo robe and a sheepskin. The buffalo robe covered more than three quarters of the office floor — it looks a lot like the brown bearskins we have at home — and he took the sheepskin into the bedroom and placed it in front of the armchair, in which he very contentedly found his place, wearing his robe and slippers, and with his pipe in his mouth. I was very comfortable on the buffalo robe with my spinning wheel, but mischievous little Christian was so often close to hurting himself on it that I had to put it away. We've hung a big quilt up on one of the walls in the bedroom — the one with the windows. Because the door from the office to the living room doesn't close completely — the house is sinking in the middle — we hung my big traveling coat across it. Living in an office and a bedroom doesn't sound too bad, but nobody who saw the space we have would say that it is too much. The space we have in these two rooms combined is sixteen feet wide and ten feet long. In the division of the rooms, the office was treated sort of like a stepmother; it's only six feet wide, while the bedroom is ten. Separating them is a thin partition with leaky boards; you can stick one, or some places two, fingers into the cracks. So it's not hard to understand how a little heating stove placed in a corner of the bedroom, between a door that leads into the kitchen and another door leading into the office (that door is always open), is sufficient to heat up these two small rooms. In the bedroom, there's just enough room for our big bed, the cradle, and two chairs. (Usually there's just one, since we don't have that many, but during this cold, Hermann has taken the armchair into the bedroom. It's placed between the end of the bed and the door to the living room — this door is usually closed, since we always use the one from the office, where my coat is hanging now.) So H. is sitting facing the office, with his back toward the window, and his feet on the stove. The bed is so close to the window that H. has to crawl over to his place when he goes to bed. I've placed a <u>small</u> table by Hermann's headboard; it's just big enough for the lamp and a book. When my lazybones goes to bed at eight o'clock in the evening or two or three in the morning, he smokes his pipe, and then messes a lot with the bedspreads, a bad habit which I always criticize him for. I guess I could make him quit the pipe, but he really enjoys it, so....

Apart from the armchair, there is also a <u>small</u> table at the foot of the bed. My bookshelf is hanging on the wall above it — the bookshelf was a gift from Governor Christie. There's a little shelf with my drawing and coloring supplies between the bookshelf and the wall with the windows. There's nothing on the wall by the headboard, since one fine day when it's raining from the East, there's a chance it would get soaked.

Now we've reached the partition; it has *Emigranten* all over it (the Norwegian paper from our press at Rock Prairie). I hung them all up last summer, including the ceiling. But it has been shrunk as much as the wall, leaving spaces for bedbugs and other disgusting creatures living there. Unfortunately, it doesn't do any good if we whitewash the cracked oak wall; it's too good a shelter for those vermin. That was my wall. It has several things on it: a portrait of Governor Christie; below that there's an Indian pincushion, shaped like a long heart with no cleft. Below that there's a drawing of Askevold, and on each side of that is a watch cushion, with Hermann's and my watches — they're in a terrible condition: the first one has stopped, and the other one I have to set ahead fifteen minutes every evening. Above this treasure hangs an excellent device — the knit carryall I got at Askevold in 1849. On it is a hook that serves as a handyman; it has a key, nail scissors, and the ball of thread I use to fasten the hem to the waist of my son's new undershirt.

NB: The window in the bedroom faces south. The office window faces east; that and a three-foot wide bookshelf take up that wall. Beneath the bookshelf is my writing desk — unpainted — and under the window, my dresser. The shelves are a foot out from the wall so that the books won't be ruined by rain coming in through the north wall. Since we got the kitchen and the little room on that side of the house, that has provided good shelter, even if there are cracks in it that let us peek into the kitchen. There are engravings hanging on the wall there, a portrait of Wexels, and a little mirror, a piece of furniture we've recently acquired. Together with the dresser, a sofa fills that side of the room. It's made of bark-covered aspen, and its pillows are the good old horsehair pillows that served me on my sleeping couch at my parents' home. They leave a little space, which is entirely filled up by the tall bookshelf, filled from floor to ceiling with carefully bound books, which are a little musty from our journey across the Atlantic. The bookshelf towers beautifully; together with the door to the living room, it takes up the western wall.

February 7 — I'm tired tonight, even though it isn't very late, which I would say is unusual, because I rarely feel like sleeping until 10-12 p.m. I'm a "night owl" — but no rule is without exceptions, and that's why I'm tired now. Nevertheless, I have to write down a tragic-comic scene that took place during the course of the day.

I'm sitting in the office, spinning — Hermann has been gone for three days — thinking about everything and anything when "Lasse," my errand boy, comes running in, crying almost desperately, "What are we going to do, *Wettle-Kossen* (the calf) has fallen into the well!" It didn't take me long to get to the well with Torbjør[259] and Lasse, and poor thing! The calf is down there, in the fifty-two-foot-deep well — it still has its head above water, but it can't keep it like that for very long. What are we going to do? "Lasse, you have to go down into the well! No men on the farm — but Thorbjør, you're strong enough to lift up, and I'll support the rope." I could see that Lasse was scared — and fearing that he might get dizzy as we lowered him down, I exclaim, "I'd rather see the calf die than you fall into the well." Thanks to God! He's down by the water now — he has the calf, and I'm calling him every minute, "Lasse, let me know when you have tied the calf to the rope!" I remain quiet for a little while, I hear splashing from down there — "Lasse! Lasse!" I yell, but he doesn't answer. I yell again and again, as loud as I possibly can — oh, how scared I was. Finally the boy calls up, "Yes, done — pull him up, but don't let go, no matter what!" "No, no, we won't, be sure, don't be afraid!" Thorbjør is pulling, and I'm supporting the rope. We probably haven't pulled more than ten feet until we hear a bump and a splash. "Lasse! Lasse!" I yell once again. "Yes, pull!" Oh my, how relieved I was to hear him answer. Always afraid of failure, I look down into the dark well and call, and I'm answered, too. But how am I supposed to describe the fear I feel now? The rope is soon up, there is the calf — it's hanging by its head, but Lasse, where is he? The calf has now reached the edge of the well; it is about to get strangled, but I'm not strong enough to pull it in, and Thorbjør has to hold the line. "Lasse!" I yell once again, in fear. Thank

God, he's answering. So, quick, take the calf, the loop is cut, and the calf is pushed into the yard — quick, lower the rope again! "Lasse! Lasse! We're lowering the rope now!" Oh, fear! The stick we forgot to fasten falls out of the loop! It might hit him in the head! But God, You held Your sheltering hand over us this time too. Lasse is answering my repeated calling. "We're pulling now, Lasse!" "Yes, yes, just don't let go!" "No, no, don't be afraid — just hang on!" Look, there he is, he'll be up soon now! "Hang on!" "Yes, just don't let go!" There, I have his arm — oh how tight I hold on to him to pull him up; he will have bruises tomorrow. "Are you hurt?" "No!" L. answers, crying as he goes over to the kitchen, rubbing his right shoulder. Only now we paid attention to the poor calf — it looked OK, except for being hauled up by its neck. But it's wet, and trembling with cold — imagine all the water it's swallowed — oh, it's probably not that filled up yet. We're rubbing it and stroking it. I go to fetch some of my Norwegian brandy, mix it with milk, and some of this warming mixture is poured into the calf. The stick had hit Lasse's shoulder, but not very hard. The calf, surprisingly enough, was not bothered by the blows on its head and back; it was able to walk fairly well, but was shivering with cold and struggling a bit because of the liquor that had made it dizzy. I think it will be all right. I came with Thorbjør when she went to give it milk tonight. It eagerly drank everything we gave it, and would probably have had more too, but we didn't dare to give it more, since it probably <u>quenched its thirst</u> in the well.

I praise You and thank You, oh God, for looking after Lasse — I guess I was inconsiderate to let him go down there! It's not really hard to be lowered down into a well like that, but the well has stones all the way around it, and a stone could easily have fallen down, and then.... It happens too often that people have to get down into their wells, not for the same reason as we, but to fetch the pail you use to fetch up water in, it often falls down in the water, both here and other places. People who are used to it don't mind going down into the well, but Lasse's situation was different. He had never done anything like that before. Oh well, it's over, and today I've been at old Christopher's to have him build a house around the well, something the congregation has been going to do for more than a year now, but what happened to the calf today was too serious to be ignored. Chickens and one pig have drowned in there before . I've run out of patience — tomorrow, I guess, we'll have a little enclosure of some sort around our well. There used to be a trapdoor over it, but it was resting on a layer of ice, and with a little push it would slide away.

March 4 — It was Monday and we sent a messanger to the post office — we got letters from home — oh, how good it is to get letters from that part of the world! It is good even if it is bad news, for the grief is also good, and it feels good to share it with everybody in Norway. This time we got the third message of grief from 1853. God called on our old grandmother the night before Christmas Eve. I was anxious as I opened one letter after the other — skimmed through one, then another one. I could tell that somebody had died, and I suspected it to be Grandmother, but I had not seen it in plain words yet; I thought about the siblings, aunts, and uncles, and I saw Cousin Preus's letter right away, so.... Finally I got hold of a letter that said right in the beginning that Grandmother was dead — I sincerely thanked God that He had shown the dear old woman mercy. I think she had experienced so much pain in this world, both for body and soul, that she was tired, and with joy and a pure, devoted heart, she could face her death. Those of us that you left behind, children, children's children (and children's children's children) will bless your memory and thank God that He has let you find rest in heaven with Jesus Christ. Yes, Father, your mercy by Jesus knows no end, and we poor sinners have to comfort ourselves knowing that our dear ones, passing away in the name of the Lord, will also find their eternal home with You. Everybody at home — even sister Hex — often wrote me before she died that Grandmother had changed a lot since I left. When you were in a good mood, Grandmother, you were often charming, but it didn't take much for you to become depressed and blue. How often I was the one to cause this change of moods in you! But I've forgotten about everything we said, and believing that a long time ago you forgave me my youthful inconsiderateness and stubbornness, you stand before me in my memory as my good old Grandmother, who did a lot for me and for my siblings, for which we sincerely thank you. Peace be with your memory, you good old woman!

Uranienborg looks different now than when I left. What will happen now — oh God — with my sisters; they're separated from each other, from aunt Lodviska — the good, dear careful aunt — from Borgen and from brother, uncles, and aunts — oh no, what will happen? God, Father, I shall not worry — You will take care of everything so wisely and well. I will ask You for one thing, though — if it is your will, then let Rosa and Bya be close to Kalla; he is the best to guide them and keep them close to You! I guess Lillemamma and Hanchen will be placed with their future in-law's. You are separating us siblings; we were so happy to be together again — yes, oh Lord, what is separation here on earth? Nothing! Nothing! As long as we live our lives in the sweet hope, for the sake of Jesus Christ, our Father wants us to be together in our heavenly home, in joy, yes, joy in the name of Jesus!

I want to write down a little poem that was printed in *Morgenbladet* and then in *Emigranten* after Hexa's death:

The 28th of June
This lively young figure
This child and this grown woman
This spirited, rich soul
This deep well of joy
Called to heaven's home so soon?

The message of death not yet conveyed, still there's life
The rose not yet parted from its stem
Though almost — still the angel of death
Has not placed its last deep kiss on her dim eyes — if we have hope
That God will once again color her cheeks with red
That are now pale — that this dim eye
Shall shine again — that rich life
Shall once again spring up as in healthy days
That God will give her back to us!

Thursday the 30th of June.
Gone — she is not here anymore — oh devastating death,
Why this flower so dear to so many,
So fresh, so pretty, so fragrant, so graceful?
Bound to this earth with such precious bonds
As wife, mother — oh, why this spirit
So young — not yet old enough for heaven?

You blind child of the earth, it was not death,
But life your rose received.
Also God found her a beauty, and
Took her home to heavenly joy.

Her walk was light and dancing,
Beautiful life ran through her veins.
Her happy laughter so often on her lips
And within reigned Christian sincerity.

So graceful to her God she must have been
Now she is resting safely in his arms
Surrounded by his love she is smiling to her loved ones here
Asking God to watch over them.

So, there is the little poem. I have finally got it down in my book. Today is the first of May 1854. When I read it in the paper last year, I put it away, planning to write it down, but I asked myself what I thought of it, and my answer was then as it is now: "Oh well, it doesn't comfort me in my grieving, even though I like parts of it." Today I feel like there is more to it, but I don't know what made me change my mind. I wonder if it's because when I said what I said, I was not yet used to the thought that God had taken my dear sister away. The author gives her much praise; what good does exaggeration do? We ought to look at mistakes, mistakes we are aware of, confess to, and forgive with all our hearts! Now when I have known for almost a year that sister is in heaven and not in Norway, she also seems more perfect than the rest of us — a better person — which is probably why I also like the little memorial better.

It was so hard for me, in the beginning, when I was writing home to my siblings, not writing to my Hexa. I often cried at the thought, and a couple of times I was close to writing "Dear sister Hex!" on the top of the sheet.

But, thanks to God, the thought of her death is no longer new to me. Since we got the message of her death, each letter has actually brought more bad news: Brother Johan (brother-in-law), Mrs. Nørgaard and three of Breder's little children, old Grandmother, and the last letter brought the message that God had taken away a little friend to us and a dear, dear son to Jørgen Breder and Pauline. Their only son, Severin — a wonderful little child — died from croup in February. If only Hermann and I, if God calls C.K. before he calls us, if only we can bear the loss with such a faith and such piety as our dear siblings at home have borne the loss of little Severin.

June 30 — Today it is exactly a year since sister Hex died — dear, dear sister! I often think of you, often talk to you, but it is such a strange way of talking — and why is that? Well, I'm too mortal to talk to you, already with God in Heaven — my thoughts are always occupied with what belongs to the perishable. When I remember our days together, I'm only concerned with what belongs to this world, though sometimes it happens that the image of our reunion in the other world stands so vividly before me that.....but, unfortunately I seldom find myself in such a state of mind, I seldom feel this longing for God, although I know that God wants us to long for him, even if our life on this earth is so happy and good as the mortal human being can ever ask for. Sometimes when I think of my death — when the time has come that death calls me — I get feverish and anxious. Shall I already be taken away from Hermann, C. Keyser, siblings, and everything I hold so dear down here ... but why this anxiety? No, I don't fear death, but I'm so happy here, I don't want to leave it ...leave it, where would you go? Do you not know, you heart of the flesh, when I die, those left on earth shall not see me again, but I would go to God in Heaven, where I shall be far happier than I have been here, and even if I leave the people I care about, God, who has cared for them and for me as well as he has, will not leave them though I do, and what good would it do them if I stayed — I'm not doing them good, but God alone is......all right, so what is this talk that you do not want to die? <u>No, I do not want to die</u> — but do you understand why I said that I was mortal? The devil fills my head with his talk about the magnificence of this world, but, praise to God, I know how to reason against it, so God's spirit can bring peace to my heart.

God can bring us death every day, but knowing that an illness that has taken many lives is imminent, I'm thinking more about it than usual — is that bad? In a couple of months I will be in the childbed again — it is so painful, but God's will be done! Hexa, you died in the childbed — so did Mother. I cannot know what God has decided for me, but His will be done — I hope everyone called to die is prepared!

There has been a lot of noise around my house these days. A mason is plastering the bedroom, and he's putting lime and sand in between the timbers on the outside. Also, I have felt uneasy; Hermann went down to Muskego six days ago, to Pastor Stub's to baptize a little girl. I was invited too, to carry the child, but I couldn't go on that trip; I can't take much traveling when I'm as big as I am now. Besides, I think wives ought to stay at home, especially when they're pregnant. Also, I have a lot to do around the house now that we have bought a farm. When H. is gone I can supervise the workers, etc., etc. For example: a couple of days ago, a man in the congregation who had just returned from an Iowa trip brought an extremely beautiful mare for Ziiølner. We were supposed to look after it until he came himself, so I put it in my neighbor's pasture. Yesterday morning Ambjørn came to tell me that the wind had blown the gate to the pasture open and the mare was gone.... Where should we look for it? Had it started on its way home, to Iowa, three hundred miles from here and on the other side of the Mississippi? Or could it be that our foals and our horse that were together with "Flora" and came with her to the gate had met her in the woods or on the prairie outside the pasture? There was a possibility, but a very small one. When our animals get away, there is such an enormous amount of land open to them that they can walk for miles and miles if they want to. Peersen had to go out and look for them. He walked and he walked all day yesterday, but in vain — neither Flora nor Bill nor any foal could be seen. None of them, although in a way that is good, it might be that they are together! Hermann was supposed to be picked up tomorrow, with Bill and the buggy, and Peersen driving; he would be waiting.

At four o'clock this morning, I woke up the boy and the hired hand—they were going out looking. Peersen left at 7 a.m. and at eleven they all came back empty-handed. What to do? Peersen had to go pick up H., he would already be in Stouthen [Stoughton] (six miles from Koshkonong parsonage). H. had to be back by tomorrow, for that is Saturday! P: you have to go to Fosmarka to rent Niels' horses. He left, but at one o'clock he came back without any horses; however, in the meantime I had been at Lars Møen's to have him go out in the woods looking for my horses. I sent for Ambjørn, asking him to come. He let me borrow his horse so that one man could use that one for the day, looking for the others, but then he said, "But ma'am, last night I saw four horses behind the big hill west of me, and I think it was that one-eared Bill of yours, the foals, and the new horse!" "How can that be possible, Peersen was over there twice yesterday?" "I'll go over there right now, and then the boy can run back to say if it's your horses." That was kind — here comes the boy. I let him go with Ambjørn, and after half an hour I see A. and the boy riding on Flora and Bill, with the foals behind them! We were luckier this time than we were two years ago, when we lost the other Flora. When P. got home he had dinner in a hurry, and then old Bill had to leave with him and the buggy. Right now they and H. are probably in Koshkonong. When they get back tomorrow, I'll get some packages my family in Xiania sent me last summer with Pastor Koren. But since everything has been very slow for the good minister with his chests and boxes, it's not so strange that I haven't gotten them until now, almost a year after they were sent. I'll take them as birthday presents, for Sunday is the 2nd of July, then it will be one year since Sister was buried and twenty-five years since I was born.

September 20 — Oh, God! Forgive me! I feel so little devotion, so little humility, so little grief for my sins! Three weeks ago you purified me with your flesh and blood — I felt so happy to have enjoyed that sacrament. I was so sure that You had forgiven me all my sins in the name of Jesus, but, oh, this notion has not been very heartfelt — I feel different now. I do not feel abandoned by You, I hope for and have faith in Christ's mercy, but my gratitude toward You for your goodness is so tepid, so dead, so indifferent — oh forgive me, oh Lord! In the name of Jesus!

Coming up now, as far as our eyes tell us, is a painful time for the body[260] — I do not feel well. Maybe I will receive a great gift from You before this day is over, oh God! Maybe You have come to fetch me. O Lord, all these thoughts; I get them so often, but they make me turn as cold as if I were dead. I will not pray any sincere prayer, I am so tired, O Lord, let me get better! Let your spirit live in me in the name of Jesus Christ — Amen!

1855

January 25, 1855 — I've thought so many times about writing in my book, but just as often something has gotten in the way. A new year has begun, in my thoughts I've thanked You, my good Lord and Father, for everything You gave me in the past year. I have talked to You in prayer, You giver of everything good, but I haven't written anything. I can't really say that I feel bad about that, but the thing is that I like to be able to sort out my thoughts on the paper every once in a while. It allows me to be by myself.... But I have already started on something quite different than what I wanted to say, so enough.... Oh, Lord God, how You have cared for me and mine in the past year with fatherly tenderness, how lovingly You have reminded us with your providence and caring, if we would only remember to add that it is all, all to the better for us, even though it often seems painful — yes, so that Your providence may bring us to a recognition of our sins! May it wake us up from our drowsy, sleepy, tepid existence, may it cause our soul more and more, through watching and prayer, to be in conversation with its God — so that with sincere love and eagerness, your Holy Ghost may lead our body to do what You find good and right, oh God!

Oh Father, help me, help Hermann, siblings, and everybody to show the tempter away when he stands at the door to our hearts with his cunning and temptations, wanting to find room inside. Give us the strength and the courage to say get away from me, Satan — we beg You, in the name of Jesus, O Lord, let us grow in faith, hope, and love each day, so that each day we will recognize our great sins, and in humility will call on You for forgiveness. Our arrogance is great, it is not easy to get rid of. If it leaves us for a minute, soon it is back again — yes, quite unnoticed, it sneaks back in. If only the door were locked with iron bands and bolts, it could not fool us. Your word, oh God, be our bands and bolts, let us by frequent use of the Word detest what belongs to the flesh, and do what the Holy Spirit commands. I cannot thank You enough, dear Lord, for graciously giving me so much of what I have prayed for in the past years — it all comes back to me — I remember so many things I prayed for that You made happen — me, unworthy sinner, has been heard for the sake of Jesus Christ — oh joy, joy! — God is watching over us!! Even a sparrow does not fall to the ground without Him knowing it — how much less would he allow a human to perish in sin without drawing him back to Himself by calling and correcting the sinner? Sometimes I feel so close to You — other times I feel far away, a stranger to You. Oh God — how wonderful, how purifying to look into Your gentle countenance. Why can't these moments always stand before my soul? Why am I so often away from You — so dead, so empty? It is the Devil in me defeating the angel — the evil spirit seeks to be the more powerful. Oh You, good Spirit, your Spirit, Lord God, be the more powerful in me, so that it may firmly show the Devil away from the door to my heart!

Dear God, in Jesus's name help us in our fight against the Devil — You will not let him be the victor in us, our own power is nothing. We would soon fall, but the Lord's sword is protecting us, to that sword Satan must surely surrender if you ask, who is this Jesus Christ? Lord of heaven's forces, our savior, mild and gentle, He will be the victor!

Lord God, You answered many of my prayers in the past year, but I most clearly remember when You gave me our dear little Pauline Rosine

— what a joyful day it was, the 21st of October. Our daughter came into this world around midday. The wonderful little girl — fine and healthy — I don't think a mother's heart is ever so thankful as when she holds her well-formed little child to her breast for the first time after her great effort and pain. Still, how faint that gratitude is compared to what it ought to be?

November 5 — I seldom write these days. Since I have two small children, I never seem to have time for anything except for my two toddlers — Christian Keyser and Pauline Rosine occupy my thoughts the entire day. Hermann and I are so fond of them!! I've been without a nursemaid almost the entire summer, and my older maid has been sick a lot, so with Sina on my arm and C.K. pulling my skirts, I've often been both nursemaid and cook. I find that pretty tough, especially when you add that Hermann has been away more than at home, which means that I have had to watch the farm, too, with boys and workers — horses, cattle and pigs, sheep, and hens. No wonder I haven't had the time to write. And when I have had a moment, I've been scribbling down some letters for siblings, family, and friends in Norway. Ziiølner and his wife came to visit us in August.[261] I was planning on having a good time, but "'Pooh!' said Peer to the king"[262] — my only maid at the time got sick, and I had to do all the work myself. Two new maids, Anne and Turi, were living here then, but then the wheat harvest started, and the two of them wanted to work outside and get half a dollar a day, something I could not pay them for doing the dishes, etc. They did the milking for me morning and evening because they were sleeping here.

Ziiølner had changed a lot since he stayed with us two years ago — he had been suffering from rheumatism for several months so he could hardly walk, and he was so skinny and stooped over that you could hardly recognize him. Elise, on the other hand, looked better than ever; she was happier, more cheerful, and the two of them seemed to love each other so very much.

Hermann and I were planning to take a trip to Iowa to visit Pastors Koren and Clausen and their wives, but it never came to anything. H. had too many other trips he had to go on, so a trip just for the pleasure of it was really out of the question. It was especially the trip to Blue Mounds that disappointed both the Korens and ourselves. Lange, who had gotten the call there, did not accept it, so Hermann had to take over as pastor there, plus the additional smaller congregations, until they get a pastor.

I was busy, too, in my own way. In addition to all the things I mentioned before, I also had to look after our garden. Because of an extremely wet summer, the weeds were outgrowing us everywhere — this summer H. and I just could not keep the garden ourselves like we have the previous years. Two times we had the new maids, Anne and Turi, weed. Once, we really fixed up our garden, mostly because Adolph Preus and his wife were coming, but then they never showed up — well, Preus came a couple of days later, but his wife….She had to stay home with the children; they had the chicken pox, poor things. My living room looked really rustic at the time; I had fresh, new aspen leaves around the walls, and a big tuft was hanging in the hole up to the attic, where the chimney comes through. In the summer, when it gets so hot that we don't need the stove, we take it out in the cowshed — there are no animals there at that time. We put the pipes up in the attic, after we have beaten them and scraped the inside with a stick. That is how we clean our pipes in America's countryside. The little brick chimney going from the attic and through the roof is never cleaned, and when the pipes leading to this are so full that there is no draft, we take them out to clean them in the yard. Only once has our brick chimney been cleaned since we moved in, and that was three years ago. I'm the one who would not accept the American custom, and to calm me down, Ziiølner had to get up on the roof, carrying a long stick with a broom attached to its end, and this remedy was long enough to reach the bottom of the chimney. I guess I'm more Americanized now — well, that's how it goes, but only in this regard — I never think about cleaning the chimney anymore.

So, my living room looked really nice, and the high church council — Hermann and Adolph Preus and three laymen — held their meeting there on the 20th of June, and the following day. At the exact same time the honorable Ellingians[263] had their annual meeting at Langeteig, so the council decided to go down there to demand an explanation from the members of that group about many false accusations they have made about false teachings, etc. Quite content with the negotiations and discussions, they returned after four or five hours, with great expectations of improvements in the Ellingians' hateful and slanderous behavior, and that they would now deal with the other branches of the church in loving fellowship, as the others treat them. The council was also hoping that the Ellingians were not far from joining our church, but there they fooled themselves. The Ellingians were just as far, if not farther, from joining after the meeting than ever before. The pastors and congregations are in a way Lutheran, but our community has the purer, truer teaching. We are "God's little flock," so no union with the "great mass" is desired — the good Ellingians use such great words to describe their community that I have difficulty finding any spirit of humility there to guide them, and isn't that what God the Father <u>wants</u> to find among his children??

That, by the way, is not the only time A. Preus has honored us with his visits this summer. He's had as many as three short trips up here, and each time Hermann has been away, so he's had to be patient and be content with my company until H. has finally come home, late at night. One of the times H. was gone and A.P. came was last spring. H. had gone to Bonnet Prairie, where he had called a meeting to meet some Methodist leaders and teachers who were going around up there, misguiding the people. Of course, when H. came home he had to say how it all went. H. was very satisfied; God had given him great help, and the three Methodist preachers had been denounced by the congregation as deceivers and false teachers. The meeting was held in the church, and three Methodist pastors attended. They had been talking a lot about how they would easily put Pastor Preus in a tight spot, but H. never felt any difficulties; on the contrary, he put his opponents on the spot more than once, so the congregation could not keep themselves from laughing and saying, "So what do you say to that?" When the discussion had been going on for an hour or two, it didn't look like there would be any improvement between H. and the Methodist pastors. H. was just trying to prove what false teachers they were for the sake of the congregation. Then a man in the congregation finally stood up, went over to H., and put his arm around his waist or over his shoulder and said, "That's enough, you don't have to keep talking to these people for our sake. We realized a long time ago that they are deceivers. Our doors will be closed for them, and we thank you for having helped us to realize what false teachers they are." With that he led H. out of the church and the congregation said as with one tongue, "Yes, yes — it's enough." I have forgotten to ask H. if they ended this meeting like they started it, with prayer and singing.

When they started the meeting, I believe they sang a hymn and H. said the Lord's Prayer. The Methodists did not seem to find this prayer sufficient. One of them came over to H. and said, "We always start our meetings with a prayer. Maybe you would allow me to say it?" H. answered that he was content with the prayer he had already said, but if the questioner felt a need to pray, he was welcome to do so. H. had hardly finished before the Methodists fell to their knees, and then there was such whining, wailing, and sighing that if you didn't know that that is how this sect shows their devotion, you'd think they were either sick or crazy. Oh, dear God, I thank you for the conviction I have in my heart that our church alone preaches the right way to salvation — Oh Father! I beg You in the name of Jesus Christ: do not take this conviction away from me, and if I should be tempted, if so Lord, be my protection and shield, let me with your word in my hand and my mouth, but most of all in my heart, stand before the tempter saying, "Jesus Christ stands by my side, for his sake only will God forgive me my sins. His blood purifies us, my own merits are none, none — but when, during my time on earth, I walk in faith, hope, and love, using God's means of grace that He gave me for my salvation — word, baptism, and communion — I shall face death fearlessly, for I will be saved!! — For the sake of Jesus."

1856

February 23, 1856 — Just as certain as it is that I haven't written anything in my book in the new year, it's certain that I've made many good promises to God in my thoughts, and prayed many a prayer to Him, for myself and my family here, for siblings and family and friends, yes for everybody. Oh, good our Father, help me in being good, let there be seriousness to my promises, and I know that You will bless them! It was with a great gratitude for your goodness in all ways, that I stepped out of the old year — but how moderate and weak is everything my heart says to You, sacred good Father. Oh, have mercy with me for Jesus's sake. During the last weeks, Lord, You have touched my heart in a powerful way. Eight to fourteen days ago, I thought You were going to take little Christian Keyser up to You. I never thought it would be so hard to say good-bye to such a little creature — but it was hard, for we had little hope, no hope, that his life would be spared. We all said our good-byes, but God let a calm sleep come to him, and for one and a half days he was in a daze, breathing heavily — and to our great joy he got better. Yes, God Father, You have given us little Christian again, so we sincerely pray for your help to raise him and Sina to be good people, so that when their time down here is over, they can be a part of your happiness, after having honored you and served fellow human beings, if their days will be more than just a few. If I tried so hard to feel God's love in all this — I prayed — I prayed, I wanted to feel happy and devoted to God's will — I said with Job, "The Lord gave — the Lord took away — blessed be the name of the Lord" I said, "Well, it is good for Christian that he may leave us now — he will not have to struggle in this world, he will be a little angel now, he can be with us every day and night, even though we cannot see him, as long as we have faith in God. I said all this as tears were running down my cheeks and my heart was filled with sorrow, but also with devotion in God's will. Hermann dear, we should not be so sad. C. will be so happy now — he will be free. C. opened his eyes and looked at Papa and Momma — we blessed him in the name of Jesus, he repeated our words, then he kissed us and Sina, and we thought he was sleeping the sleep of death. Hermann read the hymn from Gulberg's hymn book, "The light of day is gone, darkness descends upon us." While he was reading that, or a while after, I cannot really remember, C. opened his eyes again. "A little glass of water, Momma." That was more than he had said for several hours; he drank and fell asleep again. We didn't leave his bed; we expected each breath to be his last, but that that was not God's plan. And — oh dear good God — yes, it is Your unlimited love and goodness — You will forgive me for the sake of Christ, I feel like I love You more after You let me keep C. Oh, forgive, forgive, Father, I am such a great, great sinner — I feel like my love has grown. Teach me to put myself on trial, do not let the Devil defeat what is good in me, do not let him play with my heart, but be a rock that I may lean on, always and without fear, and stick to with burning love. <u>Strengthen my faith, hope, and love</u>!! C. had been sick for eight days when Hermann came home from a longer trip — during that period I sought to find peace and strength through my children, and thousands of times I told myself, "Your dear Lord is with you, is he not? Do not be so restless because Hermann is not here" — this did not always help, though, and when H. finally came home, I could really feel how weak my faith, hope, and love are, for I felt calmer, but when praying? Oh, so weak! Forgive! For Christ's sake, amen!

4th Sunday of Advent 1856[264]— Only a few days more and it's Christmas! Thursday is the day when Jesus came to this earth. Oh dear Savior — what is our love for You? Nothing! Nothing, compared to Jesus's unlimited love for us! We are but dust, and You still care for us and want us to be with You, and it is our obstinacy that causes You so much grief. Oh, help us well, Holy Ghost — be in our hearts so that we may win our heart's daily struggle against the devil — be the victor, Jesus Christ — pray, and what power does the Devil have over us? Eight days ago I confessed and then I enjoyed the Holy Communion together with my dear Hermann. God, I feel my sins weighing so heavily on my heart, but my confession is far from being as deep and serious as it ought to be. And if I should happen to really feel the heavy weight of my sins, my recognition of these sins is so incidental, so brief that — oh Lord! Thank goodness You are a <u>merciful</u> God! My joy for mercy in Jesus Christ — the hope, the hope for salvation in Him, is so strong in me that I am afraid of falling into a drowsy apathy of sins. I beg You, dear Father in heaven, that You will knock on the door to my heart — that I, by the sacred word, must be kept awake, must be eager in my prayers. Oh, if only I was not unworthy when I received the sacred sacrament — oh no, Lord, I hope not, I think not! For even though the recognition of my sins is weak and dim and far, far from what it ought to be, You are still sincere — there is no voice inside me whispering, "You are good, you are leading a proper life — you are no great sinner" No, no — praise to God, the Devil does not have such a grip on me! But there will be times like that, when he will try to snare me with such temptations.

Oh, our days down here are so uncertain, we don't know anything but the moment. Thank You, God, for each day that goes by, that I am happy and content and sharing my days with my dear Hermann, and my dear little children, Christian Keyser and Sina. Oh, if only my time with them may please You, Lord God! I often — almost always I guess — do not please You; I will really make an effort to change that, to become a better person, and You, good God, will stand by me and help me as long as my promise is serious and made in the name of Jesus. If it is so, You will add your yes and amen! In a little while our family is going to expand — oh, what would we have been, what could we have been capable of were it not for your help, oh God of mercy!!

On the Thursday before the Third Sunday of Advent, the president of our synod, Adolph Preus, came up here to visit. He was supposed to stay for eight days and travel around in the different congregations, but the weather put an end to those plans. On Saturday there was a storm with heavy snowfall, and on Sunday when there was supposed to be a service, the members of the congregation had to send their horses and sleighs back home, because they got stuck in the snowdrifts. The women had to turn back, too, but the ministers, the doctor, and the servant boy walked over to the church. The gathering that day consisted of thirteen men. Hermann and I had communion at home that day. Even if the weather had been good, I was unable to go to church because of a little accident I caused myself. A few days before A. Preus was coming to visit, I was baking some *julekake*, and *fattigmannsbakkels*[265] for the Bishop, as we jokingly call him. The entrance to the basement has recently been moved to the kitchen. My maid was going down to the basement, and she let me know she was going, but I was so occupied with my baking that I forget both maid and basement, and all of a sudden I stumbled through the trapdoor. This time, as always, You, caring, heavenly Father, were with me — You took care of me, and I did not hit myself hard, even though it seems unbelievable to us that I did not get hurt worse. Yes, we thank God for his fatherly care. I have not been able to really care for my house since then, though. I've kept to my bed more than I've been up walking, but with God's help, I will get better soon! The wife of the doctor is a good help to me around the house; she and her husband came from Norway in September this year, and have stayed with us since. Doctor Hansen[266] and his wife, two pleasant, newly married people, are very welcome.

1858-1864

The Fifth Sunday after Easter, *May* 9, 1858. It's been a long time since I last wrote in my book, and I've been through different physical difficulties since then. But my God and Father has let it all be for the better for my soul and my soul's salvation, for the sake of Christ. I thank Him for his mercy, even if I am unable to do so from the very bottom of my heart — however, God receives my thanks for Christ's sake alone.

The 13th and 14th of *January*, '57, it turned out that my fall had more severe consequences than what we first assumed. When it was time, I had violent hemorrhaging and a stillborn child. I was so weak afterward, but I loved living, and I thank God for letting me stay with Hermann and my two dear little children — the third was still lying in the cradle, so beautiful, so fine, but it was God's will that it was going back to the earth before it ever got to see the light of day. What do we really know about little ones like that? However, during my weakness it turned out that I was afraid of dying. I was always so worried, and couldn't see any other reason than my love for life and the fear of losing it. I realized that I'd been lying to myself, believing that I didn't fear death. I hope it is the joy of the life that God gave me that makes it that way, for several times later, when I was seriously ill, and especially when I got another violent hemorrhage, I thought that death was my fate, but I was calm, and I thanked God for making me strong by the hope for mercy in Jesus Christ, our Lord. So, God our Father, whatever happens to me, let me have the peace that You give my heart — let me be happy and content, whatever You put me through, for then my soul is healthy, and the fact that You let me have a weak body, is for my own good. In the name of Jesus, Amen.

Hermann and the children have all been healthy, and we have had such a good time together — many proofs of good people's love and friendship. That is also a joy to the heart — oh, let it be in humility, oh God!

25th Sunday after Trinity 1860, the 22nd of November[267] — I haven't written in my books for ages, and why is that? Have I been busier with the management of my house than I used to? It's not really that, it's probably more that I have felt like writing to others, or simply writing something else. When I have felt like writing here, it is because I have felt a need to talk to someone. Hermann is gone more than he is home. Besides, we never talk about the things I write here. I don't think I could even ever talk to him about those matters, not even while I've been sick — "why should I worry him?" is how I have been thinking. Dear God, who have taken such good care of us in all ways — both when You, with fatherly, caring reminders have put small burdens on the shoulders of this family, You have wanted us to be with You and to wake us up out of our drowsiness. And you have given us pleasures in this life, pleasures much, much greater than expected. After I had been quite weak all last summer, You gave us — dear God — on the 3rd of September 1859 a pretty little girl, who was baptized on Halloween, and was named after Mother and the two Keyser uncles who have filled the role of our parents ever since their death. Our little Agnes Wilhelma Rudolpha[268] has been in good health all the time, but she is so small and delicate, though active and healthy. And it makes me more than just a little bit happy, watching her crawl around the floor, walking where she can lean on chairs and sofas. Oh, the children you have given us, Lord God, they are a gift and a joy that we could never, ever thank You enough for, not with everything else You have given and still give. In the name of Jesus, receive our sincere gratitude, God our Father! Let us in humility recognize our guilt — let us see how bad we are! And stand by us as we raise the toddlers to adults. You can love, and God, we would really, really like to keep this gift, but if You in your wisdom see that their lives would lead them away from You and into eternal damnation —oh God, God — dear God — then take them away from this world while they are still small enough that we can hope and think that You will take them as your children — <u>that</u> must happen — Amen! Amen! — in the blessed name of Jesus! And if it is your will that we shall be together — oh help us, help us in our weakness! Amen, in the name of Jesus!

May 27, 1864 — "Here, Mrs. Preus, here is the little lock I cut of your little Carl Christie's hair before I put him into the coffin," my dear Henriette Neuberg said to me, handing me a little envelope.

The tears — they were a relief to a troubled heart, but often also unwelcome traitors, coming quickly. Today it was the longing for my little lastborn that brought them out. Dear God, You gave him to me on the 21st of October, little Sina's and Johan Wilhelm's birthday,[269] but on the following day, You had already taken the gift away from me again. His existence was short, only ten hours, but he will be longer, longer with You, dear heavenly Father, in whose fatherly arms — far healthier and better than the mother's — oh well — two — my little stillborn[270] — are resting, and before your eyes they are playing, beholding You; and then sometimes they are down here with us, together with your angels. A little lock of hair from both the children is what I have left, besides the loss of the gift, but God, You have stilled a lot of my fear and grief. Oh, how can my faith remain so weak? So often, yes, time after time — yes, daily — You give me evidence of your fatherly care and tenderness. You hear my prayers and You always help, and still I am not a firm believer, still I cannot find firmness, clarity, and fervor.

When I was lying in pain this fall — Hermann had gone to the Missouri Synod's meeting at Ft. Wayne, Indiana — the children were crying before my bed, and Henriette tried, with well-hidden anxiety and fear, to take good care of us all. I thought there were still six to eight weeks to go, but a sudden, dangerous turn in my illness told me something else. How I begged You for my life, good God — and still death seemed so right — yes, I prayed like I have never prayed before. I did not want to leave the dear little ones — the precious loan that You, merciful father, have confided me, though it would have been You who took me away from them if You had let me leave. So, let me die in the name of Jesus, if it is Your will, and let death be very dear to me, that would mean I love You more than anything else, but — but if it is not against Your wise will, I would really like to stay here. Thy will be done, though.

I cannot describe the joy I felt as I got this pain, it told me…something…well, it was too early, but as far as I understand, and understood, that was how I could get well again, and I was filled with happiness and hope in the middle of all my pain. How weak, how little faith and love, but God, You were not angry with me. You gave me strength, You strengthened my weak faith, my dim love, so that I could say, truthfully and sincerely, "Thy will be done." I was afraid of worrying those around me, so I would not tell them — neither Henriette nor my dear neighbor, a genuine Voss woman, Thorbjør Møen — "Give Hermann my love and tell him that I died in the name of Jesus." Was it strange that I had nothing more to say! No, God gave me strength — I did not worry about anything or anyone, I was so calm and happy, but the hope of surviving was always present. Message for the doctor, thirty miles from here — telegram for Hermann, it was all done right away, but the best doctor there helped me. "Really, the child is crying, isn't it?" I guess were my first words, and then a mother's gratitude. I was fine, but we needed baptismal water for the poor little thing right away — beautiful, but so small, so small. "Thorbjør and Henriette, baptize the child here by my bed." Old Throbjør's voice was trembling as she poured water over the baby's head and said the words, "I baptize you, Carl Christie, in the name of God the Father, God the Son, and God the Holy Ghost," words that were repeated in whispers by Henriette and myself. This was around nine or ten in the evening. The next morning, at about six or seven, my little Carl was no longer among us — I can still see the always-careful Henriette as she came over to the bed, saying, "I think little Carl is very ill right now." "No, not now H., he is dead." "Yes, he's dead." Then this little life was gone, and Momma was left, glad, in spite of everything, and healthy, considering the circumstances. I had my four little children with me, they cried when they saw their dead brother, but their grief didn't last for long. The doctor came in the afternoon, and later on, some guests from Madison: Borly Fleischer and others. They had no idea about my condition. It was good for Henriette, though, it made things easier. And when Doctor Hansen came — our good and faithful doctor — and said that everything was all right, and besides

The extant diary ends at this point

Part Four

Sketches by a Pastor's Wife

(1858–1870)

Reverand Hermann Preus

Sketch R1:   Begun during Christmas 1858,   Spring Prairie Parsonage

Picture: The title page of the Rolvaag collection.

Commentary: The Rolvaag book, given to the Luther College Preus Library by Ella Rolvaag Twedt, (see introduction) contained forty-seven sketches, generally from 1858-1864. It is a small pocket sketchbook, about 3 ½" by 5 ¾"

Sketch LL50: May 17, 1849

Writing on the back of drawing: Drawings by Grandmother, wife of H. A. Preus, from about 1850, and found among letters and correspondence of grandfather H.A.

Preus. Now in the possession of H.A. Preus, Calmar, Iowa Jan. 8, 1952. (In right hand corner is written) 17.5.49. L.K. indicating May 17, 1849, Linka Keyser. At that date she was living in Christiania.

Sketch R43: Our parsonage from 1852-1856. Thick bushes, thick woods

Picture: By putting together the various sketches of the parsonage, it is possible to see how the building grew over the years. (See also R16, R20, R40)

Commentary: That January 14, 1852, Herman and Linka moved into their new parsonage. They had lived from August 18, 1851, in a little room by the cows. 'It was so small that our guest and travel comrade Siølner, H., and I could not eat at one time without one sitting in the bed and that was my place."

Sketch R2: Stubs Parsonage at Coon Prairie. July 7, 1858

Picture: Linka drew this to portray their arriving at the Coon Prairie parsonage. The figure to the left is most likely Pastor Hans Andreas Stub (1822-1907) in full clerical garb waiting to greet the people in the buggy, probably the Preuses. The little boy is Hans Gerhard Stub (1849-1931), who was to become president of Luther Seminary and finally the Norwegian Evangelical Lutheran Church in America (NLC). The girl is probably his sister Mathilda.

Commentary: The dedication of the churches in West Prairie and Coon Prairie, Wisconsin, small hamlets not far south of LaCrosse, on June 26-27 was one of the first big celebrations of the Norwegian Synod. Before the festivities, which included a pastoral conference and a meeting of parochial schoolteachers, Pastor Stub wrote to the pastors inviting them and giving explicit instructions on travel arrangements. Stub wrote to Pastor Peter Laurentius (Laur.) Larsen (1833-1915), the newly installed pastor at Rush River, near St. Paul, "We will meet the day after the eve of St. John — Midsummer Eve — all of the pastors will gather in DeSoto, thirteen miles from West Prairie, Friday noon, June 25. From there you will be driven to West Prairie Friday afternoon, and after that [the dedication of West Prairie] we will come here to Coon Prairie." (February 9, 1858, Hans A. Stub to Laur. Larsen. Preus Library Archives, 96:3:7) The pastors of the Norwegian Evangelical Lutheran Church of America (Den norske Synode), informally known as the Norwegian Synod, and their families looked forward to these meetings for the fellowship they afforded them. The year before the Korens had hosted the Synod meeting at Washington Prairie. Koren had written to the pastors that their living conditions would be more like a camp meeting than a church convention because the guests would have to sleep on the parsonage floor, in the attic, or in farm buildings around the parsonage. It turned out to be a large group of pastors' families, including twenty-eight children. (September 9, 1857, Vilhelm Koren to Herman Preus. Luther College Archives.) Elisabeth, after that experience, remarked with some admiration that Han Andreas Stub (1822-1907) and his wife Ingeborg Margrethe Arentz (1815-1892) had dared to invite all the pastors and their families to come for the next summer (Letter of Elisabeth Koren to Linka Preus, November 1, 1857, Luther College Archives, 27:7:23).

Not everyone enjoyed these events: Alfred O. Erickson, in an article on Scandinavian Wisconsin, had bitter memories of those times "when our house became the rendezvous for newcomers and ministers, and many frequent synodical gatherings inflicted real hardship on our family. Our parents had twelve children, the first nine of whom were boys; Mother was timid and frail and had her hands more than full with her arduous daily tasks. And then, parading up from the railroad stations would come three or four big, fat, overfed clergymen bouncing in with agility and alacrity, throwing down their luggage, filling their pipes with strong tobacco. 'Well, here we are again!' they would exclaim as they lit their pipes and settled down comfortably." (Alfred O. Erickson, "Scandinavian Wisconsin," {*Norwegian American Studies and Records* xv 1949}, p. 185)

Sketch R3: Little Iowa Parsonage

Picture: Little Iowa Parsonage, now known as Washington Prairie parsonage, where Elisabeth and Vilhelm Koren lived, from their arrival in 1853 until it burned down in the 1870s, and then in its replacement until 1918, when Elisabeth died. This sketch shows it from the southwest, northeast of where the current church stands. The four figures approaching the house are probably the Preuses arriving at the parsonage. At the time of this drawing, Christian Keyser Preus was six, Pauline Rosina Preus (Sina), four. The Korens had only been in Iowa for five years. Paul Koren, their son, succeeded his father as pastor and continued living in the parsonage until his death in 1940.

Commentary: Linka frames the view with the burr oak trees found in abundance around Decorah. The drawing illustrates the care that Mrs. Koren lavished on the place. We know from her diary that the Korens had spent considerable time looking for the best prospect on which to build the parsonage. We cannot see, from this perspective, Mrs. Koren's garden, but we know from her diary and her many letters that she was an avid gardener. "I used to take long walks," she wrote, "and look for flowers and bushes, gather seeds, and make mental notes of what I should like to plant in the garden I eagerly looked forward to in the future." (*The Diary of Elisabeth Koren*, p. 370.)

Hannah Astrup Larsen, daughter of Laur. Larsen, the first president of Luther College, wrote for the eighty-fifth anniversary of the Korens' arrival in Iowa, that "native trees were cared for, young saplings were planted which are now great stately trees. The cultivated area was gradually extended; beds and borders blazed with color. An orchard was planted with a variety of choice trees." (*The Lutheran Herald*, 1938, p. 275.)

Sketch R4

On our journey up the Mississippi to Coon Prairie we went ashore in "DeSoto," a little, little town, where the wagons and horses stood waiting for us. A Mississippi storm squall hindered us from immediately taking the carriage road, so we waited on the grain wharf.

The pastors amused themselves by standing on the scale. Koren and Herman were the least heavy, but Gustav Dietrichson weighed more than all of them, so therefore he stood forever on the scale. The women sat and looked out at the rain. For Mrs. Brandt the time grew long, so she put on A. C. Preus's raincoat and stood there and spoke with Ottesen about how it was time to go now! 9:00 p.m., June 23, 1858

Picture: From left to right: *Linka Preus (1829-1880), Engel Brun Preus (1831-1860), {the young wife of Adolf Preus and granddaughter of the well-known bishop of Bergen, Johan Nordahl Brun , Mrs. Elisabeth Hysing Koren (1832-1918), Ulrik Vilhelm Koren (1826-1910), Mrs. Diderikke Ottesen Brandt (1827-1885), Jakob Aall Ottesen (1825-1904), Sailor, Peter Laurentius (Laur.) Larsen (1833-1915), Gustav Dietrichson (1813-1886), Adolf Carl Preus (1814-1878), Nils Olsen Brandt (1824-1921), and Hermann Amberg Preus (1825-1894).*

Commentary: Linka shows Koren's concern for his wife and children in the composition of the piece. Note also Linka's wry amusement at Diderikke's assertiveness, which caused many comments among the pastors' wives. Mrs. Caja Munch, another pastor's wife, wrote home on November 16, 1857, to say they had visited the Brandts at the Rock River parsonage. "You know, perhaps,

Diderikke Ottesen and her oratorical endowments." (*The Strange American Way: Letters of Caja Munch from Wiota, Wisconsin, 1855-1859,* trans. Helene and Peter A. Munch. {Southern Illinois University Press, 1970,} p 112.)

Sketch R5: Stopping for Water on the Way to Coon Prairie: 1858. Here we are coming in our wagon. The heat is entirely too intense so the tempting brackish water has to make do. Linka's tender throat cannot take that; she keeps with beer or wine, to the embarrassment of the others. The large stone we drove by seemed to weave in the wind." West Prairie, June 24, 1858

Picture: Linka, with another woman, is sitting in the wagon with her drink, while others are by the stream getting the brackish water. The weaving rock is Monument Rock in Vernon County, Wisconsin, near Coon Valley, a town some miles west of Westby, Wisconsin.

Commentary: The newspaper *Emigranten* reported that the heat throughout the country during that week was so fierce that many people from Brooklyn to Illinois had died of it.

Sketch R6: (Next page) Boy in yard with dogs chasing pigs, chickens, and ducks. September 1858

Picture: This sketch has no text to explain it, other than its date. The man is enjoying the commotion caused by the dog and boy as they try to stop the encounter between the dog and two pigs or wild boar.

Commentary: This could be a sketch of Herman and Christian (C.K.) working in the garden, or farmers that Linka observed in the area, but there is no way to prove that.

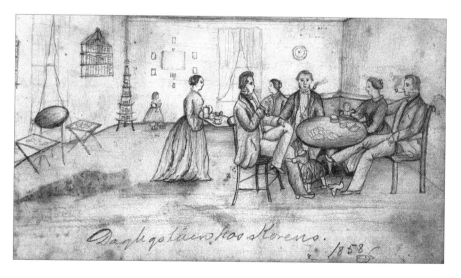

Sketch R7: Living room at Koren's. 1858

Picture: The Preuses, Korens, and Brandts in the Koren living room. Nils and Diderikke Brandt, at the time, served the Rock River, Wisconsin, congregation some miles east of Spring Prairie. The girl in the upper left-hand corner is probably Henrietta Koren, who was four at the time. Herman is the man with the long pipe.

Pauline Rosina (Sina) Preus may be the child clasping his knee. Brandt is sitting next to Diderikke who is holding their first child, Margretha. Koren is facing out. Elisabeth Koren is carrying the tray while Linka looks on. Note Linka with the tray. In her diary she comments on how wonderful it was to get her first tray so she did not have to carry out all the food and dishes separately. (Linka's Diary, p. 242.)

Commentary: After the meeting in Coon Valley, the Preuses traveled to visit the Korens in Washington Prairie while Herman attended to the business of the young synod. As one of the six pastors who had founded the Norwegian Synod, Herman's responsibilities made it necessary for him to travel widely. When he became president in 1862, an office he held until his death in 1894, his travels increased, making it necessary for Linka to manage the household on her own more than she wished. It was always a pleasure for her if she could accompany him and visit with other pastors' wives, especially her close friend, and most faithful correspondent, Elisabeth Koren.

Sketch R8: Guest room at Koren's.

Picture: Linka, Diderikke and Margretha Brandt, and Elisabeth Koren in the Koren guest room.

Commentary: The story in this picture is a bit elusive. Diderikke is standing on the bed probably putting a new candle in the sconce or extinguishing it. Mrs. Koren, the woman sitting at the left, is holding a candle to give her more light. Linka is the one holding an eye cup. Mrs. Koren has a patch over her eye. Complaints about eye disease are frequent in the letters of the women to each other and they shared the wisdom they found in a book by a Dr. Bull on the diseases of the eye.

It could be that the women needed more light to see what they were doing. Margretha Brandt, the child in the bed, has the look of one who is unable to sleep. Diderikke is the one in this group most likely to leap up on the bed and try to remedy the situation.

Sketch R9: Ole Nielson's Ferry. The steamboats leave from the wharf and we traveled over the river to Prairie du Chien. July 28, 1858, L.I.P. April 24, 1859

McGregor is a curious town. It is built in a very narrow valley, not wide enough for more than one street. It had to be dug out of the limestone and sandy ridge in order to have room for the houses which are three or four stories high. The various necessary outbuildings are thus up the hill. We counted 174 steps from the shoals up — the establishments are built on a large dry dock out on the river.

Picture: Linka pictures herself running to the bathroom in McGregor, Iowa, on the west bank of the Mississippi. Herman and Christian are following behind. McGregor was a frequent stop for the Preuses on their travels back and forth from Spring Prairie to Decorah.

Commentary: The action in the scene takes place against the backdrop of the little town on banks of the Mississippi. Linka gives us a rare visual record of the bustling young river town.

Sketch R15: See the pastors in full discussion. They are very animated. The day conference has not come to a full decision yet; therefore they continue to debate with the travel group [those who had traveled to Buffalo, Ohio, and St. Louis]. Coon Prairie. 1858

Picture: Linka notes that the pastors are in heated debate about which German-American Lutheran group they should affiliate with. There are two maps on the wall, one of Norway, the other of America. Though they had received the recommendation from Brandt and Ottesen the year before, they still had issues to address concerning their proposed alliance with the Missouri Synod. An alliance with the German Missouri Synod displeased some of the more extreme Norwegian patriots among them. Pastor Gustav Dietrichson, with his back to us, was known for his anti-German views, and made several efforts to veto any contact with them. Adolf Preus is standing beside Dietrichson. Koren is sitting at the table, smoking a pipe and facing out. Herman Preus is smoking the long pipe, one of his trademarks in the drawings. Larsen seems to be the one with the beard, facing right in the group on the right side of the table. Ottesen is seated facing left. Clausen, Stub, and Brodahl are not easy to identify as Linka did not draw them frequently. At the 1858 meeting in Coon Valley, the pastors of the Norwegian Synod had serious concerns about getting more pastors for the young church. Those present were H.A. Stub, A.C. Preus, Herman Preus, J.A. Ottesen, Nils Brandt, Gustav Dietrichson, Laur. Larsen, Peter Marius Brodahl (1823-1906), U.V. Koren, and Frederick Clausen (1810-1870).

Commentary: The need for more pastors was urgent and pleas for pastors from Norway had fallen on deaf ears. This made even more pressing a plan to build a school to train pastors. In order to do this, they had to mount a campaign to solicit funds for the school. In the meantime, however, they had to take some immediate steps to train the young men in their midst who had been called to the ministry. To that end they had sent Nils and Diderikke Brandt and Jakob Aall Ottesen, her double cousin, to Concordia Seminary in St. Louis, the Ohio Synod in Cleveland, and the Buffalo Synod in New York in order to decide which of those groups were the most appropriate for the Norwegian Synod to affiliate with. The fund they had begun for their Norwegian University, as it was called at the time, had grown to $9,800. The sum, however, was not enough to start a school. In the meantime, they planned to use the interest from the fund to pay the salary of a Norwegian professor at Concordia College and Seminary in St. Louis, the school of the Missouri Synod.

For many reasons, Ottesen and Brandt recommended that the Norwegian Synod ally itself with the Missouri Synod. Until they could start a school of their own, they decided to call a professor to go to St. Louis, live with the young boys and men, help them in their studies (all in the German language), and otherwise further the cause of Norwegian-Lutheran education in America. Laur. Larsen, who had arrived the year before, was the man they called. It was a fateful decision for succeeding generations of Lutherans. Four generations later, Linka Preus's great-grandson, Jacob Aall Ottesen Preus, would become President of the Missouri Synod, while another, David Walter Preus, became president of the American Lutheran Church.

Sketch R20: Waving good-bye

Picture: Probably of the trip west in 1858.

Sketch R12: Deep sand. Here we will get something to eat.

A railroad station where one can get supper. Brandt and Herman have discovered that one can get beer or milk, bread, and cheese in a little saloon, which they try to get for their wives and children. We are on our way from Prairie du Chien to Madison.

Picture: In this first of a two-part drawing, we see the Preus and Brandt families on their journey home, perhaps from their time in Decorah after the synod meeting in Coon Valley in 1858. The date at the bottom of the second picture is most likely the date in which Linka drew the scene. Mrs. Koren wrote to Linka on June 19, 1859, exclaiming that it had been one year since they had seen each other. (Elisabeth Koren to Linka Preus, June 19, 1859.) Brandt is leading Hermann toward the train holding tableware they borrowed from the saloon to bring food to their families. Mrs. Brandt is the woman to the left holding the child. Christian and Rosina are sitting beside their mother. Linka's very pale title says that they are in an area of deep sand.

Commentary: The Preuses and Brandts, who were fairly close neighbors, are coming traveling home from Decorah after a meeting there.

Sketch R13: (Next page) They are coming too late! January 28, 1859. Deep Sand. April 26, 1859

"All on board!" was called out and we kept on eating. Brandt and H. were off with the borrowed utensils, but had to fling them in the deep sand so that they had to throw themselves on board on the last of the cars. Deep sand by the Wisconsin River.

Picture: The man behind the two is probably the owner of the saloon, coming to claim his tableware, and maybe even the check.

Sketch R16:   Here is our dear Spring Prairie. June 1, 1859. Papa, C.K., and Sina are going to work in the garden. I am working up by the fence in the hotbeds. From 1856-1861 our house looked like this. 1859-1864 — Here is our parsonage built up to be a bit statelier.

Picture: Linka tells us exactly what this picture is about. This is from a different vantage point than the other drawings of the parsonage. (See Sketch R40, R43, R46)

Commentary: The profession of a pastor's wife, since Katie Luther, had involved managing the parsonage farm. Linka, as a pastor's daughter herself, was accustomed to the notion that the parsonage was a farm and garden for the pastor's use, much as they had in Norway, only in this case it was not the state that gave the land, but the congregation. Linka was known for her careful husbandry of the land. Elisabeth Koren, who was praised for her own management of the parsonage land, once stayed with Linka in Spring Prairie, where the two women celebrated the Korens' wedding anniversary alone. She wrote her father about the day: "Fru Linka and I observed the day as best we could. In the forenoon we sat flat on the floor with a large paper full of raisins and almonds between us; with a hammer we cracked nuts and ate, while little Christian crept on his stomach from one to the other. Fru Preus pondered what she should give me for dinner in honor of the day; however, we came to the conclusion, and wisely so, that we would not disturb the menu so beautifully arranged against the arrival of our guests. We contented ourselves with bacon, potatoes, and clabber. The day before we had baked cakes; these we enjoyed in the afternoon, and strolled about in the neat paths through the young native woodlands surrounding the parsonage." (Linka's Uncut Diary, mss. in Preus Library Archives, Letter from Elisabeth Koren, 1854.) In this sketch we see the neat paths around the parsonage.

Sketch R17: Carrying luggage to the train.

Picture: This may be a third picture in the series of Koren's meeting the visitors to the laying of the cornerstone at the new college in Decorah. It looks, however, like they are trying to make it to the train in the background, which does not fit with the other sketches. It could be a portrait of their departure.

Sketch R18: *Rock Creek Parsonage*

Picture: The Rock Creek parsonage, near Ixonia, Wisconsin, was the home of Nils and Diderikke Brandt.

Commentary: Diderikke Brandt, who was later to take a significant role as the dorm mother at Luther College when the Brandts moved to the parsonage on the college land, had studied at the Moravian School for Girls in Christianfeld, Denmark, which became a kind of finishing school for daughters of Norwegian clergy in the 19th century. There she had learned the domestic arts, modern languages, music, drawing, and conversation, skills necessary for a woman of her class. Pastors' daughters usually married pastors and carried on the cultural traditions necessary for them as leaders in the domestic lives of their women parishioners. Diderikke quickly adapted to the American frontier, bringing her skills of organization and culture to the people. Very early on she began organizing ladies' aids to support missionaries and the boys studying for the ministry in St. Louis.

Sketch R19: (Next page) Our march from Ixonia to Rock River. C.K.: Stay here. R.: Get up.

Picture: The family is on the way to Rock River from Ixonia, a town not very far from Rock River, where the Nils Brandts made their home from 1856-1865. Linka dramatizes the hearty determination of Hermann to be off, with Christian holding him back and Linka wearily resting, waiting to catch her breath, while Sina urges her on. Rosina and Christian seem to be rather young for a good long walk. Both are under six.

Commentary: Nils Brandt had lived in Rock River by himself until his marriage to Diderikke Ottesen in 1856. It was from this site that Brandt had made mission

trips to northeast Iowa in 1851 to scope out the possibilities for congregations in that area. Because of their proximity to each other, it was common for the two families to visit each other.

Sketch R21: Spring Prairie bear hunters, October 1859

Picture: This study has a quality of spontaneity and humor about it. The dog looks rather like a fox contemplating the neck of the fowl in front of it. The obvious pleasure the men are taking in themselves is amusing to Linka.

Commentary: C. K. wrote in his memoirs of Spring Prairie that Linka loathed hunting unless it was for food they needed. The diary says that Linka preserved their land as a kind of game refuge, allowing only necessary hunting. Johan Wilhelm Preus (Doktor) recalled that C.K. and Ambjørn Erickson, the neighbor boy, would bring home what food they needed for the next meal: " deer, prairie hens, wild geese, and doves." (J. W. Preus, "*C.K. Preus,* Barndomsaar," Ed. O. A. Tingelstad, O. M. Norlie, Augsburg Publishing House, Minneapolis, 1922, p. 45) Hermann, by C.K.'s description, was also a good hunter, supplying the young family with meat in their first years in Wisconsin. (Christian Keyser Preus, "Minder fra Spring Prairie Prestegaard," *Symra: En aarbog for norske paa begge sider af havet*, ed. Kristian Prestgaard and John B. Wist. Decorah, Iowa, 1906, p. 20.)

Christian Preus, in his memoirs of the Spring Prairie parsonage, remembered that many people came to the parsonage needing a place to sleep and find refreshment on their way farther west. (Preus, "Minder fra Spring Prairie Præstegaard," p. 20)

Sketch R25: Woman chopping wood

Picture: This may be a sketch of Henriette and Linka. Linka often portrayed herself wearing a scarf during her work and Henriette in fine clothes. If this is such a portrait, Linka is the one cutting the wood and Henriette, barefooted, is driving the pigs toward her. It has the same theme as the later drawing of Linka and Henriette cleaning the intestines. (See sketch N64.) It could even be the scene before the slaughter.

Sketch R26: (Next page) Trading with the Indians

Picture: Hermann trading with Indians. Linka gives us a view inside the parsonage.

Commentary: Christian Preus in his memoirs of the Spring Prairie parsonage remembers the family's contact with Indians: "Each spring and fall they would come from the North on their way to Madison and the first year they came by much more often. Once on an open place in front of our house there were four hundred encamped. Mother tried to talk to them; it didn't go well, but she traded with them for a table knife with a horn handle that she used as long as I can remember." (C. K. Preus, *Symra* 1906, p. 39.) He went on to say that their neighbor, Jørund Bergum, was "terrified of the Indians and once went out into the fields and hid all day with her children." (Ibid.) Preus recalled that "one fall the Indians had a disagreement farther north in the state and they came through the settlement with war paint on." (Ibid.)

Sketch R27: H.: There are doves for our wives. Hr. Black! L.: Five in one shot. They are coming with. Yes, in order to help them carry things home. Mrs. Black:! H.: Uffda, ????????

Picture: A man is trying to sell doves to the Preuses who are on their way. Linka is leading, Herman is carrying Anga, Sina is in the buggy, and Christian is pushing the buggy.

Sketch R37: So we are enjoying ourselves in the moonlight by throwing stones down into the Mississippi's muddy water. McGregor's Landing, 10:00 p.m. Evening of October 2, 1860. Steamboat whistle blows. The gangway is open.

Picture: This sketch shows how the young family solved the problem of entertaining the children as they were waiting for the ferry. The Preuses are returning from four weeks in Iowa with the Korens.

Commentary: Vilhelm Koren in a letter to Laur. Larsen, who had just left for Norway to recruit pastors for the immigrants, said that "Fru Preus has just been here for four weeks with her children." (Vilhelm Koren to Laur. Larsen, Luther College Archives.) According to Koren they came rather suddenly after H.A. Stub at Coon Prairie had sent Preus an urgent call saying that he was very ill and needed help with his congregation. Evidently Preus came immediately and brought his family. On October 2, 1860, Preus wrote to Larsen after their return to say that Koren had shown him the land in Decorah he thought would be best for the new preacher's school.

Linka has another woman with her; she is holding Anga, about a year old at the time. She seems to be a bit wary of what is going on. Linka is holding her hand out in the gesture mothers use to get kids to calm down — some of which C. K. seems to be understanding as he looks to her before throwing the next stone.

One thing not to miss in all these drawings is the fun the family had, both with Hermann there and without him. Whether they are skiing, sledding, or walking,

Linka always shows us a family on an adventure, enjoying each other and the adventure equally as well.

Sketch R33: *July 27, 1861* Wenn jeman eine Riese H:

Picture: This is probably the Preuses leaving Washington Prairie. They are singing the song by Matthias Claudius (1740-1813), "Urians Reise um die Welt" ("Orion's Travel Around the World"), set by Ludwig van Beethoven (Opus 52). It is still a popular travel song in Germany and Scandinavia.

Sketch R40: (Previous page) My drawing is ramshackle but that is not the case with our house. August 1864. The way our parsonage looked in 1861, after we had lived in the old house for ten years.

Summer kitchen, Cistern, Dining room, Trees and garden, Office, Guestroom, Boy's room, Kitchen, Free guest room????, *Bedroom*

Picture: The notes are self-explanatory. Christian Preus, in his Symra *lecture, remembered that the original house measured seventeen by twenty-four feet, with one and half stories, two rooms downstairs, and three on the second floor. (Preus, Symra, p. 39.)*

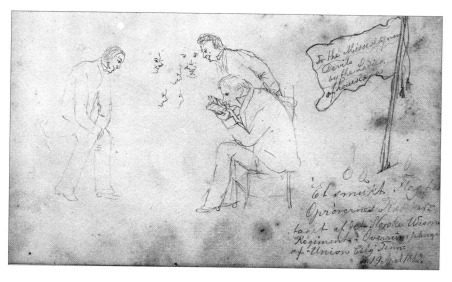

Sketch R29: To the Norwegian Devils by the Ladies of Louisiana. A handsome flag from the ranks of the rebels taken by the Norwegian Wisconsin Regiment in the taking of Union City, Tennessee, April 19, 1862.

Picture: Although not finished, the basic lines of the scene set down the story of the capture of a rebel flag by the 15th Wisconsin Regiment.

Commentary: The 15th Wisconsin Regiment has a fabled history in Norwegian Americana; it distinguished itself in battle, especially at Chickamauga, where it lost over 60 percent of its men. Its first engagements with the rebels, however, were on the Mississippi. Linka has heard the story of their valor and sketches the scene. On the 31st of March, 1862, some in the regiment attacked a rebel camp near Union City, east of Hickman, Kentucky. From Hickman, they marched to Union City, where they surprised the camp of rebels, completely routing them, and destroying their camp and its contents, capturing about a hundred horses and mules, and several wagons. Company G captured a secesh [slang term for secessionist] battle flag, which was sent to the Governor of Wisconsin as a trophy, with another, later captured at Island No. 10. The capture of the flag became a storied part of the glory of the regiment. Colonel Hans C. Heg wrote to his wife on April 15, 1862, that "we have captured three more Secesh Flags here. One has the following inscription: "Mississippi Devils," "presented by the Ladies." Linka has heard this story and her drawing records exactly what Heg wrote. The date at the bottom of the picture is likely the date she drew the sketch.

Sketch R32: Christmas Eve, Spring Prairie Parsonage, March 26, 1862

Picture: Three pastors' families together at the Spring Prairie parsonage for Christmas, 1861. Hermann is the man facing to the left, shaking hands with Mrs. Koren. The man on the left is most likely Laur. Larsen. At the time, Christian, the boy playing with the cannon, was nine; Sina (six) is probably the girl in the foreground. Anga Wilhelmina Rudolpha is two, Johan Wilhelm Preus (Doktor) six months. He is probably the baby being held by the woman, who may well be Linka, center left. Thora Larsen, four, is probably the girl facing Laur. Larsen. The woman next to Larsen, probably Karen Larsen, is also holding a baby who has not been fully drawn in. If it is the Korens, it is most likely Caroline facing Christian. Koren is facing out.

Commentary: Karen Larsen, in her biography of her father, Laur. Larsen, says that Mrs. Larsen had gone to be with Preuses for an extended period in the winter of 1861 while her husband worked at the new school in Halfway Creek, Wisconsin (Larsen, p. 150). Karen Larsen's sisters, Karine and Henriette Neuberg, both spent some time living with the Preuses, so the bond between the families grew even closer.

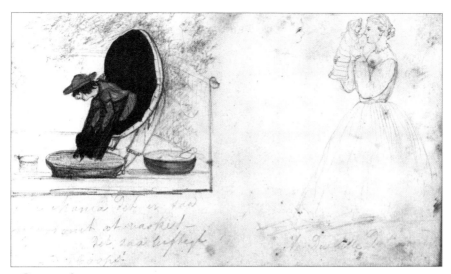

Sketch R34: Oh mama, it's so much fun to wash! And it's so airy with hoops! Oh, you little Doctor!

Picture: This sketch is of Sina, the elder daughter. In this drawing she is about ten years old and is washing clothes with the old washboard and several tubs of water. This is one of the few watercolors which Linka did. The drawing has generally subtle coloring; the green leaves in the upper and right background complement the gold in the hat and tub, but the blue in the skirt and hands blot out the detail of what she has in her hands and is too strong for the rising skirt. (See Sketch R23, R25)

Commentary: Elisabeth Koren wrote to Linka once wondering whether Linka had taken to wearing hoops. (Elisabeth Koren to Linka Preus, Preus Library Archives, 27:4:9) She had probably seen some of Linka's drawings showing the trouble hoops could cause. Hoops came in during the early '50s, just as the two women arrived in this country. It was possible to create the effect of a hoop with a stiff fabric made of horsehair and linen thread, but by the middle of the decade women could buy a series of flexible steel hoops which could be worn in a separate structure or sewn into the petticoats. In Linka's sketches of the men and women in formal dress, one can see that women are almost all wearing some kind of crinoline or hoop to puff out their dresses. Elisabeth Koren indicated she had found little use for hoops except for setting them in the garden for vines to grow around.

Sketch R35: (Next page) My sister's (husband), my brother-in-law, Kaurin's trip from the Sami (Fjelfinnen) to Kistrand Parsonage. Several have come to help Lillemamma, 1862. Christian Kaurin! Can't you take better care of your wife?! There she lies thrown out in the deep snow. Palken and Veslemor drive over her head.

Picture: Sketched after Linka had received a letter from her youngest sister, Ovidia Keyser Kaurin, (nicknamed "Lillemamma"), then living in Tromsø, describing how she and her husband, Pastor Christian Kaurin, had been going so fast on the sleigh that she got dumped. The reindeer are named Palken and Veslemor.

Commentary: The Kaurins had moved north to minister to the Sami. Kistrand is on a fjord a few miles south of Hønningsvåg, Norway, not too far from the North Cape. The drawing is interesting in that it captures a moment in the life of her sister who is far away. The quality of the coloring causes some problem in the clarity of the drawing. *Fjelfin* is the name of a strong drink preferred by the Norwegian military, but it also refers to the Sami, or Lapps. Thus its derogatory implications as a name for Sami.

Sketch R39: (Next page) A Sunday morning pleasure for Henriette and Karine and C.K. and Sina March 20, 1863.

Lovely young people. I gave Henriette, Karine, C.K., and Sina permission to take a little walk on the snow crust. And they came home sopping wet, snow in their boots. Both great and small had great fun laughing and shrieking.

Picture: Henriette, on the right, is leaning into the wind. Karine, beside her, looks more bemused while C. K. and Rosina are laughing.

Commentary: There is a poignant background to the scene, for Karine has gone to the Preuses after struggling with her situation and place in life. She knows she will marry and that her husband will probably be of her own class, but until her marriage she is forced to find lodging with a family that will have her as a governess.

En Søndagsmorgen=Fornøielse for Hes Kay Oltorine. GR 20.3.63

She has just come from living with the Korens and the Larsens in Decorah, where it had become obvious to them that she had lost her Christian faith. The pastors first noticed that she was not attending communion and began questioning her about it. Given her place in the society, and her dependence on the men in the society, all of whom were pastors, it was rather difficult for her to avoid conversations about her loss of faith. Some of the most interesting letters in the Luther College archives are those letters of Karine to Henriette in which she agonizes over her loss of faith and the condition of her soul. But even as one feels Karine's agony, one must also smile and feel some pity for this young woman whose life was completely dominated by clergy who took seriously their charge to shepherd souls. In one letter to Henriette she tells how she dreaded being with Koren because he persisted in asking her to recite the Articles of the Apostles' Creed with Martin Luther's explanation from the Small Catechism. When she was with Laur. Larsen, her brother-in-law, he forced her to think about the Articles of the Augsburg Confession. Preus was similarly inclined. They served to make her life a misery. She knew they watched her closely for any sign of a returning faith. Her main question had to do with the divinity of Christ. She could not believe in the Trinity, she wrote, because "three must be three" (October 26, 1862, Karine Neuberg to Henriette Neuberg. Luther College Archives, 4:271:25). Once she proposed the solution that she could become an Episcopalian, though she begged Henriette not to tell the preachers.

Because of her station in life and the time, she had no escape other than marriage. She did try to take some English courses at a school in Decorah named the Page Institute, but she found the classes insufferable. It helped her English, she had to admit, but she could already speak German and some French in addition to Norwegian and English. She was able to play the guitar and sing pleasingly, though she did not know how to play the piano, a fault which troubled her later on when she went to live with the Ove Hjort family at Paint Creek, one of the most cultivated of the pastor's families.

Sketch R36: Nei, I will say it straight out — you can't be the brother of the pastor, you who go and take the son from his parents just when they are in need of him!"

Here stands old Gure Hørvai shaking her finger at Nicolai because he had recruited her son to be a soldier. That was in 1862. Now in 1864 she is grieving her son's death. When he left her, he gave her a dress to wear when "Knut comes home. But now Knut is gone after the last attack on Atlanta, Georgia.

Picture: A woman in the congregation upbraiding Nicolai Preus (Hans Nicolai), Herman's younger brother, who lived for some time with Hermann and Linka until his marriage to Ludoviska Suckow. They moved to Westby, Wisconsin, where Nicolai farmed.

Commentary: This sketch portrays a drama well known during the Civil War. Those with means could escape the draft by buying volunteers. Nicolai has obviously paid for Knut to be his substitute. Later he would count himself as a veteran of the 15th Wisconsin Regiment, although his name does not appear in the rosters of the regiment. Linka, who gently jibes Nicolai in several sketches, may be making a wry comment about him by putting him in uniform. (See N65.)

Sketch AP54: (Next Page) Ow! There lies Papa with all the children on their backs. Between Norway Grove and Spring Prairie, January 10, 1863.

Picture: Norway Grove was part of the Spring Prairie congregation and is about one and a half miles away from Spring Prairie. Preus served it throughout his entire ministry, from 1851-1894.

Sketch AP54:   Everyone was on skates here, even Uncle Nicolai, with the piglets coming after him. Mama was of course not on skates, which was good. She comes behind pushing. The snow crust is not strong enough — her heavy person steps through it. But Aunt Henriette flies so that her dress flies behind her.

That day I thought the fields were covered with snow like that which met Napoleon in 1800 and that time. February 2, 1863.

Picture: This sketch, once again, pokes fun at Uncle Nicolai, and Linka's own person, this time for being heavy. Henriette Neuberg is staying with the Preuses at this time. She will remain with them for some time, because of Herman's need to travel on behalf of the synod. She helped Linka with the children and housekeeping. She was there when Carl Christie, Linka's fifth child, was born on October 21, 1863. He died ten hours after his birth. Linka is referring to Napoleon's crossing of the Alps to fight the Austrians at Marengo. Trying to get a Reserve Army of nearly sixty thousand men, with all the necessary supplies, through the deep snow of the Great St. Bernhard Pass on May 20, 1800, almost brought Napoleon to ruin. Linka's comment shows the profound impression Napoleon had made on the imagination of the people of the time.

Sketch N64: Making Sausage — The wife and governess must themselves clean the intestines in this slaughter.

Picture: In this drawing, Linka is to the left and Henriette to the right. They are engaged in the rather unpleasant task of cleaning intestines so they can be filled with sausage meat. Linka, like most of the other Norwegian American pastors' wives, used Hanna Winsnes Textbook in the Various Branches of Household Management. *First printed 1845, it contained information on how to clean and wash clothes, how to cultivate gardens, keep animals, brew wine, beer, even distill hard liquor, and how to cook and preserve food. Intended for women of the upper classes, it assumed a household full of servants and work enough to keep them busy. Before the slaughter, Winsnes advised, one must be sure to have enough wooden vessels, mended and tight, and enough lime and other chemicals in order to make the work easier. "On the first day," she wrote, "you will need at least two girls simply to wash the intestines and stomach, and if you can find a third girl, that would be even better." (Hanna Winsnes, Lærebog i de forskjellige Grene af Husholdningen 12th ed. Christiania: J.W. Cappelens, 1888, p. 101.) She also gives instruction on when to slaughter an animal who has been given something to make the bowels loose, so the intestines are easier to clearn, to slaughter in the afternoon so they can clean the intestines by daylight on the next day. Of most importance, of course, is to make sure the intestines get clean. One needs to rinse them several times in many different waters and in the last rinse one should put some celery and leek leaves to draw the smell off.*

Commentary: In this sketch one can see that Linka has clearly followed the instructions. She has a good supply of buckets and she is holding the dull knife Winsnes suggests. The spoon that is to be there is on the floor by Henriette.

The young man entering the door on the right background is perhaps one of the confirmands who stayed with the Preuses for instruction while helping the minister's family, a common practice among the Norwegian pastors' families. Winsnes suggested that there be at least two boys to hang and cut the meat. Their work, however, was to be rather separate from the work of the women. That may be why in this sketch, he seems to feel that he has intruded.

This sketch is a commentary on Wisnes: These are two fancy women, not the young girls Winsnes suggested. Linka and Henriette. Linka's sense for the scene, her awareness of its irony and the frank pleasure the two women are enjoying as they do the distasteful work, is a kind of testimony to Linka's good humored awareness of her situation in America.

Sketch N66: (Next page) Onkel Nicolai and the "Norwegian Indians"
Uncle Nicolai among the Indians and Norwegian Indians. He is going into the woods with his mosquito net on.

Picture: This sketch shows Linka's amusement with the clash of cultures. Nicolai is going out for his constitutional in the deep woods, armed with mosquito netting against the mosquitoes. In the manner of the British Colonials, he will not be stopped from his European rituals. The Indians observing him are fierce and aristocratic in their own way, every bit the equal of Nicolai in Linka's view.

Commentary: Nicolai, Herman's younger brother, came over in 1858 and settled in Coon Prairie, Wisconsin, but he stayed with Herman and Linka for some time. The group of "Norwegian Indians" in the right hand corner are so called

because they assimilated too quickly to the frontier, giving up their culture and religion, and left the Lutheran faith to become Methodists or Mormons. Though there were other applications for the term, it generally meant Norwegians who were neither Norwegian or American who lacked culture. Their mosquito netting and buckskins and rather silly appearance in the drawing show them to be people who lacked the confidence to know who they were, something neither the Indians nor Onkel Nicolai had to fear.

Sketch AP57: (Next page) A big winetapping! Sixteen to twenty jugs!! February 1863

K.: I am coming as fast as I can!

R.: Yes, mother, now Karine is coming. Can I come too?

L.: No one has called you.

    Norwegian herring, Bread, Meat, Pork, Pork, Cabbage, Wine

Picture: Linka vinting wine. Karine is carrying a pitcher into which they will pour the wine, which must then be put into flasks. On the table we can see that there is a bowl, most likely filled with the liquid mixture Mrs. Winsnes recommends for corking, and the cork lying next to it. Around the cellar one can see the kind of supplies typical for a family larder of the time. Behind Karine is a barrel filled with herring done in the Norwegian way. Atop the barrel is bread. In front of the woman are three barrels of meat, the first one salted beef and the next two salt pork, a staple of the early settlers' diet. Immediately in front of her is a keg of beer,

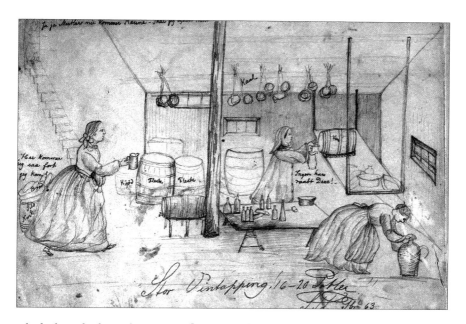

which they also brewed. Hanging from the rafters are cabbages, safe from small animals, in a place cool enough to preserve them from rapid spoilage, but close enough to the heated floor to be safe from freezing. Henriette, at the bottom right, is possibly pushing down on a cork she has just set into the large jug on the floor. The two little faces in the door show that Anga and Dr. are also fascinated by what is going on down in the cellar and would like to be with her, though they could be a trifle afraid of being in the cellar unaccompanied by an adult. Linka's droll remark, "No one has called you," is a wry comment on Anga's wish to be where the action is.

Commentary: The recipe for vinting wine in Fru Winsnes's book says that one should wait until a clear day to tap the keg, giving elaborate instructions on how to tap the bunghole. Fru Winsnes also gives precise instructions on how to cork the bottles and how to set them down in sand after the corking, somewhat apart from each other so that if one explodes, the others will not break. She includes a recipe for a liquid of resin, wax, and some tallow melted together to help the cork slip easily into the neck of the flask and seal it properly. The sketch, in and of itself, is a valid and important record of the immigrant cellar, but there is much more to it than a record of their material culture. Linka is not only interested in recording the details; she also portrays a family drama.

Sketch AP59: (Next page) Summer kitchen

Picture: The stove is Linka's focus in this sketch. Lavishing detail on it, she fills in the design handles and the kettles and pots set on top of it, even the flatiron. We

cannot tell who the men are building the lean-to on the side of the house. The children are very likely Christian and Rosina. It is possible that the other woman, carrying wood toward the stove, is Henrietta. Note the curious calves and the rest of the barnyard filled with geese and pigs. The buggy is in the carriage house, and a half door looks suspiciously like an outhouse in which someone is sitting, maybe Linka, poking fun at her own body and its physical needs Since there is no date on this sketch, it is difficult to establish when it was drawn. We can determine that it was after 1860, for in the various sketches of the house there is no summer kitchen or lean-to in the back until 1861.

Commentary: Each summer, to avoid the intense humid heat of Wisconsin, Linka, following the custom, moved the stove out into the yard. Later, the Preuses built a summer kitchen, a small shed, to keep the heat outside their small house. It was also time to clean the chimney. The way Americans cleaned their chimneys terrified Linka. "The stovepipes are placed in the attic, but only after they have been tapped on the outside and scraped on the inside with a stick. That is the way chimney sweeping is done out in the country in America. The small brick chimney which extends from the floor to the attic out through the roof is never cleaned, and when the stovepipes that lead to it become so full of soot that the draft is cut off, they are taken down and cleaned in the yard. Only once since we moved into the house has the chimney been cleaned, and that was three years ago. I was not able to endure this American custom, and finally, in order to allay my fears, Ziiølner had to get up on the edge of the roof with a twelve-foot-long pole, to the end of which was fastened a broom. This contrivance was sufficient to the very bottom of the chimney. Perhaps I have become more Americanized. If that is the case it must be in this respect alone — never any more do I think of having the chimney swept" (Linka's Uncut Diary, Luther College Archives, pp. 327-328.).

Sketch R45: Men building

Commentary: This could be a picture of the men building the summer kitchen.

Sketch R44: I snip beans and talk about the conscription, which will be on September 5, 1864. September 1864.

A Norwegian farmer is going around signing up volunteer contributions from the town's citizens of the U.S. in order to pay for volunteer soldiers so we would evade the conscription.

Farmer: So you see Mrs. Preus, the town shall send twenty-eight soldiers, so there has been a tax of $5,000 raised in order to buy volunteers. But that amount, which is what the town has imposed on itself, is too little, for one cannot get a volunteer for under $300. So I am calling upon Pastor Preus and as many as are able to to sign up for $25 again, which must be paid immediately, for people are leaving tomorrow for the North to get people.

Wife: To "buy" Volunteers? Summa summaren — in order to pay the whole bill I had to borrow $5. Hermann is not home.

Commentary: In 1864, the Union Army needed more soldiers, but could not get them without a national draft. During 1864, Lincoln issued a draft for 1,600,000 men. These conscriptions caused turmoil throughout the nation. Although the federal government had taken over the draft, the states were still encouraging volunteers. Wisconsin towns offered bounties of $300 for soldiers who would volunteer. The Norwegians had shown themselves to be willing soldiers, but this draft proved to be a burden. There is, however, a curious detachment in Linka's attitude toward the farmer. In the letters the women write to one another, one of them notes that she felt more deeply about the conflict in Schleswig-Holstein, a natural feeling given their youthful involvement with Pan-Scandinavianism of the 1850s. As Italy, Germany, and other countries had unified their different provinces to make one country, Scandinavians had made attempts to bring Denmark, Norway, and Sweden together in one kingdom. When the kingdoms of Norway and Sweden failed to come to the aid of Denmark when the Prussians attacked it, their youthful idealism suffered a terrible blow.

Sketch R46: (Next page) K.: Let me carry your luggage, Mrs. Ottensen.

Mrs. Ottesen: No, no, many thanks. It is marvelous to get out of that heat! On our trip to Iowa in the summer we met the entire Ottesen family in McGregor. That was a surprise. Everyone was going to the cornerstone-laying of our school building in Decorah. The German theologians Professor Walther and Cramer did us the honor to share in our trip and stay for the celebration.

Koren had promised to meet Walther and Cramer and us with his horse and wagons, but no one knew the Ottesens were coming. They had to go by the packed Stage. The day —June 29 — was very hot. There were twenty-eight passengers packed inside and on top of the stage. Ottesen's children stood entirely???? We followed with them, taking a

child on board with us so we were five grown-ups and five children. All of them stopped at a tavern — we were drinking beer when the stage drove by us and on to another house. Koren got Mrs. Ottesen and Miss Norman. Walther, Cramer, Hermann, and our C.K. walked a couple of miles to see if they could get a wagon.

Picture: Linka explains the sketches very well in her text. This is Koren following Mrs. Ottensen and Miss Norman offering to take their luggage.

Commentary: These two sketches, while rich with the human comedy that Linka enjoyed, are among the most important historically. The pastors and their families are gathering for the laying of the cornerstone at the new school in Decorah. Vilhelm Koren has gone to McGregor to meet their special guests, Carl Ferdinand Wilhelm Walther (1811-1887) and Friedrich August Cramer (1812-1896), the leaders of the Missouri Synod, and the theological mentors of the young Norwegian pastors. The fateful decision to send their students and professor Laur. Larsen to Concordia Seminary in 1861 which both created a bond of affection for the Germans, and alienation from the other Norwegian-American churches that were repelled by the strict orthodoxy the synod pastors began to adhere to because of this connection. (It also explains the reason two of Linka's great-grandsons, David W. Preus and Jack Aall Ottesen Preus, were presidents of the American Lutheran Church and the Lutheran Church-Missouri Synod, respectively. (See R15)

Sketch R47: K.: It's possible I have another?

Professor Walther and Cramer with Hermann wanted to make place for Mrs. Ottesen and Miss Norman and sit in an ox cart. That was unnecessary since our children were loaded upon the lumber wagon and

Pastor Koren's three-seated buggy really had place for six grown-ups. Therefore Koren had counted the German guests as extra. Koren, Walther, Cramer, Hermann.

Sketch AP61: Mama's and Auntie's evening pleasures after the children have been put to bed. April 11, 1864

Picture: Linka is on the right, Henriette on the left. Linka is playing a psalmodikon, the Norwegian version of the dulcimer, with a numbered fretboard

which generally can play both major and minor scales on one string played with a bow, as Linka is doing in this picture. Christian Preus remembered fondly that his mother played the psalmodikon until her death and that she took great comfort in it. According to him, his mother used the Lindemann Chorale Book (by Ludvig M. Lindemann, organist at Our Savior's Cathedral in Oslo at the time) when she wasn't playing by ear. (Preus, Symra, p. 27)

Commentary: A book for psalmodikon accompaniments for Norwegian hymns of the time had recently been published. It looks as though Linka is using the accompaniment book or the organ book. It was basically a play-by-number system, 1 being do, 2 for re, 3 for mi, etc., with dots for the note length. Many people played the instrument for evening entertainment, especially before the piano became commonplace in homes. Pastors brought the psalmodikon along with them in their travels from congregation to congregation in an effort to add some special accompaniment to the hymns. C. K. Preus.

Sketch AP62: Cornerstone laying, June 30, 1864

Picture: The crowd is watching from inside the building's walls as the pastors of the Norwegian Synod set into place the cornerstone of the new Main Building of Luther College in Decorah, Iowa. Walther and Cramer, seated on the left, are looking on. Laur. Larsen is the first man standing on the left. The man standing with glasses and a manuscript in his hand could be Schmidt, who had read from a manuscript. The other pastors there are Brandt, Hjort, Koren, Ottesen, Adolf C. Preus, and one other.

Commentary: The laying of the cornerstone for the new college building in Decorah brought many people to the little town on the Oneota River in Northeast Iowa. On June 30, 1864, it was reported several thousand people met at the courthouse in Decorah, across the street from the St. Cloud Hotel, where Luther College was housed at the time. From the courthouse the crowd processed across the river toward the hills in West Decorah, on the thirty-two acres that Koren had bought for $1,500 in 1860, after he and Preus had appraised its suitability for a campus. The *Decorah Republican* announced the event, praising the thrifty Norwegians for using the clay in the ground for bricks, the sand for mortar, and the stone they were digging out of the ground for the foundation. Beneath the cliff they had found an abundant supply of water. In the cornerstone, the pastors had deposited a copy of *Emigranten*, the most widely circulated Norwegian-American newspaper of the time, a copy of the *Decorah Republican*, a number of coins, a Bible, a copy of the *Augsburg Confession*, and Erick Pontoppidan's *Explanation to Martin Luther's Small Catechism*. After it was put in place, Preus hit the stone three times with the hammer beside the stone in the name of the triune God. Laur. Larsen spoke on Psalm 126, Preus gave a dedicatory address, and Koren read a short history of Norwegian emigration which Friedrich August Schmidt (1837-1928) read in English. (Schmidt was a German whose life as a theological professor in several of the Norwegian-American schools played an important part in the life of the churches founded by the Norwegians.) This too had been placed in the cornerstone.

Sketch AP63: Men in a pew

Commentary: This is probably the beginning of a sketch from the day of the laying of the cornerstone. The men appear to be sitting in a pew.

Picture: In October, 1864, the pastors of the Norwegian Synod met once again, this time for a conference at the Hjort Parsonage in East Paint Creek, Iowa. After the meeting the Preuses went to Decorah to see the progress of the new Main Building. By then, the walls had risen substantially. The inscription on this drawing, however, points to the primitive conditions that still obtained for the Larsens. It is not quite clear what she is teasing about, however. Is she saying that the pile of lumber one day will become the guest room, or that the little hut by the lumber is already the guest room? It is difficult to say. Larsen, who enjoyed the company of the Preuses, and Mrs. Larsen, whose health was never robust, carried on a warm and extensive correspondence with Linka. When Larsen had written to invite Preus to come to Decorah and bring his family along because "Decorah is large and there is plenty room," (December, 1863, Laur. Larsen to Herman Preus, Luther College Archives, 3: 18:39) Linka had made her husband respond that he was not telling the truth. At the time the St. Cloud Hotel, where the college was housed, was full to overflowing and Linka knew that people would have to double up in their beds to give them room. Furthermore, Mrs. Larsen had just given birth to a new son, Herman, and was very weak.

Commentary: The vantage of this sketch is probably somewhat behind the current Main Building, a scene frequently used in Luther College paintings. Something not to be missed is the top of the tree in the shape of a cross growing across the river valley on the hill. Karen Larsen, author of a biography of her father, noted that "One evening above the unfinished wall a rugged pine, sharply outlined against the sunset sky, stretching out it branches in the shape of a cross. He [Larsen} thought of the vision of Constantine, 'By this sign thou shalt conquer.' The tree, which stood on the bluffs beyond the river valley west of the college, was for years point out to the young people, even after it had lost its significance." (Larsen, p. 167.) There is no other visual record of this tree. The other figures in the sketch are not clear.

Sketch N16: A view of the tables at the dedication. Larsen is shaking up an Irish boy and Mrs. Koren and Brandt are going around the tables speaking to people. Several thousand people—around 8-10—had sat around the tables.

Farmwife: Yes. this is a fine arrangement, that's for sure!

Mrs. Brandt: It was good to get coffee, for it is so cold, but let us hurry so others may eat.

Professor Larsen: What are you doing that for, naughty boy! Scram, or you might get something more than cake!

Irish boy: You may empty my pockets, sir, and see all the cake I have stolen.

Mrs. Koren: It is good when one can be so content with everything, Mr. Birkrem.

Mr. Birkrem: Yes, dear Mrs. Koren. I am so pleased that we have this school ready and pleased to see the many people showing such interest in it. And then to have these 100 healthy and diligent boys seeking admission.

Out of excitement, he accidentally spills his precious coffee on Mrs. Koren's dress.

Commentary: Historically speaking, this is among the most significant of the drawings because it records a woman's view of the dedication of the first Main Building, October 14, 1865. (The south wing was not completed until 1874, and it burned down in 1889. It was replaced by a new building on the same site in 1890. It burned down in 1942 and was replaced in 1952 by the current Main Building.) The reports of the event tell who gave the speeches, on what texts, and what constituencies they represented. Some reports say that over six-thousand people attended the dedication of the Main building on October 14, 1865. Linka writes that between eight to ten thousand attended. Rain threatened throughout the program and began just as Pastor J. A. O. Ottesen concluded his final prayer. In the back of the main building, overlooking the bluff, the farmers' wives in the area had set up tables with food enough to accommodate them all. Only two-thousand were said to have eaten, the rain keeping the rest inside the building or sending the local people home early. Diderikke is her usual self, commandeering the farmer's wife next to her to get going. Professor Larsen is shaking down an Irish boy, probably from Waukon, where there was a settlement of Irish; Mrs. Koren is her usual serene self. Ole Birkrem, speaking to her and spilling his coffee on her new dress, had been a generous contributor to the college building, but who in several letters to Preus and Larsen expressed his feeling that he had not been treated right by the officials at the service. As usual, Christian is goofing off under the table. All different kinds of food are on the table. After the festivities, as darkness fell, the high windows in the building were illuminated with candles spelling out *Soli Deo Gloria.*

Sketch N10: (Next page) The Hjort Parsonage at Paint Creek, August 1866

All the children are occupied with some nosy little pigs who have run all the way from Mama's garden where they were into something they should not have gotten into. The wife herself is following them and Father is going to spade a little wherever he finds it necessary.

Picture: This drawing shows Linka's pleasure in the children when the family is on a visit to the Hjort parsonage in August 1866 just before the Preuses left for Norway. They may have come there for Karine's wedding to Dr. Jacob

Kjøns Prestegaar. Painte Creek.

Alle Bönnene ere i Aktivitet med nogle nærere Frisÿnger som have Latt, hve fra Mamas Have, om nævet antet De likke man have Fren blÿr for nÿere perfande ÿ Futter shel Shate tÿl twerpelol han fonder net n[...]

Wright Magelssen, a graduate of Rush Medical School in Chicago, who settled in Rushford, Minnesota, for a life-long practice.

The male figure on the left hand side of the house is most likely Ove J. Hjort, the pastor at Paint Creek from 1862 until 1879. It is very likely that the woman chasing the children from the garden is Mrs. Hjort who is frequently called Mama in Karine's letters to Henriette and Linka. The woman with the hat on could very well be Henriette or Karine. It is not possible to recognize the figures in the house, though one can clearly recognize most of the children.

Commentary: As she did such work, one assumes that Linka is very sensitive to the need of each child to be included. Christian is on the swing. As the oldest of the children, he would have been fourteen and he is recognizable because he the oldest boy, whose characteristic pose in these drawings is with his head down. Rosina is the girl on the far left; Lulla Hjort, who was to marry Christian ten years later, is standing with her back to us. Anga is the little girl behind the woman walking with the pigs. The other Hjort children, except for the youngest on the picture, are more difficult to name as Linka has not drawn them before. But the children would have recognized them.

Lulla Hjort Preus, the oldest of the Hjort children, wrote in a memoir of her life at Paint Creek that all of the pastors' children thought of themselves as family. They spent long weeks in the summer together and the girls traveled from home to home in order to learn certain skills from the woman of each house. All those times together served to give them a strong sense of family and encouraged intermarriage, further strengthening the bonds between each family. (Lulla Preus, "Minde fra den gamle Paint Creek præstegaard, " *Symra* {Decorah, vii 1911}, p.1

Sketch N11: Hjort Parsonage: Front view

Commentary: In the tradition of Norwegians, the pastors frequently gave their parsonages names. The Hjorts named Paint Creek parsonage *Blaasenborg*—castle of the winds. Located in a valley near Lansing on the Mississippi River, it was central to the life of the early Synod pastors: few pastors coming from Wisconsin could make the journey to Decorah without stopping off at Blaasenborg. Mrs. Koren and Mrs. Hjort were close friends and visited frequently. When Mrs. Hjort was tragically killed in a cooking accident in 1873, Mrs. Koren wrote to Linka mourning her loss saying that Mrs. Hjort had been a breath of fresh air and she thoroughly enjoyed it when she would drop in. (October 10, 1873, Elisabeth Koren to Linka Preus, J. C. K. Preus private collection.)

The Norwegian American writer Peer Strømme, (1856-) who was a student at Luther College from 1869-1876, wrote a novel in which he described a visit to the Hjort parsonage and the accomplishments of the young women, a view of culture the young boy had not had before his coming to college. While the novel does not rank with the best in Norwegian American literature, Halvor does have its charm, especially its portrait of the clergy and their families as viewed by a painfully shy farm boy of the time. (Peer Strømme, *Hvorledes Halvor Blev Prest {How Halvor became a Pastor)*. Translated by Inga B. Norstog and David T. Nelson. [Luther College Press: Decorah 1960.])

Sketch N21: (Next page) A market in New York. Fulton Market 1865.

A woman in New York: Would you like a piece of pie, Mrs. Preus?

Linka: No, thank you! These oysters taste so remarkably good!

Woman in New York: Have a seat, Mrs. Preus. Please take a seat.

Commentary: Herman had been asked by the Norwegian Synod in convention to minister to the struggling Norwegian congregation in New York for a short period. After their arrival in the city, he preached 3 times a week for the next 5- 6 weeks at the church, besides preaching at the Missouri Synod's congregation, as well as the Seaman's church. On September 21, 1865, Preus presented the congregation the constitution which Laur. Larsen had written in 1860, which the congregation had accepted. The congregation revived. Preus conducted his last service there on October 8, 1865, when ninety-five people joined the church. Some months later, Koren served the congregation, after which it called Pastor Ole Juul (1838-1903) to become its first full time pastor. Juul served there until 1876.

While Herman was engaged in his ecclesiastical duties, Linka went sightseeing. One day she convinced him it was too hot to work, so they went to Castle Garden, the place through which most immigrants of the day came, and then to enjoy the ocean and shores. They may have gone to see an exhibit of paintings from Dresden, which interested her because among her own books was a copy of sketches from the Dresden Gallery. They also saw a bit of the end of the Civil War, which she reported to her children: Regiments marching, people in Central park, including some of the first black people Linka had seen.

Fulton Market, the fishing market for the city, was well known for its oyster bars. Near the Brooklyn Bridge, on South Sixth Street in Manhattan, it was connected to the same building as the Fulton Street Ferry building. Note the young man looking toward us holding a tray with oysters on it, and the large pots for steaming the oysters.

Sketch N29: (Next page) An evening party at Hanchen and Bang's September 1867

Kalla: This "slavery in and of itself" as you say, that is sophistry. The slavery you have in America is sin. Give in, brother-in-law. On this point your wife has, peculiarly enough, the right on her side. She is a better theologian than you. What do you think, Linka? I respect you, my Sister.

Bang: Bang Bang. It is impossible for you to defend your theory.

Commentary: This drawing is most significant for those who want to know what the woman of the Norwegian Synod thought of their husbands' views on slavery. They are visiting Linka's sister, Hanchen, who is married to Hans Fredrik Bang. Herman had given lectures on the American church at the mission school in Oslo (See *Vivacious Daughter: Seven Lectures on the Religious Situation Among Norwegians in America* by Hermann Amberg Preus) where he had brought up the Norwegian Synod's position on slavery, that it was a "moral evil" but not a sin. In this opinion they were following the lead of their mentors in the Missouri Synod, whose Biblicism had convinced them that if the Bible did not say slavery was a sin, which it did not, they could not say so, even if they thought it was wrong. This got about the same reception in Norway as it had from the other Norwegian Lutheran churches in America. The uproar in the press caused Herman difficulties wherever he went in Norway, as it did the Korens when they spent some time in Norway several years later. Elisabeth complained they had to explain the issue over and over again. () The young theological students Georg Sverdrup and Sven Oftedal, who were to found the opposing Norwegian-Danish Conference some years later, never forgot Preus' comments. Linka's brother, Johan Carl "Kalla" Keyser, principal of the Nissen School for Girls in Oslo, disagrees with Herman and commends Linka for her theological position, which is not reported here or in any other extant document. Like a good lady, Linka knew she was not to express her political opinions in polite company, but her drawing is an ironic side comment on her own view and her husband's.

Sketch N38: Little Iowa Parsonage August 1866

Mrs. Koren: If we keep picking at this rate, Aunt Linka, we will soon have a basket full and will be able to get the stove good and warm so we can have dinner ready by 12:00.

Linka: Let's just keep on. Well, now I have put so much kindling into the basket that it seems odd that that it isn't full yet.

Doctor: But Mama, all the kindling is falling out again!

Picture: This sketch showing Linka and Elisabeth finding kindling is a good example of how Linka sets a story into a sketch. Linka clearly likes the boy for seeing those things and laughing. She is quick to use the moment in her sketch.

Commentary: The summer of 1866 the Preuses made a trip to Decorah which Linka documented with some of her more penetrating sketches. The Preuses were planning to leave for Norway the following November and she may have wanted to bring some of these pictures with her to show the family in Norway. There is evidence that Linka's health had deteriorated after the difficult birth of Carl Christie who died the day after being born October 20, 1863. Both she and her husband felt the need for a long rest and this was to be their fifteenth wedding anniversary celebration.

Sketch N 48: Scene from the Living Room February 2, 1868

Christian: Mama, I have done my lessons and written what I had to before Papa comes home. Can I go over to Ambjørn's and hunt?

Linka: Yes, but be careful Christian.

Anga: But I am doing the fives in subtraction.

Doctor: Anga, now I have done the Fourth Commandment.

Rosina: Uffda, this world history! I will never learn it!

Petra Brevig knits.

"Paul is the loveliest boy in the world." Da da da da.

Misses Johnson sews on my machine. Mrs. Christensen holds the yarn.

Picture: The sketch portrays the drama of the people in the room and gives us insight into the changing times. The sewing machine is a novelty to "Missis Johnson". Mrs. Koren was considered the best teacher of sewing, so several of the pastors' daughters spent time with her so she could teach them how to use the machine. Linka probably got hers soon after her return from Norway.

The other two women are making a ball of yarn. It is in the left background where we see the drama of generations that is played out against the action in the foreground. Linka is sitting at the spinning wheel, an instrument which seems to be something of an anachronism, spinning and simultaneously supervising her children's studies. Rosina's complaint about the difficulty of world history is one she repeats during her years attending the private girls' school which

Diderikke Brandt supervised for the pastors' daughters from 1873-1874 in Decorah. C. K. and Ambjørn, the neighbor boy, enjoyed hunting and the table was often graced with the game the boys would bring home. C. K. notes in his memoirs that his father was also a good hunter. Doctor is memorizing the Fourth Commandment sitting at his mother's feet learning the command that assures peaceful and prosperous family life. Christian, as a growing adolescent boy, is beginning to edge out of the woman's room, off into the world of grown men.

Commentary: The birth of Paul Arctander Preus, on April 24, 1867, while they were in Norway, meant that once again Linka was fully occupied with a baby and this time Henriette Neuberg was not there to help. She had returned to Norway some months after the Preus' departure for Norway. This sketch shows the world Linka inhabited after her return from Norway when her major responsibility with the children was educating them.

Christian at this time is a student at Luther College and he had a place, in the educational endeavors of the Norwegian Synod's educational institutions. The education of Anga and Rosina, however, posed another problem. Linka could teach them the basics, and they could learn how to be ladies from her and the other pastors' wives, but formal education for girls in the mid-19th century was a new issue. The college was specifically built to educate men for the ministry.

In 1872, Henriette and Caroline Koren, Margrethe Brandt, Rosina Preus, Emma and Thora Larsen, (daughters of Laur. Larsen) Lulla Hjort and Sara Reque, (a daughter of Luther Professor Lars Reque,) all lived together in the Brandt parsonage and took courses from the professors at the college who taught them in their spare time. They learned English, Norwegian, German, French, history, sewing, music and the art of living together as sisters. Though it was an informal and unofficial school for women, it was the first such effort on the part of the Lutheran Norwegians in this country to teach their daughters in their own institutions of higher learning. One can imagine that when the young girls learned to sew, they sat around in rooms like this one indulging in conversation, learning how to do things from their mothers or their mothers' peers, women they learned to call "Tante" (auntie).

Sketch N46:(Next page)

Brinch: Here are the Americans. Welcome, welcome.

Carl Christie: Welcome!

Tante Lodoviska: Welcome, Preus. Yes, yes. You haven't changed. I would have known you in thousands.

Wilhelm Christie: Welcome, Preus!

Doctor: Are there always so many lights in Norway at night and are there always such happy people!

Preus: So we meet again. Hello, Lodoviska; but where are my wife and children? Excuse me while I look after them. Don't ask, we'll slip out of sight.

Anga: Hee, hee, hee. Are we actually in Norway?

Kalla: Well, now, you must be Sina—you can see your Mama in you—I believe. Yes, there you are, I otherwise never would have been able to trace it out. Welcome, my dear.

Sina: Good evening! No, are you really Uncle Kalla. We see you every day on the wall at home.

Uncle Lomse: Oh, dear, at the last you come, old one. A long welcome. You are, by George, some heavier and older.

Linka: Oh, Lomse, you too have gotten old and heavy.

Sister Rosa: No, how wonderful it is that you have come. You Christian, you have gotten so big, but still I think you must get a kiss from your aunt. You can have this.

Christian: You must be an auntie person. I am acquainted with none of you, but all of you look so happy.

Commentary: A sketch of the Preus's arrival in Norway, this portrays a dramatic moment Linka will want to remember later. Each comment perfectly characterizes the person making the comment. Herman is the typical nervous in-law making his courteous greetings and looking around to see where his wife and children are and whether they need him. There is a touch of awkwardness, as though the emotion is too great and the experience too profound to be lived through without some ordinary language to keep it near what human beings can bear. This shows Linka at her dramatic best.

Sketch N52: Evening scene, July 11, 1868.

Koren: Oh, Mrs. Preus—I should ask you if you would light my cigar. (He makes the deepest bow, but does he thank me? come back later.

Henriette: It is terrible to go down with the pudding in the dark.

Linka: Take it now carefully!

Lina: Here it is coal black dark. Yes, I say so, I will spill the pudding, surely.

Mrs. Koren: Then you will have to take it up again, my child.

Sina: Mama, come with the light. Henriette you must go first down into the cellar.

Henriette Koren, Linka Koren, and Sina Preus carry the rosepudding bowl.

Picture: Trofast is ashamed though he looks so respectable. Koren lights his cigar. Mrs. Koren looks on.

Commentary: In the summer of 1868, the Preuses took another trip to Iowa. This sketch of her lighting Koren's cigar while the young girls wait impatiently for her to take the candle and go to the basement with them is a two part sketch revealing Koren as proud, in line with his reputation as the "coxcomb of the Synod."

The girls are anxious to bring their red pudding (a raspberry pudding "rødgrød") down into the cellar which is cooler than the August heat outside. They are hoping that it will set quickly so they can have some. They need a light, as well as their mother, because the dark cellar held terror for them. Rattlesnakes were not uncommon in the basements of the early immigrant cabins and some of the land around Washington Prairie is said to still have a plentiful supply. Rosina is sitting on the long benches by the tables.

The dramatic situation with the adults and the children in two different stories fulfills the requirements of genre painting that Linka had learned as a young woman.

Sketch N57: CK is under the cellar table down beneath the young girls when they come down with the red pudding where they will get a pinch in the foot and ankles and skirts. There is a shriek, howling and laughter. The evening of July 11, 1868.

Lina: Ufda, Christian. If you upset me the red pudding will end up—yes it will, Christian—it really will—you are a bad boy—the red pudding will end up on your head!

Henriette: No, Christian. Uffda, how mean you are. Uffda, you are pinching me. Uffda, how impolite you are, you terrible boy!

Picture: Christian (C.K.) is waiting for the girls under the cellar table where he is going to pull at their dresses and scare them so they will drop the pudding which they assure him he will have to lick up. Lina (Caroline) Koren almost always says "græssiligt" (awful or horrible) in her statements, and Dr. is making his wry little comments from below.

Commentary: Caroline ("Lina") Koren Naeseth remembered these times in a memoir, "A great pleasure for us were the long summer visits from the families of the ministers of Spring Prairie, Koshkonong and Painted Creek. During those visits there were often so many in the house, and it was lively both inside and out. We had a long table in the garden, around which we children stood and ate our evening meal, and drank cambric tea from small brown varnished tin cups." (Caroline Mathilde Koren Naeseth, "Memories from Little Iowa Parsonage," *Norwegian American Studies and Records*, {NAHA: Northfield, xii, 1943], p. 72).

Sketch N49: A ride in the sleigh with the pastors' wives and pastors and a single woman and Christie. If only we can get mail at the post office. February 2, 1869

Dr. Magelsson: Get up, Gulbrun, get up Truls! See, Mrs. Larsen, have you ever seen such a frisky team, see how nicely they trot. Shame on you, boys, don't gallop!

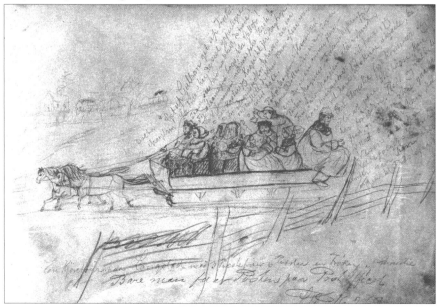

Fru Larsen: My yes, they are rather fine horses.

Pastor Magelssen throws cakes to the rear. Mrs. Magnus and Mrs. Johnson are so tightly packed in they can only eat, but not talk.

Pastor M: Who will have rolls? There is one, there is one, there is one, even more

Pastor Magnus, Miss Muhlendorf, Mrs. Sara Magelsen say all at once: I will have, I will have, they shriek, laugh and carry on...

Carl Christie appears himself to be a step child. He has too little place and he meditates on whether he should go home and falls flat on his nose causing the people to laugh at him. He waits for them at home back at the parsonage.

Commentary: One of Linka's last sketches, this shows the pastors' wives and family enjoying themselves on a sleigh ride. Dr. Jacob Wright Magelson, one of the few early Luther College graduates who did not become a pastor, was married to Karine Neuberg, Mrs, Laur. Larsen's sister at the time of this drawing. After Karine's death he married her niece, Thora Larsen, Laur. Larsen's daughter. A graduate of Rush Medical School in Chicago, he practiced medicine in Koshkonong and Rushford, Minnesota for many years. Pastor Morten Henrick Magnus (1833-1903) served the Arendal parish in Fillmore County, Minnesota. Miss Muhlendorf is the governess for the Preus children. Mrs. Sarah Stockfleth Magelssen is the wife of Pastor Kristian Magelssen, brother of J. W. Magelssen. Kristian Magelssen, a graduate of Concordia Seminary, served the Highland Prairie congregation, near Rushford.

Sketch AP69:   Eggedosis

Confusion at school because Mama has come in with eggedosis. Every birthday in the family is an eggedosis feast day when we have a plentiful supply of eggs and sugar. October 1869.

M.: Here I sit with the most serious thoughts and I am being disturbed. Come here right away. You first Mymy, and then all the children afterward.

A refreshing ?

It is so wonderfully fine that we will get eggedosis — eight and eleven are five — there you have a kick, Anga!

Anga: You are a Hottentot, Doctor, you are! Careful — Mymy will see you!

Rosina: The Hottentots? In Spring Prairie, I think —

Lina: No, Sina, let me see — the Hottentots — I thought they were in South Africa —

Paal: Mymy, take me, six, nine, four, eight

Muhlendorf: Listen now, Sina and Lina, where do the Hottentots live. There is always noise when you come in, who can manage when you carry on, Linka!

Hermann: Can I have a little?

Linka: Excuse the band on my head, but I have a toothache today. My glasses have to sit on my nose, because I have eggedosis on my fingers.

Picture: Linka is portraying the chaos that she has brought into the classroom being taught by Miss Muhlendorf. She is trying to teach them something about the Hottentot, an Afrikaans name, now considered disparaging, for the Khoekhoen people who live in northern South Africa.

Commentary: Eggedosis (eggnog) was a favorite childhood drink for these children. The interest of the family in things African, however, is keen since they all knew of Bishop Hans Paludan Smith Schreuder (1817-1882), the pioneer missionary to the Zulu whom Norwegians and Norwegian-Americans followed closely. When the first Zulu was baptized, church bells rang out over all of Norway.

Sketch AP70: Death mask. When I am dead I will look like this. I look a little more lively with my eyes open.

I will bequeath you this book, but I am no in shape to remember if it was Doktor or Anga I promised it to after my death. Now for the seven of you there are seven to share. Take half of them that are not bound as the bound were.

Endnotes

Introduction

[1] Kristiansand is the modern spelling. In the nineteenth century, the common spelling was Christianssand.

[2] *Linka's Diary: On Land and Sea, 1845-1864*, translated and edited by Johan Carl Keyser Preus and Diderikke Margrethe Brandt Preus (Minneapolis: Augsburg Publishing House, 1952), 9. Hereafter referred to as *Linka's Diary*.

[3] Aksel Arstal and Carl Just, *Oslo Byleksikon* (Oslo: Aschehoug, 1966), 327.

[4] *Linka's Diary*, ix.

[5] Ibid., xii.

[6] Elizabeth Hampsten, *Read This Only to Yourself: The Private Writings of Midwestern Women, 1880-1910* (Bloomington: Indiana University Press, 1982), 227. For a theoretical discussion of the nature of diaries, see Suzanne L. Bunkers, "Introduction to the Collection: *Diaries of Girls and Women*," <http://www.intech.mnsu.edu/bunkers/introduction.htm>, February 20, 2004. Regarding the question of reading diaries in manuscript form, see Cynthia A. Huff, "Reading as Re-vision: Approaches to Reading Manuscript Diaries," *Biography* 23:3 (2000), 505-523.

[7] Thomas Mallon, *A Book of One's Own: People and their Diaries* (New York: Penguin Books, 1984), xvi-xvii.

[8] Suzanne L. Bunkers, "Whose Diary Is It, Anyway?" <http://www.intech.mnsu.edu/bunkers/WhoseDiary.html> February 20, 2004.

[9] Suzanne L. Bunkers, "'Faithful Friend': Nineteenth-Century Midwestern American Women's Unpublished Diaries," *Women's Studies International Forum* 10 (1987), 8.

[10] Mullen discusses a variety of diarists, whom he categorizes as: Chroniclers, Travelers, Pilgrims, Creators, Apologists, Confessors, and Prisoners.

Similarly, Philippe Lejeune outlines four distinct functions of diaries: to express oneself; to reflect; to freeze time; and to take pleasure in writing. ("How Do Biographies End," *Biography* 24.1 [2001], 105-107.) As Lejeune notes, "a real diary fulfills several functions at once." (105).

[11] Margo Culley, *A Day at a Time: The Diary Literature of American Women from 1764 to the Present* (New York: The Feminist Press a the City University of New York: 1985), 8.

[12] For a more detailed discussion of his "creative editing" of the text, see Marvin G. Slind, "Constructing an Ideal Image: The Creative Translation of the Linka Preus Diary" (NAHA Norway publication 2004 — publication data not yet available)

[13] Bunkers, "Faithful Friend," 10.

[14] Mallon., 75. For a discussion of "the genesis of diaries kept for spiritual purposes," see Mallon, 105-106.

[15] Bunkers, "Faithful Friend,"14.

[16] Culley, 10.

[17] Anne Bermingham, *Learning to Draw: Studies in the Cultural History of a Polite and Useful Art* (New Haven and London: Yale University Press 2000), 128.

[18] Johan Carl Keyser Preus, *Hermann Amberg Preus: A Family History* (n.p.: Preus Family Book Club, 1966). Hereafter referred to as *Family History*.

In the original diary, Linka's husband's name is spelled Hermann. However, in American sources, including those published by his family, the spelling is Herman. This edition will use the spelling used in the original diary, Hermann, except in direct quotations from the 1952 translation or other American publications.

[19] See E. Clifford Nelson and Eugene L. Fevold, *The Lutheran Church Among Norwegian-Americans: A History of the Evangelical Lutheran Church* vol. 1, *1825-1890* (Minneapolis: Augsburg Publishing House, 1960).

The original, Norwegian-language version of O.M. Norlie's *Norsk Luterske Prester i Amerika: 1843-1913* (Minneapolis: Augsburg Publishing House, 1914), lists the early Norwegian pastors in America in the order of their arrival in the country. "Preus, Herman [sic] Amberg" is the twelfth entry in the listing. (p. 98). (The later, English version of that work, *Who's Who Among Pastors in all the Norwegian Lutheran Synods of America, 1843-1927* [Minneapolis: Augsburg Publishing House, 1928] lists all of the entries alphabetically.)

[20] Ibid., 154-155; *Family History*, 13.

[21] Ibid, 17.

[22] Ibid, 30. He died in 1983.

Linka's Diary

[1] Together with the "Jubilee Song," which follows this entry, this is the only surviving diary entry from 1844. A new diary begins on January 1, 1845. Uranienborg is currently a district in the city of Oslo. In the early nineteenth century, when it was outside of Christiania, it included a villa owned by Linka's grandmother, Dorothea Carlsen, the widow of Carl Andreas Carlsen. The house later served as a school for girls. In her diary, Linka often refers to Uranienborg as "Borgen." There was another farm near Oslo called Borgen, which now gives its name to a train station on the Kolsås and Røabanen S-train line in Oslo. However, I have found no connection between Linka's family and that farm; thus, as in J.C.K. Preus's translation of the diary, this translation will use "Borgen" as a nickname for Uranienborg. For information regarding Uranienborg and Borgen, see Aksel Arstal and Carl Just, *Oslo Byleksikon* (Oslo: H. Aschehoug & Co [W. Nygaard], 1966), 64 and 327, and **Knut Are Tvedt**, ed, *Oslo Byleksikon*, 4th edition (Oslo: Kunnskapsforlaget, 2000), 74 and 464. For a brief description of the Carlsens, see < http://www.hagerup.com/genealogy/carlsen.htm > (accessed August 16, 2004)

[2] Askevold (now known as Askvoll) is a parish in Sogn og Fjordana, north of Bergen. Linka went to live there with her aunt and uncle, Rosa (Rosalide)(1815-1898) and Johan Carl Christie (1808-1898) <http://home.no.net/mikegl/fam04420.htm>. The latter was pastor (sogneprest) of Askevold parish. Linka would help her aunt with her young children: Doris (born July 10, 1841), Wilhelm (born August 20, 1842), and Agnes (born November 17, 1845, as noted in Linka's diary entry for that day). Her aunt and uncle would eventually have five other children, the last born in 1858: Camma Maria (July 23, 1848); Hofmann, (May 15, 1849); Johan Carl, (July 24, 1851); Adolf Vilhelm,(May 2, 1854), and Rosalide Isabella (April 30, 1858) (*Digitalarchiv* [Døypte Sogn og Fjordane 1669-1895]). Although entries in the National Archives of Norway's *Digitalarchiv* spell the second child's name "Vilhelm," Linka spells it "Wilhelm."

[3] Her aunt, Lodviska Carlsen, also known as Lillebessa, or Viska (*Linka's Diary*, p. 285.)

[4] A carriage with a foldable top

[5] Ullern was the residence of Linka's aunt and uncle, Maren and Carl Carlsen. (*Linka's Diary*, p. 288).

[6] Wilhelm Adolf Carlsen, Linka's uncle (*Linka's Diary*, p. 287)

[7] The word Linka uses here is clearly *Rogen*, which does not fit with the rest of the song. *Bogen* (the book), fits. It is thus translated as such, assuming that she made a minor penmanship error.

[8] The notation, and the mark next to the word *borgerkrandsen*, are in Linka's handwriting. Her "double meaning" is unknown.

[9] *Procurator*. In the next entry, she refers to *Sorenskriver* (Judge) Landmark. The latter refers to Nils Landmark (1775-1859), who lived at Tysse, on the south side of Dalsfjorden. He was *Sorenskriver* for Sunnfjord from 1808 to 1852. He was also a *Stortingsmann* (representative to parliament). He was also a pioneer in Norwegian agriculture. There were fifteen children from his two marriages. <http://www.nrk.no/nyheter/distrikt/nrk_sogn_og_fjordane/fylkesleksikon/2103766.html> (Accessed August 16, 2004)

"Lawyer" (*Procurator*) Landmark probably refers to Johan Widing Heiberg Landmark (1802-1887), who was *ordfører* ("mayor") in Ytre Holmedal soknekommune. From 1833 to 1846, he lived at Fagervik, which had been divided from his father's land at Tysse. He was later bailiff (*fut*) in Sogn. See "Johan Widing Heiberg Landmark," http://www.nrk.no/nyheter/distrikt/nrk_sogn_og_fjordane/fylkesleksikon/1920957.html (Accessed August 16, 2004)

J.C.K. Preus's 1952 translation refers only to Judge Landmark, but in addition to using the two separate titles (*Procurator* and *Sorenskriver*), Linka's entry on January 3 refers to two separate families.

[10] *spidssleder*

[11] Johan Daniel Stub Landmark (1820-1882), another of Nils's sons by his first wife, became a parish priest (*sogneprest*). *Norsk Biografisk Leksikon*, A.W. Brøgger and Einer Jansen, ed, Vol. 8 (Oslo: H. Aschehaug & Co [W. Nygaard], 1938), pp 142, 144-146.

[12] This day's notations are set off by a marginal note, "galt" [wrong], but contain no further explanation.

[13] No first name is given for "Doctor" Landmark, but Linka is undoubtedly referring to Dr. Lars Stub Heiberg Landmark (1808-1883). He was district doctor (*distriktslege*) in Sunnfjord. See "Lars Stub Heiberg Landmark," <http://www.nrk.no/nyheter/distrikt/nrk_sogn_og_fjordane/fylkesleksikon/2103834.html>, (accessed August 16, 2004)

[14] "Fastelavn" is a combination of Christian festival and traditions from an ancient feast for spring and fertility. The Norwegian Fastelaven tradition was to go out in the woods and gather small bundles of birch branches. The belief was that people, animals, and trees would become more fertile when beaten with "livskvisten" — the twig of life. In particular, childless women were beaten. Whoever got up first on Shrovetide Sunday had the right to beat the others in the house, and then give them Shrovetide buns (fastelavnsboller) afterward. Today, "fastelavnsris" is still made, or bought, for Shrovetide, but used only for decoration.

[15] black guillemots — small black diving birds

[16] Linka describes the ribbons as "one quarter wide, and two alen long." The alen (ell) was approximately 0.627 meters, or approximately two feet.

[17] Seasoned minced meat —— often veal —— patties

[18] Her sister, Hanna Marie Keyser, also called Henny Penny (*Hønepøne*) or Hanchen

[19] Written by Sir Walter Scott in 1824.

[20] See note for January 7.

[21] "To have a long nose," means to be disappointed. In some instances in the diary, Linka accompanies that phrase with a drawing of a nose. That will be noted in the text wherever it occurs.

[22] Names for Linka's brother and sisters: "Kalle" = Johan Carl Keyser (1929-1904); Lillemamma (also "Ovid") = Ovidia (1832-1916); "Hexa" (also "Eska") = Anna Waleska (1831-1853); "Bya" = Agnes. Her two other sisters were Rosa ("Rosemette") (1837-1881); and Hanna

("Hanken," "Hanchen" or *"Hønepøne"* ["Henny Penny"]) (1840-1934). (Johan Carl Keyser Preus, *Hermann Amberg Preus: A Family History* (n.p. Preus Family Book Club, 1966), 10-11.

[23] Throughout most of the 19th century, the Norwegian Spesiedaler equaled 120 schilling (<http://www.free-definition.com/Historical-weights-and-measures.html#Monetary> and <http://www.medsca.org/measur_currency.pdf>, accessed August 19, 2004.)

[24] In the original diary, Linka left a blank space here.

[25] Earlier, Linka spelled the name Dorthe. The pronunciation would be almost the same for both spellings.

[26] *Stiftsamtmand*, defined in *A. Larsen's Dansk-Norsk-Engelsk Ordbog* (fourth edition, 1910) as "civil governor of a diocese."

Wilhelm Frimann Koren Christie (1778-1849) was the father of Linka's uncle, J. Carl Christie. A prominent political and intellectual leader in Norway, he was an important figure at the constitutional assembly at Eidsvoll in 1814, serving as first representative from Bergen. He played a key role in the negotiations for the creation of the Union with Sweden, and after creation of the new *Storting*, served as *Stortingspresident* (President of the Parliament) from 1815 to 1818. He was *Stiftsamtmand* in Bergen from 1815 to 1825, and was *Toldinspektør* (customs inspector) there from 1828 until his death in 1849. He helped found the Bergen Museum. After his death, the *Storting* allocated funds for a statue in his honor, which currently stands in front of the Bergen Museum; it was the first statue in Norway honoring an individual citizen. See "Wilhelm Frimann Koren Christie," <http://no.wikipedia.org/wiki/Wilhelm_Frimann_Koren_Christie> (Accessed August 16, 2004), and *Norsk Biografisk Leksikon*, (Edv. Bull and Einar Jansen, ed), Vol. 3 (Oslo: H. Aschehoug & Co., [W. Nygaard], 1926), pp. 13-22.

The "Landmark Family Geneology Project" <http://home.no.net/mikegl/fam04420.htm> indicates that his wife was Karen Marie Berg, and that they had one son, Johann Carl Christie (Linka's uncle in Askevold). However, according to the new edition of the *Norsk Biografisk Leksikon*, he never married, but had two sons out of wedlock. (Vol. 2, Jon Gunnar Arntzen, ed, [Oslo: Kunnskapsforlaget, 1999], p. 206 Hereafter referred to as NBL2). In addition to the numerous references to her uncle, J. Carl Christie, Linka's diary entries for July 16 and 26, 1845, refer to "his son, W. Christie" and "Wilhelm Christie (the Governor's son)."

The governor's son, Wilhelm Christie, was born in Copenhagen in 1806, and ultimately served as *"Overtoldbetjent"* (Senior Customs Official) in Bergen. He died in 1885. His wife was Anne Eline Christie, Wilhelm's cousin. (Her father was Governor Christie's brother, Edvard Eilert Christie.) (Digitalarkivet, *Gravlagde i Bergen 1881-1911*, record #s 11611 and 20364.) Edvard Eilert Christie was born in Christiansund, and died in 1831 at the age of 58; his position was listed in the burial records as *"Enkemand og Overtoldbetjent"* (widower and Senior Customs Official). (Digitalarkivet: *Gravlagde i Bergen 1816-1886*, Record #32476.)

[27] *"Gid hun nu ikke i sit 16de Aar vil hexe alt formeget."* This is a word play: *"Hexa"*— the sister's name, and *"hexe"*—witchcraft

[28] cream porridge

[29] Linka writes that the cod was "2 allen long, and 1/2 allen wide". The alen, originally based on the length of a man's arm, was approximately 0.627 meter, or approximately 2 feet

[30] Governor Christie's sister. This was apparently Catharine Elisabeth Christie, who died in 1853 at the age of 66. She is described in burial records from Bergen as *"Jomfr."* (an unmarried woman) (Digitalarkivet: *Gravlagde i Bergen 1816-1886*, record # 14865)

[31] Shepherd's horn

[32] [*vi havde Prinsessepudding til Middag*] There are two very different dishes by that name. One is a sweet dessert, made with butter, flour, eggs, and almonds, topped with a red sauce (such as strawberry or raspberry sauce). The other is served as a hot main dish item; it consists primarily of a mixture of fish, such as cod, haddock, or pollock (or a mixture thereof). It may be cooked as a loaf (as a form of *fiskepudding*) or served as fish cakes or fish balls.

Hanna Winsnes' *Lærebog i de forskjellige Grene af Husholdningen* , published in 1845, contains a recipe for "Prindsesse Budding," which is the sweet dessert variety: <http://www.dokpro.uio.no/litteratur/winsnes/frames.htm> (recipe #547) (Accessed August 30, 2004)

[33] *"knapet ¼ Al lange"* The alen was approximately 0.627 meter, or approximately 2 feet

[34] Jacob Neumann, bishop in Bergen's *Bjørgvin bispedømme*, 1822-1848. <http://www.nla.no/ojj/kirkehistorie/tabell/biskoper.htm> accessed August 18, 2004

[35] The old Norwegian Postmil or Mil was 11.295 kilometers. <http://www.maritimt.net/arkforsk/norskem.htm> (accessed August 18, 2004) Similarly, the *Dansk-Norsk-Engelsk Ordbog*, (A. Larson, ed., Copenhagen and Christiania, Gyldendalske Boghandel Nordisk Forlag, 1910) indicates that in the 19th century, a "Norwegian Mile" was "seven English Miles." Thus "¼ mile" is approximately 2.8 kilometers or 1.7 American miles.

[36] *Tollkasserer* Werner Hosewinckel Christie (1785-1877); see *Norsk Biografisk Leksikon*, (1926), vol 3, p. 3, which refers to him in the description of his son, Eilert Christian Brotkorb Christie (1832-1906)

[37] The names of Werner Christie's children and their dates of birth are: Wilhelm Friemann Koren (24 December 1825); Hans Langsted (6 August 1826); Johan Koren (20 December 1828); Andreas (30 May 1829); Anna Thue (18 March 1831); Magdalena Margaretha Koren (25 June 1834); Eduard Hagerup (8 March 1836); Werner Hosewinckel (25 Sep 1837); Benjamin Conrad (14 February 1841); Johan Andreas Budtz (4 May 1842); Hans (10 August 1843); and Cathrina Elisabeth Ulriche (13 October 1844). The spellings of the names in this entry are as written in Linka's diary. (*Digitalarkivet:* "*Døypte i Bergen 1816-1894*")

[38] Sloops sailing the northern fishing waters

[39] sunfish

[40] approximately 5.6 kilometers or 3.5 US miles

[41] shepherd's horn

[42] the German Church

[43] approximately 22.6 kilometers or 14 miles

[44] A portal of honor

[45] As noted previously, the Governor's son was Wilhelm Christie, and his brother was Werner Christie. See notes for February and May-June, 1845.

[46] This entry is followed by a small sketch of a skate

[47] Anne Thue Christie was the daughter of Customs Collector Werner Christie. (See note for May-June 1845)

[48] *"Jeg ligte ham so svert godt, ikke svert men meget godt"*

[49] *glatte*

[50] Approximately 45 kilometers or 28 U.S. miles.

[51] Jens Rennord (1780-1846), Parish Priest and then-Dean of Osen parish, died January 17, 1846. (Digitalarkivet: Burials in Sogn og Fjordane 1669-1920. [73327/196]). Ousen is now spelled Osen.

[52] Approximately 5.6 kilometers or 3.5 miles.

[53] The question mark is Linka's. Its meaning is not clear.

[54] *Provst*

[55] *Vingbaad*—J.C.K.Preus translated this as "circuit boat," and described it as "a boat provided for the exclusive use of the pastor and his crew" (*Linka's Diary*, p. 30).

[56] In the original diary, Linka drew a line, as in this translation. J.C.K Preus, however, filled in the blank, and translated the phrase as "but the Bishop also put on his chasuble."

[57] Dean Rennord died January 17, 1846. (*Digitalarkivet:* Burials in Sogn og Fjordane 1669-1920. [73327/196])

[58] Approximately 5.6 kilometers or 3.5 US miles

59 *Tossemalene*

60 Agnes

61 The night before Christmas Eve, i.e., December 23.

62 "a mile and a quarter" in nineteenth century Norwegian measurement — approximately 14.1 kilometers or 8.8 miles

63 *Floksilke*

64 A German phrase, meaning "and now nothing more."

65 Lodviska and Constance.

66 Fredrick Wilhelm Keyser (1800-1877); librarian of the University library. He never married. (*Norsk Biografisk Leksikon* (1936), Vol. 7, pp. 266-267)

67 This line is in a slightly different handwriting—a note written quickly by her sister.

68 In the 1952 translation, J.C.K. Preus notes, "A peninsula west of the city, with large woods and a picturesque shoreline, now called Bygdøy." (38)

69 Not clearly legible in original.

70 J.C.K. Preus notes that Smith (no first name indicated) was State Auditor of Christiania, and Linka's uncle by marriage (*Linka's Diary*, p. 288). In her letter of September 14, 1848, Linka refers to him as *Statsrevisor*.

71 *Speciedaler*. As noted previously, there were 120 *Skiling* [Shillings] to one *Speciedaler*

72 Oscar I (r. 1844-1859)

73 See note 1, Autumn 1844

74 *Statholder*

75 The potato blight, which resulted in the "Potato Famine" in Ireland, also caused considerable hardship in Norway.

76 German: a little doll

77 Fredrikshald, also referred to as Halden, was the home of Hermann's parents, Paul Arctander and Anne Rosine Keyser Preus. Pauline Breder (1823-1867) was one of Hermann's sisters, who was married to Jørgen Breder (Family History, p. 5)

78 The text is illegible here.

79 *Pænschekstracten*

80 In the index to *Linka's Diary*, J.C.K. Preus identified him simply as "Taulow, Professor, of Christiania" (p. 288). This undoubtedly refers to Moritz Christian Julius Thaulow (1812-1850). Born in Schleswig, and educated at Oldenburg and Kiel, Germany, he was Lektor (1839-1846) and then Professor of Chemistry (1846-1850) at the University of Christiania. Linka refers to his death in her entry of October 23, 1850) (*NBL1*, Vol. 16 [1969], p. 163). See also *Dansk biografisk Lexikon*, vol XVII <http://www.lysator.liu.se/runeberg/dbl/17/0168.html>, accessed August 20, 2004.

81 Dramatic Society

82 *Gaaseviin*

83 "*Foreningen*"; J.C.K. Preus translated this as "the Art Society" (Linka's Diary, p. 47)

84 The date notation is in J.C.K. Preus's handwriting.

85 The year is not specified, but this letter (with notations that it was written over the course of three days) was filed in sequence with other letters from 1847.

86 Johan Didrik Behrens (1820-1890), choir director and singing instructor (*sanglærer*). In 1846, he became singing instructor at the Christiania Cathedral School, and from 1847 to 1887 was Director of the *Kristiana Handelsstands Sangvorening*. The bride was Bolette Elizabeth Dorothea Matzau of Bergen (1824-1865) (*Norsk Biografisk Leksikon*, Vol. 1, pp. 409-412. [1923]). J.C.K. Preus described him as "musician and director of Norway's most famous men's quartette," (*Linka's Diary*, p. 50n).

87 The letter she refers to is apparently lost.

[83] This letter is not dated, but is filed among letters from July and August 1847. As indicated in the text, Linka has sketched a number of animals and people.

[89] The Palace was finished in the fall of 1848 (See *Oslo Byleksikon*, Revised edition [Oslo: H. Aschehoug & Co, 1966], pp. 277-280)

[90] Swedish King Karl XIV Johan (r. 1818-1844) was French. Prior to being named heir to the Swedish throne in 1810, as Count Bernadotte, he had served as a Marshall in Napoleon's army.

[91] *Skruelos*

[92] "*Veslefresken*" = Lodviska

[93] German = "nothing for me, nothing for you"

[94] See Byron Nordstrom, *Scandinavia Since 1500* (Minneapolis: University of Minnesota Press, 2000), 201-210, and T.K. Derry, *A History of Scandinavia: Norway, Sweden, Denmark, Finland and Iceland* (Minneapolis: University of Minnesota Press, 1979), 238-241.

[95] *Amtmand*

[96] Before the legislatures of Sweden-Norway approved funding for the 15,000 Swedish and 3,000 Norwegian troops, Denmark received help from 243 Swedish and 114 Norwegian volunteers. (Derry, 239.)

[97] J.C.K. Preus identified him in the index to Linka's Diary, as "Jensen, Curate P.A., 1812-1867, poet and author." (p. 286) For more information regarding Peter Andreas Jensen (1812-1867), see NBL1, Vol. 7, pp. 9-13.

[98] The word here is illegible.

[99] Several letters indicate "*Rangelborg*" or "*Ranglborg*," rather than the usual "*Uranienborg*." The Dansk-Norsk-Engelsk Ordbog, A. Larson ed., (Copenhagen and Christiania: Gyldendalske Boghandel: Nordisk Forlag, 1910) defines *rangel* as "disorderly habits" or "revelry,." and *rangle* as "rattle." As the following comments suggest, she is undoubtedly referring humorously to Uranienborg as a wild, noisy, chaotic place.

[100] J.C.K. Preus identifies "W.P." as Wilhelm Preus (*Linka's Diary*, 58).

[101] J.C.K. Preus suggests she is referring to Constance and Wilhelm Hagerup, who are also referred to in the closing paragraph of the letter. (Ibid)

[102] Wilhelm Hagerup

[103] The original diary clearly indicates "W. Christie," but there is a note in another handwriting (probably J.C.K. Preus's) indicating "Hans", and in the next sentence, the name is clearly "Hans." *Linka's Diary* presents it as "Hans Christie" (Ibid.).

[104] The original diary clearly reads, "Kjøbmand Plato," which J.C.K. Preus rendered as "Hr. Platou" (Ibid.). No further information is provided about this individual.

[105] Erik Bøgh (1822-1899).

[106] J.C.K. Preus notes that "*Møllarguten*, Torgeir [sic] Audunson, was a musical genius, one of the most celebrated country fiddlers of Norway. Poverty and lack of opportunity prevented the development of his gift. See *Eventyret Om Ole Bull* by Zinken Hopp, published in Bergen 1945. Pages 153-159" (*Linka's Diary*, 59.).

[107] Ole Bull

[108] J.C.K. Preus notes, "On the 26th of February, 1849, Linka herself becomes engaged to Herman [sic] Preus her cousin, whom she has known since childhood" (*Linka's Diary*, 62).

[109] J.C.K. Preus indicates that "Soon after the engagement, Uncle Carl Christie writes Linka that Aunt Rosa is ill, and asks if she can come to Askevold for a time. Linka decides she is more needed at Askevold than Uranienborg. However, the departure of the steamer is delayed" (Linka's Diary, p. 62).

[110] The lady against the stream. According to Professor Kathleen Stokker of Luther College, "The reference is to a fairy tale, 'Kjerringen mot strömmen,' about a wife who always, as a matter of principle, did contrary to what others, particularly her husband, wanted. The phrase is used quite regularly and to this day." (Correspondence from Kathleen Stokker, August 30, 2004.)

[111] Eggnog

[112] Born 15 May 1849.

[113] That prediction was accurate: *NBL1* Vol. 1, p. 13, and burial records from Bergen (*Digitalarkivet*: "Gravlagde i Bergen 1816-1886") list the date of his death as October 10.

[114] Johannes Wilhelm Christian Dietrichson "had been sent to America in 1844 by the Church of Norway to investigate conditions and to begin the organization of church work among Norwegian immigrants. He became pastor at Koshkonong, Wisconsin, where he founded the congregation on October 10, the same year. In 1845 he returned to Norway to report and, if possible, to arrange for the calling of other pastors to the work in the New World. When no one was ready or available, he went to America a second time, in 1846. He continued to serve the Koskonong parish and at the same time traveled widely in the new settlements, organizing many congregations. Pastor Dietrichson was now corresponding with Herman [sic] Preus about accepting a call to serve one of the parishes in Wisconsin" (*Linka's Diary*, 67n.).

Dietrichson returned a final time to Norway in 1850, and served as vicar (*sogneprest*) in Nerstrand, Ryfylke, 1851-1862, and Ø. Moland, Arendal, 1862-1876. He was then postmaster in Porsgrund, 1876-1882. He died in 1883. (O.M. Norlie, Rasmus Malmin, and O. A. Tingelstad, *Who's Who Among Pastors in all the Norwegian Lutheran Synods of America, 1843-1927.* (Minneapolis: Augsburg Publishing. House, 1928), p. 114.)

For more information regarding Dietrichson and his role in the early development of Norwegian Lutheranism in America, see E. Clifford Nelson and Eugene L. Fevold, *The Lutheran Church Among Norwegian-Americans: A History of the Evangelical Lutheran Church* (Minneapolis: Augsburg Publishing House, 1960, Vol. 1, especially pp 96-119.)

[115] *Klir, Klir*

[116] *ulydelige* The "?" is in Linka's original manuscript

[117] J.C.K. Preus describes this as "A game for two or more players. It is played with wooden pieces faced with numbers or pictures, clown, rider, house, etc." (*Linka's Diary*, p. 72n.).

[118] *Brurebør*

[119] *Frykena*

[120] *Saga om Thorvald Vidførle eller den Vidtbereiste* (1849), by Carsten Hauch (1790-1872).

[121] Spesidaler

[122] J.C.K. Preus notes, "Professor Rudolph Keyser, the historian, and Librarian Wilhelm Keyser of the Unviersity, had tutored Linka and assisted her in many ways" (*Linka's Diary*, p. 76n.).

[123] A note on the cover enclosing this letter, in J.C.K. Preus's handwriting, notes, "These are no doubt a 'first draft' of two letters written at Askevold, New Year's Eve, 1849, by Linka Keyser to her two uncles, her father's brothers: Librarian Wilhelm Keyser and historian Prof. Rudolph Keyser."

[1] Adolf Carl Preus (Hermann Preus's cousin) was born in 1814 in Trondheim, Norway, and graduated from Christiania University in 1841. He served as a teacher and then as curate (*Kapellan*). He emigrated to Koshkonong, Wisconsin, in 1850, and served as pastor there from 1850-1860. After pastorates in Chicago (1860-63) and Coon Prairie, Wisconsin (1863-72), he returned to Norway in 1872, and died there in 1878. (Norlie, et al., 463.)

[125] *Fag fat*

[126] 1/2 alen

[127] There is no further information about this child in the diary. For more information regarding Olaf Christie (1850-1924), see Øyvind Larsen, ed, *Norges Leger* (Oslo: Den Norske Lægeforening, 1996), Vol 1, 575-576, and Slekten Christie I Norge: Supplement til W.H. Christie's Geneaologiske Optegnelseer om Slægten Christie I Norge 1650-1890 (Oslo: N.p., 1964), p. 46. This baby was the son of Governor Christie's son, Wilhelm. The child was baptized in the home of Pastor Christie (*Hjemmedøbt hos sogneprest Christie*). The mother's name is listed as "Anne Eline Edvardd" (the patronymic last name thus indicating that her father's

name was Edvard). In her diary entry for July 16, 1845, Linka mentioned Anne Eline Christie, the Governor's niece. (See note for February 24, 1845) Anne Eline Edvardd. Christie was born in 1810 and died March 2, 1888. (Digitalarkivet: *Gravlagde I Bergen 1881-1911*, record # 11611.)

[128] No day indicated — last entry of the month

[129] She is undoubtedly referring to her aunt and uncle.

[130] Abbreviation for Christiania.

[131] Werner Hosewinckel Christie's children, and their dates of birth, are listed in note 37.

[132] *sur som en eddikskrukke*

[133] *han saa lapset ud og gjørde seg saa fornem*

[134] Her grandfather, Johan Michael Keyser, was bishop in Christiansand from 1805 to 1810. <http://www.nla.no/ojj/kirkehistorie/tabell/biskoper.htm> (Accessed August 26, 2004)

[135] Borgen and Uranienborg are used interchangeably in entries that follow.

[136] (?) in the original

[137] Ludvig Breder was married to Hermann's sister Elise (1819-1906). As noted previously, Jørgen was married to Hermann's other sister, Pauline.

[138] Using the informal pronoun "du" rather than the formal "De."

[139] *Linka, du er et rart Meneske*

[140] *gamle Hedenold*

[141] For a brief description of Fredrikshald, see <http://54.1911encyclopedia.org/F/FR/FREDRIKSHALD.htm> and <http://www.encyclopedia.com/html/H/Halden.asp> (Accessed August 26, 2004)

[142] This is apparently Fredrik Waldeman Hvoslef (1825-1906), who was eventually Bishop in Tromsø (1868-1876), Sogneprest in Lier in 1876), and Bishop in Bergen (1881-1898). See *NBL1* Vol. 5 (1934), pp. 408-411.

[143] Adolf Carl Preus

[144] General Domestic Handbook

[145] The disagreement concerning congregational organization is described in *Linka's Diary*, p. 108. See also, Nelson and Fevold, pp. 114-116, and J. Magnus Rohne, *Norwegian American Lutheranism up to 1872* (New York: Macmillan, 1926), pp. 76-77.

[146] This entry follows the entry for October 19. There is a note in English made by J.C.K.Preus, "Oct. 20, 1850." That is the date under which this entry is listed in the 1952 translation.

[147] *liflige*

[148] "dimisspreken" is a sermon theological candidates in Norway had to have to achieve their ecclesiastical office.

[149] J.C.K. Preus organized the original diary into twelve sections. He described Part 5 as "Smaller white handmade booklets, with penciled diary — at times only notes — from Sept 24 1850 to Feb 7 1851." Some of these entries duplicate those from same dates in Part 4. The second entry for November 10 is one such entry. Similarly, the entries for November 11-27 are all from Part 5.

In the sections that follow, where there are duplicate entries for a single date, the notes from Part 5 will be included in footnotes unless they represent dates for which there was no entry in Part 4; they will be noted accordingly. Because the passages from Part 5 are sometimes "only notes," they are occasionally not complete grammatically; the style of such entries has been left as in the original.

[150] *Spidsslede*

[151] This passage is accompanied by a sketch of a face with a long nose

[152] Wilhelm Andreas Wexels (1797-1866), priest at *Vor Frelsers kirke* (Our Savior's Church) in Oslo from 1846 until his death. He was also a poet and hymn writer. Because he was born in

Copenhagen, his Danish accent was apparently sometimes a handicap for his preaching. See NBL1, Vol. 19, pp 86-93.

[153] At least one other piece of correspondence from Linka includes a reference to herself as "*Think*." The origin of that nickname is unknown.

[154] The following entries are the concluding notes of Part 4: Most of the first paragraph is included in the 1952 edition as January 12, 1851. The section identified as February 16 is printed separately under that date in the 1952 edition, corresponding to entries in Part 5 for those dates. The sheets which she could not find are probably those from Part 5 mentioned previously.

[155] In the original, there is only a blank. The 1952 translation indicates "Melby."

[156] "*skidne Roll*" — *Linka's Diary* translates this as "some miserable gypsies," p. 118.

[157] In addition to being included within the diary, the same verse is attached as part of a letter at the end of the section J.C.K. Preus labeled "Part 5:"

> Letter from Carl Christie to Linka 19.12. –50.
>
> Little children here with me
> Quiet must you be
> Nicely on your chair must you sit
> Or else you will be hit
> On your back
> Smack!
>
> I do remember you Linka. Do not forget me, I am galloping well on Tobben

[158] *dompekjerren*

[159] The following are shorter entries for December 23 and 24 from "Part 5." in another notebook.

> "December 23— At 6 this morning from Christiania, and now at Skjeberg. The description of the journey — the dark — the crossing of Svinesund — my being reluctant to come to Skjeberg so late, at 9:30 p.m."
>
> "24th from Skjeberg — bad driving conditions — Hexa's being surprised — first H. and I, then Ovid etc. etc. The pail of eggs — and then in the evening the solemn Christmas Eve at L. Breder's — quite nice — not like at home — together with H. and two sisters, no peace! Good night!"

[160] There are a number of periods with no diary entries, during which she wrote letters to Hermann which have survived. Those will be included with the diary entries chronologically, and will be indicated by "*Letter*"

[161] Knot

[162] Mountain range in Norway.

[163] Drawing of a hat — it may be intended to be a red stocking cap [*nisselue*].

[164] J.C.K. Preus identifies her as Mrs. Breder.

[165] Pine Grove

[166] Jens Lauritz Arup, Bishop of Oslo, 1846-1874.

[167] Christiansand. Bishop Arup informed Hermann that "he would not ordain me unless there were ordained simultaneously another minister who should be engaged here at home, since he, as Bishop of Christiania Diocese, might be called on to officiate at too many ordinations, if he should permit himself to ordain me, who, he said, was none of his concern" (*Linka's Diary*, 120). Arup later agreed to the ordination, which occurred on April 30, 1851 (Ibid., 124).

[168] *Rosenfeveren* — an inflammatory skin condition

[169] This salutation and opening paragraph were written in English, as presented here..

[170] Anders Monsen Askevold (1834-1900), a prominent painter of animals and landscapes. In 1847, Governor Christie helped him study with the landscape painter Reusch in Bergen. For more information, see *NBL1*, Vol. 1 (1923), pp. 290-291. J.C.K. Preus notes, "He became one of Norway's distinguished artists" (*Linka's Diary*, p. 120).

[171] Knud Gislesen (1801-1860), perpetual curate (*Residernde Kapellan*) at Asker, 1833-1855; in 1855 he became pastor (Sogneprest) at Gjerpe, and the same year became Bishop of the Nord-Hålogaland bishopric in Tromsø, where he served until his death in 1860. (*NBL1*, vol 4 (1929), pp. 443-444.)

[172] This long letter begins on March 10, and continues over the next several days, concluding with March 14.

[173] Jacob Aal Ottesen (1825-1904), graduated from the University of Christiania in 1849, taught in Christiania 1849-1852, and emigrated in 1852. He served pastorates in Manitowoc, WI (1852-60), Koshkonong, WI (1860-91), and Decorah, IA (1894-1896). He was one of six pastors who helped found the Norwegian Synod in 1853. (Norlie, et. al., p. 448. See also, Nelson and Fevold, p. 158 ff.)

[174] First fish caught

[175] In this instance, she spells his name Vexels, while on other occasions it is Wexels.

[176] "Ovid and I are going to the summer farm"

[177] 34 el.

[178] Claus Lauritz Clausen (1820-1892), immigrated to America in 1843, was ordained by a German priest in the Buffalo synod in 1843, and served as the first pastor in Muskego, Wisconsin (1843-1845) — the first Norwegian Lutheran congregation in America — before moving to Koshkonong (1845-1846), Rock Prairie, Wisconsin (1846-1853), and St. Ansgar, Iowa (1853-1856). He served as a chaplain in the Civil War, serving with the 15th Wisconsin Regiment, 1861-1862. He also served in Philadelphia, Pennsylvania, and Blooming Prairie, Minnesota, as well as Austin, Minnesota, and Poulsbo, Washington. He was one of the three pastors who founded the Evangelical Norwegian Lutheran Church in America in 1851. Clausen died in Parson's Landing, Washington, in 1892. (Norlie, et al., p. 102.. See also Nelson and Fevold, especially pp. 82-95.)

[179] This letter was written over the course of several days. Linka noted the dates of April 3 and April 6.

[180] Nils Olsen Brandt (1824-1921), immigrated to America in 1851, and became pastor at Rock River and Pine Lake, Wisconsin, and also served in Minnesota and Decorah, Iowa. He was the first pastor from Norway west of the Mississippi. One of the six pastors who founded the Norwegian Synod in 1853, he served as its vice president (1857-1871) and as a member of the Church Council (1857 to 1882). He was also professor of language and religion, as well as the first College Pastor, at Luther College, Decorah, Iowa, from 1865 to 1882. (Norlie et al., p. 77.)

[181] *Don Cæsar de Bazan*, Original authors: Phillipe François Pinel Dumanois (1806-1865) and Eugéne Philippe Dennery (b.1812)

[182] *Procurator* Wilhelm Breder. (Linka's Diary, p. 285).

[183] According to J.C.K. Preus, "Pastor Ole Nielsen's wife was Elizabeth Christine, the oldest sister of Ludvig Breder of Halden." (*Linka's Diary*, p. 135n).

[184] J.C.K. Preus notes, "That Jørgen Ziølner had become their traveling companion was purely accidental. They had expected that another young minister, Otto C.M. Ottesen, would have occupied the cabin — there were only two — on the *Columbus*. When he was prevented from going, the space was assigned to a young stranger, the university man, Ziølner" (*Linka's Diary*, p. 135n.). According to the passenger list from the *Columbus*, there were also five other people who were listed as having cabin berths. <http://www.norwayheritage.com/p_list.asp?jo=379, accessed September 8, 2004>

Although J.C.K. Preus spelled the name Ziølner, Linka consistently spelled it Ziiølner. (It is listed as Ziølner on the transcribed passenger list cited above. An unusual name even in Norway, it would be even more so in America, where he changed its spelling to Solner. He opened a store in Dodgeville, Wisconsin, and eventually moved to Austin, Minnesota, where he owned a dry-goods store. He married Elise Bruun, whose sister Engel was married to Adolf C. Preus. (*Linka's Diary*, p. 135n. See also, *The Diary of Elisabeth Koren: 1853-1855,*

Translated and Edited by David T. Nelson [Northfield, Minnesota: Norwegian-American Historical Association, 1955], p. 202n.)

Martin Ulvestad's *Normændene i Amerika* lists two separate names which probably both refer to him: under the description of immigrants to Mower County, Minnesota, he indicates that "J. Solnes, from Kristianiakanten [the area around Christiania], was the first in the area of Lyle." (*Normændene i Amerika : deres Historie og Rekord,* (Minneapolis: History Book Company's Forlag, 1907, p. 110) But in a second volume listing immigrants alphabetically, he lists a "John Solnør" who emigrated from Christiania in 1850 [sic], and owned a "General Store" in Austin, Minnesota. (*Normændene i Amerika : deres Historie og Rekord,* Vol. 2 [Minneapolis: History Book Company's Forlag, 1907[, p. 924)

[185] The ship owner was "Consul Ole Irgens Duus, whose son, Pastor Olaus Fredrik Duus, came to America in 1854 and served Waupaca parish in Wisconsin" (Linka's Diary, p. 135 n.). The brief biographical information in Norlie, et al (p. 120), indicates that Olaus Fredrik, born in Kragerø in 1824, was the son of the Danish Consul Ole Irgens Duus.

(Olaus Fredrik Duus [1824-1893] emigrated to America in 1854, and was pastor in Waupaca Wisconsin from 1854 to 1857, and in Whitewater, Wisconsin, from 1857 to 1859, when he returned to Norway.)

[186] The passenger list for the *Columbus* includes a total of 165 passengers upon arrival in New York. <http://www.norwayheritage.com/p_list.asp?jo=379, accessed September 8, 2004>

[187] For all but the Preuses and the six other passengers who were in cabins, the passenger list notes, "Between deck and houses on deck " Ibid.

[188] Aged cheese, similar to limburger.

[189] grits, or grain porridge

[190] *selvgjort er velgjort*

[191] a brown, whey cheese

[192] Linka's July 6 entry indicates this was Anne Olafsdatter. The passenger list from the *Columbus* lists Anne Olsdatter [Dauve] as being four weeks old upon arrival in New York. <http://www.norwayheritage.com/p_list.asp?jo=379, accessed September 8, 2004>

[193] Linka calls him *"Johan hiin Svarte."* There is no indication of the reason for the nickname, whether it refers to skin color, hair or complexion, or relative cleanliness. J.C.K Preus rendered the term "Johan, the sooty."

[194] *syltede Fløde*

[195] *Aal's Memoirs*

[196] *kimminger*

[197] Her meaning here is unclear; her notation ends with three lines, as indicated here.

[198] The passenger list for the Columbus lists two women named Margit. One, twenty-seven years of age, was apparently the mother of the baby born on board, and the other was a twenty-year-old girl named Margit Rollefsdatter (with no other family name listed). There are also two other women named Rollefsdatter, which does not fit with Linka's description of Margit being alone. <http://www.norwayheritage.com/p_list.asp?jo=379>

[199] Linka's notations for the next three entries are June 1, 2, and 3, but the entries' location and contents (particularly the reference to her birthday, which was July 2) clearly indicate that it this is an error, and they should be July.

[200] "How wonderful is the country of my birth"

[201] She does not specify which temperature scale she is using. For this entry in the 1952 edition of the diary, J.C.K. Preus indicates she means Celsius; but for the December 13 entry, he converts the temperature as representing the Reaumur scale. If the degrees she indicates here are Reaumur, the temperatures are approximately 80, 72.5, and 90.5 degrees Fahrenheit, respectively. If she is using the Celsius scale, they are approximately 71, 64.5, and 79 degrees Fahrenheit, respectively.

[202] Her earlier estimates of distance simply stated "miles," but here she specifies "40 norske Mile." As noted previously, in the 19th century, a "Norwegian Mile" was approximately seven English Miles. That would place the ship at approximately 280 miles from shore. However, her other references to the relative proximity of America, and the arrival of the pilot, suggest a much shorter distance. J.C.K. Preus edited this to read, "we have forty American miles to go" which is probably more accurate. (Ibid., 178.)

[203] The passenger list includes the names of 165 passengers. <http://www.norwayheritage.com/ p_list.asp?jo=379 accessed September 8, 2004>

[204] cruet stand. In a marginal note to his transcription, J.C.K. Preus noted, "flat wheel, 'lazy susan'? caster for vinegar, etc?"

[205] In addition to this brief mention of Niagara Falls, she wrote a longer description, part of which also survives. It follows this entry.

[206] Hans Andreas Stub (1822-1907), had arrived in America in 1848. He was pastor at Muskego, Wisconsin, from 1848 to 1855, and Coon Prairie, Wisconsin, from 1855 to 1861. He was one of the three pastors who helped found the Evangelical Norwegian Lutheran Church in 1851, and one of the seven pastors who established the Norwegian Synod in 1853 He returned to Norway in 1861, but immigrated to America again in 1865, when he became pastor at Highlandville, Iowa (Big Canoe, and other neighboring congregations). He remained there until 1891. Then he returned to Norway again, this time for three years, during which he was with the Inner Mission in Bergen. In 1894, he returned to America, only to return to Norway again in 1896. In 1897, he made his last transatlantic journey, returning to serve as a pastor Emeritus in Minnesota, until his death in 1907. He was made a Knight of the Norwegian Order of St. Olaf in 1903. (Norlie, et al., 562).

[207] In the margin of his transcription, J.C.K. Preus noted, "Did Grandf. P. thus preach his first sermon in America in the old Muskego log church?—!!!"

[208] J.C.K. Preus offers the following explanation: "The Franckean Synod, organized in New York, 1837, emphasized Americanization and stressed piety, but had small regard for strict confessionalism and did not accept the Augsburg Confession. J. Magnus Rohne, in *Norwegian American Lutheranism up to 1872*, page 101," (*Linka's Diary*, 188). It is also discussed briefly by Nelson & Fevold, passim.

[209] Zouaves were originally French infantry, known for their distinctive red pants. The term came to be applied to members of other military forces who also wore red pants. For example, zouaves fought in both Northern and Southern armies at the battle of Antietam, and could be found in other units long after the Civil War. <http://www.nps.gov/archive/anti/ zouaves.htm>

[210] J.C.K. Preus identified this as "the Home of Herman's cousin, Pastor Adolph C. Preus and his nineteen-year-old wife Engel Brun, who had arrived in 1850" (*Linka's Diary*, 189n.).

[211] *Annexer*

[218] In the margin of the transcription J.C.K. Preus used for his translation, there is this note: "she was born Dec. 6, 1831, so now was 19-3/4 years old. Her oldest child was 'Ansokh,' born Aug. 22, 1851, days after Linka & Herman left Koshkonong."

[213] *ja heite niøs og nei heite nix*

[214] J.C.K. Preus's marginal note in his transcription indicates "she was a younger sister of A.C. Preus."

[215] According to a marginal note in J.C.K. Preus's transcription, "this was near Inmansville, Wisc. — now Janesville."

[216] J.C.K. Preus noted in the margin on his transcription, "so they would leave her in peace!"

[217] This entry is from the section that J.C.K. Preus had labeled part 10. The next entry was from part 9. In the margin of his transcription of this entry, he noted, "From 1st page of the blue paper booklet. Then back to first page of the bound diary — ? It was Sept. 4, 1851."

[218] J.C.K. Preus noted on his trancription, "On Monday, 4 days before Engel & A.C. Preus' first baby arrived."

[219] 6 ells.

[220] J.C.K. Preus noted in his transcription, "30 miles from Koshkonong to Spring Prairie."

[221] In his marginal note, J.C.K. Preus wrote, "arrived at Spring Prairie, Monday, August 18, 1851."

[222] Like the first entry from September, this comes from the materials J.C.K. Preus labeled part 10. In the margin of his transcription, he notes it is "continued from the blue-paper booklet, bottom of p. 1." The following entries, through July 5, 1852, are from that volume.

[223] *"gid jeg havde her en Fjerdelpart af hvad Viin de Mennesker have drukket, da skulle min Nygravede Kjelder ei staae tom og min Mand skulle hver Søndag tracteres med et Glas til Maden — Glasset skulle dog være fyldt med Druesaft, og selv ville jeg nok ogsaa have lidt med."* This last sentence seems to suggest an attitude of temperance that has not appeared previously in the diary.

[224] There is no proverb included in the diary text, but in the 1952 translation, J.C.K. Preus added the following: "Better a small fish, than an empty dish" (p. 200).

[225] This reference is confusing. In the margin of his working transcription, J.C.K. Preus notes, "Is Waleska engaged? She married Dr. Wilhelm Preus May 30, 1852." The same wedding date is not only listed in *Family History* (10), but also in *Norges Biografisk Leksikon* (1), vol. 11 (1952), pp. 174-174. Waleska died in 1853.

[226] A marginal note in J.C.K. Preus's working transcription notes, "'Bya' is Agnes, so called because she so often ran errands into town — 'Byen.'" According to *Family History*, "AGNES, the youngest of the Keyser siblings, born 1840, remained single, and lived much of her life at the home of her sister, Hanne Marie Bang and her husband, Hans Fredrik, in Drammen. She died at the age of 94" (11.).

[227] Children's names for their fingers.

[228] "Now I've made the curds and whey"

[229] "How glorious is my native land."

[230] Elf

[231] As on July 6, Linka only indicates the number of degrees, without indicating the scale being used. In the 1952 translation, J.C.K. Preus indicates Celsius for the July dates, but identifies these temperatures as being on the Reaumur scale, which he converts as "6.25 below zero Fahrenheit" and "24.25 below zero Fahrenheit," respectively. If she was referring to degrees Celsius, they would be equivalent to 1.4 degrees above zero Fahrenheit, and 13 degrees below zero Fahrenheit, respectively (Diary, 203.).

[232] A marginal note in the working transcription notes: "no doubt the oldest brother, Dr. Johan Jacob Keyser Preus +1853, and Father Preus, Overlærer Paul Arctander Preus"

[233] J.C.K. Preus converts these temperatures as "19.75 degrees below zero Fahrenheit to 24.25 degrees below zero Fahrenheit," (Diary, p. 207), which is based on the Reaumur scale. If she is referring to Celsius temperatures, their equivalents would be 9.4 to 13 degrees below zero Fahrenheit.

[234] The first entry, which J.C.K. Preus identified as Part 11, contains two brief notes, the first referring to a daguerreotype in July 1851, and the brief notation from New Year's Eve, 1851. Next to the word daguerreotype, J.C.K. Preus noted, "1851, New York," and after "letter writing to Norway," he wrote, "Spring Prairie 1851-52."

[235] Muskego

[236] J.C.K. Preus notes, "This conference was persuaded by Herman Preus to eliminate from the synodical constitution, then in the making, the Grundtvigian error which he had opposed so vigorously in his discussions with Pastor J.W.C. Dietrichson" (Diary, 209, n.). The meeting, which lasted from February 1-9, 1852, is briefly described in Nelson and Fevold, pp. 155-157.

[237] "Father"

238 Kierkegaard's *Kjærlighets Gjerninger [Works of Love]* was published in Denmark in 1847.

239 butter pudding

240 I have now made curds and whey

241 aged cheese, similar to Limburger

242 sour whey cheese

243 brown whey cheese

244 From the context of the following text, this was apparently written two days after Pentecost. However, the date she gives for the entry, *"Den 30te Mai. Pindsedag,"* was a Sunday.

245 *Gode råd* ["good advice"] or *God rådskager* was an older name for waffles. *Dansk-Norsk-Engelsk Ordbog*, A. Larsen, ed, 4th edition, (Copenhagen and Christiania: Gyldendalske Boghandel, Nordisk Forlag, 1910). Recipes can be found in Hanne Winsnes's cookbook, *Lærebog i de forskjellige Grene af Husholdningen*, recipes #512 and 513. <http://www.dokpro.uio.no/litteratur/winsnes/frames.htm>

246 pumpkins and watermelons

247 Norway

248 shock of hair: "Scruffy"

249 *Tykkemoer*

250 Christian Keyser Preus, October 13, 1852-May 28, 1921, became a Lutheran pastor, and eventually was Professor of Religion at Luther College, 1898-1921, and President of the College, 1902-1921. See *Family History*, p. 17.

251 White bear

252 *røge Thobak og drikke Øl*

253 J.C.K. Preus identifies the synod meeting as being "at Koshkonong." (*Diary*, 231.) Nelson and Fevold mention it briefly, and indicate that it "began its deliberation at East Koshkonong on February 3, 1853." (p. 158).

254 Red pudding with cream — can be made with red berries or fruit such as raspberries, strawberries, cherries, or cranberries.

255 The sister of Engel Preus (A.C. Preus's wife), she later married Jørgen Ziiølner

256 Johan Jacob Keyser Preus, 1813-1853, Hermann's oldest brother. A physician, he died in the cholera epidemic of 1853. See *Family History*, p. 4.

257 January 29

258 As noted previously, she does not indicate what temperature scale she is using. If she is referring to the Celsius scale, that equates to -7.6 degrees Fahrenheit. If it is Reamur, it is -17.5 degrees Fahrenheit.

265 In her entry of May 27, 1864, she refers to "my dear neighbor, a genuine Voss woman, Thorbjør Møen."

266 Her second child, Rosine Pauline Keyser Preus, was born October 21, 1854. She was generally known as "Sina." She married Pastor Jørgen Nordby in 1877, and died in LaCrosse, Wisconsin July 29, 1926. See *Family History*, pp. 56 -57

261 J.C.K. Preus notes, "Elise Bruun, sister of Mrs. A.C. Preus, had become Mrs. Ziølner," (Diary, 263 n.).

262 *"jo pyt sa Peer til kongen"*

263 J.C.K. Preus notes, "The followers of Elling Eilesen, the leading lay preacher among the early Norwegian immigrants, later ordained," (*Diary*, 264n.). See Fevold and Nelson, pp. 126-150.

264 December 21, 1856

265 *Julekake* (Christmas cake) and *fattigmannsbakkels* ("poor man's cookies") are popular baked goods.

266 J.C.K. Preus notes, "Dr. Søren J. Hanssen and his wife, Albertha Ulffers, served as doctor and nurse with the Fifteenth Wisconsin during the War Between the States. They established themselves at Koshkonong, Wisconsin" (Linka's Diary, 271n.).

[267]Most of the diary entry is clear: "The 25th Sunday after . . . 1860, the 22nd of November." The ecclesiastical date is not clear, however. It appears to be "Tafi," which is neither Pentacost (*Pinse*) nor Trinity Sunday (*Trinitatis*). To complicate matters even more, November 22, 1860, was a Thursday. The 25th Sunday after Trinity was November 25. J.C.K. Preus rendered this entry as "25th Sunday after Trinity, November 1860."

[268] In *Family History*, J.C.K. Preus spells her name "Agnes Wilhelmine Rudolpha Keyser Preus, known as Anga, . . . " She married Pastor Daniel Kvaase in 1862, and died in Champaign, Ill, May 12, 1927 (p. 66-67).

[269] Rosine Pauline Keyser Preus was born October 21, 1854, Johan Wilhelm Keyser Preus was born October 21, 1861, and Carl Christie Preus was born October 21, 1863. (*Family History*, 15). In the *Diary*, J.C.K. Preus notes, "Johan Wilhelm was born October 21, 1861. He was usually called 'Doctor' because he was named for his two doctor uncles." (273.)

[270] *Family History* contains the following entry: "CARL CHRISTIE PREUS, b. Oct 21, 1863; d. Oct. 22 1863. — His little headstone at Spring Prairie also has the words "and three little siblings." (15.)